Japan in the
Posthegemonic World

Japan
in the
Posthegemonic
World

edited by

Tsuneo Akaha & Frank Langdon

Lynne Rienner Publishers • Boulder & London

Published in the United States of America in 1993 by
Lynne Rienner Publishers, Inc.
1800 30th Street, Boulder, Colorado 80301

and in the United Kingdom by
Lynne Rienner Publishers, Inc.
3 Henrietta Street, Covent Garden, London WC2E 8LU

Library of Congress Cataloging-in-Publication Data
Japan in the posthegemonic world / edited by Tsuneo Akaha, Frank
    Langdon
        p.   cm.
    Includes bibliographical references and index.
    ISBN 1-55587-377-4
    ISBN 1-55587-385-5 (pbk.)
    1. Japan—Relations—Foreign countries. 2. World politics—1989–
I. Akaha, Tsuneo, 1949–   .   II. Langdon, Frank, 1919–   .
DS890.3.J356   1993
327.52'009'048—dc20   92-32013
                                                            CIP

British Cataloguing in Publication Data
A Cataloguing in Publication record for this book
is available from the British Library.

Printed and bound in the United States of America

The paper used in this publication meets the requirements
of the American National Standard for Permanence of
Paper for Printed Library Materials Z39.48-1984.

Contents

Tables and Figures

Tables

Figures

Introduction

Japan and the Posthegemonic World

Tsuneo Akaha
Frank Langdon

Since the early 1980s, theoretical expositions of the rise and fall of the historical and contemporary great powers have become a subject of heated debate among historians, political scientists, and economists. The close scrutiny has coincided with various signs of decline of the United States as a global hegemon and policymakers' concerns about the destabilizing consequences of weakening U.S. leadership in the management of global and regional problems. With the ending of the global Cold War, the collapse of the Soviet empire and dissolution of the Soviet Union, and, the outbreak of the first post–Cold War conflict, in the Gulf, the debate over the U.S. hegemonic decline has intensified and apprehensions about its policy implications have deepened.

There is no consensus as to the degree of the U.S. decline or whether the decline is absolute or relative, reversible or irreversible. Indeed, there are even some students of international political economy who reject the notion of U.S. hegemonic decline as either excessively alarmist or empirically false.[1] Even among the "declinists," there is no agreement on the possible causes of the U.S. power slide. Some observers nominate misguided policy in Washington, such as supply-side Reaganomics and excessive defense spending;[2] some attribute the slide to corporate mismanagement—for example, a lack of long-term strategy in business planning and inadequate investment in research and development (R&D);[3] and some critics lament the absence of an industrial policy including public-private sector cooperation in the United States.[4]

Other analysts find causes of the U.S. decline outside the country. For example, some have found faults with the trade practices of Japan and other export-oriented countries.[5] Some have found culprits in U.S. industries' failure to adapt to the fast changes in the structural features of the global economy, the most important element being the distribution of comparative advantage.[6] Some historians and political scientists see the excessive commitment of national resources to global political and security commitments as

1

the most important cause of U.S. decline.[7] Finally, some see the decline as a virtually inevitable phase in the cyclical rise and fall of great powers in world history.[8]

Nor is there a common understanding of the possible consequences of the U.S. hegemonic decline. Some remind us that the past periods of power transition were extremely unstable and even dangerous, with World Wars I and II coming during the period when the British hegemonic power had been spent, but the United States, the emerging global economic power, was unwilling to assume world leadership.[9] Others posit the possibility that trade, financial, and other international regimes may facilitate policy coordination among the major economic powers of the world and promote collective problem solving.[10] After all, they contend, their calculation of national interests will indicate the desirability of cooperation over discord.

It is unclear, however, that the existing international institutions, such as the General Agreement on Tariffs and Trade (GATT), the International Monetary Fund (IMF), the International Bank for Reconstruction and Development (IBRD, or the World Bank), and the United Nations, are adequate in meeting the challenges of the deepening interdependence among the national and regional economies of the world. The accelerating economic interdependence has exposed and will continue to expose the vulnerabilities of national societies and unleash potentially destructive forces of nationalism. For example, the growing sense of a loss of national control over domestic economic affairs has generated protectionist sentiments in the United States and elsewhere, and economically displaced elements in several Western European countries have incited ethnically motivated attacks on foreign residents. On the other hand, potentially constructive responses to the growing national and regional economic needs that are not currently being met by the existing global insitutions can be seen in the full integration of the European Community (EC) in 1992 and its expanded cooperation with the European Free Trade Association (EFTA), the North American Free Trade Agreement (NAFTA), the Asia Pacific Economic Cooperation (APEC) forum established in 1990, and the recently proposed ASEAN Free Trade Agreement (AFTA).

The diversity of views on the causes and consequences of U.S. hegemonic decline notwithstanding, there is an almost unanimous worldwide opinion that the management of global and regional problems in the post–Cold War era requires, at a minimum, effective and timely policy coordination and efficacious burden- and power-sharing among the United States, Japan, and the European Community. The editors of this volume believe that collective management of post–Cold War problems is both desirable and possible, but that it would require hitherto unprecedented levels of cooperation among the three power centers. Particularly crucial, we believe, will be Japan's ability and willingness to define clearly its role in the emerging new world order and to translate that definition into effective policy. Equally important will be the expectations of others regarding Japan's role and behavior in the posthegemonic world and how any discrepancies between the Japanese and non-Japanese views can be eliminated—or at least reduced—through political dialogue and policy coordination.

The collection of essays that follows represents an international collaborative effort to examine both Japan's own view of its role in the posthegemonic world and other countries' expectations regarding Japan. The geographical focus of the collective scrutiny will be on the Pacific Rim, the region of utmost importance to Japan and of growing significance to the rest of the world. Most chapter authors focus on the period of dramatic change from the mid-1980s through the beginning of 1992.

In Chapters 1 and 2, "Hegemons in History" and "Japan and Global Economic Hegemony," Philip J. Meeks (of the United States) examines the ongoing theoretical debate over hegemony and hegemons, and Japan's place in the international system. Chapter 3, by Frank Langdon (Canada), "Posthegemonic Japan-U.S. Relationship," examines the current state of U.S.-Japanese relations, the single most important bilateral relation in the region, from the point of view of U.S. interests and expectations regarding Japan's role in the posthegemonic world. In Chapter 4, "Japan's Security Policy in the Posthegemonic World: Opportunities and Challenges," Tsuneo Akaha (United States) outlines the major challenges and opportunities presented to Japanese security policy by the end of the Cold War in Asia Pacific and by the emergence of Japanese economic power as a political factor with security implications. In Chapter 5, "Japan in East Asia," David Arase (United States) examines Japan's response to the recent and ongoing changes in East Asia and posits future prospects for an expanded political and security role for Japan in the region.

Chapter 6 by Alexei V. Zagorsky (Russia) and Chapter 7 by Akaha review Japan's postwar political and economic relations with the Soviet Union and evaluate Japan's ability to respond effectively to the disintegration and dissolution of the Soviet Union as a unified state and the emergence of a postcommunist Russia as the most likely successor to the former Soviet Union. In Chapter 8 ("Japan's Foreign Policy Choices for the Twenty-first Century"), Chapter 9 ("Japan's Roles in the Posthegemonic World"), and Chapter 10 ("New Dimensions of Japanese Foreign Policy"), Zhou Jihua (People's Republic of China), Prasert Chittiwatanapong (Thailand), and Charlotte Elton (Panama) present Chinese, Southeast Asian, and Latin American views of the opportunities and challenges facing Japan's foreign policy in the posthegemonic era as well as the hopes and concerns that the expected expansion of Japan's regional and global roles are generating. In Chapter 11, "Japan as Number Two," Koji Taira examines both the likelihood and the desirability of a new world order in the image of Japan. In the conclusion, "The Posthegemonic World and Japan," the coeditors present the collective assessment of the book's contributors of the probable scope and methods of Japanese international roles and present a list of tasks Japan must undertake if it is to participate effectively and constructively in the collective management of a posthegemonic world order.

In the remainder of this introduction we set the background to the chapter-by-chapter analyses that follow. We briefly discuss the concept of hegemony (to be more closely scrutinized in Chapter 1) and introduce the debate on the U.S. decline. We then outline Japan's postwar international policy and the nation's response to the U.S. hegemonic decline since the 1960s. We finally highlight the challenges Japan faces in its relations with its Asia Pacific neighbors.

Hegemony and the U.S. Decline ──────────────────────────

Central to the debate over the U.S. decline and the posthegemonic world is the concept of "hegemony." As Meeks points out in Chapter 1, most Western analysts view hegemony in terms of the distribution of national capabilities and define a hegemon as a nation so dominant in its power—particularly coercive power, such as military—that it can dictate the terms of international relations to the other significant actors in the system. In the editors' view, however, hegemony is not a national attribute and cannot be exercised by the actor possessing a dominant set of material assets. Rather, hegemony is a set of relationships surrounding the dominant power in which the dominant actor's view of the world is more or less shared by the other significant actors in the international system. Moreover, as Robert Cox asserts, the dominant actor must be able to establish and maintain an order that "most other states [find] compatible with their interests given their different levels of power and lesser abilities to change the order." According to Cox, "The less powerful states could live with that order even if they could not change it."[11] In a hegemonic system, as Torbjon Knutsen has noted,

> The dominant power is the most efficient producer of goods in the world economy and it commands the most efficient military forces of the interstate system; the scope of its interests and involvements is coterminous with the international system itself rather than with a narrower, purely national security zone; its salience consists in the fact that no other actor in the system can ignore it and that they assess their position, role, and prospects in relations to it; it feels responsible for maintaining a world order and articulates its responsibility in universal terms.[12]

According to this definition, the United States was indeed able to establish and maintain a hegemonic system of international relations in the postwar period. Following gradual domestic economic growth prior to World War I and through the interwar and wartime military buildup, the United States emerged from World War II as the dominant world power. The United States enjoyed an unparalleled position of dominance in the world economy and an unchallenged position as a great military power in the international system. As such, the United States was able to maintain a "regime of truth and universal principles which most states found compatible with their own interests."[13]

However, maintaining the position of global dominance is an expensive proposition for any nation.[14] As Robert Gilpin points out, it requires the existence of a continuing economic surplus, which is used for the purpose of consumption, production, and protection.[15] The dominant power's inability to maintain surplus capacity leads to hegemonic decline. Gilpin maintains that the United States is experiencing this very problem. He states that the United States is caught between its many commitments and decreased power.[16] Similarly, David Calleo argues that extended military commitments and poor economic management have exacerbated the U.S. decline: "America's over-sized military commitments . . . have pressed the United States into fiscal and financial practices destructive to American, European, and global prosperity."[17]

Through a review of the history of economic change and military conflict since 1500, Paul Kennedy comes to the same conclusion about the fate of the U.S. hegemonic power. He maintains that excessive political-military commitments overseas have caused the eventual demise of all great world powers and that the United States is no exception.[18] Just as the British Empire rose and fell, Kennedy argues, the United States has declined from its hegemonic status in the immediate postwar years.

We generally agree with these assessments. We further maintain that the most desirable course for the United States would be to encourage the Japanese and the Europeans to join in a coequal, shared global leadership. We are not convinced that the U.S. decline is irreversible. We share Paul Kennedy's view that some options are available to policymakers to influence (not determine) the course of history.[19]

Japan and the Posthegemonic World

Throughout the debate over the U.S. hegemonic decline and its policy implications in the last decade, much has been made, in both complimentary and critical terms, of Japan's rapid rise to the status of a global economic power, surpassing the Soviet Union and challenging the United States. Indeed, a good part of the U.S. decline—or, more accurately, relative decline since the 1960s—has been attributed to the expansion of the Japanese economy in the manufacturing sector since the 1960s and in the high-tech and financial industries since the 1980s. However, the exalting as well as disapproving commentaries on Japan's economic record have been accompanied by stern international criticisms about the nation's apparent inability (some would argue, its lack of willingness) to play an international political role commensurate with its economic prowess. There is mounting international concern about the obvious discrepancy between Japanese economic power and political responsibility and the disturbing effects this gap has created and, if uncorrected, will continue to create in the world.

Japanese analysts have acknowledged that their nation lacks foreign policy initiatives to expand its role in international politics.[20] Some have joined foreign critics in concluding that only *gaiatsu*, or external pressures, will induce Japan to take on international responsibilities more commensurate with its economic prowess. Some Japanese researchers have also identified incongruous policymaking processes in Japan, the United States, and the EC as factors compounding the difficulty of economic policy coordination at the global level.[21]

In our view, Japan's problem is not so much a lack of debate among the Japanese about their nation's role in the posthegemonic world.[22] Nor is it a lack of willingness on the part of individual Japanese foreign policymakers to articulate their views on Japan's role in the world.[23] It is certainly not a lack of material wherewithal to back up the nation's foreign policy pursuits. What then accounts for the apparent inability of Japan to translate its enormous economic capabilities into international political influence? Part of the answer is found in the nature of the political system that has developed in postwar Japan and its impact on the policymaking process in Tokyo.

Japan's postwar international policy was characterized by: (1) a close and expanding alliance relationship with the United States, (2) a minimalist security policy based on a security treaty with the United States and maintenance of strictly defensive military capabilities, (3) an unflinching (and quite successful) pursuit of economic growth through an export-oriented development strategy, and (4) a geographical focus on the Pacific Rim region. Equally important, the conduct of foreign policy with these characteristics was supported by a fairly strong and stable consensus at home. Under these circumstances, the policymaking process in Tokyo was dominated by a fairly closed elite bureaucracy. The bureaucrats, particularly those in the Ministry of International Trade and Industry (MITI), could readily lead the as yet underdeveloped private sector in the formulation and implementation of a national industrial strategy.[24] Unfortunately, the successful pursuit of a mercantilist foreign economic policy during those years relegated the nation's contribution to the international economy to a position of minor importance.

By the early 1970s, when the nation's economy had grown to a global status, earnest discussions began on Japan's contribution to the international community. However, a series of external developments in the same decade, most importantly the two oil shocks, the sudden announcement of China-U.S. rapprochement, and President Richard Nixon's "new economic policy," caught the Japanese policymakers by surprise. They spent most of their time adjusting to the altered international environment. Japanese industries' spectacular expansion into the global marketplace also required major policy adjustments in Tokyo. Reactive (as opposed to proactive) behavior characterized the nation's foreign policy.[25] By the time the foreign and economic policy bureaucrats had made successful adjustments and appeared poised for major foreign policy initiatives, however, they found three major hurdles: the political leadership was in disarray, national consensus on international policy was fast disappearing, and international demands on Japan were overwhelming.

The instability in the political leadership was most symbolically reflected in the fact that during President George Bush's term of office, 1989–1993, there were four Japanese prime ministers, Noboru Takeshita, Sosuke Uno, Toshiki Kaifu, and Kiichi Miyazawa. Two of them were forced to resign due to scandals and one could not seek reelection because of his inability to lead the faction-ridden Liberal Democratic Party (LDP). The selection of the party's president and prime minister was more a result of factional politics within the party than an outcome of open debate on the candidates' political vision and policy course.

In the wake of Japan's rise to the status of the world's second most powerful economy and against the background of the relative decline of U.S. hegemony since the 1970s, Japan has been challenged to revise its international policy, but domestic consensus has been hard to find on many important foreign policy issues. First, Tokyo's Washington-focused foreign policy has come under increasing criticism in Japan, and Washington has similarly come under mounting domestic pressure to review what many critics view as an unfair relationship with Tokyo. Washington's incessant pressures on Tokyo concerning the issues of bilateral trade imbalance and defense burden sharing have had a polarizing effect on the Japanese debate on their international role. On the one hand, there is a widespread opinion that U.S. demands are misguided and misplaced, that they show the failure of U.S. leaders to understand the domestic causes of their own economic difficulties as well as the desire of Japan not to extend its military power beyond its territory. Japanese nationalists and other members of the media and public have countered Japan-bashing in the United States with their own U.S.-bashing. On the other hand, the mainstream Japanese politicians believe Japan should maintain a strong security alliance with the United States. To that end, Tokyo plans to pay up to 50 percent of the cost of the U.S. troop presence in Japan by 1995. Some Japanese politicians and business leaders as well as consumer advocates see a need to open the domestic market more widely, to reduce export pressure, and to stimulate domestic demand. The resulting coexistence of intransigence and acquiescence makes the policymakers' job precarious.

Second, in part due to the U.S. pressure and in part because of the conservative swing in the balance of political power in Japan since the 1970s, Tokyo has managed to boost its defense capabilities substantially. Japan today has one of the largest defense budgets in the world, and its armed forces are equipped with some of the world's most sophisticated weapons. The

Japanese Self-Defense Forces (SDF) are well on their way to being able to defend not only Japan's land territories but also its sea lines of communication (SLOCs) to a distance of 1,000 nautical miles from its shores. During the 1960s, 1970s, and most of the 1980s, the increasing Soviet military presence in East Asia strengthened the position of the prodefense forces in Japan. At the same time, however, the perennial sense of resource vulnerability among the Japanese and the relative success of Tokyo's economics-first foreign policy in the earlier decades assured a popular support for the idea of economic, as opposed to military, security. The ill-defined relationship between the two aspects of security found its way into the concept of "comprehensive security policy" that Tokyo has adopted since the 1980s. Balancing economic and military security measures is a task that goes beyond the current ability of the Japanese policy bureaucracy, which is characterized by vertical lines of authority and the absence of effective interagency coordination.

Third, the oil crises, the Cambodian conflict, the protracted Iran-Iraq war, and the political crises in the Philippines—all in the wake of declining U.S. power in East Asia throughout the 1970s and most of the 1980s—challenged Japan's international policy, which had been geared more toward economic growth than crisis management. Tokyo's response to these developments was to attempt to translate its growing economic power into political influence. In the Arab-Israeli conflict, Japan adopted a pro-Arab position at the risk of alienating Israel; during the first Gulf war, Tokyo maintained diplomatic and commercial ties with both Tehran and Baghdad and unsuccessfully attempted an intermediary role; in Southeast Asia, Japan extended the largest part of its official development assistance (ODA) to the Philippines and other members of the Association of Southeast Asian Nations (ASEAN) and supported ASEAN's push for a comprehensive political settlement of the Cambodian conflict. However, these policies had limited, if any, impact on the course of the regional conflicts. More recently, Tokyo has begun to interject explicitly political and strategic considerations into its ODA policy and, as noted below, has begun disbursing economic aid to countries considered of strategic importance to the United States. Tokyo has also decided to base its ODA decisions in part on such political factors as defense spending, arms export policy, and democratization efforts in the countries receiving or wishing to receive Japanese assistance. However, these policy changes are not necessarily based on a strong national consensus.[26]

Fourth, the focus of Japan's international policy has also begun to widen, going beyond Asia Pacific. Japan's position as the world's leading creditor and trade-surplus nation, with $261.7 billion in external credits and $95 billion in trade surplus in 1988, has given Tokyo an unprecedented opportunity to extend the geographical reaches of its international policy. The most visible change in this regard has been the disbursement of Japanese ODA to such far-flung countries as Pakistan, Turkey, Egypt, Kenya, Zimbabwe, Jamaica, Sudan, Poland, Hungary, Panama, and Nicaragua. The Japanese ODA program, the largest in the world for the first time in 1989, the second largest in 1990 (after the U.S. program), and again the largest in 1991, has become an important instrument of Japan's global policy. Prime Minister Noboru Takeshita expressed Tokyo's expanding international perspective in an International Cooperation Initiative in 1988, and his successors have actively followed the program. The initiative calls on Japan to strengthen its contribution to international peace, to expand its ODA, and to promote international cultural exchange. A major component of the new policy is to expand Japanese contributions to the United Nations and its peacekeeping and humanitarian activities. In 1989 Japan became the third largest financial contributor to UN peacekeeping operations behind the United States and the Soviet Union. Japanese financial (and in some cases, personnel) contributions have gone to the Good Offices Mission in Afghanistan and Pakistan (UNGOMAP), the Iran-Iraq Military Observer Group (UNIIMOG), the Interim Force in Lebanon (UNIFIL), the Disengagement Observer Force (UNDOF), the UN Peace Keeping Force in Cyprus (UNFICYP), the Transition Assistance Group in Namibia (UNTAG), the UN Observer Group in Central America (ONUCA), the UN Observer Mission in Nicaragua (ONUVEN), and most recently to the UN Transition Authority in Cambodia (UNTAC). Japan's contributions to UN refugee and reconstruction programs, amounting to $259 million in 1990, have also gone beyond the Asia Pacific region. The UN High Commissioner for Refugees (UNHCR) and the UN Relief and Works Agency for Palestine Refugees in the Near East (UNRWA) have been the major recipients of Japanese financial support. As well, there is much talk about Japan's desire to become a permanent member of the UN Security Council.

These changes in Japanese international policy since the 1960s have taken place in the context of several major trends at the global and regional levels. Most importantly, the deteriorating domestic condition and the weakening international position of the superpowers have resulted in a reduction of global tension of an unprecedented scale. Its impact appeared immediately in Europe, where the superpower conflict had created the most clear-cut regional cleavage, ideologically and geographically. In contrast, the thaw in the global Cold War has had a less dramatic, if equally important, impact on the Asia Pacific region. This has been partly because the superpowers placed their priorities first on Europe and partly because the heterogeneous background and character of Asia Pacific relations have allowed neither a simultaneous nor a uniform response from the regional powers to the changes in superpower relations. This has complicated Japan's foreign and security policy options.

Since the end of the 1980s, coinciding with the end of the global Cold War and the diminution of the perceived Soviet threat to the West, some in the United States have called for a major review of the U.S.-Japanese security alliance. And some have maintained that the overall political interests of the two countries require the broadening of bilateral cooperation to include not only bilateral issues but also regional and global political, security, and economic problems.[27] Others have warned that the two countries might drift apart unless the existing security arrangements were revised into a more mutual and balanced one with reciprocal defense obligations and more equal burden sharing.[28] Still others have observed that the overall political interests of Tokyo and Washington are so closely intertwined that the two sides are unlikely to change the existing alliance structure for the foreseeable future.[29]

On the economic front, despite some signs of improvement in bilateral trade, strains in the Japan-U.S. relations have grown. Japan's trade surplus with the United States dropped from $56.3 billion in 1987 to $41.1 billion in 1990, thanks in part to the expansion of domestic demand in Japan. By mid-1991, however, the trend had shifted toward a bigger trade gap and demand for imports had fallen. Moreover, the dramatic increase in Japanese direct investments in the United States, from $10 billion in 1986 to $26 billion in 1989, had created a specter of Japanese economic "invasion" of the United States. Without a doubt, the most important key to Japan's constructive international policy in the posthegemonic era hinges on its ability to manage its political and economic relations with the United States. A complicating factor is the disappearance of the Soviet Union as a unified state and the dramatically reduced threat, if any, that the former Soviet republics now pose to the security of the West.

The first pronouncements of the Soviet post–Cold War policy toward the Asia Pacific region came in Mikhail Gorbachev's Vladivostok speech in 1986 and his Krasnoyarsk speech in 1988. The Soviet leader's top priority in Asia Pacific was rapprochement with China, and any improvement in Soviet-Japanese relations had to wait. Nor could Tokyo respond favorably to Gorbachev's proposals for a comprehensive regional security framework, arms control, and confidence-building measures (CBMs) when Washington had only begun to review its global strategy. In the assessment of the Japanese defense policymakers, the quantitative reductions in the Soviet Far Eastern and Pacific forces were more than compensated by qualitative improvements.[30] Politically, Tokyo and Moscow were deadlocked in the intractable problem of the "Northern Territories," and the stagnant economic ties between the two countries offered no assistance in breaking the deadlock. In contrast, Japan's Northeast Asian neighbors quickly moved from animosity and hostility to reconciliation and cooperation. Moscow and Seoul established diplomatic ties in the fall of 1990, and China and South Korea set up trade offices in each other's capital in the winter of 1990 and established diplomatic relations in 1992.

The Korean situation has presented both a challenge and an opportunity to Japan. The fast pace of Soviet–South Korean rapprochement surprised Tokyo. It was, however, a welcome development, as Tokyo soon began talks with Pyongyang to establish diplomatic relations. North Korea wanted to counter the recent diplomatic feats of its southern rival and also wished to tap into Japanese economic resources to save its devastatingly backward economy. Japan, for its part, wanted to prevent further isolation of North Korea and its potentially destabilizing effect.[31] Fortunately, Washington, Moscow, and Beijing welcomed Tokyo's efforts. Tokyo has approached Pyongyang cautiously so as not to hurt the interests of its allies and friends. Japan shares the international concern over Pyongyang's refusal to commit itself formally and unequivocally to the full safeguards inspections of North Korean nuclear facilities by the International Atomic Energy Agency (IAEA). Eventually, the international pressure was instrumental in the December 1991 conclusion of a North Korea–South Korea treaty of reconciliation and nonaggression, which renounced armed force against each other, and in the Seoul-Pyongyang agreement the same month to make the Korean peninsula nuclear-free. Although details of the agreement are yet to be worked out, Washington and Tokyo have welcomed the accord.

There are now enhanced opportunities for Tokyo to contribute to the implementation of the security and confidence-building measures developing on the peninsula. The most urgent task for Tokyo is to normalize its relations with Pyongyang and assist North Korea economically but to do so without harming its relations with Seoul. Tokyo understands Seoul's concern over the issue of Japanese compensation for North Korea for Imperial Japan's colonial control of the Korean peninsula and has repeatedly rejected the North Korean demand for postwar damages, hinting instead at the possibility of badly needed economic assistance to North Korea. Tokyo is equally cognizant of Seoul's concern that Japanese economic aid to North Korea might be used in Pyongyang's military buildup. Lastly, the South Korean concern about the North's references to "one Korea" in its dealings with Japan was eliminated in September 1991, when both North Korea and South Korea were admitted into the United Nations. Thus, yet another obstacle to Japanese–North Korean rapprochement has been removed. Interest is also growing in Japan and Korea (both North and South), as well as in China and the former Soviet Union, to bring their economies into closer association. Although there remain many obstacles to the establishment of what some call a "Japan Sea-rim economic zone," support for the idea is likely to grow among the coastal regions facing the Sea of Japan.[32]

Japan's relations with China have been affected surprisingly little by the recent global trends, with the bilateral ties developing more according to a logic of their own. Tokyo has welcomed and supported Beijing's modernizations program and open-door policy since the early 1980s. However, in the wake of the crackdown of the democratic movement at the Tiananmen Square in June 1989, Japan joined the Western sanctions against China by suspending a $5.9 billion aid program that was due to start in fiscal year 1990 and by barring all high-level contacts. After Beijing took several steps in response to the Western criticisms of its human rights violations, Tokyo sought to restore normal relations with Beijing. At the Houston summit in

July 1990, Prime Minister Kaifu sought the other Western leaders' understanding toward Japan's "special relationship" with China and soon thereafter announced planned resumption of untied yen loans. In September, Tokyo also lifted the ban on high-level diplomatic contacts with Beijing.[33] By the summer of 1991 Japanese-Chinese relations had returned to the pre-Tiananmen level. Prime Minister Kaifu visited Beijing in August, marking the first visit to China by the top leader of a major industrialized democracy since June 1989, and in October 1992 the Japanese emporer visited China. Barring major incidents in China, it is likely that the bilateral political relations will continue to improve and economic ties expand beyond the current level, with two-way trade reaching more than $20 billion.

There are a number of issues that could dampen Japan's relations with China, however. Potentially troubling issues include the territorial dispute over the Senkaku (Tiaoyu) Islands in the East China Sea, the development of a Chinese blue-water navy, Beijing's apprehensions about the growing military power of Japan, the continuing struggle over who should succeed Deng Xiaoping, and the severe financial shortages and debt problems Chinese partners of Japanese businesses are facing under Beijing's antiinflation policy instituted in the fall of 1988.

Tokyo's minimalist security policy and economically oriented and Asian-focused foreign policy seem to have been vindicated by the deepening relations between Japan and the ASEAN countries. Since the announcement of the Fukuda Doctrine in 1977, Tokyo has aggressively (and for most part, successfully) cultivated friendly ties with the ASEAN members. Japan has generally viewed national and regional economic development as essential to the political stability of the region and the Southeast Asian leaders have also seen domestic resilience as the most important aspect of their national security. Moreover, Japan has consistently supported the ASEAN policy in favor of a comprehensive political settlement of the Cambodian conflict and pledged its support for and participation in the UN-administered postwar settlement in Cambodia and postconflict reconstruction of the Indochinese economies. Of some concern to the ASEAN countries, however, is the possibility that some of Japan's ODA and investments in the region might be diverted to Vietnam.

As protectionism in the industrialized world has grown, Japan's expanding domestic markets for Southeast Asian exports have begun to have political significance. Should the Uruguay Round of GATT negotiations fail to resolve the most contentious trade issues in agricultural trade, that would have far-reaching implications for the export-dependent ASEAN economies. Therefore, Japan's role in the global talks and its role as an export market for Southeast Asian products cannot be underestimated. The presence of Japanese direct investments in ASEAN countries, particularly in the manufacturing sector, has also grown, thereby accelerating the integration of the region's economies. However, the resulting Japanese dominance has generated some anti-Japanese sentiments. The region's externally oriented economies are increasingly affected by economic developments beyond Southeast Asia. Southeast Asians are concerned, for example, that the APEC forum, established in 1990, may undermine the degree of influence the ASEAN forum has accorded them vis-à-vis Japan. These considerations clearly call for better communication and more effective consultations between Japan and the ASEAN countries.

From this brief overview of the opportunities and challenges that face Japan, it is clear that at the dawn of the posthegemonic era the nation has a daunting task. In the following analyses, the authors delve further into the expectations of the Pacific Rim countries and Japan's performance in the fast-changing regional environment, and assess Japan's potential as a major political power in the posthegemonic world.

—————————————————————————————— *Notes*

1. Joseph Nye, Jr., *Bound to Lead: The Changing Nature of American Power*, New York: Basic Books, 1990; Bruce Russett, "The Mysterious Case of Vanishing Hegemony; or, Is Mark Twain Really Dead?" *International Organization*, vol. 39, no. 2 (Spring 1985), pp. 207–231; Susan Strange, "The Persistent Myth of Lost Hegemony," *International Organization*, vol. 41, no. 4 (Autumn 1987), pp. 563–571; Samuel Huntington, "The U.S.—Decline or Renewal," *Foreign Affairs*, vol. 67, no. 2 (Winter 1988/89), pp. 76–96

2. See, for example, Robert Gilpin, *The Political Economy of International Relations*, Princeton, N.J.: Princeton University Press, 1987; Seymour Melman, "Economic Consequences of the Arms Race: The Second-Rate Economy," *American Economic Review*, vol. 78, no. 2 (May 1988), pp. 55–59; Seymour Melman, "Limits of Military Power: Economic and Other," *International Security*, vol. 11, no. 1 (Summer 1986), pp. 72–88.

3. See, for example, William S. Dietrich, *In the Shadow of the Rising Sun: The Political Roots of American Economic Decline*, University Park, Pa.: Pennsylvania State University Press, 1991.

4. See, for example, ibid.; Robert B. Reich, "Why the U.S. Needs an Industrial Policy," *Harvard Business Review*, vol. 60 (January–February 1982), pp. 74–81; Chalmers Johnson, ed., *The Industrial Policy Debate*, San Francisco: Institute for Contemporary Studies Press, 1984.

5. Karel van Wolferen, *The Enigma of Japanese Power: People and Politics in a Stateless Nation*, New York: Alfred A. Knopf, 1989.

6. See, for example, David Calleo, *Beyond American Hegemony: The Future of the Western Alliance*, New York: Basic Books, 1987; Robert B. Reich, "Making Industrial Policy," *Foreign Affairs*, vol. 60 (Spring 1982), pp. 852–881; Clyde V. Prestowitz, Jr., *Trading Places: How We Allowed Japan to Take the Lead*, New York: Basic Books, 1988; Michael Moffit, "Shocks, Deadlocks, and Scorched Earth," *World Policy Journal*, vol. 4, no. 4 (Fall 1987), pp. 553–582

7. Paul Kennedy, *The Rise and Fall of the Great Powers*, New York: Random House, 1987.

8. See, for example, ibid.; Immanuel Wallerstein, *The Politics of the World-Economy*, Cambridge: Cambridge University Press, 1987.

9. Charles Kindleberger, *The World in Depression, 1929–1939*, Berkeley: University of California Press, 1974; Robert Gilpin, *War and Change in World Politics*, Cambridge: Cambridge University Press, 1981, p. 17.

10. See, for example, Robert O. Keohane, *After Hegemony: Cooperation and Discord in the World Political Economy*, Princeton, N.J.: Princeton University Press, 1984.

11. Robert Cox, "Production and Hegemony: Toward a Political Economy of World Order," in Harold K. Jacobson and Susan Sidjanski, eds., *The Emerging International Economic Order*, Beverly Hills, Calif.: Sage Publications, 1982, p. 45.

12. Torbjon Knutsen, "Hegemony in the Modern International System," paper delivered at the 1986 annual meeting of the American Political Science Association, Washington, D.C., August 28–31, 1986, p. 15.

13. Ibid., p. 13.

14. Gilpin, *War and Change in World Politics*, p. 17.

15. Ibid., pp. 156–157.

16. Ibid., p. 187.

17. Calleo, *Beyond American Hegemony*, p. 215.

18. Paul Kennedy, *The Rise and Fall of the Great Powers*, New York: Random House, 1987.

19. This assessment is shared by Richard Rosecrance, who has observed that the United States stands at the divide between a "trading" path to national growth and a "political-territorial" course of foreign policy. See Richard Rosecrance, *The Rise of the Trading State: Commerce and Conquest in the Modern World*, New York: Basic Books, 1986.

20. An insightful review of the debate in Japan over its role in the emerging new world order is found in Kenneth B. Pyle, "The Burden of Japanese History and the Politics of Burden Sharing," in John H. Makin and Donald C. Hellmann, eds., *Sharing World Leadership? A New Era for America and Japan*, Washington, D.C.: American Enterprise Institute for Public Policy Research, 1989, pp. 41–77. For an articulate advocacy of an expanded Japanese role in the collective management of global problems, see Takashi Inoguchi, *Tadanori to Ikkoku Haneishugi o Koete: Tenkanki no Sekai to Nihon* [Beyond free-ride and unilateral prosperity: The world at a turning point and Japan], Tokyo: Tōyō Keizai Shimpōsha, 1987; Kuniko Inoguchi, *Posuto Haken Shisutemu to Nihon no Sentaku* [The emerging posthegemonic system: Choices for Japan], Tokyo: Chikuma Shobō, 1987.

21. Chihiro Hosoya et al., *Nichi-bei-ō no Keizai Masatsu o Meguru Seiji Katei* [The political process surrounding the economic frictions among Japan, the United States, and Europe], Tokyo: National Institute for Research Advancement, 1990.

22. Some of the most recent examples include Hideo Sato, "Japan's Role in the Post–Cold War World," *Current History* (April 1991), pp. 145–148, 179; Takashi Inoguchi, "Change and Response in Japan's International Politics and Strategy," in Stuart Harris and James Cotton, eds., *The End of the Cold War in Northeast Asia*, Boulder, Colo.: Lynne Rienner Publishers, 1991, pp. 192–216; Masaru Tamamoto, "Japan's Uncertain Role," *World Policy Journal*, vol. 8, no. 4 (Fall 1991), pp. 579–597; Koji Taira, "Japan: An Imminent Hegemon," *The Annals of the American Academy of Political and Social Science*, vol. 513 (January 1991), pp. 151–163; Yoichi Funabashi, "Japan and the New World Order," *Foreign Affairs*, vol. 70, no. 5 (Winter 1991/1992), pp. 58–74; Miyohei Shinohara, "Japan as a World Economic Power," *The Annals of the American Academy of Political and Social Science*, vol. 513 (January 1991), pp. 12–24.

23. Indeed, there have been numerous proposals for Japan's enhanced international roles, some put forth by government agencies and advisory committees and

some by private groups and individuals. A few recent examples include Seiichi Kondo, "Nihon wa Gaikō Taikoku ni Nareruka" [Can Japan become a major diplomatic power?] *Gaikō Forum*, no. 37 (October 1991), pp. 69–80; Hiroaki Fujii, "90-nendai no Kokusai Keizai to Nihon no Yakuwari" [International economy in the 1990s and Japan's role], *Gaikō Forum*, no. 28 (January 1991), pp. 46–55; Takakazu Kuriyama, "Sekai Shin-chitsujo no naka no Nichibei Kankei: Gurōbaru Pātonāshippu o Motomete" [Japan-U.S. relations in the new world order: In search of a global partnership], *Gaikō Forum*, no. 38 (November 1991), pp. 16–26.

24. Chalmers Johnson, *MITI and the Japanese Economic Miracle: The Growth of Industrial Policy, 1925–1975*, Stanford, Calif.: Stanford University Press, 1982.

25. For an excellent collection of essays on Japanese foreign policy during this period, see Robert A. Scalapino, ed., *The Foreign Policy of Modern Japan*, Berkeley: University of California Press, 1977.

26. For a dissenting voice, for example, see Tsuneo Iida, *Nihon Keizai wa Doko e Ikunoka: Ayaui Yutakasa to Hanei no naka de* [Where is the Japanese economy headed? Amidst precarious wealth and prosperity], Tokyo: PHP Kenkyūjo, 1986.

27. Makin and Hellmann, *Sharing World Leadership?*

28. Pyle, "Burden of Japanese History."

29. Donald S. Zagoria, "Major Power Relations in East Asia," in Robert A. Scalapino and Gennady I. Chufrin, eds., *Asia in the 1990s: American and Soviet Perspectives*, Berkeley, Calif.: Institute of East Asian Studies, 1991, pp. 49–59.

30. Bōeichō, *Boēi Hakusho* [Defense white paper], Tokyo: Okurashō Insatsu-kyoku, 1990, pp. 44–59.

31. North Korea's trade with Japan amounted to $502 million in 1989, only one-sixtieth of the South Korean–Japanese trade. Hisane Masaki, "Expectations Mount for Kanemaru Trip to N. Korea," *The Japan Times*, Weekly International Edition, September 24–30, 1989, p. 3.

32. For a discussion of this concept in Japan, see Kazuo Ogawa and Teruo Komaki, *Kan Nihonkai Keizaiken* [Japan Sea-rim economic zone], Tokyo: Nihon Keizai Shimbun, 1991; Takeo Touma, *Ugokihajimeta Kan Nihonkai Keizaiken* [The Japan Sea-rim economic zone beginning to move], Tokyo: Sōchisha, 1991; Kenji Nakano, *Hokutō Ajia no Shimpū: Kan Nihonkai Shinjidai no Genten o Saguru* [A fresh wind in Northeast Asia: Exploring the origins of the new era of the Japan Sea-rim], Tokyo: Jōhō Kikaku Shuppan, 1991.

33. Japan was also encouraged by the normalization of China's relations with Indonesia and Singapore in August 1990.

Chapter 1
Hegemons in History
Philip J. Meeks

This chapter focuses on a number of issues related to the concept, definitions, and problems of hegemony. It argues that the concept of hegemony, which in the original Greek implied only "leadership," has traditionally meant "dominance," particularly military dominance. The increasing interest in economic sources of international power over the past thirty years, however, has changed the definitions and use of the concept of hegemony. The traditional preoccupation with military dominance of most scholars writing on this topic has been increasingly challenged by political economy scholars, including some who have tried to conceptualize systems of international economic leadership/hegemony that do not rely upon the ability to project military power throughout the globe. The debate over hegemons and their role in international relations has also frequently been an intensely ideological one. Neorealists, neoliberal idealists, and neo-Marxist advocates (as well as their historical predecessors) all fundamentally disagree about both the causes and the consequences of the uneven distribution of power among contemporary nation-states as well as their historical predecessors.

The first part of this chapter surveys and examines a number of different perspectives concerning the definitions of hegemony and their relationship to concepts of power. Subsequently, there is a brief summary of the ideological differences concerning hegemony and dominance in international relations. The second part of this chapter examines a number of specific countries and historical periods in which hegemony has been alleged to have occurred, as well as claims to uniform causes and consequences that link some of these cases. Particular attention is focused on the cases of nineteenth-century Britain and twentieth-century United States, which have received the predominant amount of contemporary attention.

The conclusion of this analysis proposes that our understanding of hegemony, particularly economic hegemony, in the decade ahead should be transformed from notions of single country dominance to notions of collective international leadership. Dominance in international relations usually is accompanied by resentment and conflict. Claims that dominance produces desired stability have often been self-serving nationalist claims by those who benefit from or agree with the interests of the hegemon. Leadership, on the other hand, is demonstrated by building consensus whereby all major participants have an important role in international decisionmaking. This type of leadership/cooperation system may be seen as ushering in a "posthegemonic" world order, or substantially changing the concept of hegemony. It will remain hegemonic insofar as a relatively few wealthy and powerful countries will continue to establish the "rules" by which international relations will normally operate. Furthermore, vigorous economic competition for markets, trade, and finance are likely within the collective hegemony.

Japan will certainly play a crucial role in this transformation of international relations in the decade ahead. A more specific analysis of this transformation will be presented in Chapter 2.

Hegemony and Power

According to Joseph Nye, power in international politics is like the weather: Everyone talks about it, but few understand it.[1] Actually, far more agreement exists about the dynamics of weather than about the dynamics of power among nations. And it is difficult to effectively control either power or the weather at a given place or time for national or international goals.

Just as it is difficult to obtain a consensus on the nature of power and its dynamics in international relations, it is difficult to obtain a consensus on the nature of hegemony. The study of historical and contemporary hegemony deals with the unequal distribution of power among nations. Hegemonic theories purport to explain how and why some countries have obtained a preponderant degree of power vis-à-vis other nations and the consequences of this preponderance for international relations.

The literal meaning of "hegemon," taken from the Greek, means "leader." A leader can guide or conduct without dominating. Leadership and its authority to influence vary widely from culture to culture. Perhaps the popularity of this concept among British and U.S. scholars tells us more about British-U.S. culture than it does about the multiple definitions of leadership implied by the term "hegemon." Hegemony does not necessarily imply only one nation-state. Leadership can be collective. It can be exercised by a small group of states. Indeed, it need not be a nation-state. An international organization or an international regime may be able to exert the crucial leadership necessary to guide a system or to maintain maximum feasible benefits.

Hegemony can also be usefully seen in the context of a balance-of-power system. The hegemons may be one or more crucial states and/or international organizations, which can act as the balancers in a potentially unstable political or economic system. Equilibrium may depend upon their leadership, but they are not responsible for the entire dynamics of the system.

Hegemonic theories of such authors as Robert Keohane, Robert Cox, Bruce Russett, and Susan Strange have emphasized a situation in which one state is dominant in all aspects of power and influence—military, economic, political, and even cultural.[2] Other authors, such as Duncan Snidal, have allowed for more narrow definitions in which a nation may dominate in only one sphere of influence.[3] Snidal asserts, however, that if a state's capacity for dominance is in the military arena it should be described as a "coercive" leadership system, whereas economic dominance requires a "consent" leadership system.

In spite of the application of the term "hegemony" to virtually any analysis of power and leadership in recent years, it remains for many theorists a fundamentally military concept derived from the classical Greek system of city-states. In this approach, hegemony is often defined as "conflicts precipitated by the military effort of one dominant actor to expand well beyond the arbitrary security confines set by tradition, historical accident, or coercive pressures."[4] Yet, as Nye argues, "no modern state has been able to develop sufficient military power to transform the balance of power into a long-lived hegemony in which one state could dominate the world militarily."[5]

There have been many attempts to "graft" this concept/paradigm onto the historical experiences of Great Britain in the nineteenth century and the United States after World War II, but there has always remained a difficulty in clearly distinguishing the economic and the military characteristics of power in the analysis of hegemony. The dawn of the nuclear era and Cold War bipolarity merely reinforced the military preoccupation until the unprecedented postwar economic growth and resource crises of the 1970s began to attract more attention from international relations scholars.

As nuclear stalemates and even conventional military failures by the superpowers became commonplace in the 1960s and 1970s, many political scientists focused on economic control as the key to hegemonic dominance. In Immanuel Wallerstein's terms:

> Hegemony in the interstate system refers to that situation in which the ongoing rivalry between the so-called "great powers" is so unbalanced that one power is truly *primus inter pares*; that is, one power can largely impose its rules and its wishes (at the very least by effective veto power) in the economic, political, military, diplomatic, and even cultural arenas. The material base of such power lies in the ability of enterprises domiciled in that power to operate more efficiently in all three major economic arenas—agro-industrial production, commerce, and finance. The edge in efficiency of which we are speaking is one so great that these enterprises can not only outbid enterprises domiciled in other great powers in the world market in general, but quite specifically in very many instances within the home markets of the rival powers themselves.[6]

At the same time, Wallerstein is more careful than others in distinguishing between hegemony and omnipotence:

It is not enough for one power's enterprises simply to have a larger share of the world market than any other or simply to have the most powerful military forces or the largest political role. I mean hegemony only to refer to situations in which the edge is so significant that allied major powers are *de facto* client states and opposed major powers feel relatively frustrated and highly defensive vis-à-vis the hegemonic power. And yet while I want to restrict my definition to instances where the margin of power differential is really great, I do not mean to suggest that there is ever any moment when a hegemonic power is omnipotent and capable of doing anything it wants. Omnipotence does not exist within the interstate system.[7]

Unfortunately, the 1970s also witnessed dual crises in international relations theory in both politics and economics. Political scientists debated dependency, then hegemony, then regimes, without fundamentally rethinking the historical and technological conditions that have changed the classical ideologies of capitalism and socialism. Economists debated Marxist, Keynesian, and monetarist theories of growth, development, and distribution, without fundamentally reconsidering the nature of the state and public policy in an increasingly complex and crowded international environment. International political economy became an increasingly popular field just as its theoretical foundations began to crumble away.

In one of the best recent works on hegemony, however, Nye makes careful distinctions between power "resources" and power "conversion" or mobilization.[8] Power resources come from the capabilities that states possess as measured in so-called "objective" units such as military weapons and personnel, territory, natural resources, economic production, financial capital, advanced technologies, and so forth. Power conversion is the ability to use these power resources in order to affect the behavior and decisions of other countries or to structure the costs and benefits of the entire system of international relations.

Another interesting dimension is the appropriateness of any given type of power in a given historical or particular context. Nye gives the example of the 1860s, when Germany pioneered the use of railways to transport armies for quicker victories. In turn, the increasing use of railroads in continental Europe as a means of mobilizing armies helped deprive Britain of the luxury of relying upon the naval technologies it had mastered in an earlier era. The inability or unwillingness to use nuclear military force in the post–World War II era remains an even more powerful reminder of this situation.

Nye also emphasizes both the dynamic and the relative nature of power in international relations. He claims that raw materials and heavy industry are less critical indices of economic power, for example, than they were in the nineteenth century. Instead, it is information and professional and technical services that are crucial. Unfortunately, this "postindustrialist" thesis is not examined in depth, nor is there even a superficial attempt to estimate the relative importance of industry versus services and/or information as power resources.[9]

Strange argues that much of the confusion over the nature of power and possible hegemony results from the failure to distinguish between structural power (military or economic) and relational power.[10] In her definition, structural power is the "power to shape and determine the structures of the global political economy."[11] Relational power refers to the ability to use power in order to affect the behavior and decisions of certain countries or to structure the costs and benefits of bilateral or multilateral political, military, or economic relations in a certain way—but not the entire system of international relations.

For Strange, one of the dilemmas of either form of power is the fact that "the power to exploit others, whether the exploitation is economic or political, is not inconsistent with the possibility that power will ricochet back on its possessors to their ultimate disadvantage."[12] She believes that structural power is obviously more important; hence her conclusion with regard to the present world financial system that "Japanese power in finance is relational only whereas that of the United States is structural. The process of equalization if it ever happens will take a long time and would involve radical reform of the international economic organizations over which the U.S. still has constitutional veto power."[13]

Although there is no consensus about the general nature and consequences of hegemony in international relations, most theorists ultimately fall into one of three camps: egalitarian, elitist, or middle ground. Egalitarian theorists believe that hegemony on the whole is bad because hegemons usually use their power for selfish, nationalistic reasons that rarely promote world security and/or prosperity. Hegemons, according to this view, attempt to dictate or dominate the goals and actions of international politics in ways to derive maximum benefits for themselves, while passing off maximum costs to the less powerful nations of the world.

Elitist theories of hegemony usually focus on the benefits of order and stability that result from one or more hegemonic powers. They believe that nations become hegemons in the same way that elites form in societies—by being the best at what they do. Disproportionate power is the appropriate reward, according to this view, for those elites and/or nations who are the most efficient at obtaining and/or utilizing resources. Just as in the case of wealth, elitist proponents of hegemony believe that the risks of leadership and initiative will not occur if power is distributed evenly among actors. While most elitist theorists will admit that nations seek to create a world order in their own image and with goals and values that may be uniquely national, they are quick to point out the universality and/or desirability of these goals for other nations. In any case, elitists often believe themselves to be "realists" and argue that altruism among nations is a noble but unnatural virtue, and a stable, if unequal, order is preferable to the equality and stagnation of anarchy.

Although there is a strong temptation to cast hegemonic theorists into one or the other extreme camp, it must be recognized that most theorists actually fall into the middle-ground camp, which recognizes the advantages and disadvantages of both positions. Many in this fuzzy middle ground may lean more strongly in one direction or another, depending upon the period of history being studied or the countries involved. The theoretical price to be paid for staying in the fuzzy middle ground is acceptable for those unwilling to commit themselves to a clearer but more radical perception of the causes and consequences of the inequality of power among nations. The large number of theorists in the middle also indicates the lack of consensus and/or evidence about the true nature of hegemony.

Not surprisingly, most middle-ground hegemonic theorists are from Europe, the United States, or Japan. Most elitist theorists are also from these relatively powerful and wealthy countries, which derive substantial benefits from the current inequalities in the contemporary world system. Although many egalitarian theorists are critics of their own country's disproportionate power, it is fairly safe to say that most Third World scholars are egalitarians. The emergence of dependency analysis from Third World scholars in the past thirty years is primarily a radical egalitarian response from these theorists to addressing the basic causes and consequences of hegemony in international relations. Casting the hegemony question in terms of imperialism and/or neo-colonialism is preferable for those theorists from developing countries whose peoples have suffered under recent or past domination. It is rare to find a Third World scholar who will publicly extol the virtues of imperialism and/or hegemonic power, but it is not difficult to find Third World governments willing to attempt to establish regional hegemonies and to attempt to pass on the relative exploitation and disadvantage they have suffered at the hands of the most powerful nations to the weakest countries in their areas of the world.

Equally at the heart of the ideological debate about hegemony is the debate over the vices and virtues of capitalism. The virtue of capitalism is competition, which presumably creates the lowest and fairest prices and gives the greatest incentives to maximize production. The greatest vice of capitalism is inequality, not just in the relative distribution of wealth but of the very means of survival. The strongest survive and the weakest die. This is true not just for firms but also for people. And in the words of the great historian Fernand Braudel, "capitalism implies above all hierarchy, and it takes up a position at the top of the hierarchy, whether or not this was created by itself."[14]

This raises the crucial question of whether a hierarchical imperative of capitalism creates hegemony in a unique and fundamental way or merely affects the relative power and influence hegemons now have compared to precapitalist hegemons. Can the Soviet Union prior to its recent dissolution as an anticapitalist state be considered a hegemon? What is the essential and definitional difference between a "superpower" and a hegemon?

The history of hegemonies has also been inextricably linked to the rise and decline of empires and imperialism. There is not enough time or space to review even superficially the major theories of imperialism of the past century. Suffice it to say that, whereas hegemony deals with the rise and decline of power within and among nation-states and imperialism deals with the motivations for the creation, administration, and expansion of colonial areas, both hegemony and imperialism are about the acquisition and maintenance of global power and wealth. The ideological judgments of the value and consequences of imperialism, especially capitalist imperialism, are very similar to those regarding hegemony.

Some theorists have emphasized the political motivations for empire and/or hegemony, including the prestige of the sovereign and/or nation-state. Other theorists have stressed military interests, including both basic warrior satisfaction in dominance and conquest as well as strategic defense. Cultural theories of imperialism, including zeal for religious crusades and linguistic pride, have also enjoyed some popularity from time to time. However, economic explanations for empire and hegemony have dominated the twentieth century. From J. A. Hobson to Paul Kennedy, the rise and decline of nations and empires is primarily attributed to a variety of economic factors and explanations.[15] As Robert Gilpin and others have suggested, this is because the technology of production introduced in the Industrial Revolution made great wealth possible through trade and investment.[16]

Adapted to the contemporary discussion of hegemony, Hobson would presumably attribute predominance in global affairs to the nation that could most effectively limit its domestic consumption and use its "excess" goods and capital to penetrate and control the economies of other countries. Simultaneously, it could also invest in the most advanced and efficient technologies of production at home to assure maximum competitive advantage in foreign trade. This penetration, however, has not been as extensive in developing countries as it has been in advanced industrial states. Currently, approximately three-fourths of all trade and two-thirds of all foreign investment occur in and between advanced industrial states. No doubt Hobson would find it difficult to explain today how and why advanced industrial countries have not needed to conquer each other to achieve this, and how recipient countries consistently try to outbid each other with government subsidies to attract foreign investment.

Most ideological arguments, to use an old cliché, add more heat than light to the understanding of the complex problem of power in international relations. We still lack a clear understanding of the relationship between the economic and military sources of power as they relate to hegemony. There is no consensus on how capitalism and/or imperialism determine or are affected by hegemony. The search for general theories ultimately comes down to the consideration of relatively few historical cases.

Hegemons and History _____

Explanations for the growth and decline of power within and between countries have provided much, perhaps most, of historical scholarship. Although most theses are multicausal and multidimensional, inevitably one factor is given more weight than others. The perception of national interest and the prime objective of foreign policies are determined by the ruling elites in virtually all countries. Traditionally, national security and military power have been given top priority. According to Gilpin, this is because

> prior to the modern age, particularly prior to the Industrial Revolution, conquest of territory was the primary means by which a group or state could increase its security or wealth. In an era of relatively stable technology and low productivity gains in both agriculture and manufacturing, a group or state could best increase its wealth and power by increasing its control over territory and conquering other peoples. In fact, until the technological revolution of the late eighteenth century, the international distribution of territory and the distribution of power and wealth were largely synonymous.[17]

According to Wallerstein's economic definition of hegemony, in which there is a simultaneous advantage in production, commerce, and finance, hegemony has been rare and short lived. In fact, Wallerstein claims there have been only three modern instances of hegemony—in the Netherlands in 1620–1650, in Britain in 1815–1873, and in the United States in 1945–1967.[18] From his neo-Marxist perspective, Wallerstein has described these hegemonic eras as ones in which economic dominance was accompanied by an ideology of global economic liberalism, although these countries made exceptions to their general antimercantilism when it was in their self-interest. Hegemony was further reinforced with global military power and secured by long world wars (1618–1648; 1792–1815; 1914–1945). The consequence of these long conflict phases was a major restructuring of the interstate system (Westphalia, Concert of Europe, United Nations, and Bretton Woods) in tune with the need to stabilize the world's order with the interests of the hegemonic power. Finally, as the power of the hegemon slowly declined, "contenders for succession" emerged (England and France after Dutch hegemony; Germany and the United States after British hegemony; and Western Europe and Japan after U.S. hegemony), with the eventual winner seeming "to use as a conscious part of its strategy the gentle turning of the old hegemonic power into its 'junior partner'."[19]

Christopher Chase-Dunn generally agrees with Wallerstein's three modern hegemonic periods and with his triad of productive, commercial, and financial dominance, but he stresses that productive efficiency must be reinforced by state power:

> The creation and maintenance of economic preeminence requires the political and military capacity to preserve a domestic class structure favorable to capitalist accumulation, innovative production, and the prevention of external restrictions on flows of capital or goods. In this sense political-military power is a necessary but not a sufficient basis for the attainment of hegemony in a capitalist world-economy.[20]

Chase-Dunn makes the crucial distinction that mere ability to collect large amounts of taxes is insufficient to categorize state strength. Hegemons, like the Dutch and English during their respective periods, must be able to mobilize the resources of economic elites in times of national emergency by convincing them that their economic interests are as much at risk as the power and prestige of the state. Modern hegemonic states also seem to have a relatively egalitarian and pluralistic domestic political system compared to other rival states. Chase-Dunn points out that these characteristics can be advantageous in the world economy because "this pluralism allows rapid adaptation to changes in the interests of classes in the center coalition, as well as some flexibility in response to the demands of workers and farmers."[21] In other words, not only do hegemons have stronger home markets because of relatively more equal distributions of income, but they also are more effective in capitalizing on national allegiance in pursuit of military expansion and/or foreign economic policy.

Chase-Dunn also helpfully characterizes hegemonic periods by contrasting them with "normal" nonhegemonic periods. The periods in between these hegemonic ones have been characterized, he says:

> by a relatively equal (multicentric) distribution of military power and economic competitive advantage among core states, and by relatively higher levels of conflict and competition within the core . . . these periods were characterized by more bilateral and politically controlled relationships between core and the periphery in which each core state attempted to monopolize exchange with its "own" colonial empire.[22]

Another related historical treatment of hegemony groups past periods of political-economic dominance into periodic movements in which power rises and declines. These movements are purported to be based upon economic cycles. The longest and best known of the economic cycles are the Kondratieff price cycles, which are roughly fifty years in length. George Modelski has proposed five hegemonic cycles since the end of the fifteenth century.[23] Each long cycle begins with a global war and reordering of power. Eventually it loses legitimacy and power, and the decline of the hegemon sparks another global war.

Modelski starts with Portugal as the hegemon from 1494 to 1580. Portugal emerged from a period of global warfare from 1494 to 1516; its influence rose from 1516 to 1540 and then declined until 1580. Next, the Netherlands emerged as global leader after wars from 1580 to 1609. Dutch predominance continued from 1609 to 1640 until its decline in 1688. Britain began the first of its two hegemonic periods after the wars from 1688 to 1713. Its height of predominance ran from 1714 to 1740 and was over by 1792. After the Napoleonic wars of 1792–1815, Britain again resumed the role of world leader until its peak in 1850, and then slowly declined until 1914 and World War I. Like Wallerstein, Modelski sees 1914–1945 as a more or less continual period of global war, which initiated the U.S. century of dominance. According to Modelski, U.S. hegemony was strongest from 1945 to 1973 and has been declining ever since. If his theories and projections are correct, another period of global warfare will occur sometime in the early twenty-first century. But would this mean a second century of U.S. dominance or a new hegemon such as Japan, Germany, or a united Europe?

Paul Kennedy, in his best-selling book *The Rise and Fall of the Great Powers*, deals with the same general theme and historical periods (since 1500) as do Wallerstein and Modelski.[24] However, he puts less emphasis on the notion of hegemony per se and is not particularly interested in following the imperative of capitalism thesis of Wallerstein or the Kondratieff cycles of Modelski. Instead, he focuses on the relationship between economic resources and the quest for military dominance. He is very careful to warn his readers about overgeneralizing about trends derived from so few cases, but he generally subscribes to the "imperial overstretch" theory of hegemonic decline. In his view, economic wealth fuels military expansion and conquest by a "great" power. Eventually, however, the imperial or foreign commitments eat away at the economic and technological base of a country. If a country expands too much, its military overseas commitments will weaken its economy and competitiveness and it will inevitably decline. He details this dilemma in greatest length for Spain, the Netherlands, France, Britain, and the United States.

Macrohistorical theories such as those by Wallerstein, Modelski, and Kennedy are helpful in the understanding of general relationships between economic and military power in determining the hierarchy of nations over time. The study of hegemony, however, is not like the study of war per se in that it lacks both detailed historical evidence before 1500 and a sufficient number of national cases to test a powerful general theory. The case can be made that before 1500, city-states like Venice or Genoa acted like regional hegemons within their spheres of influence. Many of these cities had powerful economic elites but they came to power before the true development of a capitalist world economy. Their domination was more politicomilitary and more independent of economic interests than later cases. Because these city-states were also preindustrial, they were much less able to use technological innovation to accelerate their sources of power and advantage.

The military, economic, and technological revolutions of the past five hundred years make it extremely difficult to compare the power relations of preindustrial, precapitalist hegemonic states with states that developed after these fundamental changes in the world economy. Even the Dutch case in the late seventeenth and early eighteenth centuries, although Wallerstein and Chase-Dunn make credible arguments for it fulfilling the minimum modern requirements of hegemony, is probably best seen as occurring in a transitional period between earlier city-state hegemons and modern nation-state hegemons. Amsterdam was never higher than fourth among core cities in terms of population, compared to London and New York.[25] Violet Barbour, Braudel, and Peter Burke all provide substantial arguments and evidence that Amsterdam is more correctly seen as the last great city-state than as the first hegemonic nation-state.[26]

Ultimately, most scholars are forced to concentrate on the two most recent cases of hegemony—Britain in the nineteenth century and the United States in the twentieth century. The rise and decline of any future hegemonic powers will have to be understood in terms of what we can learn from these two cases. Therefore, we will now turn to a brief consideration of these two countries and look at the major similarities and differences between them.

_____ *Pax Britannica*

In his introduction to *Industry and Empire*, E. J. Hobsbawm states why nineteenth century Britain has long been considered the archetypal case of modern economy.

> There was a moment in the world's history when Britain can be described, if we are not too pedantic, as its only workshop, its only massive importer and exporter, its only carrier, its only imperialist, almost its only foreign investor; and for that reason its only naval power and the only one which had a genuine world policy. Much of this monopoly was simply due to the loneliness of the pioneer, monarch of all he surveys because of the absence of any other surveyors. When other countries industrialized, it ended automatically, though the apparatus of world economic transfers constructed by, and in terms of, Britain remained indispensable to the rest of the world for a while longer.[27]

British dominance of the international economy in the nineteenth century rested primarily on two factors. First, the British efforts in the pioneering of industrial technology gave it a fifty- to sixty-year head start in industrial investment and production. Second, the British had a vastly superior merchant fleet. Britain's advantages in shipping were not, however, due so much to technological superiority (French and U.S. ships were consistently more advanced), but rather to the sheer size of her fleet and "the preference of British shippers (even after the abrogation of the Navigation Acts, which protected the industry heavily) for native ships."[28]

The British economy exhibited progressive dominance in all three of Wallerstein's economic sectors, starting with cotton textile production. By the middle of the nineteenth century, England was producing and exporting a wide variety of machinery and industrial goods, as well as railroads and steamships. The role of Britain's international financial institutions in financing trading ventures, railroads, and ships was clearly evident by the end of the nineteenth century.

The early British industrial economy relied for its expansion chiefly on international trade. This was both a policy choice and a natural necessity. British supplies of industrial raw materials, with the exception of coal, were not very significant. Moreover, from the middle of the nineteenth century onward, the country's agriculture could neither feed the domestic population nor supply crops such as cotton, which were essential for the textile industries. Britain was in a position to develop its international trade both because of early monopolies in various industrial products, and later because of relations with the underdeveloped overseas world, which Britain established between 1870 and 1915.[29]

Britain was also able to expand so rapidly because of British naval strength, which made competition difficult for rival trading countries. English economic self-interest in suppressing the slave trade is well documented as is Britain's relatively greater effectiveness in combating piracy. Even when they were not totally effective, the British left a powerful inhibiting impression. As Kennedy puts it:

> the continual presence of the Royal Navy's warships off African and other coasts immeasurably strengthened Britain's influence in those regions, added several useful naval bases to the Empire and confirmed the impressions of European and native observers that an "informal rule" actually existed.[30]

By the beginning of the twentieth century, however, the effects of Britain's industrial pioneering and trading dominance were largely negative. Britain's economy remained dependent upon earlier industrial technologies and production equipment, whereas other and newer industrial economies could learn from the failures of the early processes and invest in newer, more productive techniques. These developments were particularly disturbing in the most basic industrial sector of iron and steel, in which most innovations came from or were developed in Britain (for example, the Bessemer converter in 1856, the Siemens-Martin open hearth furnace in 1867, and the Gilchrist-Thomas basic process in 1877–1878), but British industry was reluctant to apply these new technologies.

Why Britain did not adapt its domestic industrial structure to changing technology has been much debated. Whatever the reasons, it is evident that behind this industrial decline lay at least four fundamental problems: (1) lack of technologically innovative investment in the domestic economy, (2) sharp increases in public and private consumption, (3) problems of low productivity, and (4) sociopolitical conflict created by persistent inequalities in the distribution of wealth. Various analysts and historians have given different weights to each of these factors in explaining Britain's hegemonic decline, but most agree that all four factors have been important.[31]

The failures of the domestic economy increased Britain's vulnerability to external constraints. These external constraints included Britain's limited reserves, a consistently unfavorable balance of payments, and loss of much of its extensive international financial and resource holdings in the eventually independent developing countries. For nearly a century, observers of British international relations have been split over whether economic or political factors were more important in accounting for Britain's decline. Others have insisted that Britain's decline was more relative than real. They posit that Britain's early hegemony developed largely in a relative economic and military (naval) vacuum, and by the beginning of the twentieth century, many other industrial countries (especially the United States, Germany, and Japan) had "caught up." Nationalism and anti-imperialist sentiments in the twentieth century unquestionably took their toll on British overseas power and influence.

Although "imperial overstretch" theories of British decline have an intuitive appeal, critics of the theory rightly point out that British defense expenditures were, on average, only 3 percent of gross national product (GNP) from 1860 to 1914. Indeed, total government expenditure as a percent of GNP was significantly less than 10 percent for the same period. However, by 1913, two-thirds of British exports were going to what today would be considered developing countries. Likewise, 47 percent of total British foreign investment in 1913 (3.7 billion pounds sterling) was in the British Empire, including 10.1 percent in India and Ceylon and 9.8 percent in South Africa. An additional 20.1 percent was invested in Latin America, and half of the British investment in Europe was in czarist Russia. All of these investments, along with those in the United States, Canada, and Australia/New Zealand, were severely weakened by the economic depression in the 1920s and 1930s, as well as by the overvaluation of the pound. Britain's economic problems of the post–World War II era were further worsened by the combination of foreign economic policies designed to protect sterling and the financial connections of the City of London banking community, and domestic welfare policies designed to soften the blow of obsolescent industries on Britain's working class.

———————————————————————— *Pax Americana*

Much has been made of the similarity between nineteenth-century British hegemony and post-1945 U.S. hegemony. On the surface, both countries appeared to be dominant economically as well as militarily during their respective periods of hegemony. The respective currencies of these countries were the international reserve currency of their time. Both countries were able to capitalize on the weaknesses of their rivals as much as on their own strengths to achieve hegemony. However, the actual dimensions of U.S. dominance were unprecedented in absolute terms.[32] The United States accounted for one-half of the world's manufactured goods, one-third of the world's exports, and two-thirds of the world's gold reserves. It had the world's most powerful navy and air force as well as a monopoly on atomic weapons.

In fundamental ways, however, the United States was domestically and diplomatically unprepared for U.S. world hegemony after World War II. As Kennedy aptly describes it, "Like the British in 1815, the Americans in their turn found their informal influence in various lands hardening into something more formal—and more entangling; like the British, too, they found 'new frontiers of insecurity' whenever they wanted to draw the line."[33]

Despite many similarities, however, there is ample evidence that the cases of British and U.S. hegemony are fundamentally different. Nye, Keohane, and Russett all make convincing arguments about this comparison. In the total size of economy, volume of manufacturing, military spending, and even industrial productivity, Britain was never as superior to the rest of the world as the United States was after 1945.[34] Nor was the United States as dependent upon overseas possessions, foreign trade, and investment as Britain was in the nineteenth century.

In a recent study, Karen Rasler and William Thompson test the proposition that rich and powerful countries like Britain and the United States spend too much and, consequently, undermine the economic foundations of their hegemonic success.[35] In particular, they attempt to critique Gilpin's model of hegemonic decline.[36] At the heart of Gilpin's model are the relationships among protection (the costs of national security and the security of property rights); consumption (the public and private use of resources, goods, and services); and investment (economic resources returned to the economy to improve productivity and efficiency). The basic problem for hegemons, according to Gilpin, is that expenditures for protection and consumption rise over time at the relative expense of investment and hence of productivity. Without maintaining or improving economic productivity, the chances for sustained economic growth and wealth are diminished.

Rasler and Thompson also examine a similar hypothesis by C. M. Cipolla, which uses many of the same variables but with different conclusions.[37] According to this model, hegemonic or imperial expansion leads to greater organizational complexity and foreign hostility. As economic benefits of predominance are achieved, they produce a higher standard of living and private consumption. The key for Cipolla, however, is the domestic response to greater foreign hostility and competition. If the response is to reinvest the economic gains of hegemony in greater productivity rather than to consume them, then maintenance of hegemony is likely. If the opposite response takes place, which Cipolla predicts is more likely for a variety of social and psychological reasons, then relative efficiency and competitive advantage are diminished.

Rasler and Thompson acknowledge the generic difficulties in the hegemonic literature distinguishing cause from effect. They maintain that structural models inevitably require the specification of the presence as well as the absence of linkage among the variables.[38] In their analyses of Britain from 1831 to 1913 and of the United States from 1950 to 1986 they find that private consumption has played a significant role in the U.S. case but not in the earlier British case. They conclude, therefore, that "neither public nor even private consumption propensities are either necessary or sufficient factors in the relative decline of modern lead economies."[39]

The literature for and against the apparent decline of U.S. hegemony has been as heated and prolific as it has been for the analysis of British decline. Kennedy, Gilpin, and David Calleo present somewhat different arguments, but all essentially agree that the United States is now in a period of hegemonic decline.[40] Calleo sums up well both the causes and consequences of this argument:

> Hegemony has a tendency to break down because of the absolute or relative weakening of the hegemonic power itself. A hegemon in decay begins to exploit the system in order to compensate for its progressing debility. Present events appear to fit this pattern all too well. Under the mantle of Pax Americana, the rise of Europe, Japan, China, and other developing states has made American predominance increasingly strained. As a result, today's historic challenge lies in adapting the postwar system to the decline of American predominance and to the rise of middle range powers—old and new—not only in the First World but also in the Third World. The danger is not merely that America's lingering hegemony will collapse, but that the attempt to hang on to it will ruin the chances for stability in a more plural system.[41]

Joseph Nye is one of a few analysts who disagree that U.S. power is declining, and yet he predicts that U.S. hegemony is not likely to continue in the future.[42] He stresses that, although the fragmented structure of world politics among different complex issues has made power resources less transferable from one issue to another, the United States is as strong or stronger than any potential international rivals.

The key to his argument is his separation of the sources of power into tangible (or hard) power resources and intangible (or soft) power resources. In his assessment of tangible resources, he ranks the United States strong in all four categories: basic resources, military, economic, and science/technology. Likewise, in his intangible list, the United States is strong in national cohesion, universalistic culture, and international institutions.[43] Among his other major power contenders (the Soviet Union, Europe, Japan, and China), every other contender except the Soviet Union has at least one dimension in which they are "weak" and at least one other dimension in which they rank only "medium."

The former Soviet Union was ranked strong on military and basic resources but only medium on the other five dimensions. Europe's disadvantages, according to Nye, are a "medium" military and "weak" national cohesion. Japan is held to be "weak" in military, and only "medium" in universalistic culture and international institutions. Meanwhile, China is rated "weak" in science/technology and "medium" on the other dimensions, except for basic resources and national cohesion which are rated "strong."

One can somewhat easily forgive Nye for his ratings of Soviet power, given the changes that have occurred in the two years since the book was written. Today, one would have to downgrade the economic, national cohesion, and universalistic culture power resources of the former Soviet Union and its presumed successor, the Commonwealth of Independent States or Russia, to "weak" and possibly even the military to "medium." It also seems unfair to rank the regional identity cohesion of Europe with national identity cohesion of the other four contenders. Even so, many might argue with the assessments that European identity is "weak" and that U.S. national cohesion is "strong." Perhaps both should be rated "medium," even if U.S. cohesion is stronger than European cohesion. Likewise, it seems to be an overstatement to characterize the U.S. economy as "strong" and therefore roughly equivalent to Japanese economic power.

A more detailed examination of the components of economic power is contained in Chapter 2. The important point to reiterate is Nye's claim that "power is becoming less fungible, less coercive, and less tangible."[44] Nye's arguments on fungibility, concerning transferability of military power to economic issues and/or economic power to military issues, has much validity. The U.S. experience in the Gulf War with Iraq makes it difficult to determine whether the war was fought primarily for economic motives and/or whether the prospect of the United States having to bear the full cost of the war would have vetoed the military response.

Nye qualifies his claim about power being less coercive by including the proviso "at least among the major states."[45] "Less coercive" here means presumably only the use of military force. One could easily argue that the use of economic coercion has risen dramatically. Nye claims that the use of military force by the United States, for example, against weak Latin American countries such as Nicaragua and Panama, is now more costly. However, the United States still seems as willing as ever in the past decade to resort to military force even if the costs are higher.

It is most difficult to accept Nye's claims about the substantial influence of "soft" intangible power. He claims that U.S. popular culture, embodied in products and communications, is a major source of power. Although he recognizes an "element of triviality and fad in popular behavior," he tries to claim trends of greater popularity in U.S. films, clothes, and music, especially to international youth, as a source of U.S. power.[46] Surely, it is equally or more persuasively explained as an adolescent sign of unconventional behavior protesting forced conformance with one's own national culture. Nye is more than just idealistic when he claims that democracy and human rights are "American values." U.S. openness to immigrants may be a source of cultural strength compared to that of Japan. However, it is questionable to claim that U.S. openness to ethnic cultures is the reason why so many of the world's poor are prepared to risk their lives to go to the United States.

More helpful is Nye's analysis of the relative nature of power. The focus of the book *Bound to Lead* is on the debate over the U.S. decline of power, but presumably it could also be applied to a rise of power. Nye states unequivocally:

> Absolute decline, in which there is a loss of critical power resources or of the ability to use one's own resources effectively, is less common than relative decline in which the power resources of others grow greater or are used more effectively. Neither type of decline requires nor implies domestic decay.[47]

The reverse corollary of this hypothesis would also seem to imply that absolute gains in power may have less to do with the gain of critical power resources or of the ability to use them than in either the decline of others' resources or in their slower ability to acquire them. Furthermore, neither form of relative advantage requires or implies domestic growth in power resources or their effective utilization. Indeed, this is Nye's fear:

> The United States has both the traditional hard power resources and the new soft power resources to meet the challenges of transnational interdependence. The critical question is whether it will have the political leadership and strategic vision to convert these power resources into real influence in a transitional period of world politics. . . . The twin dangers that Americans face are complacency about the domestic agenda and an unwillingness to invest in order to maintain confidence in their capacity for international leadership. Neither is warranted. The United States remains the largest and richest power with the greatest capacity to shape the future.[48]

⸻⸻⸻ *Hegemony and International Economic Regimes*

Hegemonic stability and international regimes have been two related themes in the literature on international relations in the past two decades. Both themes have focused primarily, although not exclusively, on the questions of hierarchy, order, and cooperation in the international political economy. As Joanne Gowa has pointed out, much ink has been used on three analytical issues: (1) hegemonic self-interest in free trade, (2) the nonexcludability of free trade, and (3) the necessity of a hegemon in collective goods problems.[49]

Hegemonic theories have been concerned with the roles played by certain nation-states during historic periods to bring equilibrium and political leadership to the international system. Some authors have bemoaned the inability or unwillingness of certain nation-states to bear the costs of international leadership, whereas other authors have focused on the biased ways in which hegemonic powers have pursued national interests under the guise of international leadership.

International regime analyses have focused on international "institutions" (which are conceived as sets of behaviors consistent with norms appropriate to recognized international roles) and on international "organizations" (which are tangible actors that have staff, offices, resources, and equipment). This distinction between patterns of behavior and physical entities has opened new theoretical horizons about the causes, motivations, and effects of compliance with international norms.

Theories of hegemony and international regimes have wrestled with the notion of international public goods. Public goods are held collectively, are indivisible, and are nonexcludable (nuclear security), but are not necessarily positive (pollution). Because the goods are nonexcludable, there is a collective action disincentive and a "free rider" problem. A stable system of international free trade is claimed by many authors to be an international public good. Charles Kindleberger has argued that because of the collective action disincentive, a hegemon must exist in order for the system to come into being.[50] Many regime theories dispute this assertion and show how a "critical mass" of actors (usually states) may reach a consensus to form a regime because they have a common incentive to see that the collective good is provided, even if they have to bear the full costs of providing something they cannot prevent other states from sharing.

The decline of military competition between the United States and the Soviet Union, coupled with a conscious effort over the last decade by the Group of Seven (G7) nations to harmonize economic relations, provide an excellent opportunity to speculate about the possible emergence of a new type of hegemony or a broad economic regime. Historically, hegemons have been single states (city-states or nation-states) that have had an overwhelming advantage in military and/or economic power. As observed earlier, in the agricultural era, military dominance was crucial to a hegemon's power so long as conquest of land was the only real means by which to increase production and obtain resources. There has been an increasing tendency in the industrial era for military power to reinforce or strengthen economic power, as industrial technologies could create higher standards of living without the need for land conquest. Instead, naval strength became the key to maintaining trade empires across the globe. Britain's strength then declined (because of anticolonial sentiments and domestic unwillingness to bear the high costs of empires) and the devastation of World Wars I and II left the United States in a position to assume both economic and military hegemony. The military competition of the Cold War greatly taxed the resources of both the United States and the Soviet Union while Japan and Europe rebuilt their economies with newer technologies and lower defense costs. Ultimately, the military competition between the superpowers destroyed both the political and economic system of the Soviet Union and changed the United States from a world creditor into a world debtor. Much of that debt was and is financed by the Japanese, whose economic growth and domestic propensity to save provided their country with an unprecedented position of international financial leverage.

Over the course of nearly twenty years, the United States, Japan, Canada, and the largest countries of Europe have learned the necessity of collective economic agreements. This need began with the energy crises of the 1970s and continued through various attempts to coordinate economic boycotts and sanctions. Mutual vulnerabilities and interdependence with developing countries concerning debt, trade, environment, and labor issues have further reinforced the need for "economic regimes." Although the United States was willing and in the best position to be the hegemon/protector in military defense of the advanced industrial states, this role became increasingly unpopular domestically as other advanced countries with lower defense costs developed and used new advanced technologies to catch and pass the United States in trade competition. Even though the end of the Cold War should allow the United States to greatly reduce its defense expenditures, it is financially too weak to attempt to reassert itself as the economic hegemon of the world. The strength of Western Europe and Japan necessitates the formation of a collective economic hegemony instead of a single country hegemony as in the past.

A collective economic hegemony constructed by the major nation-states is also the logical response to the ever-growing power and questionable national loyalties of the world's multinational corporations (MNCs). For decades these multinational corporations have been able to play national rivalries against each other and utilize to their own advantage gaps in various international legal and economic jurisdictions. Although many of their activities have been applauded and encouraged by the leading advanced industrial states, there have also been "outlaw" MNCs whose irresponsible and selfish behavior has been difficult, if not impossible, to control.

At the end of a remarkable century it is time to rethink and explain the political and economic interactions among nations and the consequences of these relationships. It is long past time for a new transsubjective perspective. It is time for international relations theory to gather its energy for a quantum leap to a new set of paradigms and propositions.

Ultimately, it may be most helpful to view hegemony not as a unique and more or less rare condition in international relations but as one end of a continuum of "powerfulness" and "powerlessness" of nation-states. Hegemony can helpfully be seen as a position on the high side of the international power continuum:

Subjugation	Dependence	Interdependence	Hegemony	Omnipotence
least power				**most power**

Hegemony, whether military and/or economic, may be merely regional, more broadly hemispheric, or truly global. Hegemony is always relative to both the power capabilities of other nation-states and to the power conditions at large in the international system. These conditions have changed frequently and dramatically in history. As we have already seen in the cases of the United States and Britain, future conditions of hegemony are likely to be unique to both historical conditions and national strengths and weaknesses relative to global rivals.

Hegemony since 1500 has been defined almost exclusively in terms of single nation-states. Although many authors have described how trans-national actors and international governmental organizations have diffused much of the power of would-be national hegemons since World War II, there has been little serious discussion about the possibility of, or conditions favoring, transnational or multinational hegemons in the future. Will it be useful to describe "issue" or "sectorial" hegemonies by countries even if they are not predominant in all or even most dimensions of global power and/or influence? As the Cold War fades and if substantial disarmament continues throughout the coming decade, will economic dominance be the only relevant sphere for measurement? Perhaps a century from now we will still have no greater consensus on understanding the nature of global power (or the weather) than we do today. If so, it will probably not be because of a dearth of political and economic analyses. The quest for understanding the causes and effects of dominance across human history is as old and captivating as the quest for dominance itself.

Conclusion _____

As is shown in the other chapters of this book, Japan's economic growth and prosperity have brought it unprecedented wealth. Indeed, Japan may have accomplished more through peaceful economic relations in the post–World War II era than it could have hoped to accomplish through military conquest and empire earlier in the twentieth century. If there had not been a war in the Pacific and if Japan had attempted to control all of China and East Asia for the past fifty years, Japan might have found itself today like Britain. Instead of unprecedented wealth and an increasingly successful image as a peaceful country, it might have been even more hated and feared than either the United States or the former Soviet Union.

Japan's wealth has, in turn, transformed its relations with every other region of the world. Its position as the world's most important creditor has brought new responsibilities and new dilemmas. Japan's leaders are anxious to transcend the perception of its foreign policy as mere "checkbook diplomacy." It is no longer comfortable with its previous position as "little brother" with the United States. Nor is it comfortable, however, with some U.S. images of it as an ambitious, selfish state anxious to seize the crown of world hegemony for itself. It has, in its own eyes, earned a more respected position in the world's international financial institutions, such as the IMF and the World Bank. In spite of its self-imposed military limitations, it probably deserves a permanent seat on the UN Security Council. In order to assume and maintain its image as a global power, Japan is fully prepared to venture beyond its preeminent position in East Asia and play a more influential position in all of the world's regions.

Japan understands the value and necessity of teamwork. Although it has a closer and more significant relationship with the United States than with Western Europe, it shares with the Europeans the understanding of collective leadership. Like the Europeans, Japan is skeptical of domestic politics in the United States, which assigns most of the blame for its economic difficulties to foreigners. Also more like the Europeans than the Americans, the Japanese understand that the enormous economic challenges of the next several decades must be faced through carefully negotiated collective agreements rather than through short-sighted national efforts.

——————————————————————————————— *Notes*

1. Joseph Nye, Jr., *Bound to Lead: The Changing Nature of American Power*, New York: Basic Books, 1990, p. 25.

2. Robert O. Keohane, *After Hegemony: Cooperation and Discord in the World Political Economy*, Princeton, N.J.: Princeton University Press, 1984; Robert Cox, *Production, Power, and World Order: Social Forces in the Making of History*, New York: Columbia University Press, 1987; Bruce Russett, "U.S. Hegemony: Gone or Merely Diminished, and How Does It Matter?" in Takashi Inoguchi and Daniel Okimoto eds., *The Political Economy of Japan*, vol. 2, Stanford, Calif.: Stanford University Press, 1988, pp. 83–107; Susan Strange, "The Persistent Myth of Lost Hegemony," *International Organization*, vol. 41 (1987), pp. 551–574.

3. Duncan Snidal, "The Limits of Hegemonic Stability Theory," *International Organization*, vol. 39, no. 4 (Autumn 1985), pp. 579–614.

4. Charles Doran, *The Politics of Assimilation: Hegemony and Its Aftermath*, Baltimore, Md.: Johns Hopkins Press, 1971, pp. 19–20.

5. Nye, *Bound to Lead*, p. 41.

6. Immanuel Wallerstein, *The Politics of the World Economy*, New York: Cambridge University Press, 1984, pp. 38–39.

7. Ibid., p. 39.

8. Nye, *Bound to Lead*.

9. Ibid.

10. Susan Strange, *States and Markets*, New York: Basil Blackwell, 1988.

11. Ibid., p. 24.

12. Susan Strange, "Finance, Information, and Power," *Review of International Studies*, vol. 16 (1990), p. 267.

13. Ibid., p. 273.

14. Fernand Braudel, *The Perspective of the World*, vol. 3, New York: Harper & Row, 1984, p. 65.

15. J. A. Hobson, *Imperialism—A Study*, London, 1902; Paul Kennedy, *The Rise and Fall of the Great Powers*, New York: Random House, 1987.

16. Robert Gilpin, *War and Change in World Politics*, Cambridge: Cambridge University Press, 1981.

17. Ibid., p. 23.

18. Wallerstein, *The Politics*, pp. 40–41.

19. Ibid., pp. 42–43.

20. Christopher Chase-Dunn, *Global Formation*, Cambridge, MA: Basil Blackwell, 1989, p. 170.

21. Ibid., p. 175.

22. Ibid., p. 165.

23. George Modelski, "The Long Cycle of Global Politics and the Nation-State," *Comparative Studies in Society and History*, vol. 20 (1978), pp. 214–235.

24. Kennedy, *The Rise and Fall of the Great Powers*.

25. Chase-Dunn, *Global Formation*.

26. Violet Barbour, *Capitalism in Amsterdam in the 17th Century*, Ann Arbor: University of Michigan Press, 1963; Fernand Braudel, *The Perspective of the World*; Peter Burke, *Venice and Amsterdam: A Study of 17th Century Elites*, London: Temple Smith, 1974.

27. E. J. Hobsbawm, *Industry and Empire*, New York: Penguin, 1968, p. 1.

28. Ibid., p. 179.

29. Ibid., p. 135.

30. Paul Kennedy, *The Rise and Fall of British Naval Mastery*, London: Ashfield Press, 1986, p. 166.

31. Philip Meeks, "The Politics of Corporatism and International Economic Relations in the United Kingdom, West Germany, and France," unpublished doctoral dissertation, Austin: University of Texas, 1980, p. 169.

32. Kennedy, *The Rise and Fall of the Great Powers*, p. 357.

33. Ibid., p. 359.

34. Nye, *Bound to Lead*; Keohane, *After Hegemony*; Bruce Russett, "The Mysterious Case of Vanishing Hegemony; or, Is Mark Twain Really Dead?" *International Organization*, vol. 39 (1985), pp. 207–232.

35. Karen Rasler and William Thompson, "Relative Decline and the Overconsumption-Underinvestment Hypothesis," *International Studies Quarterly*, vol. 35 (1991), pp. 273–294.

36. Gilpin, *War and Change*.

37. C. M. Cipolla, "Editor's Introduction," in C. M. Cipolla, ed., *The Economic Decline of Empires*, London: Methuen, 1970.

38. Rasler and Thompson, "Relative Decline," p. 282.

39. Ibid., p. 288.

40. Kennedy, *The Rise and Fall of the Great Powers*; Gilpin, *War and Change*; David Calleo, *Beyond American Hegemony*, New York: Basic Books, 1987.

41. Calleo, *Beyond American Hegemony*, p. 149.

42. Nye, *Bound to Lead*.

43. Ibid., p. 174.

44. Ibid., p. 188.

45. Ibid., p. 190.

46. Ibid., p. 194.

47. Ibid., p. 16.

48. Ibid., pp. 260–261.

49. Joanne Gowa, "Rational Hegemons, Excludable Goods, and Small Groups: An Epitaph for Hegemonic Stability Theory?" *World Politics*, vol. 41 (1989), pp. 310–311.

50. Charles Kindleberger, "Hierarchy Versus Inertial Cooperation," *International Organization*, vol. 40 (1986), pp. 841–848.

Chapter 2
Japan and Global Economic Hegemony
Philip J. Meeks

This chapter analyzes the various arguments and perspectives surrounding the concept of hegemony in order to assess whether Japan is or is becoming a hegemon in the international political economy. The first part of this chapter argues that Japan may be emerging as a key player in a new type of leader/hegemon–system/regime, even though it does not yet possess the type of military power believed by many to be a prerequisite for international hegemony. Japan's extreme dependence upon foreign sources for its raw materials, however, leaves it vulnerable to naval blockades. If the United States were to decide to try to weaken and/or economically blackmail Japan militarily in order to obtain more favorable trading conditions, Japan would be forced to rethink its military strategy and weapons strength. With the former Soviet Union no longer a military threat, both the United States and Japan will undoubtedly reassess the nature of their military relationship.

The second part of this chapter examines Japan's position on five different dimensions of international economic power. The argument made is that although the salience and the weights that should be allocated to these five factors are constantly changing and difficult to predict, Japan is surging forward on most, if not all, dimensions. Japan's potential for international hegemony may depend more upon how aggressively other nations, especially the United States, respond to Japan's growing strength than upon the prospects of maintaining the successful domestic economic policies that have been crucial to its international economic competition. For at least the next decade or two and maybe longer, Japanese economic strength will depend upon U.S. goodwill and a benign U.S. foreign policy. A long and persistent decline in U.S. international economic strength and/or the rise of relatively closed and hostile regional trading blocs may spell the end of these presently positive relations. For the foreseeable future, Japan will not be in an economic position to dictate terms to the United States or, for that matter, to the European Community countries. Similarly, however, if Japanese economic strength continues to grow on its present course, it will "be able to say no" to any conditions dictated to it by any other country in the world. However, equally important will be whether Japan can or will "say yes" to new global responsibilities beyond those of "checkbook diplomacy."

In the conclusion to this chapter, this analysis proposes that hegemonic stability theories be transformed from the traditional Anglo-American dominance notion of international leadership to ones more consistent with Japanese notions of collective leadership. In Japan, leadership is demonstrated by consensus-building strategies in which all major participants have an important role in the process. As Japan's unique characteristics and power in the international economy, particularly in international finance and multinational corporations, grow stronger, it may be able to exert a more positive and collective notion of international economic relations. Fears of emerging Japanese international economic hegemony may tell us more about U.S. desires for continued dominance than about either the capabilities or the intentions of the Japanese. For their part, the Japanese already recognize their vulnerability with regard to not only raw materials but also current liberal U.S. foreign economic policies. Japan will need to continue to diversify its economic relationships as much as possible, particularly in developing countries and in Eastern Europe, if it wants to decrease its dependence on the United States.

The Economic-Military Equation in Japan's International Relations _____

Hegemonic theories have been concerned with the roles played by certain nation-states during historic periods to bring equilibrium and political leadership to the international system. Some authors have bemoaned the inability or unwillingness of certain nation-states to bear the costs of international leadership, whereas other authors have focused on the biased ways in which hegemonic powers have pursued national interests under the guise of international leadership. Many classical theories of hegemony center upon the military strength of the hegemon. Some see economic strength as a crucial determinant of building a dominant military capability, and, conversely, others see a dominant military capability as the key factor in perpetuating economic hegemony.

The raging controversy about Japan's new role in the international system may provide the opportunity for a new formulation of the military-economic equation. Japan's rising economic prominence in international relations in spite of its lack of offensive military power, together with the probable demise of the Cold War between the United States and the former Soviet Union, gives us a clue that a new type of international system may be emerging. Maybe now that the United States has emerged victorious from an international military conflict and redeemed its self-image, tarnished by the war in Vietnam, it can stop worrying about whether it is a classical hegemon (with either a benign or coercive face) and get on about discovering a new era of international relations. Just as hegemony and hierarchical patterns of relations between states have been socialized after international conflicts have restructured national roles,[1] it is now time to see whether the emergence of Japan as an "economic superpower" can tell us anything about the new era we may be entering.

Much has been made, both inside and outside of Japan, about article 9 of the Japanese constitution, which bans warfare and the maintenance of an army. The existence of this article of the constitution has not prevented Japan from currently spending more than $32 billion annually on defense.[2] Japan today spends more money on defense than any country except the United States and the former Soviet Union. Its 246,000 regular armed forces are well equipped with 1,200 main battle tanks, 17 submarines, 6 destroyers, 60 frigates, more than 500 combat aircraft, and 72 armed helicopters. Proponents of more military spending in Japan, however, question whether Japan could effectively defend itself alone against either of the Koreas, much less against China or even a drastically weakened Russia. The question no longer is whether Japan will rearm, but to what degree and for what purposes.

In their controversial book, *The Coming War With Japan*, George Friedman and Meredith Lebard put U.S. military hegemony in the post–Cold War world on a collision course with Japanese economic interests:

> The essential political and military fact in the world today is the domination of the seas by the U.S. Navy. All of the world's oceans belong to one country: America. This is a novel fact in recorded history, a goal Britain strived to attain for a century without success. This means that, should it choose to do so, the United States can determine the pattern of world trade, dictating what goes where and how. If this is intolerable for Japan, then Japan must try to challenge that power, at least in the Pacific.
>
> The desire for Japan to control its own destiny cannot be achieved without displacing the United States Navy from its preeminent role in the Pacific. This cannot be done without generally undermining American power throughout the world's oceans. The Japanese political and military challenge cannot be achieved unless the United States contents itself with becoming a hemispheric rather than a global power. After nearly a half century of refusing to take this role vis-à-vis the Soviets, it is unlikely that the United States will accept the role vis-à-vis the Japanese.[3]

The security of Japanese raw material trade routes is of legitimate concern both inside and outside the country. More than 70 percent of Japan's oil imports has to pass through the Straits of Hormuz and 88 percent of its oil imports has to pass one of three other straits: Malacca, Sunda, or Lombok. Japan will need friendly relations with the three countries closest to this latter group of straits—Indonesia, Malaysia, and Singapore. In order to reduce its potential vulnerability to these choke points, Japan must diversify its sources and cut back on its reliance on crude oil from the Gulf. Malaysia and Indonesia have some proven reserves but they are relatively small compared to Japan's potential needs. A logical choice would be Siberian fields in north-east Russia. A Russian economy desperate for capital and goods and a Japanese economy hungry for energy imports appear to be an attractive match now that the military threat from the Russians has substantially declined. China is another important potential supplier. Although there is less threat to sea-lanes from these countries, there are considerable doubts about the political stability of these countries.

It would be a mistake, however, to overemphasize Japanese trade vulnerabilities. With a domestic economy of $3.2 trillion in 1990, Japan has a total trade of only $523 billion, or 16.3 percent of the total economy. Total imports from the Middle East accounted for only $31 billion in 1990. Even the substantial conflict during the Gulf War in 1991 and the cutoff of Iraq and Kuwait as suppliers hardly affected Japanese oil imports. In a worst case scenario, a total cutoff of trade with the United States would represent a combined trade loss of $91 billion in exports and $53 billion in imports. Japanese banks and corporations, however, hold up to $800 billion in U.S. currency and bonds, stocks, and securities, not to mention real estate and plant facilities in the United States. The consequences of a trade war with Japan initiated by the United States could be more devastating for the United States than for Japan. It would also probably provoke a world economic crisis that would dwarf the depression era of the 1920s and 1930s. In short, for the United States, an all-out economic war with Japan is just about as unthinkable as an all-out nuclear war was with the Soviet Union.

For the past forty-five years, Japanese defense policies have been built upon U.S. security guarantees. Security has been narrowly defined in terms of protecting Japanese national territories. Every Japanese government has agreed with this limited definition of security as a defense against a conventional invasion of the homelands, within which there is unlikely to be any military danger from any country that could not be met by the Japanese Self-Defense Forces.[4] There has been persistent pressure from the left in Japan to cut all military ties with the United States, but this debate seems to be fueled much more by pro-nationalist and anti-American sentiments than by universal acceptance of pacifism. The recent Gulf War and collapse of Soviet military power should have provoked a much more serious dialogue about future Japanese security options. Instead, the debate over Japanese defense policies continues to take place on a highly emotional and moral plane when it occurs at all.

It is not within the purview of this analysis to examine in depth the domestic and foreign reasons for Japan's unique perception of national security. This subject is treated elsewhere in this book. Most, if not all, Japanese seem to believe that Japan's national security, as well as the contribution Japan makes to international security, rests upon Japanese economic stability and international interdependence in trade, capital, and technology.[5] In the eyes of many Western critics, Japan's approach to security issues has been much more akin to that of an international trading company than that of a powerful nation-state.[6] Perhaps even more importantly, any fundamental shift in Japanese defense policy toward a substantial new role in Pacific security could bring about domestic political unrest that would not only threaten the scandal-ridden Liberal Democratic Party's tenuous grip on political power but also undermine the economic coalition of interests that has provided Japan with its unprecedented economic prosperity.

Japan has gone much further than the United States or Western European countries and refrained not only from arms exports to communist countries and those under United Nations arms sanctions but even from exporting weapons to developing countries where there is significant likelihood for international conflicts. Under Prime Minister Takeo Miki in the mid-1970s, Japan extended its arms export limitations to include equipment related to the manufacture of arms and arms-related technologies. From 1978 to 1988, the highest amount of arms exports for a single year was only $310 million in 1983. The total amount of arms exports for that period amounted to only $1.7 billion compared to $107.7 billion for the United States, $34.5 billion for France, $18.3 billion for Britain, and $17.5 billion for East and West Germany combined.[7] Whereas other advanced industrial countries have eagerly profited from arms sales to unstable developing countries, Japan has refrained. Japan may have made a far greater contribution to world security by omission than by any amount it might have spent to improve its own military capability.

The most likely scenario for the 1990s is that Japan's defense expenditures, in spite of its naval and raw material vulnerabilities, will grow by only about 4 percent annually and stay close to the 1 percent of GNP figure that has received consensual domestic support. This certainly means that Japan will not be in a position to use its military forces to break up blockades or to intervene in some Asian ground conflict. Its military forces will not be able to effectively increase its economic power in Asia, much less in the rest of the world, but neither will defense expenditures take away from Japan's domestic economic strength nor provoke substantial political unrest.

Japan's Power in the World Economy

Economists and political scientists of all major ideological and theoretical perspectives for more than thirty years have tried to fit the postwar economic development of Japan into one or more of their favorite hypotheses, in spite of their logical contradictions. The Japanese experience has been described as both deviant and compliant with neoclassical, Marxist, and monetarist theories.[8] Its management style is and is not the key to its success.[9] Japan's new financial success is a threat to the United States and taking over its future.[10]

Japan is also weak and vulnerable to natural resource cutoffs and consequently no threat at all.[11] Perhaps no state has grown so rich so fast and hence confused everyone including the Japanese.

This analysis looks briefly at five different dimensions of Japan's international economic power and influence: (1) size of domestic economy, (2) nature of corporate structure and financial influence, (3) strength and size of international trade, (4) strength and diversity of advanced technologies, and (5) amount of foreign economic assistance. Although all of these factors are well known, their interrelationships, and in particular their basis for international power and leadership at any given historical moment, are not.

The salience and weights that should be allocated to these factors are constantly changing. The importance of one's domestic economy, for example, is determined by both domestic factors and international factors. If a country is rich and not dependent on international trade, then that country may be economically strong and independent of the international economy. That country, however, may be neither helped nor hurt by its independence. If a nation, on the other hand, is resource dependent, as is Japan, then it may be vulnerable to the rise or decline of natural resource prices.

Japan has clearly benefited from comparatively low oil prices in the 1980s, but like other advanced industrial countries it has had to deal with domestic producers who have been unable to compete and therefore have had to be subsidized. In some ways, the economic independence the United States has enjoyed in the past century has made it less vulnerable but also less disciplined. For many economies in the world, those that can utilize the discipline and competition of the world market conditions are in a better position to profit from interdependence than those economies that are less vulnerable. Japan, through its industrial and export policies, has been able to turn its raw materials vulnerability into an economic advantage and source of influence vis-à-vis countries in Southeast Asia that provide raw materials and energy to Japan. This economic discipline is further reinforced in Japan by a Confucian culture that values self-restraint and social discipline, in marked contrast to the U.S. culture.

The key to international preeminence, therefore, is the ability of a country to take advantage of those international economic forces that are the most crucial to international economic competition at any given time. Classical economic theories have emphasized the size of the domestic economy and economies of scale, together with international trade, as the primary factors in establishing international economic power and influence. Some early Marxists, notably Lenin, emphasized that international finance capital may ultimately be more important than international trade in achieving international economic dominance. However, Lenin's predictions seemed inaccurate, or at least premature, in the first half of the twentieth century—an era dominated by nationalist competition among the wealthiest nations, not by internationalist financial "conspiracies." Furthermore, the experience of the depression in the 1920s and 1930s further reinforced beliefs that conflicts over trade—not finance—were most threatening to stable and prosperous international relations.

The rising importance of the role of international finance, multinational corporations, and advanced technologies in facilitating the operations of the international economy may not have been fully appreciated before the last ten to fifteen years. Capital transactions—both foreign exchange and international lending—have now replaced international trade as the most significant factors in the world economy. On a given day there can be as much as $700 billion in foreign exchange available for manipulation. Total world trade has grown in response to GATT reforms and other trade regime norms to nearly $6 trillion annually, and liquid and semiliquid international finance factors amount to more than $13 trillion. Equally important, international financial assets can be transferred much more quickly electronically to respond to international economic conditions. International trade can be and has been slowed more often by transportation factors and by political obstacles than by problems of international capital. This means that global corporations that are primarily financial, such as banks and holding companies, have clear advantages over more traditional manufacturing or natural resource–based corporations. Japan's role as arguably either the most or at least second most important creditor in the world takes on even more importance in view of the dominant influence of finance in the contemporary world economy.

The fundamental changes in international monetary regimes in the mid-1970s further strengthened international financial forces. The "floating" international currency regime since the 1975 Smithsonian Agreements has limited government actions to manage exchange rates and has turned over most of the control to international market forces. Even though there is still little research on the political roles of national central bank intervention and enforcement of international bank regulations, there is some question as to whether central bank interventions are motivated primarily by concerns to maintain currency value and stability or by other national domestic and foreign economic policy priorities.[12] The same can be said for multinational corporations, widely acknowledged to be motivated by corporate priorities and interests rather than by interests determined by the political leadership of the countries in which they are headquartered. Again, modern electronic communication technologies facilitate the ability of these corporations to evade control by national governments. If taxes or other regulations are viewed as too restrictive, then pulling up stakes is far easier for financial corporations than for traditional manufacturing or mining companies.

_____ *Japan's Domestic Production Power*

Domestic economies, particularly in the advanced industrial economies, are still crucial factors in the assessment of international economic strength. For Immanuel Wallerstein and world systems theorists as well as for more conventional political economists, national power begins with the strength of domestic production.[13] The U.S. economy alone accounts for a quarter of the world's economy and remains 45 percent larger than second-place Japan (see Table 2.1). In fact, if one sets aside the unusual case of the Soviet economy, the U.S. economy remains almost as large as the sum of the next three largest competitors (Japan, Germany, and France), and, until the recent German reunification, the United States had more than 10 million more in population. The openness of the U.S. domestic economy to most international trade makes it even more significant as a contributor to the world economy. Although it is premature to speculate extensively, a North American free trade zone including Mexico and Canada will only enhance the contribution (and vulnerability) of the United States in the world economy. That openness is, of course, to a great extent a condition of policy choices made by recent political administrations and cannot be taken for granted if political conditions change.

The enormous advantage of a large unified economy has not been lost upon the Europeans, who stand at the threshold of their bold new 1992 initiative. The top five economies of the European Community together represent nearly 22 percent of the world's economy. Although recent political

Table 2.1 Comparative Gross National Expenditure and Industrial Production, 1965–1990

Country	1965	1970	1975	1980	1985	1990
Gross National Expenditure (US$ billions)						
United States	705.8	1,015.5	1,598.4	2,732.0	4,014.9	5,465.2
Japan	90.8	202.7	498.3	922.5	1,346.9	2,961.0
Germany	114.6	184.6	418.4	817.1	626.4	1,512.5
France	99.2	145.5	343.1	669.7	523.1	1,175.3
United Kingdom	101.8	125.4	238.9	537.8	462.9	977.3
Italy	62.8	107.9	211.7	453.8	467.7	948.0
Canada	52.3	83.8	166.1	258.3	298.6	477.7
Brazil	42.9	41.8	122.6	242.1	211.1	433.3
China	n/a	n/a	153.4	286.1	284.3	363.7
Netherlands	18.9	31.8	87.2	169.7	126.1	223.1
Industrial Production Index (1985 = 100)						
United States	53	63	69	88	100	114
Japan	27	56	61	84	100	125
Germany	64	83	84	98	100	117
France	57	73	84	99	100	112
United Kingdom	73	83	85	93	100	109
Italy	51	73	79	104	100	118
Canada	49	62	75	86	100	108
Netherlands	52	69	86	95	100	109

Source: IMF, *International Financial Statistics Yearbook, 1991.*
Note: n/a = not available

changes in Eastern Europe and especially German reunification may temporarily complicate the process of European unification, in the long term there are even greater possible positive economic consequences for the whole region than were thought feasible only five years ago.

Although Japan's domestic economy has grown faster than those of either the United States or Western Europe and is now the second largest in the world, it is difficult to see how Japan in the next decade will be able to expand its domestic economy through comparable new regional economic regimes. Political and economic difficulties and barriers in its two largest Asian neighbors, China and India, are not likely to provide much more than modest trade increases. Equally difficult would be an economic merger between Japan and the ASEAN countries, which are strongly united by fear of further Japanese economic dominance in Asia.

However, it would be equally wrong to ignore the long-term future of the general Pacific Rim area. If substantial regional and semiclosed blocs do emerge in Europe and North America, then pressure for a comparable Pacific region may overcome present reluctance. The already substantial interdependence between Japan and its Asian trading partners could be the foundation for such a regional partnership if there were the political will and/or necessity. Perhaps more importantly, the prospects for internal domestic economic growth for Japan seem much better than for the United States. If Japan's domestic production continues to grow at more than three times the rate of the United States, as it did during the 1980s, then Japan will surpass the United States as the largest economy in the world by the year 2002.

_____ *Japan's Corporate and Financial Power*

One of Japan's present advantages comes from the strength of its global corporations. As seen is Table 2.2, for the years 1989–1991, of the top 1,000 global corporations, Japan has 987 (32.9 percent of 3,000) of the top corporations and 40.3 percent of their total market value. Although the actual number of firms is less than the U.S. total, their value is greater by more than $1,078 billion. In comparison with the entire European Community, Japan has 45.3 percent more of the largest firms (the EC has 697) and 121.6 percent greater market value (the EC value is $3,607 billion).

Of the top twenty-five most valuable global corporations, as seen in Table 2.3, 11 are Japanese, and of those eight are financial institutions. Of the fourteen largest banks and financial institutions, Japan has twelve and the United States has none. Of the fifty most valuable corporations in the world, the twelve largest banks in Japan from 1989 to 1991 had a total market value of $1,562 billion, compared to $1,024 billion for the top seven Japanese manufacturing and utilities corporations. These assets actually declined recently for many companies because of a significant stock market decline in early 1990, which wiped out 30 percent of the Nikkei stock market average.

Table 2.2 Top 1,000 Global Firms by Country, 1989–1991

Country	1989 Firms	1989 Value (US$ billions)	1990 Firms	1990 Value (US$ billions)	1991 Firms	1991 Value (US$ billions)	Total Firms 1989– 1991	Total Value (US$ billions)
Japan	345	2,998.6	333	2,649.9	309	2,346.5	987	7,995.0
United States	353	2,069.3	329	2,288.5	359	2,559.3	1,041	6,917.1
United Kingdom	93	451.3	89	546.6	94	614.9	276	1,612.8
Germany	30	151.0	41	270.3	39	248.6	110	669.9
France	31	114.8	42	205.7	40	183.8	113	504.3
Canada	31	114.6	25	111.0	25	119.2	81	344.8
Switzerland	12	72.9	13	110.8	11	102.1	36	285.8
Italy	15	66.1	26	122.4	19	84.1	60	272.6
Netherlands	11	66.0	14	90.3	13	94.0	38	250.3
Sweden	19	56.8	20	73.6	17	68.6	56	199.0
Australia	14	57.0	15	56.8	15	63.9	44	177.7
Spain	11	46.4	12	52.3	13	58.9	36	157.6
Hong Kong	12	38.6	13	46.3	15	61.6	40	146.5
Belgium	10	30.3	11	36.3	10	34.6	31	101.2
South Africa	4	15.3	5	24.6	6	27.2	15	67.1
Singapore/ Malaysia	4	11.1	4	13.1	6	17.8	14	42.0
Denmark	2	4.2	4	11.8	6	15.8	12	31.8
Norway	1	4.6	1	6.5	1	6.2	3	17.3
Austria	0	—	3	8.3	3	7.3	6	15.6
Finland	5	11.2	1	2.0	1	2.1	7	15.3
New Zealand	1	2.5	1	2.6	1	2.9	3	8.0
Ireland	0	—	2	4.7	1	2.0	3	6.7

Sources: Business Week, various annual issues.

Nippon Telegraph and Telephone, world leader in market value for the past three years, actually lost $45 billion in 1990 and another $15 billion in 1991 but remained ahead of second-place Royal Dutch/Shell by $191 billion for the period 1989–1991.

The role of transnational corporations blurs the distinction between the power and influence a country obtains from the sheer size of its domestic economy and the influence it may have in other countries through foreign direct investment. The extent of influence a country may have on the economy of another country is dependent upon the willingness of multinational corporations to bend toward the foreign policy wishes of their home country rather than toward the host country. The imprecise evidence we have on this would seem to suggest that home country loyalty may not be very important. However, it may also be true that relative to other multinational corporations, particularly U.S. and British firms, Japanese MNCs may be more likely to factor in Japanese foreign policy goals when they are clear and explicit. If this is true, then the greater involvement of Japanese multinationals in the United States and elsewhere will further multiply Japan's economic power and potential political influence.

Other significant factors in the world economy are the foreign assets and

Table 2.3 Top 50 Global Firms by Market Value, 1989–1991

Firm	Country	1991 Rank	1991 Value (US$ billions)	1990 Rank	1990 Value (US$ billions)	1989 Rank	1989 Value (US$ billions)
Nippon Telegraph and Telephone	Japan	1	103.00	1	118.79	1	163.86
Royal Dutch/Shell	Netherlands/U.K.	2	72.91	4	67.14	10	54.36
Exxon	U.S.	3	72.81	6	60.00	8	54.92
General Electric	U.S.	4	67.45	5	62.54	12	49.39
Industrial Bank of Japan	Japan	5	64.18	3	67.61	2	71.59
Philip Morris	U.S.	6	63.33	16	39.11	19	32.14
International Business Machines	U.S.	7	60.77	2	68.89	6	64.65
Fuji Bank	Japan	8	58.68	8	53.17	4	67.08
Mitsubishi Bank	Japan	9	58.08	12	47.17	7	59.27
Dai-Ichi Kangyo Bank	Japan	10	57.38	11	49.57	5	66.09
Sumitomo Bank	Japan	11	56.39	7	55.81	3	69.59
Sanwa Bank	Japan	12	49.94	14	45.60	13	49.29
Mitsui Taiyo Kobe Bank	Japan	13	48.69	10	49.80	24	29.69
Wal-Mart Stores	U.S.	14	48.55	22	31.89	40	21.49
Merck	U.S.	15	46.01	18	32.72	25	27.52
Toyota Motor	Japan	16	44.01	9	50.44	11	54.17
Bristol-Myers Squibb	U.S.	17	42.45	21	32.13	85	14.39
American Telephone & Telegraph	U.S.	18	40.43	13	46.96	16	38.12
British Telecommunications	U.K.	19	40.03	27	29.15	31	24.29
Coca-Cola	U.S.	20	38.26	23	30.42	39	21.50
Tokyo Electric Power	Japan	21	37.53	15	41.68	9	54.46
Du Pont	U.S.	22	33.16	29	27.98	28	26.08
Nomura Securities	Japan	23	30.80	19	32.54	14	44.44
British Petroleum	U.K.	24	30.61	25	29.55	33	24.15
Johnson & Johnson	U.S.	25	30.18	47	21.28	68	16.45
Glaxo Holdings	U.K.	26	30.02	53	19.68	74	15.92
Long Term Credit Bank of Japan	Japan	27	29.79	20	32.44	22	30.85
Proctor & Gamble	U.S.	28	29.49	32	26.78	60	17.40
Hitachi Ltd.	Japan	29	27.73	17	33.04	17	35.82
Mobil	U.S.	30	26.42	34	25.67	43	21.15
General Motors	U.S.	31	26.40	26	29.45	29	25.25
Amoco	U.S.	32	26.16	30	27.34	35	22.93
Allianz Holding	Germany	33	26.15	35	24.98	101	13.25
Tokai Bank	Japan	34	26.10	38	23.52	23	30.54
Chevron	U.S.	35	25.91	36	24.94	52	18.90
GTE	U.S.	36	25.91	48	21.13	61	17.33
Matsushita Electric Industrial	Japan	37	25.46	24	29.63	18	35.70
Pepsico	U.S.	38	24.89	54	19.48	87	14.22
Unilever	Netherlands/U.K.	39	24.07	44	22.15	66	16.60
BellSouth	U.S.	40	24.04	31	27.10	32	24.17
Nippon Steel	Japan	41	23.19	28	28.17	15	41.48
Abbott Laboratories	U.S.	42	22.73	78	16.57	98	13.35
Nestle	Switzerland	43	22.03	41	22.81	96	13.39
Kyowa Saitama Bank	Japan	44	21.83	137	10.62	124	11.50
Eli Lilly	U.S.	45	21.24	45	21.82	79	15.19
Minnesota Mining & Mfg.	U.S.	46	20.92	65	18.39	70	16.09
Kansai Electric Power	Japan	47	20.62	37	24.80	21	30.89
Daimler-Benz	Germany	48	20.52	42	22.58	86	14.36
Bank of Tokyo	Japan	49	20.46	57	19.12	36	22.46
Waste Management	U.S.	50	19.97	63	18.63	120	11.79

Sources: Business Week, various annual issues.

Table 2.4 Deposit Banks' Foreign Assets and Liabilities, 1976–1990 (US$ billions)

	1976	1977	1978	1979	1980	1981	1982
World							
Assets	702.7	890.5	1,191.4	1,495.2	1,833.3	2,192.0	2,373.3
Liabilities	745.6	931.7	1,213.1	1,566.9	1,898.2	2,244.3	2,395.9
Advanced industrial countries							
Assets	526.80	663.50	896.10	1,138.3	1,371.3	1,611.3	1,743.8
Liabilities	530.80	659.20	859.90	1,135.2	1,355.3	1,562.5	1,662.9
United Kingdom							
Assets	145.61	171.53	217.69	285.49	356.32	432.71	462.82
Liabilities	154.52	183.66	226.89	304.43	377.71	451.40	489.64
United States							
Assets	72.68	88.05	130.05	156.57	203.98	292.85	401.53
Liabilities	71.15	87.33	101.08	141.00	151.45	189.92	254.55
Japan							
Assets	21.65	21.69	33.69	45.44	65.67	84.61	90.95
Liabilities	29.04	28.58	39.01	50.49	80.21	100.39	100.02
Switzerland							
Assets	55.48	70.73	91.53	118.27	139.69	163.45	162.40
Liabilities	43.73	54.20	70.79	88.24	108.58	134.80	141.20
France							
Assets	41.29	72.69	108.88	137.59	160.21	158.09	162.96
Liabilities	51.50	66.84	95.24	119.65	146.68	153.79	164.67
Cayman Islands							
Assets	22.00	31.49	49.03	61.81	84.53	109.57	125.96
Liabilities	22.06	31.13	48.59	64.65	83.40	107.92	120.07
Luxembourg							
Assets	38.17	51.19	68.90	95.09	104.83	114.20	109.71
Liabilities	35.12	48.21	64.01	89.51	98.45	106.70	102.57
Germany							
Assets	48.23	58.27	73.21	82.56	85.17	84.54	81.73
Liabilities	30.20	38.37	57.93	76.70	72.09	66.80	64.69
Hong Kong							
Assets	12.42	17.47	20.88	25.60	35.77	47.59	58.23
Liabilities	9.20	13.07	16.39	21.15	32.62	45.28	54.12

Source: IMF, *International Financial Statistics Yearbook*, 1991.

liabilities held by the world's banks. These funds continue to grow and for the most part represent money largely outside the control of governments. These are foreign assets and therefore they can be seen as an interesting secondary measure of international confidence in the financial management and regulatory environment of these countries. As expected, most of these funds are in advanced industrial countries (ADCs), and they have been very consistent, ranging from 74.9 percent of the world total in 1976 to 75.6 percent by 1990 (see Table 2.4).

Great Britain and the infamous City of London financial community remains the world leader in bank foreign assets. Unlike the market value of Japanese corporations, which is in many cases heavily based upon the value of expensive Japanese real estate, these assets represent tangible capital. The

1983	1984	1985	1986	1987	1988	1989	1990	1976–1990
2,457.3	2,531.4	2,978.1	3,736.4	4,751.8	5,128.1	5,831.6	6,783.6	44,876.7
2,504.0	2,605.3	3,030.4	3,815.1	4,909.0	5,350.9	6,094.5	7,113.8	46,418.7
1,795.8	1,841.2	2,224.2	2,842.7	3,633.7	3,867.6	4,376.10	5,128.50	33,660.9
1,740.7	1,831.0	2,195.3	2,845.6	3,708.1	4,050.6	4,609.40	5,443.60	34,190.1
485.21	489.71	590.07	715.56	875.22	882.66	923.59	1,068.95	8,103.1
519.63	538.22	625.74	758.93	927.46	961.77	1,028.07	1,201.30	8,749.4
433.13	443.37	446.78	506.70	549.56	608.04	661.72	654.29	5,649.3
305.78	338.12	381.26	477.22	572.95	645.26	713.61	726.55	5,157.2
109.06	126.92	194.62	345.33	576.83	733.69	842.06	950.58	4,242.8
106.65	127.05	179.31	345.99	592.03	772.42	879.72	958.48	4,389.4
162.38	161.83	205.46	253.44	331.95	319.06	355.60	444.05	3,035.3
137.48	134.59	163.79	193.72	247.88	243.46	280.46	352.97	2,395.9
156.32	158.64	184.38	217.99	290.10	299.72	358.90	458.71	2,966.5
167.07	174.37	197.18	228.29	296.36	315.90	384.69	518.99	3,081.2
131.28	143.59	167.20	199.83	242.53	290.73	341.95	389.40	2,390.9
130.45	138.84	162.17	187.54	233.31	259.38	327.46	401.02	2,318.0
103.24	101.71	130.95	171.69	226.52	232.01	280.19	355.12	2,183.5
94.97	93.35	117.20	151.90	197.77	199.24	241.43	308.09	1,948.5
74.76	75.23	112.93	178.48	232.61	230.05	295.29	394.78	2,107.8
57.92	58.22	75.77	101.29	131.38	131.00	159.90	226.37	1,348.6
67.56	78.75	101.17	155.23	266.05	309.74	355.64	463.79	2,015.9
59.63	65.94	83.33	125.78	229.43	269.58	310.13	402.69	1,738.3

total value of these assets deposited in British banks was $1,069 billion in 1990 (see Table 2.4), representing 15.75 percent of total world assets in this category. The British have led in this category for many years, and although present assets have increased by 634 percent since 1976, they are down from the 20.7 percent share they were fourteen years ago. External assets of Japanese banks, by contrast, are estimated by the IMF to be more than $950 billion in 1990, up from only $21 billion in 1976. Japanese market shares of these assets have risen from only 3.08 percent in 1976 to 14.01 percent by 1990. The Japanese assets passed those of the United States in 1987. Although the value of these assets in the United States went up by 800 percent, from $72.68 billion in 1976 to $654.29 billion by 1990, U.S. shares of these assets decreased from 10.3 percent to 9.6 percent.

Bank foreign liabilities represent the opposite side of the ledger. World-wide in 1990, liabilities exceeded assets by $330 billion. Great Britain accounted for 40 percent of that, with foreign liabilities exceeding foreign assets by $132 billion. Japan's deficit was very small, at only $7.9 billion, whereas the U.S. deficit was $72.2 billion. Germany, by contrast, had a foreign asset surplus of $168.4 billion with assets of $395 billion and liabilities of slightly more than $226 billion.

There is not enough space to discuss a number of other important trends in this area, but it is noteworthy to consider the significant deposits being made in a number of international banking centers in microstates such as Luxembourg, the Cayman Islands, Hong Kong, Singapore, and the Bahamas in addition to the traditional banking haven, Switzerland. In 1988, these six centers accounted for $1,500 billion, 30.6 percent of total foreign assets deposited.

Japanese Trading Power

World trade has been the most discussed international economic factor for most of the twentieth century. The collapse of international trade between World War I and World War II is still being analyzed, whereas the growth of international trade since World War II has been seen as a primary reason for the unprecedented prosperity in advanced industrial nations for the past four decades.

Even after adjustments are made for inflation, the growth of world trade during the past forty years has been truly phenomenal. Most of this trade continues to be among advanced industrial countries. Advanced industrial states have remained remarkably constant at the 70 percent level for most of the past forty years. Only in 1975–1979 did their share drop to only 63 percent of trade for that five-year period. Included in these figures is trade between ADCs and LDCs (less developed countries), but dependency theorists will point to the fact that the huge increase in the volume of world trade in the past forty years has not significantly increased South-South trade percentages.

Although the GATT regimes and various bilateral and multilateral treaties have unquestionably helped the increase in world trade, this has not been without political costs and tensions. The most recent GATT discussions, which centered on agriculture and trade in services, have revealed just how explosive domestic political pressures can be. In many respects, given the enormous losses in traditional industrial employment in the United States and Western Europe during the past twenty years, it is remarkable that there have not been more serious trade wars to date.

Despite domestic myths and rhetoric to the contrary, the United States still led the world in international trade volume for the past forty years. Its exports for 1960–1989 were slightly more than $3.75 trillion (12.35 percent of the world's total), and its imports were almost $4.9 trillion (15.6 percent of the world's total). Even for the five-year period of 1984–1989, U.S. exports were just slightly more than second-place Germany's and more than $228 billion greater than that of Japan. What is better known, however, is the U.S. appetite for imports, which totaled nearly $5 trillion from 1960 to 1989 and more than $2.1 trillion in 1984–1989 alone. This left the United States with a huge $1.1 trillion trade deficit for the past forty years, 89 percent of which was accumulated during the 1980s.

Japan has been seen as the major winner in the trade game, but it has actually accumulated only a $428 billion surplus in the past forty years compared to Germany's $509 billion. From 1960 to 1989, Japan exported more than $2.5 trillion and imported $2.1 trillion. Germany exported more than $3.3 trillion and imported more than $2.8 trillion. This means that Germany traded $1.5 trillion more than Japan in the past forty years. Japan's surplus, however, represents 9.1 percent of its total volume, compared to Germany's surplus, which is 8.2 percent of its volume. Equally significant was that German trade was only 17 percent less than the combined trade of both Britain and France.

These trade figures must also be measured in relation to the total size of the country's economy. It is surprising that Japan's dependence on world trade, as measured by percentage of gross domestic product (GDP) in 1989, is only 17.0 percent, only slightly more than the 16.4 percent for the United States. This compares with 85.7 percent for the Netherlands, 45.8 percent for Germany, 44.5 percent for Canada, 42.4 percent for the United Kingdom, 35.3 percent for France, and 31.8 percent for Italy. These countries are far more dependent on world trade than the United States or even Japan and have had to make many more painful economic adjustments than the United States has. They have also restricted their consumers' choices far more than in the United States, where citizens have been a far more important force in defeating import restrictions than Japanese lobbyists have been.

A summary of Japan's regional trade figures from 1980 to 1990 (Table 2.5) shows the proportions of trade between ADCs and LDCs. For the decade, 56 percent of exports went to ADCs and 55 percent of imports came from LDCs. Overall, this resulted in a $463 billion trade surplus of which $241 billion was accumulated in just three years (1986–1988). Within Asia, Japan accumulated an overall surplus of $107 billion from 1980 to 1990. Exports of $594 billion to this region represented roughly 27 percent of Japan's total exports, and imports of $488 billion represented roughly 28 percent of total imports. By contrast, trade with other developing regions of the world was small, except for imports from the Middle East, which were more than $333 billion, or 19 percent of total imports, from 1980 to 1990.

The ranking of Japan's specific trade partners on different dimensions from 1972 to 1990 (Table 2.6) gives a more informative understanding. The United States was clearly the largest single trading partner for Japan, with

Table 2.5 Regional Trade Summary, 1980–1990 (US$ billions)

	1980	1981	1982	1983	1984	1985	1986	1987	1988	1989	1990	1980–1990	Percentage of Total
Total													
Exports	130.441	151.495	138.385	146.965	169.700	177.164	210.757	231.286	264.856	273.932	287.851	2,182.832	100.00
Imports	141.296	142.866	131.499	126.437	136.176	130.488	127.553	151.033	187.378	209.715	235.368	1,719.809	100.00
Balance	−10.855	8.629	6.886	20.528	33.524	46.676	83.204	80.253	77.478	64.217	52.483	463.023	
Advanced industrial countries													
Exports	59.124	70.283	65.497	75.199	94.751	102.797	131.062	142.554	160.083	165.811	168.492	1,235.653	56.61
Imports	47.470	49.370	46.356	47.801	52.985	51.680	60.591	69.888	92.742	104.780	118.100	741.763	43.13
Balance	11.654	20.913	19.141	27.398	41.766	51.117	70.471	72.666	67.341	61.031	50.392	493.890	
Less developed countries													
Exports	61.124	70.099	63.051	67.399	70.929	70.192	75.679	85.524	101.063	105.197	116.272	886.529	40.61
Imports	89.129	88.553	80.722	76.929	81.420	77.041	64.694	78.191	91.331	101.246	113.345	942.601	54.81
Balance	−28.005	−18.454	−17.671	−9.530	−10.491	−6.849	10.985	7.333	9.732	3.951	2.927	−56.072	
Africa													
Exports	5.254	6.311	4.820	4.046	4.030	2.939	3.418	4.783	4.681	4.439	4.697	49.418	2.26
Imports	3.986	4.202	3.512	3.000	2.850	3.009	3.610	3.852	3.934	4.066	3.693	39.714	2.31
Balance	1.268	2.109	1.308	1.046	1.180	−0.070	−0.192	0.931	0.747	0.373	1.004	9.704	
Asia													
Exports	31.518	34.533	31.500	40.015	44.577	46.826	52.914	62.564	77.443	82.626	90.146	594.662	27.24
Imports	34.693	35.179	33.284	33.639	38.218	37.509	36.081	47.220	58.886	64.982	68.074	487.765	28.36
Balance	−3.175	−0.646	−1.784	6.376	6.359	9.317	16.833	15.344	18.557	17.644	22.072	106.897	
Middle East													
Exports	14.152	17.365	16.605	16.812	13.893	11.985	9.535	8.869	9.051	8.115	9.422	135.804	6.22
Imports	44.612	42.445	37.594	33.737	32.915	30.056	18.585	20.296	19.474	22.792	31.282	333.788	19.41
Balance	−30.460	−25.080	−20.989	−16.925	−19.022	−18.071	−9.050	−11.427	−10.423	−14.677	−21.860	−197.984	
Latin America													
Exports	8.331	9.853	8.601	5.798	7.650	7.450	8.423	8.037	8.556	8.783	9.658	91.140	4.18
Imports	5.514	6.445	6.088	6.279	7.033	6.126	6.014	6.208	8.060	8.495	9.409	75.671	4.40
Balance	2.817	3.408	2.513	−0.481	0.617	1.324	2.409	1.829	0.496	0.288	0.249	15.469	
USSR/COMECON													
Exports	3.688	4.184	4.693	3.790	3.260	3.589	3.945	3.242	3.804	3.585	2.914	40.694	1.86
Imports	2.355	2.428	2.046	1.785	1.734	1.794	2.372	2.827	3.409	3.605	3.859	28.214	1.64
Balance	1.333	1.756	2.647	2.005	1.526	1.795	1.573	0.415	0.395	−0.020	−0.945	12.480	

Source: IMF, *Direction of Trade Statistics Yearbooks, 1980–1991.*

Table 2.6 Ranking of Trade Partners, 1972–1990 (US$ billions)

Rank	Country	Total Trade	Country	Exports	Country	Imports	Country	Balance
1	United States	1,306.382	United States	850.722	United States	455.660	United States	395.062
2	Saudi Arabia	252.261	South Korea	136.469	Saudi Arabia	189.387	Hong Kong	85.286
3	South Korea	222.518	Germany	127.355	Indonesia	153.986	Germany	61.140
4	Indonesia	204.238	Hong Kong	101.360	Australia	128.160	South Korea	50.420
5	Australia	203.272	United Kingdom	89.259	United Arab Emirates	97.575	Singapore	49.851
6	Germany	193.570	People's Rep. of China	88.500	People's Rep. of China	89.008	United Kingdom	48.336
7	People's Rep. of China	188.508	Taiwan[a]	84.894	South Korea	86.049	Taiwan[a]	35.148
8	Canada	149.625	Canada	77.431	Canada	85.547	Netherlands	34.253
9	Taiwan[a]	134.640	Germany	75.112	Germany	66.215	Thailand	22.357
10	United Kingdom	130.182	Iran	64.078	Iran	58.013	Belgium/Luxembourg	19.362
11	Hong Kong	117.434	Malaysia	62.874	Malaysia	56.273	Soviet Union	11.926
12	United Arab Emirates	116.413	Taiwan[a]	50.252	People's Rep. of China	49.746	People's Rep. of China	10.492
13	Singapore	105.011	United Kingdom	48.043	United Kingdom	40.923	France	8.173
14	Malaysia	93.917	France	45.477	France	34.651	Philippines	0.809
15	Iran	84.374	Soviet Union	43.388	Soviet Union	33.551	India	0.561
16	France	77.475	Switzerland	42.824	Mexico	30.879	Mexico	-2.558
17	Soviet Union	75.658	Brazil	37.644	Italy	29.407	Italy	-2.944
18	Thailand	73.729	Singapore	29.303	Switzerland	27.580	Switzerland	-7.809
19	Switzerland	53.949	Philippines	26.740	Brazil	25.931	Brazil	-11.053
20	Philippines	52.671	Iran	26.361	Malaysia	25.686	Malaysia	-18.629
21	Netherlands	52.523	Switzerland	23.070	Canada	24.969	Canada	-21.469
22	Brazil	47.761	Italy	22.025	India	21.111	Iran	-31.652
23	Italy	46.994	India	21.672	Mexico	20.637	Australia	-53.048
24	India	42.783	United Arab Emirates	18.838	Hong Kong	16.074	United Arab Emirates	-78.737
25	Belgium/Luxembourg	39.244	Brazil	18.354	Belgium/Luxembourg	9.941	Indonesia	-103.734
26	Mexico	38.716	Mexico	18.079	Netherlands	9.135	Saudi Arabia	-126.513

Source: IMF, *Direction of Trade Statistics Yearbooks*, 1979–1991.
Note: a. Taiwan data for 1982–1990 only.

$1,310 billion in total trade and an overall surplus for Japan of $395 billion for this period. Saudi Arabia was Japan's second largest trading partner for the past eighteen years, with $252 billion in total trade but with an overall deficit of $126 billion. Thus, almost 32 percent of the total surplus gained from the United States was taken up by trade deficits from Saudi Arabia alone. Combined with the deficits for mostly energy and raw materials from Indonesia, the United Arab Emirates (U.A.E.), Australia, and Iran, Japan's total trade deficit from these five countries was $394 billion, almost exactly equal to the surplus with the United States.

The still unappreciated lesson for the United States, however, is the extent to which trade competition is highly sensitive to exchange rates and currency values. The U.S. business and financial community have complained for years about the effects of the budget deficit on the value of the dollar, but one suspects that the U.S. public has only been inclined to hear this as corporate fear about more taxes. Even more sophisticated international economists still debate the relative importance of exchange rates versus labor costs in determining trade success. Productivity does matter, but a strong or weak currency can still make a significant difference and, more importantly, because foreign exchange and currency factors are highly unstable in short-term markets, they can be much more difficult to control. The U.S. public is also largely unaware of the ways in which the use of the dollar as a reserve currency in the world economy has shielded them from painful devaluations that would have pushed import prices much higher. Since the reinstitution of the floating currency regime, however, this insulation is no longer as effective as it once was.

The scope of this analysis is too limited to discuss in detail the roles of interest rates in establishing the values of currencies, but these too have their influence. Interest rates are usually set by a combination of market and government forces. Again we return to the political versus economic roles of central banks or unique institutions such as the U.S. Federal Reserve Board. With money market interest rates in 1989 of 9.22 percent in the United States versus 4.87 percent in Japan and 6.59 percent in Germany, one can easily see the relative weaknesses and strengths of these currencies as well as the potential effects on domestic investment in these countries.

Japan's strong performance in international trade greatly increases its position of influence in the world economy. This might be discounted somewhat if it were not for its additional strengths in its domestic economy and corporate/financial sectors. The combined power Japan gains from all three of these sources is the foundation for Japan's potential as an economic hegemon or at least co-equal partner with the United States for international economic leadership. The prospects for continuing or increasing its relative influence in the world economy depends upon our last factor, technological advancement.

_____ *Japanese Technology Power*

A final but difficult factor to incorporate into an assessment of international economic power and influence is the role played by advanced technologies. Advanced technological research has witnessed a veritable revolution of scientific discoveries in the past fifty years, beginning with the atomic fission process in the early 1940s. Information technologies, biotechnologies, material processing, and a host of other discoveries in transportation, communications, and manufacturing have emerged as a result of unprecedented public and private investments in personnel and facilities.

Technological development and diffusion is always a controversial subject because of the competitive atmosphere in which it takes place and because of the prospects of enhanced power and wealth that come as a result of technological mastery and marketing. The problems of developing and marketing the most lucrative and useful technologies involve countless choices about appropriate sectors of the economy to be transformed and the most effective levels of public versus private risk- and reward-taking. Whereas developing countries continue to decry their problems of technological dependence and underdevelopment, virtually all of the advanced industrial countries are publicly voicing their own concerns about maintaining technological competitiveness in the contemporary global economy.

Considerable problems concerning international technological assessment and its ramifications are related to important misunderstandings regarding the nature of technology and its applications. Technology can be differentiated from basic knowledge by defining technology as information that can be used to produce something. The crucial distinction for purposes of the international economy, however, is between proprietary and nonproprietary technologies. Only a fraction of today's research and development activity would take place if technological research were for the sake of science alone. As advanced technologies continue to reshape political and economic power in the world, the battle between those countries with successful and profitable research enterprises and those countries hoping to profit from that research at the lowest cost to themselves will be focused on the nature and extent of proprietary rights and guarantees for technological research information, products, and services.

Precise statistics on national expenditures on research and development have only recently begun to be collected by the Organization for Economic Cooperation and Development (OECD) and a few other governmental organizations. Approximately $300 billion is spent annually on total research and development (R&D) in the advanced industrial states, where advanced technologies are primarily created. The United States spent $136 billion in 1988 and $145 billion in 1989, which represents approximately 45 percent of all R&D expenditures for advanced countries. By contrast, Japan spent only $51 billion in 1988 and nearly $58 billion in 1989. On a per capita basis (see

Table 2.7 Gross Domestic Expenditure on R&D, 1985–1989

Country	1985	1986	1987	1988	1989
		Per Capita (US$)			
United States	484.9	503.2	523.2	553.4	582.2
Japan	331.8	342.0	376.4	416.0	471.0
Germany	327.5	n/a	378.3	399.5	431.4
France	264.1	272.8	291.2	312.1	338.1
United Kingdom	255.1	273.9	282.6	297.9	n/a
Italy	122.8	129.8	144.6	159.4	179.7
Canada	218.4	232.7	236.4	246.2	256.1
		As Percentage of GDP			
United States	2.93	2.91	2.87	2.83	2.82
Japan	2.81	2.79	2.86	2.91	3.04
Germany	2.71	n/a	2.86	2.83	2.88
France	2.25	2.23	2.28	2.29	2.32
United Kingdom	2.31	2.34	2.25	2.20	n/a
Italy	1.12	1.14	1.19	1.23	1.29
Canada	1.41	1.44	1.38	1.35	1.33

Source: O.E.C.D., *Main Science and Technology Indicators*, 1991.
Note: n/a = not available

Table 2.7), however, Japan spent $471 in 1989—nearly 81 percent of the U.S. expenditure and 9.3 percent more than Germany. Trends for R&D spending as a percentage of the domestic economy, moreover, show that of Japan increasing from 2.81 percent of GDP in 1985 to 3.04 percent in 1989, whereas that of the United States has declined from 2.93 percent to 2.82 percent for the same period.

The general structure of industrial policies influences the high-technology strategies chosen by different governments. In the U.S. experience, the growth points of high-technology research have not been designed by the government, but have been left to private firms or state and local governments to compete by packaging tax and utility savings. In Japan, the combination of private competition among larger firms and the "critical sectors" strategy of technological promotion pushed Japan to the front of the group in certain key niches (especially robotics). In West Germany, massive amounts of government spending decentralized through the Lander and into the private and public research centers has yet to really help Germany keep pace with the United States and Japan. France has had very limited success in certain government-sponsored "national champions." Britain and France, like the United States, spend significant amounts of research and development resources on defense and aerospace, often with unproductive results. In the United States the percentage of total government R&D appropriations spent on defense from 1986 to 1990 has been in the 65–69 percent range, whereas in Britain it has been 45–49 percent, and in France it is closer to 34–37 percent. Unfortunately, there are no available estimates for Japan, but it seems very likely that they are very low.

The incentive for the costly experiments in the production of basic scientific knowledge always has depended largely on financial considerations. Rarely do appeals for grants or programs for research rely on humanitarian grounds to convince public or private benefactors. Profitability may be a long-term rather than a short-term prospect, but research and development costs usually must be recovered in some fashion. The key to profitability, however, depends upon the proprietary nature of the ownership of the knowledge and a means of receiving compensation for the acquisition of that knowledge. The protection of the rights of the producers of technological information and the terms of negotiation under which it is exchanged or sold have become highly politicized. Different national laws regarding technological research producers' rights and the limits on licensing agreements have been particularly difficult obstacles to the establishment of more liberal international guidelines on the transfer of technologies. Current international agreements on international trading practices are focused on specific products and are incapable of dealing with questions concerning the exchange or sales of lucrative information.

The consumer orientation of Japanese demand-driven technological innovation has meant that the greatest gains have come in the enhancement of intermediate products and adaptive marketing rather than in original creativity. Although Japanese nationals in recent years have applied for as many patents as those in the United States and the European Community combined, Japan is still not a significant supplier of technology. Only 15 percent goes to the United States and a third to all advanced nations. Two-thirds of Japanese technological exports are middle- and lower-scale industrial ones sent to less developed countries. The results of Japanese technology in South Korea and Taiwan have been quite impressive.

Unlike the United States, Japan has not unleashed a wave of multinational corporations to exploit their technologies. Instead, they have been generally content to keep their high-technology industries at home. The enormous flow of U.S. technology to Japan in the 1950s and 1960s compounded the one-way nature of Japanese technology markets. The barriers to doing business were very difficult. Distribution systems were run by national business groups that have traditionally been closed to foreigners. The Japanese markets seemed more alien, remote, and limited in profit potential compared to Western Europe and Canada. The prospect for U.S. managers of easy quick income from technology sales already written off as R&D expenses was attractive, and the Japanese were eager to buy.

Japan's successes with its well-directed industrial policies toward targeted "critical" sectors served the country well during the 1970s. The Japanese system has not highlighted the role of smaller-scale firms, as in the United States, but instead has established about two hundred technical and managerial laboratories as outlets for diffusing technology to small industry. The "export to survive" trade mentality of the Japanese has reinforced the intensity of technological diffusion and adaptation.

Lower profit margins and more concern for long-term market shares have helped provide more money for private research and development in Japan. Estimates of funds available range from 3 to 6 percent more than in other advanced industrial states. Dividends are generally measured as a return on capital at par value rather than as a percentage of earnings. Consequently, the Japanese are much more interested in sales than they are in earnings. Quality control methods have helped enormously. Several hundred thousand of these groups are broadly distributed. The results of their findings and discussions are disseminated through contacts within the national engineering associations.

Japan, more than most countries, has also stressed education policy and an effort to substantially upgrade the mathematics and science skills of the entire population. Heavy use of the media to promote educational skills of the general public is combined with support for continual education for scientists and engineers. Very high levels of capital investment in Japan also contribute to the modernization and promotion of higher levels of technology. A perfect example of the capital-intensive nature of Japanese technology is the field of robotics. Japanese "robot-fever" has drawn an emerging consensus that industrial robots will be the key to industrial competitiveness in the future. By 1980, it took only two-thirds as many Japanese workers and only two-thirds as many hours to produce the same number of cars that U.S. producers were sending out. The key was industrial robot spot welders. By the end of the 1970s, Japan had six times as many of these machines as their U.S. rivals. Japan seems to believe that robots are the key to international economic competition in the next fifty years and is gambling that its early lead will give it an insurmountable advantage in the decades ahead.

But Japan has not solved all of its problems. It has yet to establish a more powerful and creative research base. It has been much more effective at technology dissemination than innovation. There have been significant examples of failures of industrial sectoral support in such fields as aircraft development, construction equipment, chain saws, plate heat exchangers, and marine engines. In addition, there have been other difficulties of government and business conflicts of interest in some of the metal and synthetic fibers industries as well as in other areas, which have impaired the development of sectoral policies.

Japan knows that it will meet heavier competition from the United States and Western Europe in high-tech industries in the future. With its much lighter defense burdens a sore point, Japan will also be pushed to make more national sacrifices to foster fairer and freer international technology transfer and investment. As less formal barriers to entry and trade become more important to trading regimes in the future, governmental assistance to high-technology development will become more controversial and disputed. Japan already has the advantage of last position in governmental spending for industrial R&D promotion and is much less vulnerable to this claim than its rivals. Japan will also be likely to continue the successful sectoral policies in various knowledge-intensive industries in the future. Already high-speed computers, oceanic and space development, aircraft, optic fibers, and ceramics have been given new attention.

The behavior of Japanese multinational corporations will be extremely important to international economic relations and technology transfer. If MNCs continue to expand direct investment in the United States and elsewhere and allow domestic markets to be more open to other multinational corporations, there may be greater common interests. The Japanese gamble on robotics may be one of the most important decisions for the rest of the century. If they are right, their economic performance in the 1990s will continue to provide unprecedented affluence and stronger market positions. If they are wrong, and it takes much longer than anticipated to develop assembly-capable robots, then much of the effectiveness of governmental action will have been wasted.

_____ *Japanese Foreign Aid*

The final aspect of Japan's influence in the contemporary world economy concerns foreign economic assistance. In 1989, Japan passed the United States to become the world's largest donor of foreign economic aid (see Table 2.8), even though the $8.9 billion for that year represented a 2 percent decrease from 1988. The Japanese government, however, increased its economic foreign aid by 10 percent for 1990 to just under $10 billion and seems determined to establish this assistance as one of the major pillars of its foreign policy. The 1990 levels of economic foreign aid still represent only 0.33 percent of Japan's GDP and are lower levels than most European countries but are nevertheless an attempt to mute criticism that Japan has been too self-centered and nationalistic.

Japan's foreign aid program in the 1950s began as a form of war reparations; by the 1960s it was linked to export promotion and raw materials imports from Asian nations. Throughout the 1970s, the trade linkage to foreign aid was expanded to some African countries with large trade deficits with Japan and to the Middle East, where economic aid projects were traded for oil contracts.[14] As Japan emerged as the world's largest creditor in the 1980s, Japan not only became more generous in its direct aid to developing countries but also more liberal with long-term development loans. Many Japanese politicians believe that in the future economic aid will greatly increase Japanese influence in international relations and be a more acceptable means of leverage than the military aid given by the United States and the Soviet Union during the Cold War.

Table 2.8 Official Developmental Assistance, 1970–1989

Country	1970	1975	1980	1985	1986	1987	1988	1989
			Total Net Flows (US$ billions)					
Japan	0.458	1.148	3.353	3.797	5.634	7.342	9.134	8.949
(% OECD total)	6.57	8.28	12.28	12.90	15.36	17.65	18.98	19.16
United States	3.153	4.161	7.138	9.403	9.564	9.115	10.141	7.676
France	0.971	2.093	4.162	3.995	5.105	6.525	6.865	7.450
Germany	0.599	1.689	3.567	2.942	3.832	4.391	4.731	4.949
Italy	0.147	0.182	0.683	1.098	2.404	2.615	3.193	3.613
United Kingdom	0.500	0.904	1.854	1.530	1.737	1.871	2.645	2.587
Canada	0.337	0.880	1.075	1.631	1.695	1.885	2.347	2.320
Netherlands	0.196	0.608	1.630	1.136	1.740	2.094	2.231	2.094
Sweden	0.117	0.566	0.962	0.840	1.090	1.375	1.534	1.799
Total OECD	6.968	13.855	27.296	29.429	36.663	41.595	48.114	46.697
			As Percentage of Donor GNP					
Sweden	0.38	0.82	0.78	0.86	0.85	0.88	0.86	0.97
Netherlands	0.61	0.75	0.97	0.91	1.01	0.98	0.98	0.94
France	0.66	0.62	0.63	0.78	0.70	0.74	0.72	0.78
Canada	0.41	0.54	0.43	0.49	0.48	0.47	0.50	0.44
Italy	0.16	0.11	0.15	0.26	0.40	0.35	0.39	0.42
Germany	0.32	0.40	0.44	0.47	0.43	0.39	0.39	0.41
Japan	0.23	0.23	0.32	0.29	0.29	0.31	0.32	0.32
United Kingdom	0.41	0.39	0.35	0.33	0.31	0.28	0.32	0.31
United States	0.32	0.27	0.27	0.24	0.23	0.20	0.21	0.15

Source: IMF, *World Development Report*, 1990.

Although the contribution of foreign aid to development in the Third World is often seen as minimal compared to direct foreign investment, many Japanese see foreign aid not as altruism but as a form of investment. Tadashi Ikeda has summarized this attitude in Japan:

> Today, with relations between nations growing increasingly interdependent, the contributions that one country makes to other countries or to the world as a whole also benefit that country itself; it is hard to draw a clear line between self-interest and altruism. In this sense, we would probably interpret "international contributions" to refer basically to the necessary expenses of Japan's guaranteeing itself the continuation of its present security and economic prosperity while maintaining the existing international order.[15]

Conclusion: Japan, Global Economic Hegemony, and the Future

Recently, William Pfaff has joined the chorus of those who are calling upon scholars of international relations to redefine world power. In the past, he says, the category of "great power" was associated with invulnerability.[16]

Clearly, the age of economic and military invulnerability has passed. If hegemony is equated with invulnerability, there may never be another hegemon in international affairs. According to Pfaff, "National power as such rests on a triad: military power; economic power, incorporating technological leadership or competitiveness; and finally social cohesion and public consensus on national goals."[17]

This chapter has not directly addressed the need to redefine military power—only that the notion of hegemony has been heavily influenced by notions of military power. The United States remains the world's most important military power, although there is no consensus about whether it is sufficiently invulnerable to compare it to military dynasties of the past. The United States was the first to develop the weapon that may put true military invulnerability out of the reach of any contemporary nation-state.

This analysis has addressed the changing nature of international economic power and the need to treat it differently than classical economic treatments of national economic power. A more comprehensive analysis would need to prioritize more carefully the appropriate weights given to each of the five factors treated here. There may still be other factors that merit consideration. The argument made here is that the salience and weights that should be allocated to these factors are constantly changing, and any country's potential for international hegemony in the world economy will depend upon how well it maintains and improves its current position on these important dimensions relative to its international competition. Vulnerability may violate older notions of hegemony and great power status but it may also provide the discipline and vitality necessary to prevent or at least slow down the decline of hegemony.

This chapter also has not addressed the question of national cohesion and public consensus on domestic and/or foreign policy roles. But it is appropriate to mention that the U.S. consensus still remains weak on foreign economic goals even after the military victory against Iraq. Most telling is the lack of consensus on an energy policy that would reduce the dependence on foreign oil. Western Europe's resolve to push ahead with full economic union will be forcefully challenged by German reunification, events in Eastern Europe, and continued British reluctance to surrender monetary sovereignty. European reluctance to more forcefully trim its agricultural subsidies to allow a new phase of trade liberalization may be the harbinger of the inward regional attitude feared by some. Japan may have the most consensus on its foreign economic policies in spite of recent instabilities and leadership crises in the ruling Liberal Democratic Party.

It is certainly premature to declare Japan as the next economic or even financial hegemon if one uses the dominance notion of hegemony. Japan has obtained an unprecedented amount of financial and economic influence in the United States. There continue to be those in the United States and elsewhere who will try to revive bitter feelings left from Japanese militarism earlier in this century together with a jealousy toward its contemporary economic accomplishments. Others, such as Pfaff, will more subtly claim that Japan's lack of international ambition, cultural uniqueness, and historical isolation will permanently disqualify it from assuming a more dominant role, even if its wealth continues to grow unabated.

All of this misses, in my opinion, the hidden wisdom in Japan's example for the rest of the world. Japan's tradition of collective leadership and consensus building is sorely needed in today's world. Its pragmatism is indeed strategic, as the Schmiegelows would say.[18] It prefers long-term strategies to short-term profits, which is the way the world needs to be managed. Japan has eschewed the pursuit of military power, which is not only helpful for world peace but is also a wiser use of resources. For those imprinted with coercive models of hegemony, Japan will thankfully never achieve whatever elusive dominance may have been held by Britain and the United States in their heyday. But for those who yearn for a return to a more constructive notion of leadership in a world of complex interdependence, Japan's ascendence may be exactly what the world needs.

Notes

1. G. John Ikenberry and Charles Kupchan, "Socialization and Hegemonic Power," *International Organization*, vol. 44 (1990), pp. 283–316.

2. International Institute for Strategic Studies, *The Military Balance, 1991–1992*, London: Brassey's, 1991.

3. George Friedman and Meredith Lebard, *The Coming War With Japan*, New York: St. Martin's Press, 1990, pp. 12–13.

4. Donald Hellmann, "Japanese Security and Postwar Japanese Foreign Policy," in Robert A. Scalapino, ed., *The Foreign Policy of Modern Japan*, Berkeley: University of California Press, 1977, p. 329.

5. Masataka Kosaka, *Japan's Choices*, New York: Pinter, 1989, p. 86.

6. Hellmann, "Japanese Security," p. 325.

7. United States, Arms Control and Disarmament Agency, *World Military Expenditures and Arms Transfers*, Washington, D.C.: U.S. Government Printing Office, 1990.

8. Karel van Wolferen, *The Enigma of Japanese Power*, New York: Alfred Knopf, 1989; Michele Schmiegelow, "Cutting Across Doctrines: Positive Adjustment in Japan," *International Organization*, vol. 39 (1985), pp. 261–296.

9. James Abegglen and George Stalk, *Kaisha, The Japanese Corporation*, New York: Basic Books, 1985.

10. Daniel Burstein, *Yen! Japan's New Financial Empire and Its Threat to America*, New York: Simon and Schuster, 1988; Douglas Frantz and Catherine Collins, *Selling Out*, Chicago: Contemporary Books, 1989.

11. Bill Emmott, *The Sun Also Sets*, New York: Random House, 1989; Deborah Haber, "The Death of Hegemony: Why Pax Nipponica Is Impossible," *Asian Survey*, vol. 30 (1990), pp. 892–907.

12. Ethan Kapstein, "Resolving the Regulator's Dilemma: International Coordination of Banking Regulations," *International Organization*, vol. 43 (1989), pp. 323–347.

13. Immanuel Wallerstein, *The Politics of the World Economy*, New York: Cambridge University Press, 1984.

14. Xiaoming Zhou, "Japan's Official Development Assistance Program," *Asian Survey*, vol. 31 (1991), p. 341.

15. Tadashi Ikeda, "Japan's International Contribution," *International Affairs*, Spring-Summer 1989, p. 19, quoted in Xiaoming Zhou, "Japan's Official Development Assistance Program: Pressures to Expand," *Asian Survey*, vol. 31, no. 4 (April 1991), pp. 344–345.

16. William Pfaff, "Redefining World Power," *Foreign Affairs*, vol. 70 (1991), p. 36.

17. Ibid., p. 36.

18. Henrik Schmiegelow and Michele Schmiegelow, "How Japan Affects the International System," *International Organization*, vol. 44 (1990), pp. 553–588.

Chapter 3

The Posthegemonic
Japanese–U.S. Relationship

Frank Langdon

The Varied and Contradictory Relations

To better evaluate the relationship of Japan and the United States in the post–Cold War period, one needs to view their changed relations broadly, both historically and in regard to their international environment. Their historical relations provide a surprisingly varied and often contradictory relationship. The United States first played an important role as a military threat to Japan as the first of the major powers to force Japan open to the world in 1853 after centuries of self-imposed isolation. The so-called "black ships" of U.S. Commodore Matthew Perry enabled him to extract Japan's adherence to its first modern international treaty. Japan opened up some of its ports to foreign commerce, an action that started that country on its road to modern industrial development and the status of a great world power. The theme of military and economic threat is interwoven throughout the relations of Japan and the United States for the last century and a half.

The first treaties with the Western powers were unequal: they gave foreigners a stranglehold on the commerce of Japan by a fixed low tariff and they permitted foreigners to remain under their own laws and courts in Japan. Such extraterritorial privileges to foreigners would never have been granted to Japan in North America or Europe. Initially, foreigners dominated the foreign trade. Japan created its great trading companies to recapture some of its own trade. The subsequent defensive protectionism of Japan probably owes its origin to the need to regain control over its own commerce in those early years. Japan began the sixty-year struggle to free itself from those foreign economic and political controls soon after Perry left Japan. The fierce competition within Japan for market share in some manufacturing sectors has periodically spilled over into its trade abroad and threatened to wipe out European and U.S. industries as it did in the 1970s and 1980s.

However, in the late decades of the nineteenth century Japanese foreign relations were particularly favorable as the United States proved to be a guide and teacher—along with other Western powers—in the setting up of modern communications, industries, and education in the island empire. By the turn of the century, Japan had plunged into the Western imperialist rivalry to seize or control the rest of East Asia. The rivalry was played out for trade, political privileges, and territory in Korea, China, Taiwan, the Philippines, and Southeast Asia. The Chinese made only timid attempts under the Ching dynasty to follow Japan's example of modernization and self-strengthening but could not protect itself against the Western assault in which Japan participated.

The United States devised the doctrine of the "open door" in China in a rather ineffectual attempt to use international diplomacy and law to keep China's trade accessible to all foreign countries, and it opposed the attempts of Japan to obtain exclusive economic and political controls there. During World War I the United States managed to use diplomacy to keep Japan from completely dominating the government in Beijing. The U.S. open-door doctrine for China contained some liberal trading ideas that became important following World War II.

Japan was strongly motivated to obtain exclusive rights in Korea and China and to remove the Western privileges there. After a war with China in the 1890s over dominance of Korea, Japan clashed in another war with Russia over exclusive rights in Manchuria in 1904 and 1905. It was U.S. President Theodore Roosevelt, an admirer of the "plucky Japanese," who mediated the peace terms at Portsmouth, New Hampshire. Thereafter, the United States feared the Japanese regional challenger to the Western powers and championed China against Japan. Meanwhile, Japan went on to absorb Korea and then Manchuria, and then it invaded the rest of China in 1937.

When Japan threatened to seize the Western colonies in Southeast Asia as well, the United States under President Franklin Roosevelt, a cousin of Theodore Roosevelt, joined in economic sanctions with Canada, Britain, and the Netherlands to cut off supplies of oil and other essential raw materials needed by Japan's war machine. Tokyo was faced with the fateful choice of giving up its aggression in China or waging war with the United States and Britain. Therefore, Japan began the war in the Pacific with a surprise attack on Pearl Harbor, much as it had in the Chinese and Russian wars. Many Japanese blame President Franklin Roosevelt for starting the Pacific war by forcing the issue with an Allied embargo, which threatened to halt Japan's army and navy. Thus began the military struggle with the United States for hegemony in the Asia Pacific region. The relationship had finally turned into that of enemy combatants. After almost succeeding in driving out most of the Western powers from East Asia and the Western Pacific, Japan went down to defeat and for the first time in its history was occupied by a foreign power.

Thus, in the early history of Japan-U.S. relations, the role of the United States varied greatly from military threat to guidance to competition to enmity. It also included economic as well as military conflict. Japan had been allied with Britain in the early part of the twentieth century against Russia. But Canada, then an integral part of the British Empire, was afraid it might get caught on the wrong side if a war finally broke out between the United States and Japan. It did not want to be allied through Britain with Japan, which would leave Canada open to conquest by the United States. Britain reluctantly canceled the Anglo-Japanese alliance at Canada's behest in the early 1920s.

The Cold War Relationship

The Japan-U.S. relationship after the wartime defeat in 1945 was characterized by punishment and democratization of Japan largely at the hands of the United States on behalf of the Western allies. The Cold War came to Europe with the formation of the anti-Soviet military alliance in Europe and the Atlantic, the North Atlantic Treaty Organization (NATO), in 1949. In the same year the Cold War came to Asia with the Chinese communists' defeat of the Chinese nationalists, who had become the chief Asian ally of the United States. The undisputed hegemon at that time, the United States, took the lead in quickly terminating the Japanese occupation and bringing about a conciliatory peace treaty with Japan, which the Soviets and Chinese communists refused to sign. By 1950 Washington had quietly junked the punitive peace treaty it had planned to impose. In 1951 it signed a security treaty simultaneously with a new conciliatory peace treaty, making Japan the chief U.S. ally in Asia. In the Cold War period from 1949 to 1989 U.S. military competition with Japan had disappeared and economic differences were replaced by close cooperation, particularly in the first half of that period.

Japan's role as an ally was quite different from that of other U.S. allies in NATO or in the Asia Pacific region. The other allies were prepared to fight alongside the United States, not only in their own territory but elsewhere in their region as well. Korea contributed troops to the Vietnam War as did Australia and New Zealand to aid their U.S. ally. But Japan's treaty obligations are much more limited. It was expected to join with U.S. forces only to defend Japan itself if threatened or attacked. It is not an exaggeration to say that after the Pacific war the whole nature of Japan was transformed in respect to military affairs. It was completely disarmed by the punitive policies of the occupation. The new constitution, crafted almost wholly by the U.S. occupation commander and his staff, liberalized the political system, outlawed war, and, most unique of all, forbade even the maintenance of armed forces. In addition, the Japanese public had become thoroughly disillusioned with their former military leaders, whom they blamed for the death and destruction inflicted on their country. The country became pacifist and antimilitaristic in its outlook. The situation was a kind of ironic trading of places by Japan and the United States. Prior to the attack on Pearl Harbor, most of the U.S. public had been quite isolationist and pacifist. But the attack reversed those attitudes overnight, enabling the United States to play a decisive role in World War II, both in Europe and in the Pacific. In the Cold War, the United States was prepared to fight almost anywhere to defeat the threat of communist expansion.

Only a few of Japan's older nationalist politicians were at first prepared to support rebuilding a strong military force like a major power or one prepared to fight outside Japan. Reluctantly, in the face of U.S. pressure, the Japanese government slowly rebuilt limited armed forces, called the Self-Defense Forces, to evade the constitutional restriction. The numbers of armed personnel remain smaller than those of any of Japan's neighbors. Although Japanese military capability has increased with the most modern, mainly defensive equipment, the number of military personnel has remained relatively stable for decades. It is so difficult to recruit volunteers in Japan that the authorized number of armed men has never even been reached.

Nor has there ever been a political consensus in support of the Self-Defense Forces. The socialist and labor parties of the NATO allies early in the Cold War accepted the necessity of armed defense and alliance against the communist threat, but not so in Japan. Hence, Japan remains divided over defense policy. The Social Democratic Party of Japan, the main opposition party, and especially its left wing, are the most opposed to Japan's allied military role. The party considers the Self-Defense Forces to be contrary to the constitution. They wish to phase out the security treaty with the United States. The political division keeps the Japanese armed forces limited in number, in military role, and in equipment compared to all other major powers. The contradictory nature of Japan's defense policy is not only in the conservative government's defense cooperation with the United States as an ally, but in the unusual limitations due to only weak public support and outright opposition from some parties and their supporters to Japan's Cold War allied role.

In the first half of the Cold War the United States was not troubled by the small role of the Japanese armed forces, which was mainly a symbolic commitment by Japan to Western allied objectives in the region. The term "ally" was seldom heard in Japan until the 1980s because it smacked of the aggression under the old Japanese imperial military. During this period the most valuable military role Japan had was as a secure key basing area. It enabled the United States to follow a forward deployment policy to deter or threaten its nearby opponents. The United States used Japan militarily to put its weapons and forces close to potential enemies in the Soviet Far East, Korea, China, and Vietnam. With the United States committed to the defense of allies such as South Korea, Taiwan, the Philippines, or South Vietnam, it was an ideally located place from which to back up its exercise of military power in the Western Pacific and East Asia or even the Middle East. The U.S. Seventh Fleet, homeported in Yokosuka, near Tokyo, has been used throughout the region, as well as the Indian Ocean, the Bay of Bengal, the Arabian Sea, and the Gulf. Japan, for its part, was doubly defended by the sea between it and the continent and by the United States and its other allies remaining at a safe distance from Japan. The close presence of Soviet forces on territory still claimed by Japan in the northern islands or across the Sea of Japan was the greatest threat to Japan and to the U.S. forces based there. But Japan was conveniently close to the potential enemies for ready use of all of the advanced weapons of the United States. The support of Japan's advanced industrial economy was also valuable for repair, supply, and other services.

To a considerable extent Japan's governing conservatives papered over the lack of domestic political consensus on defense policy and clung success-fully to power by emphasizing economic growth in the 1960s. It was possible to mobilize the entire spectrum of politics behind an economic growth objec-tive until the shocking results of extensive mercury poisoning compelled political compromise with environmental safety in the 1970s.

Under the occupation and during the early Cold War, Japan was depen-dent on the United States for food and major raw materials, which reestab-lished and deepened old trading ties, especially when former continental sup-pliers were cut off by the allied embargo on trade with communist countries. The close economic interdependence that developed with the United States was greatly accelerated by the welcome extended to Japanese trade in the more open U.S. market economy. The conversion of the United States to free trade principles strengthened its allies and cemented their defense coopera-tion. The resulting great increase in world trade strengthened the U.S. economy, too. The worries of U.S. officials in the early days of the occupa-tion that backward Japan might be unable to create a viable economy were quite misplaced.

The second half of the Cold War ushered in frequent skirmishes in a kind of subsurface economic Cold War between the United States and its own military allies, particularly Japan. The United States became increasingly intolerant of Japan's trade competition. Angered by Prime Minister Eisaku Sato's failure to persuade Japanese textile makers to cut back on their ex-ports, President Nixon used the old "Trading with the Enemy Act" to levy a large surcharge on all the allies' exports to the United States. He used liberal entry to the U.S. market as a club or sanction against his shocked allies. U.S. trade officials were also angry about a small $1 billion trade surplus with the United States in Japan's favor for the first time. All the allies were compelled to revalue their currencies upward to get the surcharge removed. The lowered value of the dollar reduced their exports so the United States could restore its customary trade surplus.

But the skirmish against Japan was not purely an economic one. It was accompanied by a new military strategy that depended on China, not Japan. U.S. hostility toward communist China was replaced by close cooperation with that country to better oppose the Soviet Union. In the 1970s China seemed almost to have replaced Japan as the chief U.S. Asian ally, the second greatest shock to Japan after the trade surcharge attack. Nixon had already warned his Pacific allies that they could no longer expect the support of U.S. troops to defend them as they had in the Korean and Vietnam wars with the communists. He then reduced the military budget, as Eisenhower had done after the Korean War.

During the second half of the Cold War the United States was increasingly troubled by trade friction with Japan and the NATO allies, whose exports to the United States were apt to be more competitive and whose own markets were not as open to U.S. trade as that of the United States was to them. The United States demanded and obtained restrictions on Japanese exports such as textiles, steel, electronics, and automobiles, especially in times of recession when U.S. unemployment rose and weaker industries could not compete. The friction increased in volume and coverage, with huge U.S. government debts and the corresponding leap in trade deficits by 1983.

The 1985 dollar devaluation greatly stimulated U.S. export trade. Also, investment in U.S. assets became only half as expensive for Japan. Fueled by excess private savings and by inflation in the value of Japanese stock and real estate, capital poured out of Japan into foreign investment and securities for several years. Those Japanese funds proved very popular with U.S. and other foreign borrowers, particularly the U.S. Treasury. Large Japanese investors bought a big share of U.S. Treasury bills to help finance the huge U.S. budget deficit and enormous military spending. The debt was increased by lowering taxes in accord with popular monetary theories. Contrary to the theory, tax revenues from increased investment and production did not balance the large increases in spending. For their part, forty-four of the states maintained offices in Tokyo, largely to channel as much Japanese capital as possible into direct investment in the industrial development of their individual states but with little thought of the likely long-term ill effects.

Far from happy with those developments of increasingly close economic interdependence, some members of Congress and the media took the lead in raising the specter of a "Japanese economic threat." Japanese investors bought a majority share in the group owning the Rockefeller Center in New York and major Hollywood studios and entertainment conglomerates. *Newsweek* magazine likened this to "buying America's soul," its cover appropriately showing the Statue of Liberty clothed in a Japanese kimono. Significantly, the ownership by Britain of a much larger share of U.S. assets aroused no criticism at all. Also, in the 1980s the (by then) large permanent trade deficit with Japan leaped in size and multiplied several times, becoming a symbol of "unfair" Japanese trade. Thus, the relatively close allied harmony between the United States and Japan in the first half of the Cold War was increasingly marred by the economic friction of the second half.

Post–Cold War Defense Relations

After 1989, the disappearance of the Soviet threat and the friendly cooperative policies with the Western allies adopted by the Soviet successor states
have completely changed the basic character of global and Asia Pacific affairs that had existed for the forty years of the Cold War. The United States is
left as the sole superpower with a huge warmaking machine, the chief purpose of which has suddenly disappeared. Most of the NATO allies, as well as
the Commonwealth of Independent States (CIS, the loose association of successor republics to the Soviet Union), are making force reductions, scrapping
old equipment, and planning to destroy some of their nuclear weapons. In the
United States, those industries that have been devoted to making weapons
and preparations for war, and the millions of people who have been employed
in those industries, are resistant to sharp cuts at their expense. Nevertheless,
the Pentagon planned an overall reduction of 25 percent in personnel in the
first half of the 1990s but less in the Western Pacific, where the numbers
were already small. Of the 135,000 forward deployed U.S. forces in Asia,
14,000 to 15,000, or about 11 percent, were to be eliminated in the first phase
to 1993. Greater incremental reductions are expected in the next phase of two
years, and then reductions will continue for the third phase in the second half
of the 1990s if circumstances permit.[1]

Up to the year 2000, the U.S. Department of Defense expected the U.S.
presence in Japan would still include "a homeported aircraft carrier, strategic
lift aircraft, and postured Air Force strike assets to fulfill regional and global
missions and to honor treaty commitments."[2] U.S. military planners considered the forward deployed U.S. forces in Japan to be essential because of the
geostrategic location of their bases there and their cost effectiveness over any
other location. The United States is committed to defend Japan jointly with
the Japanese Self-Defense Forces under their Mutual Security Treaty.[3] But,
as indicated above, those forces are also for regional and global missions, the
most important reason for the U.S. military presence. The chief value of the
treaty for the United States was the provision by Japan of forward military
bases for maximizing U.S. military influence in the region. In the first half of
the Cold War, during the wars in Korea and Vietnam, the defense of Japan
was incidental to U.S. military operations nearby in the region, but later the
U.S. bases in Japan significantly enhanced the U.S. global reach, as could be
seen in the repeated dispatch of Seventh Fleet units from Japan to the Middle
East.

As might be expected, military leadership in both countries pointed to
the still formidable Russian forces adjacent to Japan, which they insisted
were too large to be needed purely for defense in spite of Soviet and Russian
force cuts and scrapping of old equipment.[4] Of course, those forces in the
Russian Far East were created to be an effective defense against the strong

U.S. forces in the Pacific, some of them based in Japan as well as in Korea, the Philippines, Alaska, the central Pacific, and the U.S. West Coast. If relations between the United States and Russia continue to be friendly, and defense against each other clearly unnecessary, the Russian Pacific forces should be reduced greatly, as should the U.S. forces.

If the United States hopes, as government officials seem to, to continue to exercise strong influence globally and in the Asia Pacific region, its forces based in Japan probably do maximize its regional influence and its influence on Japan, at least psychologically. If they are only to be used in "policing" small aggressive powers, they could probably do so as well from Hawaii, Guam, or Palau bases, or simply by using the civilian port facilities of friendly countries. They could call in to Japan with or without bases or a security treaty. In place of the Philippines, Singapore has already agreed to provide some naval port services despite some grumbling from its ASEAN partners. The Pentagon phrased the U.S. regional role this way:

> In spite of a real and/or perceived reduction of the Soviet threat, what has previously been a traditional aspect of our military presence in the region— the role of regional balancer, honest broker, and ultimate security guarantor—will assume greater relative importance to stability. Over the next decade [the 1990s], as a new global order takes shape, our forward presence will continue to be the region's irreplaceable balancing wheel.[5]

The post–Cold War purpose for the U.S. forces in the Asia Pacific region has shifted from deterrence against the former Soviet forces "to localize and minimize hostilities while providing us necessary diplomatic leverage for conflict resolution."[6]

There is a contradiction in the continual U.S. pressure to encourage Japan to increase its defense expenditures and at the same time express caution about becoming too strong by acquiring a "power projection" capability.[7] Japan already contributes more to the cost of U.S. forces stationed in Japan than does any other ally. Japan's current forces are well structured to meet its defense commitments and there is no need to increase them beyond updating and improving mainly defensive equipment. Its air and naval forces are intended to operate with U.S. units only in the direct defense of Japan or defense of the two countries' merchant ships and war ships, by antiair and antisubmarine warfare, out to 1,000 nautical miles from Japan. The U.S. carrier force, its Japan-based fighter bombers, and its marine amphibious units exist mainly to project offensive force in the region or assist in the support of Japan's own self-defense when it is not strong enough to resist an attack by itself alone.

If the United States were to reduce some of its global power projection capability in order to decrease military expenditures and accept a smaller East Asian and global military influence, it could reduce or pull back its forces to its own territory in the central Pacific. Considerable economic and political influence would remain, even in a world where economic prowess is more important than military superpower capability. That is not to assume major power military conflict in the region cannot reappear. But in the 1990s most of the countries in the region are consumed with the desire to strengthen their economies, and Japan is consumed with the desire to supply the principal motive power for the regional economic development and integration. As is amply demonstrated in the next chapter, on Japan's expanded security role in the region, Japan is using its economic strength and diplomacy to stabilize and improve interstate relations. Regional reliance on military power decreased in the early 1990s. Arms increases in China, Japan, and Southeast Asia look mainly defensive rather than like an arms race. Japan's economic "weapon" of financial aid seems more effective in ensuring regional security than superpower military weapons.

Japan's policies of avoiding the buildup of offensive armaments likely to threaten its neighbors and rejecting nuclear weapons are well entrenched in a democratic Japan.[8] The fear that a departure of U.S. military units from Japan would prompt its increase of armaments as a superpower seems exaggerated. It would take a great change in Japan's political system or some serious new military threat to stimulate a strong rearmament policy in Japan. As in the United States, in Japan, too, the end of the Cold War has prompted strong demands to reduce military spending. But, only the usual increases in defense spending have been curtailed. The defense increase in the 1992 budget was only 3.8 percent, compared to 5.5 percent in 1991, the smallest rise in twenty years, and some planned weapons acquisition had to be reduced.[9] The prime minister promised to reduce by a trivial amount the 1990–1994 midterm defense buildup plan by subtracting 100,000,000 yen, a full 0.44 percent reduction!

The prime minister and defense minister both promised a major review of the current five-year defense buildup plan as well as the national defense program outline, established in 1976, on which it was based.[10] Due to the unpopularity of military life in affluent Japan, the Ground Self-Defense Force (GSDF) had recruited less than 83 percent of its authorized strength in 1992.[11] It prompted the governing Liberal Democrats to offer to cut the authorized GSDF from 180,000 to 150,000 to cool opposition demands for defense budget cuts, but that would only confirm the status quo, which is a force already less than 150,000. Rather than weapons, acquisition of which was slowed, the new budget improved the enlisted men's living conditions to keep up recruitment from the diminishing eligible age group.

The U.S. Congress and the Pentagon were dissatisfied that Japan did not buy more expensive military equipment from the United States to reduce its huge trade deficit, especially when U.S. ships and weapons were such a bargain, generally costing only a fraction of what it cost to make them in Japan. Furthermore, such a move would increase the interoperability of both countries' forces. But the lower cost and trade balance advantage did not apply to the airwarning and control system aircraft that Japan intended to acquire from the United States as the centerpiece of new equipment for the 1991–1995 midterm buildup plan. Modified Boeing 767 planes were offered by the United States at about $450 million each, nearly double what Japan had expected to pay.

Although pressure persists from the U.S. Congress to increase Japanese military spending to assume a fairer share of the common military burden, the end of the Cold War has removed much of the rationale for the size of that burden, which was to deter and defend against the powerful former Soviet Union. Why Japan should increase its military spending when the Cold War and the Soviet Union are gone is not even seriously questioned, let alone answered adequately by the spokesmen for either government. When other serious regional tensions are also being enormously reduced and there are no short- or medium-term military threats, better answers are needed for a future hostile Russian regime or regional major power conflict. What needs to be answered is why they should not be reduced.

Post–Cold War Economic Relations

The economic friction between Japan and the United States, which grew during the second half of the Cold War, assumed greater prominence by the early 1990s. Particularly during the world recession of 1991 and 1992 and the Bush reelection campaign, Japan became a convenient whipping boy for those calling for protection against Japan's adverse economic impact on the United States. After the Cold War and the virtual disappearance of the Soviet threat, the diminishing rationale for Japan-U.S. military cooperation no longer compensated for the hostility aroused over trade, nor, apparently, did the global economic partnership, which was the positive contribution of the Japan-U.S. trade and investment relationship.

The costs from Japanese competitive imports, which displace U.S. workers, are concentrated in certain parts of the country or in certain industries, in which they are felt immediately and trigger protective action from politicians and trade officials. The benefit of cheaper or better quality goods is spread widely and diffused through the population, which does not feel impelled to act to protect the extra expendable income or diversity of choice due to foreign products. U.S. officials have responded to the plight of the injured firms by punitive tariffs on Japanese exports and those of other allies such as Canada.[12] They have attempted to use U.S. antitrust law to harass Japanese companies with branches in the United States for unfair trade practices abroad.[13] Those actions even prompted formal government protests from both Europe and Japan.[14] One Japanese business leader, Akio Morita, the founder and head of Sony Corporation, made it his one-man mission to urge the U.S. public to wake up and rally to maintain their important manufacturing industries, preferably by investing more in them at home rather than in cheaper labor locations such as Southeast Asia or Mexico. He believed manufacturing is the basis of a nation's economy and should not be given up.[15]

In the United States the value of manufacturing output has increased and productivity is growing rapidly. Although U.S. productivity growth did decline in the 1960s and 1970s, it spurted ahead in the 1980s at a rate of 3.4 percent a year, contrary to the prevailing belief about the decline of the U.S. economy. In fact, it pulled ahead of both Japan and Germany.[16] The U.S. total trade deficit so decried by U.S. politicians dropped to $72 billion by 1991, less than half the 1987 level. Admittedly, the deficit with Japan did not decline by very much, even with the much lower dollar exchange rate since 1985.

However, the volume of U.S. manufactured exports shot ahead, rising 90 percent over the 1986 rate.[17] Those figures suggest that the declinists and Morita's worries about the failure of the United States to keep its essential manufacturing capability are exaggerated. A striking example was the U.S. iron and steel industry, which was unable to compete internationally for decades and received a great deal of protection negotiated by the U.S. government. Between 1986 and 1991, that industry managed to quadruple its exports, which indicates the improvement in competitiveness. But the major Japanese steelmakers had a hand in it as they formed joint ventures with U.S. steel firms to transmit their technology. Their direct investment paid off with the help of the lower dollar and improved productivity.[18] The Japanese steel companies also tried to improve the Canadian steel industry, but with poor results.

U.S. exports of aircraft, electrical machinery, pharmaceuticals, telecommunications equipment, and clothing all more than doubled in those five years from 1986 to 1991. U.S. goods are the cheapest among the advanced industrial countries, and U.S. productivity is the highest. Japanese automakers' joint ventures with U.S. auto companies have helped the U.S. companies. Ford has planned to export U.S.-made cars to Europe and to Japan by 1992.[19]

Electronics companies such as Apple Computer Inc. are teaming up with the Japanese not only because they have superior manufacturing expertise but also because they have the capital to invest in production. Japanese companies did capture the lion's share of the most popular mass-produced microchips, leading Washington to extract an agreement from the Japanese government to try to give U.S. companies at least 20 percent of its market, which proved very hard to reach. Nevertheless, the American companies have maintained their ability to trailblaze, whereas the Japanese pack mentality constantly has caught them up in overproduction of the same products, even in computer hardware. The biggest Japanese companies lost money during the 1991–1992 slowdown when their home market shrank. U.S. computer manufacturers are increasingly penetrating the Japanese market.[20]

Despite the positive side of Japanese trade with and investment in the United States, the negative side received the most attention. Within Japan, rivalry between companies producing the same product creates excessive competition to gain a larger market share. The overproduction drives them into overseas markets in North America and Europe, where the same cut-throat competition ensues. Foreign producers are apt to be devastated, as in the television industry. Most U.S. production was quickly wiped out or took refuge in Southeast Asia, where labor was much cheaper. Although television recorders were invented in the United States, it was Japan that developed and produced them. But these circumstances have also worked in reverse: The U.S. firm, Intel, took up the development of the "flash" memory microchip that Toshiba invented but was too risk-adverse to develop. When it took off in popularity, Intel had 80 percent of the market share.[21]

Almost as serious as the backlash in the United States against Japan caused by its competitive exports was the dissatisfaction with the difficulty of exporting to the Japanese market. For decades, European Community trade officials complained about Japan's trade barriers. The U.S. trade representative[22] and the Department of Commerce were the shock troops for the economic counteroffensive. Thus, in the early 1990s in trade talks between Japan and the United States, monopolistic Japanese business practices and economic structural barriers to imports became the focus of Japan-U.S. negotiations. What was demanded were major changes in Japanese business culture itself. One unique aspect of Japan's trade was the lack of intraindustry trade. Intraindustry trade is typical of exports of developed countries except for Japan. Normally, the manufacturers in the country importing a very competitive foreign product try to find something else to produce, usually an improved or somewhat different product in the same industry. They then export some of their new product to the other country. Japan seems not to want to import such products. The result is a lack of the usual reciprocal trade within the same industry—intraindustry trade—in which other advanced countries indulge. In the other foreign countries the original importing country's industry is not wiped out and it continues to employ its assets and workers with little major economic or social welfare loss.[23]

Canada and the United States both manufacture steel and cars and export them to each other, as is also the case for the United States and Europe. But Japan, whose most valuable export to Canada, the United States, and Europe is autos and auto parts, imports almost none of these from Canada and very few from the United States or Europe.[24] In quite a few major Japanese export industries, the smallness of intraindustry trade is unique, suggesting an unusual reluctance to import from abroad, and making the trade very one-sided. It might also account for the more disruptive impact of Japan's competitive exports. Korea, which is consciously following the Japanese pattern of industrial development and has more overt trade barriers than Japan, has a greater degree of intraindustry trade than does Japan.

The ultimate contradiction in the Japan-U.S. relationship in the 1990s is the officially blessed global partnership that coexists with what approaches a trade war with each other. In 1992, 70 percent of the U.S. public, egged on by the media and hypercritical politicians, viewed the strong economic penetration of Japan as a serious threat.[25] On the other hand, 50 percent of those in the same poll thought that "Japan is being blamed unfairly for a trade crisis that is really the fault of the United States," in comparison to only 35 percent who thought so in 1985. Despite some nationalistic backlash in Japan to the hostile criticisms coming from the United States, the Japanese public is slow to become anti-U.S. U.S. culture, from hamburgers to rock music, remains popular in Japan and keeps the younger generation, at least, under its spell. But Japanese leaders increasingly have become aware that they have a serious problem with the major Western powers.

The 1992 trade white paper issued by the Japanese Ministry of International Trade and Industry has proposed discarding the objective of economic growth, the one goal everyone could previously agree on in Japan for the past thirty years. It urges making the improved quality of life the objective of Japan, a striking about-face for the ministry credited with orchestrating Japan's postwar trade offensive abroad. Prime Minister Miyazawa was already using it as the slogan of his administration. Japanese companies were urged to stop their expansion-first policies and conduct their business so as to harmonize with international society. The white paper stated that the government must increase domestic demand so as to benefit Japanese consumers and encourage the participation of foreign firms in Japan to make foreign trade more reciprocal. It criticized the way Japan's firms set aside capital funds to invest and create high growth rates when they should be shared with workers and investors much more generously.[26] Employees and stockholders were formerly willing to forgo short-term benefits, but now they wanted shorter working hours and more short-term profits. Needless to say, the former style of business behavior caused enormous imbalances in trade and innumerable disputes with foreign countries.[27] The Japanese ambassador to the United States, Takakazu Kuriyama, the previous top career official in the foreign ministry, when he started out on his tour of duty in Washington, said he didn't blame U.S. business for resenting cutthroat Japanese competition and he recognized the damage it did to the United States.

Because of the severity of the friction, Japan's government had already been grudgingly responding to U.S. officials' demands to modify its monopolistic practices at home. That behavior not only kept out cheaper foreign exports, but hurt its own consumers, who were increasingly irritated by the unreasonably high prices in Japan. Indeed, some Japanese exports sold for much less in New York than in Tokyo.[28]

In addition, many changes within and without Japan not subject to government control are reducing the one-sided economic advantages Japan had in the late 1980s. Japan's economy changed structurally with the wringing out of the inflation in the stock and real estate market called the "bubble economy" in 1991 and 1992. Japanese foreign investment was no longer virtually costless for large investors, and the domestic and foreign interest rate spread was reduced, in turn reducing the incentive to invest abroad so much of the smaller pool of capital. The severe setbacks in the early 1990s for many Japanese companies forced them to disinvest abroad, especially in real estate. Rather ineffectual curbs to the shocking abuses in the stock market and financial institutions were attempted by the government in the face of the finance ministry officials' reluctance to cooperate. Also, there has been some crossover of Japanese collectivist business practice such as closer producer-supply networks, or *keiretsu*, adopted in the United States. The U.S. automakers together with their suppliers introduced the Japanese just-in-time system of close-coordinated production between their firms. They even began to design and produce components cooperatively in what was a more flexible form of vertical integration than cartels or takeovers.[29]

Economic contradictions were rife in the early 1990s. At the same time as Japan-U.S. governmental friction was high and the thesis of U.S. decline was fashionable, the U.S. manufacturing base was strengthening and economic cooperation was growing between the two countries. Although in the long term the United States must increase public and private investment and strengthen its labor base, it is probably still the strongest of the advanced countries. It is number one in national economic size and potential. The editors of the British magazine *The Economist* consider the United States the most innovative and productive country in the world. Furthermore, increased linkages between major firms of both Japan and the United States, representing older industries as well as high-technology sectors, are strengthening the U.S. firms. Examples can be found in steel (National Intergroup–Nippon Kokan) and automobiles (GM-Toyota), as well as electronics (Motorola-Toshiba), machine tools, and chemicals (DuPont). Far from rich Japanese buying up the United States or reducing all of its citizens to peons slaving for them, as the fear-mongers would have it, the greater impact of the positive side of the economic relationship should become clearer as U.S. firms rise to the challenge of Japanese competition, which has as its weakness characteristics such as herd mentality and lack of innovation.

There is general harmony between Japan and the United States in their relations with respect to the Asia Pacific regional economic activities. Japan is rapidly expanding its regional economic and political influence in both commercial and security spheres, and the United States remains the only other major player as a trading nation, investor, and military great power. The rapid spurt of Japan's influence in Asia Pacific in the second half of the 1980s has tended to obscure the still important U.S. economic role there. The U.S. market still tends to be more open to Asian exporters than that of Japan. Japan is still hobbled by its nontariff market barriers. In this sphere the roles of the United States and Japan are complementary more than competitive.

Probably the worst outcome of the trade friction would be a more severe form of U.S. protectionism, the chief victim of which would probably be the United States itself. Although protectionism does afford quick relief to the believed-to-be injured party, its long-term effect is apt to damage the United States more than Japan.[30] That has been true of restrictions on Japanese auto exports. Protection also further erodes the liberal international economic order, such as the GATT system, and increases the tendency toward a world economic system made up of competing protectionist trading blocs.

It is far too soon to believe that the United States will need to resort to increased protectionism and is too weak to protect itself through its own economic strength. And it is far too soon to condemn Japan as such a great threat to the independence and well-being of the United States, and, presumably, to Japan's other trading partners as well.

The End of U.S. Hegemony

The end of U.S. hegemony really began in the 1970s, when the U.S. allies, and especially Japan, had restored and expanded their economies. Greatly aided by U.S. funds and up-to-date technology, they were able to catch up quickly and even get ahead of the United States, as evidenced in the developments in the steel industry. Those countries were actually helped by the wartime destruction because they replaced old industrial equipment with the most advanced new facilities and had to reorganize, thereby eliminating old inefficiencies and older conservative management. Hence, direct U.S. assistance was no longer necessary in the economic sphere, and that source of U.S. influence was reduced. Gratitude is apt to be a transient feeling. Therefore, it is striking that Prime Minister Miyazawa did express strong thanks for the earlier U.S. postwar help when President Bush similarly made his pilgrimage to Tokyo to get assistance for the troubled U.S. automobile industry in early 1992. It, perhaps, reflects Miyazawa's own political background. He was a young assistant to Hayato Ikeda, the finance minister, in Washington in 1950 when Ikeda was negotiating the terms of Japan's future military force in return for U.S. economic help to Japan, which had not yet recovered from wartime devastation.

It was no accident that the 1970s was also the time when Nixon inaugurated economic warfare against his allies. Concomitant with the reduction of the allies' economic need, détente broke out with China and Russia, heralding the time when the communist threat would virtually fade away. Nixon and Secretary of State Henry Kissinger, backing out of the Vietnam War and enlisting Chinese help against the Soviet Union, had less need for their allies and could discipline them with impunity. It left Japan reeling from the unexpected treatment. Canada and the NATO allies were equally bowled over by the economic disciplining to which they were subjected, but at that stage they quickly complied with U.S. demands to revalue their currencies to favor U.S. trade. Japanese textile makers quickly agreed to curb their competitive exports to the United States. So Nixon and Kissinger won that first round.

Only the continuation of the Cold War in the security sphere concealed the extent to which the allies were already trading places with their U.S. mentor in economic affairs. Once Gorbachev brought the Cold War to an end in the 1980s, hegemony was clearly over with the most important basis of it—the common Soviet threat—gone. However, economic pugnacity only increased in a vain effort by the United States to regain the kind of leadership or control over its allies that it once enjoyed when it could induce them to agree to something like the Tokyo Round of international trade negotiations. By the 1990s the lack of U.S. leadership in the crucial sphere of global economic management was only too obvious in the way the international negotiations to reform the world trading system under the GATT stumbled on inconclusively year after year.

The idea has occasionally been mooted that Japan and the United States might revive a kind of world hegemonic diumvirate together, perhaps inspired by frequent reference by officials in both countries to their "global partnership."[31] Miyazawa's idealistic hopes for a harmonious relationship were expressed by the prime minister on January 10, 1992, when he told a conference that the Tokyo Declaration on the Japan-U.S. Global Partnership, which he and President Bush had just approved, was "aimed at confirming the global responsibility of both Japan and the United States in constructing the framework of a new world order of peace and democracy."[32] It is probably true that U.S. military superiority and Japan's economic superiority would nicely complement each other. As the countries with the largest and next to the largest economies in terms of gross national product, they already dominate a large share of the world economy between them, accounting for 40 percent of total global production and 20 percent of world trade, to say nothing of their extensive regional and global influence. Although Japan might temporarily be willing to play the part of number two, it is difficult to believe it would not want to be treated as an equal in the long run and would be unwilling to permanently continue the subordinate diplomatic role it has long followed under the United States. After all, such a situation would ignore the century and a half of Japanese struggle against Western domination of the Asia Pacific region, which is what the Pacific War was about. Similarly, the United States is far from agreeing to share its independence in decisionmaking with Japan, even if it is in an uneasy state of interdependence with it.

As for Japan replacing the United States as a new global hegemon, it would have to reproduce something like the status of the United States during the early Cold War. To do so would require the following steps: (1) It would have to build a technically superior military arsenal, including a full range of nuclear weapons. (2) It would have to throw open its market widely, like the

United States did—and still does to a surprising extent. (3) The Japanese people would have to be persuaded to reduce some of their customary close personal and business ties to let foreign products compete more freely in Japan. (4) Government leaders would have to more fully admit to, and make greater restitution for, those war crimes or acts of oppression for which the neighboring countries have still not forgiven them. (5) Japan would have to demonstrate the kind of regional and global leadership in political and economic affairs that the United States displayed in its peak hegemonic phase in the early Cold War. Without a strong incentive such as a Cold War to stimulate such a program, it would be difficult to carry out, and probably impossible in the present international environment, in which the Western major powers are strong and unthreatened.

The above is not meant to hold up the United States as a paragon of virtue. Far from it. But the foreign perceptions of Japan would have to change greatly as well as Japan's policies and actions. In an era when great military power may be less necessary, Japan might not need to acquire the capability of a military superpower if it demonstrated the economic and social characteristics of the good hegemon by providing the kind of global leadership that produced needed public goods, either alone or in coalition with others. It must be said, however, on Japan's behalf, that the seeds of such a program can be seen in its proclaimed desire to make an international contribution to peace and to regional and global prosperity. Its increasingly active economic aid program is also a step in the right direction.

The global role of the United States in the post–Cold War period is that of the strongest of the major powers rather than a hegemon that can provide the kind of economic and military benefits or public goods that it was able to do in the immediate post–World War II period. In military affairs its weapons are the most advanced of any country and it maintains military facilities in most parts of the world. But the European NATO allies as well as Japan could probably acquire the same level of armaments if they wished to do so. They already have modern advanced weapons and military forces, and they have the economic and technical capacity to create more. The most formidable weapons of the former Soviet Union are still in existence, although they are being shared among the successor republics. As the Soviet forces are gradually absorbed or replaced by the new military organizations of the successor states, Russia will be the strongest and have a major part of those forces. It already occupies the Soviet Union's place in the Security Council of the United Nations as one of the five permanent members.

Even during the Cold War, the United States did not rely on itself alone. It depended on its allied coalition with the democratic European states and its mainly bilateral alliances in the Asia Pacific region to augment its military power and supply overseas bases and local forces to help to oppose the Soviet Union and other communist countries. Similarly, as late as 1991 in the war against an apparently strong regional power in the Middle East, the United

States managed to put together a coalition of allies and friendly states to eject Saddam Hussein's forces from Kuwait and protect Saudi oil from the clutches of the Iraqi dictator. The economic and military sanctions against Hussein were also supported by resolutions of the United Nations Security Council, which has seldom been able to function so supportively. However, significantly, the United States demanded that the financial costs be borne by the rich allies such as Japan and Saudi Arabia.

The present seven major powers consist of the United States, Britain, France, Russia, China, Japan, and Germany. If they continue to cooperate, they might be able to function as a central coalition to direct or strongly influence world peace and to prevent international conflict, and especially to prevent conflict among themselves.[33] Their early post–Cold War behavior in the United Nations suggests that as long as they can cooperate together they might be able to make that organization more effective as an international peacekeeper. Ideological conflict among them is at a low level. Both Russia and China are fully occupied with economic reform and growth and heavily dependent on the Western five for economic assistance and cooperation. If they all could work together internationally, they might be able to replace the more usual balancing of power among rival major powers and their allies. The balance-of-power, international-type system has seldom prevented major wars. A cooperative central coalition might reduce the danger of major power wars. However, the threatening proliferation of "weapons of mass destruction" may enable the minor powers to challenge the others or upset any major power balances. Major new conventional and unconventional weapons are already available to smaller powers.

The U.S. hegemonic leadership in the early Cold War did not depend wholly upon its military power or that of its allied coalition. The leadership it exercised depended heavily upon the economic benefits it provided. Direct economic benefits to allies as well as more broadly shared public goods won cooperation from the other weak and demoralized countries in the creation of the leading liberal global and regional trading and financial institutions. It provided grants and loans to strengthen its allies and opened its enormous consumption-oriented market to them. The resulting economic benefits in addition to the military ones provided the basis for U.S. hegemony. Major U.S. products and technology were either superior or sufficiently competitive in that period that the United States had little fear from the large influx of its allies' and other countries' products. Its budget was not preempted by huge debt payments. The United States itself shared in the prosperity from the growth of world trade.

The U.S. allies, such as Japan and Britain, no longer need U.S. assistance. On the contrary, they have been investing in and lending money to the United States, some of which enables it to finance its huge military budget by going into debt instead of paying for it through taxes. The U.S. state governments and the taxpayers are also borrowing to finance their excessive consumption and speculation instead of saving and investing productively themselves. With the decline of the military threats to its allies, those countries have neither military necessity nor economic necessity to prompt them to be as cooperative as they once were. On the contrary, their devotion to the present global liberal institutions is suspect, to judge from the refusal of the European Community, Canada, and Japan to reduce their agricultural protection.

The consequence of the present circumstances is that harmony in resolving bilateral problems or those of global importance, such as reform of the trading system under GATT or managing world resources, is increasingly difficult to achieve. The attitudes of the United States and its policies are no longer the same. The trade war among the U.S. allies threatens to replace the old Cold War against the communists. In other international problems, such as the unprecedented ten-year global negotiations for a law of the sea, in which the United States played a major role, the Republican administrations since 1978 have refused to sign the Law of the Sea Convention. They fear putting resources of the deep sea under a world body, which would actually be the first step in a world government exerting authority over that portion of the globe occupied by the sea beyond national territorial limits. In the preliminary negotiations for the United Nations Earth Summit in 1992, the United States strongly opposed any set limits for cutting greenhouse gas emissions by the year 2000 to avoid any binding commitment. Those attitudes and behavior of the U.S. government are hardly those of a benevolent global hegemonic leader in the handling of global public goods or the global commons.

Then there is the often debated question of whether the United States is still a hegemon and whether it is in a permanent decline. It has been argued both ways. It is plausible to ascribe much of the debt-ridden, poorly maintained U.S. economy to unwise policies and poor leadership of both government and business, with or without the impact of Japan. After all, it took the stimulus of a world war to really get the U.S. economy out of a depressed state in the 1940s. It is even possible that tax increases and policies to encourge government and private saving would be sufficient to enable the U.S. government to go on spending nearly $300 billion a year on defense, reduce its debt, beef up its economic infrastructure, and make considerable headway on some of its biggest social problems of inner-city poverty and inefficient lower education. There is no substitute for good political and economic leadership to undertake something like that, nor is it at all beyond the capacities of the United States.

_____ *Conclusion*

This chapter has concentrated on the Japanese-U.S. relationship in economic and military affairs in the Cold War and post–Cold War eras. It has also sketched in some relevent historical background. It puts the relationship in context with the other major Western powers and with hegemonic and posthegemonic times. The attempt has been to illustrate the extraordinarily long, varied, and contradictory nature of the relationship in order to make its present status clearer. The most important conclusions that emerge are how favorable international conditions are in the 1990s for a positive and constructive attempt to create a new world order in which both the United States and Japan would play key roles. But there is little sign of willingness to go beyond rhetoric about a new world order or global partnership. The strained economic relations between these two countries and the declining liberal international economic order militate against those constructive visions. The United States has become economically combative internationally and increasingly absorbed domestically. Also, serious global economic problems are crying out for attention, and the only possibility for tackling them successfully is by major power cooperation, which does not appear forthcoming soon. Perhaps it will take a global environmental crisis as serious as a Cold War to supply the stimulus and leadership needed. There is no present-day hegemon to rescue us, no deus ex machina.

Notes

1. U.S. Department of Defense, "A Strategic Framework for the Asian Pacific Rim: Looking Toward the 21st Century," pp. 13–14. Mimeo.

2. Ibid., pp. 19–20.

3. Martin E. Weinstein, *Japan's Postwar Defense Policy, 1947–1968*, New York and London: Columbia University Press, 1971. See Appendix B: Treaty of Mutual Cooperation and Security Between the United States and Japan, Signed at Washington, D.C., January 19, 1960, Article V, p. 140.

4. The 1991 Japanese defense white paper said the Soviet forces deployed in the Far East are far stronger than necessary for defense, requiring Japan to maintain a strong military. Bōeichō, *Bōei Hakusho, Heisei Sannenban*, [Defense white paper, 1991], Tokyo: Okurashō Insatsukyoku, 1991, p. 195. The Commander in Chief of the Soviet Navy said, "By the year 2000, the number of naval vessels will be cut by 20 percent to 25 percent, but the navy's might will be maintained at the level of defense sufficiency." "Defense Paper Endorses Sending SDF Overseas," *Daily Yomiuri*, July 28, 1991, p. 1.

5. U.S. Department of Defense, "A Strategic Framework," p. 10.

6. Ibid., p. 10.

7. Ibid., p. 18.

8. Japan does tolerate port calls and homeporting of nuclear-armed U.S. naval units afloat, but most of the nuclear arms are scheduled for removal by the United States.

9. "Kokkai Bōeihi Kōbō ga Shōten" [The Diet: Focus on the battle over defense expenditures], *Yomiuri Shimbun*, January 25, 1992, p. 2. See also Chapter 4 on Japan's expanded security role.

10. "Bōei Keikaku no Taikō" [National defense program outline], document #23, in Bōeichō, *Bōei Hakusho*, pp. 244–249, also see pp. 100–105.

11. "Defense Agency Plan Aims to Attract More Recruits," *Daily Yomiuri*, May 4, 1992, p. 2.

12. John Saunders, "U.S. Wields Protectionist Club," *Globe and Mail*, May 2, 1992, p. B2. Frank Rutter, "All That's Missing From the War with Japan is the Shooting," *Vancouver Sun*, February 15, 1992, p. A12.

13. "Hills Pushes for Tougher Antitrust Policies," *Daily Yomiuri*, April 28, 1992, p. 1; Joseph P. Griffen, "Countering U.S. Antitrust Offensive," *Nikkei Weekly*, May 2, 1992, p. 7; and Saunders, "U.S. Wields Protectionist Club."

14. "OECD Komyunike An, Bei 'Han-torasutohō' Ikigai Tekiyō, Nichiō Kyodō de Hihan" (In an OECD draft communiqué Japan and Europe together criticize the extraterritorial application of U.S. antitrust law), *Yomiuri Shimbun*, May 3, 1992, p. 1.

15. Akio Morita, "Don't Just Stand There, Manufacture Something, Simply Doing the 'Money Shuffle' Saps North America's Talented Managers," *Financial Post* (Toronto), June 21, 1991, p. 7.

16. "Shed No Tears for Uncle Sam," *Globe and Mail*, January 25, 1992, p. B17; reprinted from *The Economist*, the noted British weekly magazine. In 1990, U.S. labor costs per hour in manufacturing were lower than most rich countries: $15 in the United States, $16 in Japan, and $23 in Germany.

17. Ibid. The U.S. share of the industrialized world's manufactured exports rose to an estimated 18 percent in 1991, ahead of Japan's 17 percent. The U.S. share advanced from only 14 percent in 1987.

18. Ibid. See also Dorothy Christelow, "Believe It or Not, Joint Ventures Do Help U.S. Industry, It's not True That We Lose out When We Join Forces with the Japanese," *Current News*, March 1990, no. 1836, pp. 9–10; reprinted from *Newsday*, February 19, 1990, p. 41. The U.S. steel companies still demanded protection from low-priced foreign steel. "Kōban Danpingu Beisha Teiso e" [U.S. firms file dumping charges against steel sheet imports], *Yomiuri Shimbun*, May 9, 1992, p. 1.

19. Ford has planned to export Taurus and Sable models with right-hand drive to Japan and Europe. U.S. auto companies for years have refused to make right-hand-drive cars for the forty countries that drive on the left, such as Japan and Britain. But Ford did make them for a time in the 1950s. "Ford Car Models to Go Foreign," *Globe and Mail*, May 2, 1992, p. B3.

20. In the fourth quarter of 1991, Apple's computer sales captured 33 percent of the Japanese market when overall sales of personal computers dropped 17 percent. Jacob M. Schlesinger, "Japanese Short-Circuited," *Globe and Mail*, May 2, 1992, p. B4. From the *Wall Street Journal*.

21. Ibid.

22. The U.S. trade representative was the title of Carla Hills under the Bush administration. She has a trade office separate from the Department of Commerce.

23. Edward J. Lincoln, *Japan's Unequal Trade*, Washington, D.C.: The Brookings Institution, 1990, pp. 39–60.

24. "Ford Car Models to Go Foreign."

25. Karl Schoenberger, "Poll: 7 of 10 Americans Regard Japan as a Threat," *Daily Yomiuri*, February 13, 1992, p. 1; Murray Campbell, "Japanese Gain Is American Pain," *Globe and Mail*, February 3, 1992, p. B2.

26. Japan had been investing in its own plant and equipment the equivalent of trillions of dollars in the 1980s at the same time that it was investing so much abroad. In the second half of that decade, Japan invested 35.6 percent of its gross national product whereas the United States invested only 17 percent. In 1990, Japanese firms paid out 30 percent of after-tax profits in dividends, whereas U.S. firms paid out 83 percent to shareholders. Michael Harrison, "U.S.-Style Capitalism 'Dusty Relic,'" *The Financial Post* (Toronto), April 13, 1992, p. S10, a review of Lester Thurow's *Head*

to Head: The Coming Economic Battle Among Japan, Europe and America, Toronto: Macmillan of Canada, 1992.

27. For extracts of the white paper, see "Tsūshō Hakusho" (trade white paper), *Yomiuri Shimbun*, May 9, 1992, p. 8.

28. "Price Gap Study Touches Heart of Structural Barriers Issue," *Japan Times*, September 28, 1989, p. 8. This is a report of a study of the economic planning agency in Japan that compared retail prices of the same designer-brand imports in Tokyo, New York, Paris, Düsseldorf, Sydney, and Seoul. The foreign cities' prices were uniformly much lower than Japan's for exactly the same items.

29. The Japanese economist, Ken'ichi Imai, recommends Japanese companies in major *keiretsu* groups draw up codes banning unfair reciprocal transactions and root out factors driving them into cutthroat competition. Ken'ichi Imai, "The Legitimacy of Japan's Corporate Groups," *Economic Eye*, Autumn 1990, p. 20.

30. It must be admitted, in the interests of balance, that Japan did succeed in building up its economic strength by the heavier protectionism it practiced in the early Cold War period, as did South Korea. Japan still protects its weaker uncompetitive industries both directly and indirectly, but so does the United States and virtually every other country, at least to some extent. If Canada had not used protectionism, it would not have an automobile industry, currently its biggest manufacturing industry and largest export earner.

31. In May 1992, Vice President Dan Quayle used such a reference in the press briefing before his trip to Japan. Shinzo Yoshida, "Quayle Urges Larger Role for Japan in U.S. Missions," *Daily Yomiuri*, May 10, 1992, p. 1.

32. The Tokyo Declaration of President Bush and Prime Minister Miyazawa on January 9, 1992, goes on to state, "The two governments resolve to join in a Global-Partnership . . . to help build a just, peaceful and prosperous world and to meet the challenges of the 21st century." *Daily Yomiuri*, January 10, 1992, p. 1. The full text in Japanese of the declaration and the action plan to improve trade relations appears on pages 6, 7, and 9 of *Yomiuri Shimbun*, January 10, 1992.

33. Richard Rosecrance proposes that a central coalition of the major powers could form a more permanent "concert" of powers to keep the peace, such as existed only briefly after previous great international wars. Richard Rosecrance, "A New Concert of Powers," *Foreign Affairs*, vol. 71, no. 2 (Spring 1992), pp. 64–82.

Chapter 4

Japan's Security Policy in the Posthegemonic World: Opportunities and Challenges

Tsuneo Akaha

The Cold War has virtually ended in Asia Pacific, although remnants of the East-West ideological conflict are still visible in parts of the region, particularly in Korea and, to a lesser extent, in Indochina. Although attempts at specific predictions about the future direction of the regional security situation are hazardous at best, the end of the Cold War surely requires major adjustments in the security policy of Japan, an economic beneficiary of the U.S.-led Western alliance during the Cold War era. How Japan will respond to the opportunities and challenges of the post–Cold War world will have important consequences not only for Japan but also for its Cold War allies and adversaries.

The purpose of this chapter is to offer a brief outline of the likely direction of Japan's security role in post–Cold War Asia Pacific and the implications for Japan's relations with the other regional powers. First, I briefly outline the general regional trends that are developing in the post–Cold War era and discuss their implications for Japan's security environment. I then examine Japan's response to the changing security atmosphere. Finally, I offer some preliminary conclusions about the prospects for an expanded regional security role for Japan.

It is argued in this chapter that in the posthegemonic era Japan's military capabilities are likely to be limited to those necessary for the defense of its home islands and 1,000-mile sea-lanes and that the nation's resource commitment even to this circumscribed defense mission will be subject to close domestic and regional scrutiny as the military threat from the former Soviet Union further dissipates. It is also argued that Japan will continue to increase its diplomatic and economic efforts to reduce regional tensions and promote political stability. Tokyo and Washington will manage to maintain their bilateral security alliance for the short to medium term, but long-term prospects will be increasingly uncertain as the prospects of a common regional or global security threat diminish. The gradual withdrawal of U.S. military presence and security commitments in the region will force Japan and other regional powers to explore alternative or complementary security arrangements and measures, but the region's stability requires U.S. participation in any framework that may be contemplated by Asian powers. Japan will continue to explore an international security role for itself in those areas that require the least amount of change in its constitutional, legal, and political systems, such as a noncombat role in UN-sponsored peacekeeping efforts.

The End of the Cold War and the Changed Security Environment

The end of the Cold War entails four developments at the global level: (1) the disappearance of the capitalist-communist ideological conflict as the most important source of political division at the global and regional levels; (2) the structural transformation of the international political economy from superpower-centered bipolarity to multipolarity characterized by more diffuse power distribution and more complex patterns of cooperation among the major powers; (3) the primacy of economic development both as a foundation of political legitimacy domestically and as a determinant of the pattern of international relations; and (4) the rise of nationalism as a powerful force in international relations and often frustrating efforts at international cooperation.[1] Each of these features of the post–Cold War world has profound implications for Japan's security environment.

First, in the absence of a Soviet threat to U.S. interests in the region, the United States will gradually reduce its military presence there. The U.S. role in the Asia Pacific region will gradually change from that of an eager and determined provider of security for its political allies and friends to that of a "balancer" and "power broker." U.S. security commitments will be redesigned to prevent any power from seeking hegemonic dominance in the region and restructured to maintain the freedom of navigation and other insurances of an open region in which the political and economic interests of the United States and its economic partners will remain substantial. Barring unforeseeable developments in the region, it is highly unlikely that the United States will seek to reestablish the extensive and costly military presence it had maintained at the height of the Cold War. Tokyo and Washington will have to make the necessary adjustments in bilateral security relations and for regional security purposes.

Second, although the United States will be a major power broker in the Asia Pacific region, it will increasingly rely on the cooperation of other regional powers to contain sources of instability. For example, it is already apparent that the future security situation on the Korean peninsula depends not only on the direction of U.S.-Russian relations but on the logic of bilateral relations between Seoul and Pyongyang and their respective relations with Tokyo and Beijing. Likewise, successful UN-sponsored administration of Cambodia until 1993 and political stability of the country beyond 1993 require the convergence of political-security interests of China, the United States, the former Soviet Union, Japan and, of course, the ASEAN countries. In these developments, the United States and Japan no longer see China and Russia as destabilizing factors but requisite participants in the process of conflict resolution and stability building. Japan's security role, whether explicitly sought or imposed on Japan by external circumstances, is bound to grow, and Japan and its neighbors will have to reach some understanding on what Japan may or may not do in this area.

Third, the already substantial interdependence among the Asia Pacific region's capitalist economies will further deepen as their markets become integrated through fast-expanding trade, investment, and technological exchanges across national boundaries. The transnationalization of factors of production, aided by technological revolutions, is fast breaking down national barriers to market integration, creating new prosperity and distributing expanded wealth across national borders. The crossnational processes are limiting the effectiveness of an insular, nationalist approach to economic development and social well-being. This has prompted the region's governments to step up their efforts to institutionalize channels and means of international cooperation, as exemplified by the formation of the Asian Pacific Economic Cooperation in 1990, following a decade-long discussion among the members of the Pacific Economic Cooperation Council (PECC). The 1992 ASEAN decision to develop an ASEAN Free Trade Agreement represents a major effort among the Southeast Asian countries to enhance cooperation among the subregion's economies. These efforts have been intensified in response to the fear that the full integration of the European Community in 1992 and the success of the ongoing negotiation for a North American Free Trade Agreement may reduce nonmembers' access to the European and North American markets.

Japan will play a pivotal role in the process of institutionalization of economic cooperation in Asia Pacific. The region's smaller countries have turned increasingly to Japan both as the region's most important spokesperson at global economic forums and as the locomotive of regional economic dynamism. Japan will need to step up policy consultation and cooperation with the United States and the other APEC members, but at the same time will have to actively promote policy consultation/coordination at the subregional level through the ASEAN Post-Ministerial Conference (PMC), with AFTA members, and in a Northeast Asian economic forum that may develop in the not too distant future.[2] Given Japan's global economic presence, Tokyo must lead the Asia-Pacific countries' campaign for "open regionalism."[3]

The fourth major trend in the post–Cold War world is the rising tide of nationalism that will likely frustrate attempts at institutionalizing global and regional cooperation. Nationalism is on the rise among the developing capitalist countries and the more insular socialist countries that are being liberated from the constraining effects of the Cold War obligations and commitments. In the face of ever-stronger transnational forces, which impinge on domestic social, economic, and even political developments, the developing countries' sense of loss of control over their own fate is likely to grow. Nationalism is a powerful force. It may be mobilized for the attainment of national socioeconomic goals or it may be exploited for divisive purposes by those segments of a society who feel disadvantaged in the sharing of the benefits of growing economic interdependence.[4] Balancing political and economic development is an extremely difficult task in an authoritarian society, as has been amply demonstrated in China. With Japanese economic dominance evident throughout Southeast Asia and likely to grow in Northeast Asia, Tokyo must see to it that its official economic assistance and Japanese private investment will contribute to economic development that is politically fair and sustainable. Japan's comprehensive security policy, with an accent on economic security and with ODA as a key component, has largely been successful in cultivating the view in the region that economic development promotes political stability and political stability enhances national security.[5] Japan must further proceed along these lines.

Dissolution of the Soviet Union and Projected U.S. Force Reduction

Today there are no near-term prospects of an open conflict among the major powers in the Asia Pacific region.[6] As a result of the demise of Soviet control over Eastern Europe in 1989 and the dissolution of the Soviet Union in December 1991, the strategic threat of the former Soviet Union against the United States, Japan, and other Western powers has virtually disappeared. However, the demise of the Soviet Union has not had a uniform impact on defense planning in the United States and Japan.

In general, the U.S. public no longer views the former Soviet Union as a threat to its security. Pending successful if slow and painful political and economic reforms in the former Soviet Union, Russia is expected to cease to be a destabilizing force in the long run. In April 1990, the Pentagon announced its plan to substantially reduce the number of U.S. military personnel in Asia Pacific. During the first phase, within three years, the number of personnel stationed in Japan, Korea, and the Philippines were to be cut by a total of 14,000–15,000 (12.3–13.1 percent) from the March 1990 level of 114,079. During the second phase, within three to five years, the Pentagon might undertake additional incremental reductions in combat forces in Korea and Japan.[7] However, Japanese defense planners were less sanguine in their assessment of the security situation in Northeast Asia. In the 1991 defense report, they called for continued "vigilance" against the qualitatively improved forces of the former Soviet Union, presumably under Russian control.[8] Barring a major breakthrough on the territorial dispute between Moscow and Tokyo, and without a mutually acceptable framework for confidence- and security-building measures (CSBMs) including the demilitarization of the disputed islands, the Russian forces in its Far Eastern region will for the near term remain a source of security concern among Japanese defense policymakers.[9]

For the medium term, the United States plans to retain a sizable military presence in the Asia Pacific region, thus assuring Japanese defense planners that neither quick buildup of their defense capabilities nor immediate establishment of an alternative regional security arrangement would be necessary. Washington is generally pleased with the improvements Tokyo has made in its defense capabilities in recent years, but it wants Tokyo to further increase its share of the defense burden financially, to purchase more U.S. weapons both for U.S. business reasons and for interoperability purposes, and to contribute more to the sharing of the cost of defense technology development. U.S.-Japan security relations are increasingly affected by economic and technological considerations, and this trend is likely to grow for some time.

Over the long haul, the United States will face some difficult choices. If the postwar containment policy, undergirded as it was by the extensive U.S. military presence and sustained political commitments in the region, represented the single most important change in the foreign policy of the previously isolationist United States, the disappearance of the Soviet threat globally and the substantial reduction in the Russian threat to U.S. interests in East Asia and the Pacific will likely bring about a change of equally historic importance in the U.S. policy toward the region. However, as long as the U.S.-Japan security alliance remains intact, Washington will need to respond to Tokyo's security concern vis-à-vis the Russian Far Eastern forces by maintaining a U.S. military presence at reduced yet significant levels. Nonetheless, political and economic developments within the United States may dictate further U.S. force reductions and result in a popular demand for an expanded military role for Japan. A larger military role for Japan may not necessarily be in the long-term interest of the United States, however, inasmuch as one cannot rule out the possibility that Tokyo and Washington may develop a major disagreement on geostrategic requirements of the region's security or the Japanese may wish to expand their military responsibilities far beyond the U.S. wishes and expectations.[10] Alternatively, Washington may need to develop a regional or subregional security framework within which to address post–Cold War security concerns of Japan and other regional powers.

A formidable problem remains, however, regarding the Russian and U.S. forces in Northeast Asia and the Western Pacific. As long as the U.S. forward-deployed forces remain in the area, the asymmetry in security requirements between the land-based Russian forces and the offensively deployed maritime forces of the United States will continue, and major naval arms control agreements between Moscow and Washington will be difficult. This strictly military problem could be eliminated if and only if the strategic rationale for the U.S. forward-deployment policy disappeared. The forward deployment of U.S. forces in the region has been an important pillar of the U.S. global strategy. The forces have been conceived and structured for two purposes: (1) deterrence against the Soviet Union on the premise that a military confrontation in Europe between the U.S.-led NATO forces and the Soviet-led Warsaw Pact forces would automatically trigger a U.S. military engagement of the Soviet Union on the Pacific front, and (2) prevention of the emergence of an Asian regional power with hegemonic designs. The first of these contingencies is no longer relevant today with the conclusion of the Intermediate Nuclear Forces (INF) Treaty and the Strategic Arms Reduction Treaty (START), the demise of the Warsaw Pact, the development of the Conference on Security and Cooperation in Europe (CSCE), and the dissolution of the Soviet Union. However, the second possibility cannot be ruled out.

If the Japanese should come to view the U.S. military presence in and around their territory as a strategic design to prevent them from pursuing any hegemonic aspirations in the region, this would have complicating and possibly even destabilizing consequences for the U.S.-Japan alliance. Even though Tokyo professes no such designs at all, the right-wing and left-wing elements in Japan might try to exploit the increasingly nationalistic sentiment among the Japanese against the Japan-U.S. alliance. Under those circumstances, even pro-U.S. conservatives in the country would find it difficult to justify security cooperation with the United States, which, among other things, requires the Japanese to pay by the mid-1990s up to 50 percent of the total cost of maintaining U.S. forces in Japan. How could the Japanese agree to finance a foreign presence whose very purpose was to contain them?

To avoid these difficult and potentially destabilizing consequences, Tokyo and Washington may find it both necessary and desirable to develop a regional or subregional security framework within which to accommodate Japan's security concerns and at the same time prevent a feared Japanese "breakout." The need to develop a regional security framework is recognized at the top level in Tokyo.[11] However, the great diversity in the political background, historical experience, and economic development among the countries of the region would make it virtually impossible in the near future to construct an overarching regionwide security framework with official membership and formal obligations—in effect, an Asia Pacific version of the CSCE. Because the process of postwar reconciliation between the wartime enemies was soon disrupted by the commencement of the Cold War, which pitted the capitalist and the socialist countries of the region against each other, Asian countries never had an opportunity to develop a regionwide, genuine dialogue concerning the lessons of World War II. After the war, the Asian peoples never had an opportunity to bare their hearts and souls to each other in the kind of reconciliation that might have healed their wounds and ameliorated their mutual suspicion and animosity. Whether the United States—the architect of containment policy—had hegemonic designs or not, its military and political presence in Asia in the Cold War decades obviated the development of any regionwide forum for political dialogue. Virtually every international scheme that was attempted in the region during those years, be it the Southeast Asian Treaty Organization (SEATO), the Asian Development Bank (ADB), ASEAN, or a U.S.-led bilateral security alliance, either presumed adversarial relations among the Asian countries or was designed to promote cooperation among some Asian countries to the exclusion of others. As a result, genuine reconciliation did not take place between the Japanese and their neighbors, and suspicions, apprehensions, and distrust about the Japanese continue to this day. A spring 1992 public opinion poll in South Korea revealed, for example, that 67.4 percent of the respondents disliked Japan. Of those polled, 26.1 percent felt upset by the mere mention of the word "Japan," 66 percent said they should be on their guard against Japan, and only 18 percent believed their country should establish friendly ties with their former colonial master.[12]

Under these circumstances, any attempt to establish a formal regional security organization with the powerful Japan as a key member would run up against formidable opposition in many countries of the Asia Pacific region. A less unrealistic yet still daunting task would be to develop a forum for security consultations without formal obligations or membership for Northeast Asia and another for Southeast Asia. The Northeast Asian forum would include Japan, the United States, Russia, South Korea, and possibly China as key participants, and the Southeast Asia dialogue would involve Japan, the United States, the ASEAN countries, Vietnam, and, ideally, China. Such arrangements would certainly require close consultations and cooperation between Washington and Tokyo and trust-building, broadly based interactions between the Japanese and their Asian neighbors.

A key question would be whether China would agree to participate in such arrangements. On the one hand, substantially improved Japanese relations with a nonthreatening Russia and Chinese participation in a Northeast Asian security forum designed in part to ensure friendly Russian-Japanese relations would be a major boon to China, whose leaders strongly desire a stable regional security environment that will allow them to pursue domestic economic reform and development. Chinese participation would also ensure that subregional security consultations were not targeted against China's interests but rather helped to prevent a possible Japanese attempt to fill the regional power vacuum, which many Chinese analysts believe is being created by the drawdown of U.S. forces in the wake of the end of the Cold War. Moreover, assuming Japanese-Chinese economic ties continue to expand, the Chinese should find less cause for concern in the development of subregional frameworks for security consultations in which Japan played a key role. On the other hand, given their perennial concern for political independence, the

Chinese might not wish to participate directly in regional or subregional security arrangements, even if they were of an informal, strictly consultative nature.

Another important question is whether Japan and Russia can overcome their historical animosities and agree to participate in a Northeast Asian security forum at a time when they cannot seem to find a mutually acceptable compromise on the most important bilateral issue—the status of the Northern Territories. As detailed in Chapter 6 by Zagorsky and Chapter 7 by Akaha, the territorial dispute has prevented Tokyo and Moscow from taking full advantage of the opportunities for cooperation that the end of the Cold War has presented. Moreover, as I mentioned earlier, the Japanese continue to harbor security concerns about Russia's military policy in its Far Eastern region. As well, Tokyo remains reluctant to give serious consideration to Moscow's repeated call for the establishment of an Asian security system. The ideas that Gorbachev outlined for his proposal for Asian security at his address before the Japanese parliament on April 17, 1991, indicated that Moscow's contemporary thinking had little to do with the concept of Asian collective security that Leonid Brezhnev had enunciated in 1965, with a clearly anti-Chinese intent. However, Japan remains highly skeptical about either the applicability of the CSCE formula, which seems to have inspired Gorbachev's Asian security concept, or the proposal's implications for the U.S. naval strategy in the Pacific. Most other Asian countries share these concerns as well.

Should efforts at regional or subregional security consultations fail, historical rivalries and animosities might tempt the region's potential hegemonic powers—Japan and China—to pursue a more autonomous approach to national security. Such a development would entail, quite likely, the beefing up of Japanese and Chinese defense capabilities, locking these countries in an arms race from which neither side would gain in security. This would be most destabilizing for both Northeast Asia and Southeast Asia, regions in which Japan and China have major stakes and interests.

Japan's Security Role in Northeast Asia

In contrast to Europe, where the end of the Cold War has unleashed the destructive forces of nationalism and ethnic tensions, Asia Pacific is witnessing a general lessening of political tensions, although the conflict in Korea continues and the future of postconflict Cambodia remains far from certain. The security outlook of Asia Pacific depends increasingly on whether Japan can translate its economic power into a stabilizing political influence. Improving relations among the Northeast Asian powers—Russia, China, South Korea, and the United States—are slowly easing Japan's security concerns, but further improvement in Japan's immediate security environment is clearly desirable.

First, as noted earlier, the dissolution of the Soviet Union has had only a limited impact on Japan's security concerns vis-à-vis its northern neighbor, and their relations remain both strained and restrained. On the one hand, Russia is clearly desirous of closer relations with the United States and no longer intent on threatening Japan, Washington's closest ally in the region. Moreover, Russia desperately needs capital and technological inputs from Japan. On the other hand, Japanese and U.S. defense policymakers are agreed that the force level in Russia's Far Eastern region far exceeds its defense needs. As well, the impasse on the Northern Territories dispute has prevented the two sides from starting a new relationship free of mutual suspicions. Although Russia stands to gain substantially from Japanese economic assistance and, more importantly, from Japanese private investments, particularly in the resource-rich but infrastructure-poor regions of Siberia and the Russian Far East, a major breakthrough on the territorial issue is highly unlikely in the near future. As discussed in Chapter 7, Moscow's options are severely limited against the background of rising Russian nationalism; the political struggle among the conservative, moderate, and liberal forces in the country; and the growing rift between the increasingly conciliatory Russian government (particularly its Foreign Ministry) and the hardening political leadership in Sakhalin, which has administrative authority over the southern Kuril Islands.

Second, the Korean peninsula continues to be a source of concern to Japanese defense planners. Tokyo shares with Washington, Moscow, Beijing, and Seoul an interest in a stable Korean peninsula and desires the termination of the ideological and political conflict that has long divided the North and South Koreans. Tokyo wants to see a credible and stable rapprochement between Pyongyang and Seoul. If immediate national reconciliation is difficult, Tokyo at least wants to avoid the destabilizing consequences of an isolated and unpredictable Pyongyang. Two major sources of security concern to Tokyo are the suspected nuclear development and the uncertain post-Kim leadership succession in North Korea. A nuclear-armed North Korea would be a direct threat to Japan's security.[13] Tokyo wants to use what leverage it has in its talks for the establishment of diplomatic ties with Pyongyang and to secure North Korea's unequivocal pledge not to develop nuclear arms. Japan supports the full safeguards inspection by the International Atomic Energy Agency, begun in the spring of 1992, in compliance with the Nonproliferation Treaty that Pyongyang signed in 1985.[14] Japan also wants to see the implementation of the 1991 Pyongyang-Seoul agreement on a nuclear-free Korean peninsula, including mutual inspection and verification. Although by no means promethean, Tokyo has hinted at exploiting the potential of its enormous economic resources in inducing conciliatory changes in Pyongyang. Japanese aid to the backward and failing North Korean economy is clearly conditioned on the establishment of diplomatic relations between the two countries, and the diplomatic recognition is tied to the nuclear issue. On the second security concern, that is, the possible destabilizing consequences of power transition in Pyongyang, Tokyo unfortunately has no more influence than any other country.

Third, Japan's relations with China have improved substantially since they normalized their diplomatic relations in 1978. Above all else, China's economic needs and Japan's interest in a politically stable and economically growing China have supported the two countries' growing contacts. The view in Tokyo is moderately optimistic about the future bilateral relations. Particularly encouraging are the growing signs that the leadership in Beijing intends to maintain and further promote the introduction of the principles of market economy to support the nation's modernization and the widening support for the establishment of a "socialist market economy" in China.[15] There are several issues of concern to Japan, however. The most immediate worry has to do with the continuing uncertainty as to the post-Deng power succession in the context of the delicate and difficult balance between political and economic liberalization. Second, Tokyo views with some concern Beijing's expressed interest in developing a blue-water navy. Third, the territorial dispute between Tokyo and Beijing over the Senkaku Island (Tiaoyu Tai) remains a potentially disruptive issue, as demonstrated by Tokyo's vocal protests over the explicit reference in Beijing's territorial sea law, adopted in February 1992, to the disputed island as Chinese territory.[16]

In summary, for the foreseeable future, the formidable political problems in Korea and China are likely to limit Japan's direct contributions to the peace and security of Northeast Asia. If the United States and Russia could agree to Northeast Asian arms control, if the obstacles to political reconciliation among the Northeast Asian powers could be removed, and if the prospects for internal political stability improved, Japan, by virtue of its enormous economic resources, would have the potential to become a very important player in the development of a framework for security consultations in Northeast Asia.

Japan's Security Role in Southeast Asia

Much like those in Northeast Asia, developments in Southeast Asia are generally encouraging. Although uncertainties remain, the political settlement of the Cambodian conflict is a welcome development, and Tokyo is determined to play a key role in the postconflict reconstruction of the wartorn country. Tokyo is also encouraged by the deepening thaw in Indochinese-ASEAN relations and Sino-Vietnamese rapprochement, both facilitated by the end of the war in Cambodia. In the fall of 1992, Japan sent Self-Defense Force personnel to Cambodia in support of the UN Transitional Authority in Cambodia (UNTAC), the first time Japanese troops had been deployed overseas since the end of World War II.

For much of the postwar period, Japan needed little in the way of an independent strategy for defending and promoting its interests in Southeast Asia. Instead, it relied on U.S. leadership in seeking stability in this sub-region. Even the announcement of the Nixon doctrine in 1969 did not immediately prompt any serious search for a Japanese political policy toward Southeast Asia. Only after Japan's growing economic presence in the area generated adverse reaction, such as the anti-Japanese demonstrations in Thailand and Indonesia during Prime Minister Kakuei Tanaka's tour of Southeast Asia in 1972, did Tokyo begin to pursue an activist policy in the area. The U.S. defeat in the Vietnam War also forced Tokyo to formulate an explicit policy toward the region. Hence, the Fukuda Doctrine was announced in 1977.

Fortunately, Tokyo's adoption of a "comprehensive security policy" in the early 1980s corresponded closely to the ASEAN countries' pursuit of "national and regional resilience," with an emphasis on domestic economic growth and political stability as an approach to national security. This conceptual congruence enhanced the role of Japanese economic assistance in the region.[17] Economic aid and private investments, despite their shortcomings, were the single most important contribution that Japan had made toward the dynamic economic development and resulting political stability in the region.

On the political front, Tokyo long supported ASEAN's call for a comprehensive political settlement to the Cambodian conflict and closely coordinated its approach toward Vietnam with the ASEAN countries. For example, in deference to ASEAN, the Japanese government had refrained from providing any economic assistance to Vietnam from 1974 to 1992. In July 1992, Tokyo announced it would extend 840 million yen in humanitarian aid for the repair of a hospital in Ho Chi Minh City.[18] As discussed below, however, Tokyo's desire to participate directly and actively in the UN peacekeeping operation in postconflict Cambodia was long frustrated by its failure until spring 1992 to win parliamentary approval for the dispatch of SDF personnel to Cambodia.

International support for a Japanese security role in Southeast Asia is slowly growing. There was a generally favorable response among ASEAN countries to the dispatch of Japanese minesweepers to the post–cease-fire Gulf. Japan's patient and quiet diplomacy, in concert with the ASEAN countries, to bring the warring factions to a negotiating table and promote a comprehensive political settlement of the Cambodian conflict also won some praise among political observers in Southeast Asia.[19] In February 1992, the head of UNTAC, UN Under Secretary-General Yasushi Akashi, called on Tokyo to make substantial contributions to the UN-sponsored peacekeeping operation in Cambodia, including participation in a 3,000-member police force.[20] In June 1992, Prince Sihanouk asked Tokyo to dispatch Japanese personnel to Cambodia as part of UNTAC.[21] In June 1992, Tokyo hosted an international conference on the economic reconstruction of Cambodia. The countries and international organizations participating in the conference revealed that of the $879 million they were scheduled to provide by the end of 1993, Japan's contribution amounted to $150 million, by far the largest contribution by any single country.[22] Although, as Prasert Chittiwatanapong details in Chapter 9, ASEAN countries were initially cool to Tokyo's suggestion that the ASEAN PMC should be used as a forum for political and security consultations, by 1992 ASEAN had placed security issues on its formal agenda. The ASEAN foreign ministers' meeting in Manila in July 1992 adopted a resolution calling for a peaceful resolution of the territorial dispute over the Spratly Islands between China, Taiwan, Vietnam, the Philippines, and Malaysia. They also issued a joint communiqué urging all factions in the Cambodian conflict to observe the Paris peace accord, which recognized the Supreme National Council (SNC) as the only legitimate body of authority in Cambodia and expressed full support for the activities of UNTAC.[23]

Tokyo welcomes the signs of improving relations between Vietnam and the ASEAN countries as a factor contributing to the peace and stability of the area. Given the centrality of ASEAN in Tokyo's policy toward Southeast Asia, Japan will continue to coordinate its approach to Vietnam with the ASEAN countries. Once Tokyo normalizes its political relations with Hanoi, however, it is quite conceivable that Japan will quickly become Vietnam's most important trading partner, as was the case in the wake of the end of the Vietnam War in 1975.[24] In the early 1990s, Tokyo began encouraging Japanese private companies to establish a business presence in Vietnam, and several firms responded favorably. Japanese economic assistance will no doubt play an important role in the economic reforms under way in Vietnam and will contribute to the political stability of Southeast Asia.

Lessons of the Gulf War and Japanese Participation in UN Peacekeeping

The 1990–1991 Gulf War was the most important test of Japan's post–Cold War security policy, and its consequences are still being felt in Tokyo. The war tested Japan's willingness and ability to assume an expanded security role, it strained Japan's alliance relations with the United States, and it challenged Tokyo's policymaking ability in the face of an international crisis.

The crisis taught Tokyo at least four important lessons. First, Tokyo realized the need to develop a politically sustainable arrangement for burden-sharing with Washington. The Gulf War demonstrated, on the one hand, that the United States was no longer able to finance a military campaign against a small regional power by itself and also required UN-backed justification for its action, and, on the other hand, that the United States wanted Japan to undertake more than what the U.S. public criticized as Japanese "checkbook diplomacy." Second, Tokyo realized that its consensus-based decisionmaking process was too cumbersome and time consuming to respond quickly to a crisis. Third, Tokyo came to realize the need to articulate more effectively its security needs and security policy goals to the international community, particularly to Japan's neighbors in Asia Pacific. When Tokyo was debating the ill-fated peacekeeping bill during the crisis, many of Japan's Asian neighbors expressed concerns about the rising Japanese military power. However, Tokyo was successful in obtaining understanding and cooperation from the Philippines, Malaysia, and Singapore for its decision to dispatch minesweepers to the Persian Gulf following the termination of the conflict. Fourth, and most important, Tokyo realized the need to contribute more actively and visibly to a post–Cold War international security system with a view to deterring aggression and limiting the potential destructive power of belligerents through various arms control measures.

The Kaifu government failed to win parliamentary approval of its recommendations for Japanese military involvement in the UN peacekeeping effort in 1991. The most formidable obstacle came from the opposition parties and the majority of the public who believed the dispatch of SDF personnel overseas would violate article 9 of the Japanese constitution. After twenty long months of on-again-off-again parliamentary debate, the Miyazawa administration on June 15, 1992, forced the passage of a bill authorizing the dispatch of up to 2,000 members of the SDF to UN-sponsored peacekeeping activities. In the face of the opposition-controlled upper house, however, the government was forced to accept opposition parties' demands for severely restricting the Japanese peacekeeping role. The role of SDF personnel in UN peacekeeping activities would be limited to noncombat support functions, including logistical support, medical assistance, and election monitoring carried out by peacekeeping missions under UN command. SDF participation in more hazardous UN operations, which might require the use of small weapons in self-defense, would require additional legislation. Also, the bill requires an implementation review after three years.[25] These restrictions are generally in line with the measured support among the public for Japanese participation in international peacekeeping. In a January–February 1991 poll by the prime minister's office, for example, 45.5 percent of the respondents showed strong to moderate support for SDF participation in international peacekeeping activities provided such participation did not involve the use of force, and 37.9 percent were opposed to any involvement in international peacekeeping activities.[26]

How will the lessons of the Gulf War be translated into policy beyond Cambodia? There are three essential conditions for an expanded security role for Japan. First, it must be based on a stable national consensus that can be developed only on the basis of sustained national debate on the long-term security needs of Japan as well as those of its neighbors. The weak political leadership and the deep pacifism among the Japanese public are likely, for the foreseeable future, to prevent Tokyo from abandoning its postwar security policy defined strictly in defensive terms. If political leaders are successful in educating the public to the international expectations regarding Japan's international role, the government will have a much better chance of winning parliamentary approval for a security role for the nation beyond Asia Pacific.

Second, a regional security role for Japan must be acceptable to the other Asia Pacific nations, and this requires the kind of broadly based dialogue between the Japanese and their Asian neighbors that currently does not exist. Japan's international security role will be less troubling if Japan can convince its Asian neighbors that its security role will be expanded only within the framework of a UN-sponsored peacekeeping operation and that it will be undertaken only after close consultations with those neighbors. For the time being, the self-imposed limits on Japanese participation in UN-sponsored peacekeeping activities must be strictly observed.

Third, a regional security role for Japan must be developed with close and visible consultation with the United States. Although U.S. pressures will be necessary for Japan to find an international security role more commensurate with its economic power, excessive *gaiatsu* (external pressures) may backfire. One solution, albeit a time-consuming one, may be for Japan and the United States to develop a more broadly based political dialogue on a visibly more equal basis.[27] Such a dialogue should include not only defense and foreign policy planners but legislators, academics, journalists, and other influential opinion makers in both countries. Expanded and improved communication is all the more urgent in the face of the Japan-U.S. economic frictions that are likely to continue for many more years.[28]

Japan's Growing Role in the United Nations _____

A Japanese security role outside the framework of UN peacekeeping will continue to be problematic, both domestically and internationally. This means that the legal foundation, international political support, and financial basis of the UN peacekeeping activities must be firmly established. It is imperative that the United States and the other permanent members of the UN Security Council reach a consensus on a UN-based collective security system, in accordance with chapter 7 of the UN Charter. Article 9 of the Japanese Constitution is interpreted as being in full accord with the collective security system originally envisaged by the framers of the UN Charter. Unfortunately, the East-West confrontation during the Cold War prevented the United Nations from developing such a collective security system. The world body instead developed more ad hoc peacekeeping operations in response to international crises during the Cold War years.[29]

Whether the United States and the other permanent members of the Security Council can agree on a permanent collective security arrangement remains highly uncertain. Among the many obstacles, the continuing economic difficulties in the United States and the former Soviet Union are likely to dampen public support for substantially enlarged financial contributions that a permanent collective security system would require. Nor is there willingness on the part of former Cold War adversaries to place their soldiers under a unified UN command. Most permanent members of the Security Council will also want to retain their right to veto any UN military role that might impinge on their interests. For example, it would be quite unrealistic to expect a U.S. endorsement of the engagement by a permanent UN military force in some crisis in Latin America or active Russian support for a similar UN involvement in one of the former Soviet republics.

Tokyo is interested in a stronger and more effective United Nations, particularly in the area of conflict monitoring and prevention. For example, in September 1991, Foreign Minister Ichiro Nakayama proposed the establishment of a "conflict-prevention system" to improve the UN Secretariat's ability to monitor potential areas of conflict and enhance preemptive diplomatic measures, much like the "preventive diplomacy" advocated by the second UN Secretary-General Dag Hammarskjöld.[30]

Since joining the United Nations in 1956, Japan has been a strong advocate of nuclear disarmament, calling on the nuclear weapons states—including its ally, the United States—to ban the testing of weapons of mass destruction. More recently, Japan has been stepping up its effort to enhance its global role through UN diplomacy. In 1985, Japan successfully proposed the establishment of a special UN panel to consider how to reform the organization's administrative and budgetary processes. Japan actively participated in the drafting of committee recommendations, putting pressure on the United States and other member states to make their assessed contributions to the world body. Back in 1985, Japan also successfully resisted the U.S. urging to join Washington and London in withdrawing from the United Nations Educational, Scientific, and Cultural Organization (UNESCO).

In addressing the General Assembly in September 1991, Foreign Minister Nakayama urged the deletion of references in the UN Charter to Japan and Germany as "enemy states" on the grounds that the world situation had changed dramatically since 1945, when the Charter was adopted.[31] Moreover, in January 1992, Prime Minister Miyazawa called on the representatives of the UN Security Council attending a special summit to "consider thoroughly ways to adjust [the UN] functions, composition, and other aspects so as to make it more reflective of the realities of the new era," a statement generally interpreted as an expression of Japan's desire to become a permanent member of the Security Council. Although there is strong resistance among the permanent members to any revision of the Charter at this time, the status of Japan and Germany in the United Nations is not merely a question of prestige or symbolism but an issue of substantive political consequence. If the United Nations is to become a central part of the post–Cold War order in response to the dramatically altered realities of the world, the question cannot be long ignored.

In the meantime, Japan will carry on an increasingly visible campaign to secure enhanced status in the United Nations by taking concrete steps to demonstrate its contribution to the world body. Particularly important will be Japan's financial contributions to the increasingly costly UN peacekeeping activities. The UN peacekeeping effort in Cambodia was projected to cost $1.9 billion, and the Yugoslavian operation to cost another $634 million. The total cost of eleven UN peacekeeping operations was estimated at $3.7 billion in 1992 alone. The United States owed the United Nations $377 million in back dues for peacekeeping. Secretary of State Baker asked Congress for $810 million for UN troops due for deployment in Cambodia and Yugoslavia, but there was substantial resistance among the legislators who were under public pressure to address domestic economic ills. In contrast, in March 1992, Tokyo indicated it would contribute about $25 million as its share of the $200 million requested by the United Nations to finance startup costs for UNTAC.[32]

Expanding ODA Versus Growing Restraints on Defense Buildup _____

More extensive and more visible than Japanese contributions to the UN peacekeeping effort is Tokyo's official development assistance as a part of its comprehensive security policy. In 1989, Japan became the largest ODA donor in the world, with an $8.97 billion disbursement, surpassing that of the United States. The nation's enhanced position in this area was supported by favorable public opinion, with 42.4 percent of those polled by the prime minister's office in 1989 approving of the amount of Japanese ODA, 39.4 percent advocating a larger sum, and only 8.2 percent preferring a lower level of support.[33] Although Japan lost the top ODA position to the United States in 1990, it regained the title in 1991, with a total ODA disbursement of $11.3 billion (0.32 percent of GNP), an increase of 19.6 percent over 1990.[34] There is no doubt that Tokyo plans to further increase the level and improve the quality of its economic assistance to developing countries and to do so with increasingly explicit political-strategic considerations.

Tokyo has responded to the long-standing criticism about its Asia-focused ODA program by gradually increasing the proportion of its aid extended to non-Asian countries. For example, 64.8 percent of Japan's bilateral ODA in 1986 went to Asian countries, but by 1990 the proportion had declined to 59.3 percent. The Middle East, Africa, and Europe increased their shares from 8.8 percent, 10.9 percent, and 0.1 percent in 1986 to 10.2 percent, 11.4 percent, and 2.3 percent in 1990, respectively.[35] The proportion of Japanese aid that is "tied" has also declined. For example, according to the Japanese Foreign Ministry, almost half of Japan's ODA loans were tied in the mid-1980s but by 1990 the percentage had dropped to 15.6 percent. The Foreign Ministry also estimates that the percentage of loan-funded procurements that went to Japanese businesses—long a target of international charges of "de facto tying of aid"—had declined to only 27 percent in 1990 from 67 percent in 1986.[36]

Most importantly, by the late 1970s Tokyo had abandoned its traditional aversion to the explicit incorporation of political-strategic considerations into its ODA policy. After the Soviet invasion of Afghanistan in 1979, Japan visibly increased its assistance to Thailand, Pakistan, and Turkey—countries described by Tokyo as "bordering conflicts." In May 1981, Prime Minister Zenko Suzuki gave official endorsement to the concept of comprehensive security and at the same time declared Japan would strengthen its aid to "those areas which are important to the maintenance of world peace and stability." Included in this category of areas were the ASEAN countries, China, Egypt, Kenya, Zimbabwe, Jamaica, and Sudan. In 1984 the Foreign Ministry added South Korea, Somalia, and Tanzania to this list. The list has since been extended to include Jordan, Turkey, the former Soviet Union, Poland, Hungary, Czechoslovakia, Romania, Panama, and Nicaragua. Following Iraq's invasion of Kuwait in August 1990, Japan committed $2 billion in economic assistance to the "frontline states" of Egypt, Jordan, and Turkey. By 1991 Tokyo had extended more than $2 billion in financial and technical assistance to Poland, Hungary, Czechoslovakia, and Romania to support the Eastern European countries' effort to move toward market economies. In April 1991, Tokyo agreed to provide about $6.3 million to establish a fund for Eastern Europe within the European Bank for Reconstruction and Development (EBRD). In addition, in October 1991, Tokyo announced a $2.5 billion package of export insurance and economic assistance for the former Soviet Union.

In April 1991, Tokyo adopted new ODA guidelines, which would take into consideration the military and the political policies of the nations receiving or asking for Japanese economic aid. Factors to be considered in this new framework include military spending, the production of weapons of mass destruction, arms trade, democratization, human rights, and market-oriented economic reform. So far, however, the application of the new guidelines has been rather inconsistent. For example, Tokyo suspended economic assistance to Myanmar following human rights violations in that country in 1989, but it resumed ongoing projects and continued such assistance despite the military's refusal to transfer power to the opposition party, which won elections in May 1990. Tokyo banned all aid to Haiti following the overthrow of the democratically elected government of Jean-Bertrand Aristide in September 1991. In his talks with Chinese Premier Li Peng in August 1991, Prime Minister Kaifu mentioned his government's new ODA guidelines and urged that Beijing adhere to the Nuclear Nonproliferation Treaty and restrict military expenditures and arms exports. But the Japanese leader lifted the post-Tiananmen suspension of large-scale economic aid to Beijing, citing a "special relationship" between Japan and China.[37]

These limitations notwithstanding, Japan's burgeoning ODA power is likely to increase both in level and in political significance in contrast to that of the United States, suffering visibly diminishing public support for foreign aid. In December 1991, Tokyo decided to boost its ODA to about $7.1 billion in fiscal year 1992, an increase of 7.8 percent over the previous year. This was expected to enable Tokyo to meet its goal of disbursing a total of $50 billion in ODA during the period 1988–1992.[38]

In contrast to the continuing strong domestic support for foreign economic aid, Tokyo's defense spending is beginning to come under stricter scrutiny in the wake of the end of the Cold War. Defense spending had received a favorable treatment in the government's budget decisions since the 1970s. By the end of fiscal 1990, Tokyo had accomplished most of the personnel and equipment procurement objectives contained in the 1976 National Defense Program Outline. As late as July 1990, in view of the continuing qualitative improvements in the Soviet forces in the Soviet Far East, the Japanese National Security Council (NSC) urged that the fiscal 1991–1995 defense buildup plan continue to modernize the SDF and qualitatively improve weapons systems. Trends began to shift in 1990. In December of that year, the Kaifu administration adopted a new five-year defense buildup plan, which would increase the defense spending by a mere 3 percent annually before adjustment for inflation. This contrasted sharply with the 5.4 percent increase the fiscal 1986–1990 plan had achieved. Nonetheless, the fiscal 1991–1995 plan authorizes the procurement of thirty-six vehicle-mounted multiple-launch rocket systems, four airborne warning and control system (AWACS) aircraft, two Aegis destroyers, and other advanced weapons systems by fiscal year 1995.[39] The December 1990 decision also called for a review of the fiscal 1991–1995 defense buildup plan in summer 1993. In December 1991, Tokyo approved a 3.8 percent increase in the defense spending for fiscal year 1992 (to $33.7 billion), the smallest rise in thirty-two years.[40] This limited increase resulted in several procurement cuts in fiscal year 1992. Among the "casualties" were one of two planned P3C antisubmarine warfare helicopters, eight of twenty-eight projected Type-90 tanks, one of two scheduled Patriot surface-to-air missile batteries, six of ten expected AH-1S antitank helicopters, and four of eleven planned F-15 fighter aircraft. Further cuts were expected by defense planners. Moreover, in view of the dissolution of the Soviet Union and the end of the Cold War, the NSC decided in December 1991 to push the review of the five-year defense buildup plan one year ahead of schedule. Some Japanese policymakers have also suggested that the end of the Cold War has rendered the 1976 National Defense Outline obsolete.

_____ *Conclusions*

The foregoing analysis suggests that the most likely scenario for the development of an international security role for Japan will include the following elements. First, Japan's military capabilities are likely to be limited to those necessary for the defense of its home islands and sea-lines of communication out to a distance of a thousand nautical miles from its shores. Second, the nation's resource commitment even to this circumscribed defense mission will come under greater scrutiny as the military threat from the former Soviet Union further dissipates. Third, beyond the limits of its defense perimeter, Japan will continue to increase its diplomatic and economic efforts to reduce regional tensions and promote political stability. ODA will grow further in importance and Tokyo gradually and cautiously will apply its recently adopted approach of conditioning the level and terms of ODA on the political and military policies of the recipients of Japanese aid, although how successful or how uniform its application will be remains to be seen. Fourth, Tokyo and Washington will manage to maintain their bilateral security alliance for the short to medium term, but long-term prospects will be increasingly uncertain as the likelihood of a common security threat of a regionwide, much less global, nature emerging diminishes. Fifth, as the U.S. military presence and security commitments in Asia Pacific gradually diminish, Japan and other regional powers will explore alternative or complementary security frameworks with U.S. participation. Because formal security arrangements are extremely difficult in the highly diverse political environment of the region, the most promising avenue will be security consultations in loosely organized subregional frameworks. Participants will go to great lengths to avoid the impression of exclusivity, much less alliance, against other regional powers that may decide not to participate. Sixth and finally, Japan will continue to explore and cultivate an international security role for itself in those areas that require the least amount of change in its constitutional, legal, and political systems. UN-sponsored peacekeeping efforts will be the ideal candidates for financial, technical, and logistical support from Japan. Although in the immediate future Japan's debate on the constitutionality of an SDF participation in UN peacekeeping is unlikely to produce a definitive and popular government position, over time noncombat participation is likely to be accepted by the Japanese people and by their Asian neighbors. As Japan's UN contributions accumulate over time, the nation will press harder and harder for a revision of the UN Charter to secure for itself a permanent seat on the Security Council.

The restrictive characteristics of Japan's post–Cold War security policy will no doubt help ease the apprehension among that nation's neighbors about its potential military power. On the other hand, the strictly circumscribed security policy will be criticized by some foreign observers as unworthy of the global economic giant that is Japan. Whether Tokyo will succeed in pursuing the politically and economically expanded but militarily restricted security role during the remainder of the 1990s and beyond depends largely on two things. First, it will depend critically on whether the United States and other big powers can collectively develop regional security frameworks to contain the rising ethnic tensions and nationalist conflicts. The most disturbing in this context will be the escalation of a regional conflict into a crisis similar to that which transpired in the Gulf in 1990 and 1991. Second, Japan's performance in international security will depend on whether Tokyo can articulate its own view of the post–Cold War world, including what it realistically can do and cannot do with respect to its regional and global security roles. In this respect, the continuing absence of an effective political leadership in Tokyo cannot but cast a dark shadow on its ability to communicate with the rest of the world.

Notes

An earlier version of this chapter was presented at the annual meeting of the International Studies Association, Atlanta, Georgia, April 1–4, 1992.

1. For a similar reading on general trends, see Robert A. Scalapino, "The United States and Asia: Future Prospects," *Foreign Affairs*, vol. 70, no. 5 (Winter 1991/92), pp. 19–40.

2. An informal group, the Northeast Asian Economic Cooperation Forum, was formed in 1991 among academics, business representatives, and government officials acting in a private capacity from Japan, the Russian Far East, China, North and South Korea, the United States, and Mongolia. The concept of a Japan Sea Rim economic zone is attracting increasing academic and business interest in Japan. See, for example, Kazuo Ogawa and Teruo Komaki, eds., *Kan-Nihonkai Keizaiken: Hokutō Ajia-Shiberia Jidai no Makuake* [A Japan Sea Rim economic zone: The dawning of a new northeast Asia-Siberia age], Tokyo: Nihon Keizai Shimbunsha, 1991; Takeo Toma, *Ugokihajimeta Kan-Nihonkai Keizaiken: 21 Seiki no Kyodai Shijō* [A Japan Sea Rim economic zone beginning to move: A gigantic market of the twenty-first century], Tokyo: Sōchisha, 1991.

3. "Open regionalism" is an approach to regional economic development that attempts to accelerate market and institutional integration within the region without reducing the access to the regional market for countries outside of the region. I learned much about the concept from the series of seminars on this theme held at the Asia Foundation, San Francisco, February–March 1992. "Open regionalism" was the theme of PECCIX in San Francisco in September 1992.

4. Scalapino discusses the problems associated with weak political institutions in many Asian countries. See Scalapino, "The United States and Asia," pp. 23–25.

5. For an extended discussion of Japan's comprehensive security policy and its applicability in East Asia, see Tsuneo Akaha, "Japan's Comprehensive Security Policy: A New East Asian Environment," *Asian Survey*, vol. 31, no. 4 (1991), pp. 324–340.

6. Scalapino, "The United States and Asia," pp. 19–40.

7. As of March 31, 1990, the Department of Defense had 297,987 military personnel and 36,410 civilian employees assigned in the Pacific theater. Of these, 52,770

were in Japan, 46,476 in Korea, and 14,833 in the Philippines. See General Accounting Office, *Military Presence: U.S. Personnel in the Pacific Theater*, Washington, D.C.: Government Accounting Office, 1991, pp. 4, 27, and 44.

8. *Defense White Paper, 1991*, Tokyo: Defense Agency, 1991.

9. See, for example, Kiyoshi Araki, "Japan's Security Policy in the Regional and Global Context," *RIIA Discussion Paper 37*, London: The Royal Institute of International Affairs, 1991; Shigeki Nishimura, "Military Balance in Northeast Asia," *IIGP Policy Paper 46E*, Tokyo: International Institute for Global Peace, February 1991; Shigeki Nishimura, "Transformation of the U.S.-Japan Defense Posture: The New Soviet Challenge," *IIGP Policy Paper 65E*, Tokyo: International Institute for Global Peace, October 1991.

10. For this concern, see Zbigniew Brzezinski, "The Consequences of the End of the Cold War for International Security," *Adelphi Papers*, no. 265 (Winter 1991/92), p. 13.

11. Prime Minister Miyazawa stated in June 1992 that a new Asian security framework was needed that called for participation by Japan, the United States, China, and the former Soviet Union. *Asahi Shimbun*, June 24, 1992, p. 2.

12. *The Japan Times Weekly International Edition*, March 23–29, 1992, p. 2.

13. Yasuhide Yamanouchi, "Japan's Security Policy and Arms Control in North East Asia," *IIGP Policy Paper 60E*, Tokyo: International Institute for Global Peace, October 1991, p. 1.

14. In an attempt to put additional pressure on Pyongyang, Prime Minister Kaifu announced at the UN Conference on Arms Reduction held in Kyoto on May 27, 1991, that Japan would seek to expand criteria for inspection under the IAEA framework, which would include more forceful verification of treaty violations. See Yamanouchi, "Japan's Security Policy," pp. 1–2. See also Ryukichi Imai, "Revision of International Atomic Agency Safeguards," *IIGP Policy Paper 59E*, Tokyo: International Institute for Global Peace, June 1991; Ryukichi Imai, "Expanding the Role of Verification in Arms Control," *IIGP Policy Paper 72E*, Tokyo: International Institute for Global Peace, February 1992.

15. *Asahi Shimbun*, July 16, 1992, p. 11.

16. *Asahi Shimbun*, February 27, 1992, pp. 1 and 3.

17. Akaha, "Japan's Comprehensive Security Policy," pp. 337–339.

18. *Asahi Shimbun*, July 22, 1992, p. 2.

19. See, for example, Chapter 9 in this volume, by Prasert Chittiwatanapong.

20. Margo Grimm, "Japan Seeks Greater Role in Cambodian Reconstruction," *JEI Report*, no. 6B (February 14, 1991), pp. 6–7.

21. *Asahi Shimbun*, June 20, 1992, p. 2.

22. *Asahi Shimbun*, June 23, 1992, p. 2.

23. Ibid., p. 6.

24. For a detailed analysis of Japanese-Vietnamese relations in the postwar period, see Masaya Shiraishi, *Japanese Relations with Vietnam: 1951–1987*, Ithaca: Cornell University Southeast Asia Program, 1990.

25. Barbara Wanner, "UN Peacekeeping Support Bill Becomes Law," *JEI Report*, no. 23B (June 19, 1992), pp. 5–7.

26. *Seron Chosa* [Public opinion survey], Tokyo: Sōrifu Kōhōshitsu, August 1991, p. 10.

27. For an argument in favor of a more equal relationship, see Richard Holbrooke, "Japan and the United States: Ending the Unequal Partnership," *Foreign Affairs*, vol. 70, no. 5 (Winter 1991/92), pp. 41–57.

28. On the need to broaden bilateral communication, see James A. Baker III, "America in Asia: Emerging Architecture for a Pacific Community," *Foreign Affairs*, vol. 70, no. 5 (Winter 1991/92), pp. 9–11.

29. See the dialogue between Mizuo Kuroda and Soji Yamamoto in "Kokuren Heiwaiji Katsudō Sankamondai o Megutte" [On the issue of participation in UN peacekeeping activities], *Gaikō Forum*, no. 32 (May 1991), pp. 45 and 47.

30. Barbara Wanner, "Japan Views Leadership Opportunities Through the United Nations," *JEI Report*, no. 10A (March 13, 1992), p. 5.

31. For a succinct summary of Japan's diplomatic activities in the United Nations, see ibid., pp. 1–11.

32. *Japan Times Weekly International Edition*, March 16–22, 1992, p. 2.

33. Akaha, "Japan's Comprehensive Security Policy," p. 332.

34. *Asahi Shimbun*, June 19, 1992, p. 1.

35. Margo Grimm, "Japan's Foreign Aid Program: 1991 Update," *JEI Report*, no. 45A (December 6, 1991), p. 9.

36. Ibid., p. 6.

37. Foreign Ministry spokesman Taizo Watanabe admitted that the new economic aid policy is more a principle than a "very strict law" and it will be applied on a "case-by-case basis." Ibid., p. 12.

38. Margo Grimm, "Foreign Aid Boosted in Japan's FY 1992 Budget," *JEI Report*, no. 1B (January 10, 1992), p. 10.

39. Barbara Wanner, "Japan's Defense Procurement and Planning Complicated by Global Changes," *JEI Report*, no. 38A (October 11, 1991), pp. 4–5.

40. The Defense Agency had sought a 5.4 percent increase. Barbara Wanner, "FY 1992 Defense Budget Reflects Tight Money and Changing Global Conditions," *JEI Report*, no. 1B (January 10, 1992), p. 11.

Chapter 5

Japan in East Asia

David Arase

The issue I would like to explore in this chapter is Japan's changing relationship with East Asia, a region encompassing the Korean peninsula, China, Indochina, Burma, and the ASEAN member countries. Japan's emergence as an economic superpower has given it a natural leadership role in the process of Asian regionalization, and the question is how Japan is taking up the challenge. The implications for the global political economy and the role of the United States in Asia are likely to be profound.

The collapse of the Soviet Union and the demise of the communist challenge mean that the underlying rationale for the old Cold War system of alliances and informal alignments in East Asia is obsolescent. It also makes more salient the fact that Japan has grown from a mere 10 percent of the U.S. GNP in 1960 to more than 60 percent of the U.S. GNP in 1992. Compared with the United States, Japan has a higher per capita income, greater growth performance, and perhaps a more competitive industrial economy. A structural change of this magnitude cannot fail to give Japan greater leadership in East Asia.

Change is already evident in Japan's relations with the United States, which are changing from that of a client to that of an equal power. For each country this change may have quite different meanings. The United States demands change in some of Japan's basic economic and security policies, whereas Japan wants to be consulted by the United States in issues of global management as well as to have the power to say no to some U.S. demands.

From a theoretical perspective, one might characterize the changing bilateral relationship as a shift from bandwagoning to balancing behavior,[1] or, alternatively, a shift from free-riding to negotiated burdensharing.[2] "Balancing behavior" implies the possible development of great-power rivalry—with all that that entails—whereas "burdensharing" implies continued close partnership and the absence of fundamental antagonism.[3] Whatever the final outcome, change in the relationship is being driven by the changed structure of international relations.

Japan's relations with the rest of East Asia are also changing, but in a more amicable direction. Others in the region are increasingly reliant on Japan, thus creating a condition for vast improvement in Japan's heretofore strained relations with its neighbors.

Structural Change in Northeast Asia —————————————

As a preface to a discussion of Japan's post–Cold War role in East Asia, it may be worth recalling the structure of the Cold War. From the Korean War until 1971, the Cold War boundaries in Northeast Asia were clearly drawn at the thirty-eighth parallel in the Korean peninsula and in the straits between China and Taiwan. The Korean War produced these boundaries as well as the Western assumption that the states on the communist side of the divide constituted a monolithic bloc implacably hostile to the West. The Sino-Soviet split that opened within a decade of the Korean War cast doubt on this assumption, but it was not until 1969 that its falsehood was conclusively demonstrated by Sino-Soviet armed border clashes.

From 1972, China opened relations with the West out of fear of a Soviet military threat and in pursuit of its own ambitious domestic modernization program. This replaced the bloc confrontation model with the U.S.–China–Soviet Union "strategic triangle" in Northeast Asia. China's ability to exploit the new situation was slowed by domestic turmoil caused by the rise and fall of the Gang of Four, but by 1978, when Deng Xiaoping gained a firm hold on leadership, the new agenda was clear. By signing the 1972 Shanghai communiqué with the United States and the 1978 Peace and Friendship Treaty with Japan, which contained the antihegemony clause directed against the Soviet Union, China dropped even the pretense of fraternal relations with the Soviets, won the removal of U.S. security commitments to Taiwan, and gained normalized relations with the United States and Japan.

The one communist East Asian regime with whom China maintained the pretense of fraternal solidarity was North Korea, also known as the Democratic People's Republic of Korea (DPRK). To achieve its own security and modernization aims, China needed an ability to promote stability on the Korean peninsula and to prevent the establishment of a Soviet military presence there. In addition, being a nation divided by the Cold War, China had an interest in backing Korean reunification efforts that would not undermine its own reunification policy toward Taiwan. Accordingly, China continued to avoid direct official dealings with South Korea, also known as the Republic of Korea (ROK), while covertly beginning indirect trade with it in the late 1980s.

The Soviets responded to the unfavorable shift in the Northeast Asian strategic triangle by replacing the détente of the early and mid-1970s with a policy of military and diplomatic intimidation of China, Japan, and the United States. This only succeeded in renewing the Cold War and strengthening a strategic counteralignment from the late 1970s whose axis was Beijing-

Seoul-Tokyo-Washington.[4] As China dropped objections to Japanese rearmament and welcomed closer military ties between the Nakasone, Chun, and Reagan administrations, North Korea perceived a greater threat and moved closer to the Soviets by reaching new military cooperation agreements.

Thus, by the mid-1980s the crux of the renewed Cold War in Northeast Asia was back at the thirty-eighth parallel where it had all begun in 1950. Here was where the nuclear-armed United States, China, and Soviet Union could fall into direct conflict due to circumstances beyond their ability to predict or control.[5]

The transformation of Northeast Asia began when a new leadership in the Soviet Union under Mikhail Gorbachev arrived in 1985 bent on a radical program of domestic reform that would require a peaceful environment and unobstructed access to the global economy. Accordingly, Soviet policy in Northeast Asia worked to reduce the risk of war along the Chinese border and in the Korean peninsula. The purpose was to turn Soviet territory in Asia from a liability into an asset by engaging the countries of the economically dynamic Asia Pacific region in new economic and political cooperation.[6]

Concrete indications that the Cold War in Northeast Asia was ending included the 1987 INF agreement, which among other things banned modernized Soviet intermediate-range nuclear ballistic missiles from the Soviet Far East and Siberia; the withdrawal of Soviet troops from Afghanistan in 1988, which removed one of China's so-called "three obstacles" to normalized relations with the Soviet Union; and the 1988 Olympic Games held in Seoul, which saw the participation of both China and the Soviet Union. A successful official visit to Beijing by Gorbachev in May 1989 put Sino-Soviet relations on a peaceful course, and the June 1990 informal meeting between President Roh Tae-woo of South Korea and President Gorbachev, which took place in San Francisco, only could have happened after the end of the Cold War in Northeast Asia.

With largely successful efforts by China and the Soviet Union to resolve their ideological and border disagreements, followed by the demise of the Soviet Union in 1991, the Cold War cleavages in Northeast Asia, as elsewhere, have become obsolete. The old lineup of the Soviet Union and North Korea versus the United States, Japan, and the ROK—with China leaning away from the Soviets and toward the West[7]—is gone. The DPRK is the clearest loser in the process of dismantling the Cold War because it still lacks normalized relations with the ROK, Japan, or the United States, and has strained relations with its only remaining former ally, China.

New Pressures on Japan

The most outstanding structural development in Northeast Asia affecting Japan is the emergence of the ROK as a regional actor. The old Cold War confrontation left the ROK opposed by China, the Soviet Union, and the DPRK, and highly dependent on the United States. In the post–Cold War order, however, the ROK is winning the cooperation of the Russians and Chinese in many important areas, and the political and military threat of the DPRK is nullified if nuclear weapons are taken out of the picture.[8] The United States is cooperating with ROK wishes for greater autonomy by reducing its military presence and turning over military command functions to the South Koreans.[9] All this means that the ROK, with its industrialized economy and potent military capabilities, is free to turn its energies outward in pursuit of a greater regional and global role. The effort is apparent in the ROK's successful bid to join the UN and OECD, its increasingly active role in Pacific economic cooperation fora such as APEC, and its successful efforts to become a regular ASEAN dialogue partner.

This development creates a new agenda item in the region: How will the more powerful and independent ROK, or perhaps even a unified noncommunist Korean peninsula, be incorporated into a stable regional order? A secure and prosperous ROK benefits the United States, China, and the former Soviet Union by letting them disengage from their direct confrontation in the Korean peninsula. Moreover, an autonomous ROK promises to be an important economic partner of China and the former Soviet Union, and perhaps even a security cooperation partner as well. A more secure and autonomous ROK security posture also coincides with the U.S. interest in reducing its military forces in the region. With lower costs and risks in the Korean peninsula, the U.S.-ROK bilateral mutual security treaty is of greater net value to the United States.

For Japan, however, the benefits are less clear. Japan's risk of getting caught in a superpower conflict is lower, but "local" instability on the Korean peninsula still could easily affect Japan's security. In addition, this ROK emergence affects Japan differently because Japan is restricted by its constitution to local defense in security matters, whereas in contrast the ROK is not forbidden to enter military alliances or regional security agreements from a legal or political standpoint. And unlike Japan, which has a ban on exporting weapons, the ROK can produce and transfer advanced weapons. In terms of military capability, the ROK does get more "bang for the buck," with roughly 750,000 soldiers on active duty versus 250,000 for Japan, thirty-four major ROK warships versus sixty-eight for Japan, and 469 combat aircraft (including F-16s) versus 387 (including F-15s) for Japan.[10] Economically, however, the ROK has only about 7–8 percent of the GNP of Japan and spends about 39 percent of the amount Japan does on defense.

In view of the remaining threat from the DPRK and the size of the Japanese economy, prudence would dictate that the ROK should not do anything to provoke Japan into rearmament. But bilateral economic frictions are chronic and serious, and anti-Japanese sentiment in Korea cannot be easily dismissed. Repeated Korean demands for apologies from Japan for the past, an end to discrimination against ethnic Koreans in Japan, compensation for Korean victims present during the bombing of Hiroshima, and the return of Korean art treasures stolen during the Japanese colonial period are signs of unresolved animosity, and in the background there is an unresolved territorial dispute over the island of Tokto, or Takeshima, in the Korean Straits. Given the unhappy history of past relations, and the fact that the United States may no longer be able to dictate the actions of either party, Japan will have to treat cautiously the emergence of this new regional actor.

Japan has a similar problem with the Russian Federation. New Russian warships and submarines that have been in the pipeline are nearing completion, and many could be deployed in Northeast Asia as replacements for existing vessels. Although the Russian fleet will be downsized,[11] the new vessels may actually enhance certain Russian naval capabilities. Meanwhile, the collapse of the Soviet Union, a reduced scope of Russian naval activity, and the completion of the U.S. naval modernization program give the United States a more benign and confident assessment of the situation. The result is likely to be less U.S. pressure on Japan to rearm.

The Japanese threat perception stems most immediately from the unresolved dispute over island territories in the vicinity of Hokkaido and blocks the signing of a peace treaty ending World War II between Japan and the Soviet Union. The dispute stems from the Soviet occupation of the islands at the close of the war and the subsequent claim of Soviet sovereignty based on an Allied agreement at Yalta that the Soviets should gain (or from the Russian viewpoint, regain) the Kuril Islands. The Japanese claim that Imperial Russia recognized these islands as part of Japanese territory in treaties signed in 1855 and 1875, but the Russian response is that the Treaty of Portsmouth (1905), which redrew territorial boundaries between Japan and Russia, nullified the previous treaties, and that in any case Japan's unconditional surrender binds Japan to the Yalta agreement.[12]

The islands are not a vital interest for either side, and notwithstanding certain military, economic, and social issues connected with these islands, a purely bilateral resolution of the dispute incorporating demilitarization of the islands without the intrusion of issues relating to the U.S. presence in Japan is possible in the post–Cold War environment. The inability to resolve this issue is not to be blamed on a persisting Cold War, but instead on the present-day legacy of relations between the Russians and Japanese scarred by unresolved conflicts. As with the Koreans, the Japanese have had bitter relations with the Russians predating the Cold War. As the post–Cold War order unfolds, the retention of superior military force in Russian hands, even as Japan's capabilities remain limited, puts Japan at a disadvantage—a position that could be compounded if the Russians and Koreans succeeded in forging better links with each other than either has with Japan. This is a possibility skillfully raised by Gorbachev's meetings with Roh in June 1990 (just after Roh had left Tokyo) and in April 1991 (just after Gorbachev had left Tokyo). The

Japanese, however, remain intransigent over the islands dispute and may make additional demands for arms reductions before Japan will extend large-scale economic cooperation to the Soviets.

The trend in U.S.-Japan relations also shapes Japan's post–Cold War orientation. The bilateral friction caused by the Gulf crisis of 1988 and the subsequent 1990–1991 Gulf War showed how difficult it has been to find a new basis for close political partnership. Added to this are various economic frictions between the United States and Japan, which already have had a corrosive effect on mutual perceptions. Finally, the United States has announced a drawdown of forces stationed in Asia due to budgetary restrictions, the closing of U.S. bases in the Philippines, and a reduced perception of threat. The overall impact on Japan of chronically troubled bilateral relations and a reduced U.S. security role in the region could be to leave its regional interests more exposed. Thus, in spite of—or perhaps because of—the end of the Cold War, Japan may have good reasons to gradually build up its conventional military capabilities and seek a more active regional security role.

Japan's Regional Diplomacy

It is significant that the first official overseas trip of the new Japanese emperor was to Southeast Asia in 1991; the second was to China in October 1992. The apologies for Japan's wartime behavior the emperor has already made and will make to Japan's Asian neighbors, along with those of recent Japanese prime ministers, show a more serious attempt to put the past to rest and to prepare for a new, more positive regional diplomacy.

The new regional diplomacy has three mutually reinforcing themes. One theme is leadership in organizing an expanding regional economy. This is illustrated by Japan's large official development assistance flows to the region and its strong support for institutions promoting regional cooperation, such as the informal Pacific Economic Cooperation Council, the Asian Pacific Economic Cooperation forum, and the Asian Development Bank, for which Japan is by far the single largest provider of funds.

Another theme is greater Japanese contributions to peace and security in the region. Japan desires a direct role in the resolution of conflicts on the Korean peninsula and in Indochina, and this underlies Japan's efforts to get a permanent seat on the UN Security Council and to broaden the role of the Self Defense Forces to include peacekeeping operations (PKO). This desire for a greater role in regional peace and security issues also partially explains the continued gradual buildup of the SDF and its proposal at the 1991 ASEAN Post-Ministerial Conference to turn the annual event into a forum for security discussions.

The third theme is greater independent leadership in the East Asian region.[13] This is a natural corollary of the vision of Japan's role in a tripolar order as articulated in a speech by Prime Minister Kaifu at Strasbourg,[14] and of Japan's desire for a "global partnership" with the United States. As former Vice Foreign Minister Takakazu Kuriyama explained in an interesting paper laying out Japan's diplomatic strategy, "today, the time when Japan could take for granted an international order sustained by U.S. strength . . . is long past. The two nations . . . are in a position to share responsibilities for world peace and prosperity together with Western Europe. This is precisely what is meant by the 'global partnership'." He also noted that "movements to establish a new order [are] also evident in the main theater of Japan's foreign policy—the Asia and Pacific region."[15]

Japan's economic power allows the ability to pursue a new agenda—particularly in the Asian region where Japan's economy is so predominant (see Figure 5.1).[16] To understand Japan's capabilities, it might be useful to examine its economic relationship with China, Japan's only serious rival for leadership in the region. Although China is a nuclear-armed military power, the U.S. nuclear umbrella, Japan's military capabilities, and China's own growing economic dependence on Japan neutralize any Chinese threat to Japan's military security. With regard to economic strength, China has only one-eighth of Japan's GNP, and although China's population vastly exceeds that of Japan, it is a liability because it makes China the poorest nation in East Asia in per capita terms. In important ways, China must be a follower not a leader.

Contrary to popular perception, Japan is not very vulnerable to economic blackmail or pressure from any nation in Asia, including China. Japan is less dependent on trade (total trade equals 17 percent of GNP) than is China (26 percent of GNP). The total of their two-way trade was about $19 billion in 1988, only about 4 percent of Japan's total trade, but more than 18 percent of China's total trade. For China, this trade yields much-needed hard currency and vital technologies for its modernization. The structure of this trade also shows Japanese leverage: in 1989 more than two-thirds of China's exports to Japan were nonstrategic foodstuffs, textiles, and manufactured products; more than 80 percent of Japan's exports to China were chemicals, machinery, and fabricated metal needed to keep China's industrialization projects moving forward. The one strategic item China exports to Japan is oil. But Japan gets less than 7 percent of its total oil imports from China. Thus, the economic relationship is asymmetrical: Japan may be sensitive to Chinese trade sanctions, but China is the one who would be vulnerable to Japanese sanctions.

In the area of direct investment, China is heavily dependent on Japan, the third-largest foreign investor in China after Hong Kong and the United States. According to Chinese figures, cumulative Japanese investments total $2.64 billion in 951 projects. Also, China is heavily dependent on Japanese official development assistance. In 1987, Japan gave $553 million in bilateral ODA to China, or 64.3 percent of China's total bilateral ODA.[17] These funds

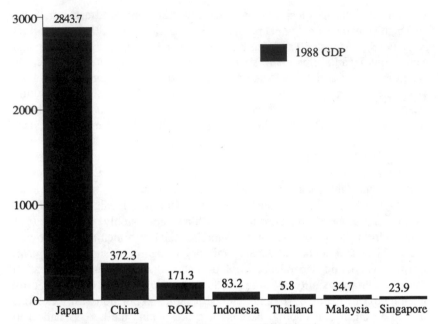

Figure 5.1   GDP of Selected Asian Countries (US$ billions)
Source: World Development Report 1990, Washington, D.C.: World Bank, 1990, Appendix.

are crucial to China. They are counted as revenue in the government's capital budget every year and so are needed for fiscal "balance," especially in the reform era, which has created a loss of revenue and a tremendous budget deficit for the authorities in Beijing.

The fact that Japan's GNP is more than three times as large as the combined GNP of all the other lower- and middle-income countries of Asia indicates the degree of economic leverage Japan has over any single country in Asia including China. This suggests that Japan, without in any way being selfish or crudely interventionist, can link its resources to a wide range of issues without risking a strategic setback.

How is Japan using its new power and influence? Signs of more independence from U.S. policy are emerging in Japan's approaches toward such issues as human rights and security, and Japan's diplomacy toward particular East Asian countries and regional groupings yields particular examples.

Japanese Policy Toward the Two Koreas _____

Japan succeeded in gaining greater involvement in the resolution of conflict in the Korean peninsula by starting official bilateral negotiations over normalization with North Korea in 1990—despite the misgivings of the United States and South Korea. Japan abandoned its postwar diffidence to gain direct involvement there, and it did so through a solo initiative to get the North Koreans interested in Japanese economic assistance.[18]

After China and the Soviet Union ignored North Korea's plea to boycott the 1988 Seoul Olympics, North Korea's fear of total isolation and economic collapse facilitated Japan's direct involvement into peace and security issues in the Korean peninsula. In 1990 the DPRK contacted Japan's ruling Liberal Democratic Party leadership through the intermediation of the Japan Socialist Party (JSP) and renewed an offer made the previous year to return two Japanese sailors imprisoned by the DPRK on spying charges in exchange for the start of official talks with Japan. The offer was accepted, and in September 1990, Shin Kanemaru, a senior leader in the ruling Liberal Democratic Party, flew to Pyongyang with Makoto Tanabe, vice-chair of the JSP (now renamed the Japan Social Democratic Party) and thirteen government officials. Kanemaru gave Kim Il-sung a letter from Prime Minister Toshiki Kaifu containing expressions of regret over past unhappy relations, and on behalf of the LDP, Kanemaru signed a declaration with Tanabe and Kim that promised normalization talks with the DPRK and monetary compensation for damages inflicted on Korea in both the prewar and postwar periods. In addition, an agreement to open direct flights and satellite communications was reached. In return, Japan gained the release of two Japanese sailors imprisoned on spying charges by North Korea in 1983.

The Japanese opening to the DPRK appeared surprisingly narrow and awkward in that it seemed to offer the DPRK important concessions without gaining any promise of changed policies by the DPRK, and it was inconsistent with ROK and U.S. policies toward the North. The ROK objected to the communiqué signed by Kim, Kanemaru, and Tanabe because of the promise of compensation for damages suffered by the DPRK in the postwar period, a consideration not given to the ROK at the time of normalization; and it denounced the idea of giving the DPRK compensation before normalization took place. In addition, no conditions regarding the inspection of nuclear facilities, the sponsorship of terrorism, progress in North-South talks, or tension reduction at the demilitarized zone were attached to the compensation or normalization process, and this reportedly also raised concerns in the United States.[19]

Fundamentally, the ROK was concerned lest Japan's initiative undercut its carefully planned strategy of forcing the DPRK into meaningful bilateral talks. The ROK feared that Japan would relieve the DPRK's isolation and give it enough money to allow it to resist external pressures for change. In addition, Japan's sudden initiative threatened the ROK's control over the peace process on the Korean peninsula, and some South Koreans even suspected this was Japan's true objective in order to keep the Koreans a weak and divided nation.

The Japanese response was that this initiative was not binding on the government of Japan because Kanemaru was merely a politician acting on his own initiative. When Kaifu paid an official visit to Seoul in early January 1991, he reassured the ROK by giving a pledge to accept all ROK demands regarding the Japan-DPRK normalization talks to start at the end of that month. Nonetheless, what concerned the South was the fact that the bureaucracy and all the political parties in Japan except for the Japanese Communist Party immediately welcomed the start of normalization talks as a step long past due.

The five main demands presented to Kaifu during his visit to Seoul were (1) full consultations with Seoul regarding Japan-DPRK normalization talks, (2) Japanese support for progress in the North-South dialogue, (3) a demand that Japan press the North to agree to nuclear inspections, (4) no payment of compensation before normalization, and (5) efforts to open up North Korean society to the outside world.[20] When official talks began in Pyongyang at the end of January 1991, the Japanese position reflected Kaifu's pledge.

The effect of the opening is clear: Japan now has a direct role in the ongoing effort to improve the peace and security situation in the Korean peninsula. Together with prime ministerial talks with the South, the Japan-DPRK talks began a process of opening up the North, which may promote pragmatic reform and ideological deradicalization, and this allowed both China and the Soviet Union to take a further step away from the DPRK without fear of leaving it in dangerous isolation. The talks give Japan leverage not only over the North but over other actors because they must now involve Japan in the successful management of Korean affairs. Japan has introduced conditions for normalization desired by the ROK and the United States, but to preserve its options Japan has not officially linked its conditions to those of either country.

Policy Toward China

Japanese policy toward China has also been distinctive both before and after the events of 1989. By 1988, Japan and China had negotiated a huge ODA loan package for the 1990–1995 period, allocating roughly $1 billion per year for large-scale aid projects. Then came the events of June 3–4, 1989, in Tiananmen Square. The Japanese prime minister's initial reaction was: "We do not have the slightest idea about taking punitive actions."[21] Western pressure delayed the aid package, but by the 1990 Western summit, Japan announced the ending of sanctions. The ODA package was reinstated in toto, and another bilateral trade agreement worth $8 billion was signed. The official rationale was regional stability, but more to the point was Japan's shift of attention to China as an attractive site for trade and investment, especially the Guangdong–Hong Kong–Fujian area, which the Nomura Research Institute estimates will grow 9.8 percent annually for the next decade.[22]

What do the Japanese hope to gain from this approach to China? After stating that Japan should overlook China's violations of democratic norms, and that the United States lacks the economic power to play the role of the world's policeman, the former Japanese ambassador to China (1984–1987), Yosuke Nakae, stated, "It is certain that without friendly and cooperative relations between Japan and China there can be no support for peace, stability, or prosperity in Asia."[23] Without a good political relationship with China, Japan cannot hope to win widespread acceptance as a leader elsewhere in Asia, much less preserve its security environment. As a first step, the Japanese hope to resolve the bitter legacy of Sino-Japanese relations through bilateral economic cooperation. As long as China does not threaten its security, Japan appears willing to support the present regime no matter what the other Western countries do. In return, the Chinese government no longer dredges up the wartime reparations issue and otherwise shows a willingness to forget the past.[24]

This approach also serves Japan's broader economic and military security interests. By creating greater economic interdependence between Japan and China, the likelihood of military conflict is reduced and China would be less likely to form a combination against Japan. At the same time, by incorporating the coastal areas of China into an East Asian economic region dominated by Japanese trade, finance, and technology, Japan's own economic and political foundations are broadened. With a stable society producing a GNP eight times as large as that of a backward and domestically troubled China, Japan can remain confident that for the foreseeable future economic interdependence between Japan and China will be asymmetrical, with Japan holding far more cards than China.

These hopes, however, must be tempered by the realization that the Chinese people have not forgotten the past and do not feel comfortable in the role of a follower of Japan in Asia, no matter what agreements are reached with the present Chinese leadership. This situation will likely persist, as Japanese Diet member Shintaro Ishihara indicated when he stated in a 1990 *Playboy* magazine interview that the Rape of Nanking was a fabrication, and important elements in Japan have yet to show sincere contrition to the Chinese for the past.

In addition, the unresolved Chinese reunification problem, as well as China's involvement in other island territorial disputes, has the potential to disrupt Japan's security environment. China reserves the right to use force to protect its sovereign claims over Taiwan, the Paracel Islands, the Spratly Islands, and Senkaku Island (or Tiaoyutai Island). Only in the latter case does this directly conflict with a Japanese claim, but insofar as these unresolved issues give China a reason to build naval capabilities sufficient to disrupt Japan's vital sea-lanes,[25] and could tempt China to use force, Japan's interests are vitally engaged. As in the case of the ROK, however, this will cause

China to be cautious in the use of force because it does not have an interest in provoking Japanese rearmament.

Policy Toward Southeast Asia

Japan evinced a cautious approach to Burma (now Myanmar) after the mass killing of prodemocracy students by the military in the summer of 1988. Japan cut aid but without mentioning the violation of human rights. In February 1990, Japan recognized the State Law and Order Restoration Council (SLORC), and, under prodding from Japanese aid contractors, resumed stalled aid projects worth more than $1 billion. The May 1990 elections resulted in a defeat for the military, which then arrested the leaders of the opposition, among them Aung San Suu Kyi, the still-imprisoned winner of the 1991 Nobel Peace Prize. Japan has continued to give special debt relief packages to the Burmese regime, even though it was known that the regime was somehow financing large-scale purchases of arms.[26]

Japan has been engaged in unprecedented diplomatic activity to gain a peacebrokering role in Indochina, but so far with only limited success. As in the case of Korea, Japan has been disadvantaged by the fact that it is neither a permanent member of the UN Security Council, nor is it able to extend military assistance. Although many in Japan wished to participate in UN peacekeeping operations in Cambodia, Tokyo was long frustrated by the failure to pass legislation authorizing this through the Diet until June 1992. Japan's two most significant achievements have been the 1990 Tokyo meeting of the Cambodian factions (the first significant peace conference held in Japan since 1945), and the chairmanship of the Paris Conference's subcommittee on the rehabilitation of Cambodia.

Nonetheless, Japan has gained economic interests and influence there. Japan now is Vietnam's largest trading partner and is in the process of starting aid projects and oil development activities with Cambodia. Japan also will work with the ASEAN members in rehabilitating and developing Indochina.

Japan has fostered the process of dependent development in ASEAN by directing a significant part of its trade and capital to its members, especially after the yen appreciation and Japan's capital surplus opened new opportunities for Japanese investment. The impact has been large: according to the Japanese ambassador in Bangkok, Hisahiko Okazaki, without foreign investment in Thailand, most of it Japanese, the growth rate would have been 2–3 percent instead of the 12 percent it got in 1989. In 1989 a new Japanese factory opened up every four days, and in 1990 the rate increased to two every five days.[27]

Through a program of coordinated aid, trade, and investment policies initially dubbed The New Asian Industrial Development (AID) Plan, since 1987 the Japanese govenment has been engaged in bilateral policy dialogue with the ASEAN members over foreign investment laws, infrastructure development, local industrial development plans, and technical assistance in order to facilitate Japanese direct investment. The intent is to create what MITI calls a horizontal division of labor in Asia. This effort is being accelerated by sizable bilateral ODA packages as well as multilateral aid mechanisms such as the $2 billion Japan-ASEAN Fund.

In 1987, Prime Minister Noboru Takeshita signed the Fund agreement at ASEAN's Manila Summit and thus won ASEAN's endorsement of Japan's intention to represent Asia at Western summit meetings. This willingness to follow Japanese leadership is strengthening, as indicated by Malaysia's persistent call for a Japanese-led East Asian Economic Grouping (EAEG).

East Asia as a Region

Japan's regional diplomacy is suited to the needs of the region's governments and Japan's own strengths. As the region's largest economy and the world's largest exporter of capital, Japan remains at the core of economic regionalization, but Taiwan, South Korea, and Singapore are also making important contributions. In 1988–1989 those countries committed $8 billion in direct investment to the ASEAN Four (Malaysia, Thailand, Indonesia, and the Philippines), and Hong Kong alone sent $6.6 billion to China.[28] Also, the region's developing countries, including the communist ones, are avowedly developmental and increasingly open to international investment and trade. As these nations cooperatively develop vast underutilized human and natural resources, the long-term growth prospects appear to be the best of any region in the world.

This process of regionalization is now strong enough to have immunized East Asia from the ill effects of the U.S. recession. The Asian Development Bank estimates that in 1991 Asia, excluding Japan, grew 6.2 percent, in contrast to 0.4 percent globally and actual negative growth in the United States. In 1992 the estimate is 6.5 percent for Asia and 2.3 percent globally. This contradicts the notion that when the U.S. economy sneezes, the dependent East Asian economies catch the flu. Japan helps to explain this turnaround performance: for example, in Hong Kong Japanese banks now make 61 percent of all loans issued there, as opposed to only 5 percent for U.S. banks.[29]

Some have attempted to explain East Asia as a region linked by a common cultural identity or tradition. The region is certainly culturally different from the West, but this does not diminish the fact that the region encompasses a very disparate mixture of religions, languages, nationalities, and ways of life, which have been and will remain the seed of violent conflict within the region. The so-called cultural factor will, if anything, have to be overcome if regionalization is to find stronger institutional expression.

A firmer basis for a regional identity under Japanese leadership is the shared set of political problems and interests in the region. Each regional member faces a similar fundamental political dilemma: how to reconcile rapid growth and structural transformation with continued political stability and legitimacy.

The East Asian states,[30] whether communist or capitalist, all share a strong developmental orientation—a conscious organization of state structures to plan and implement accelerated development, with the deliberate neglect of such areas as political representation and the legal protection of individual and group rights. The East Asian capitalist developmental state, as Chalmers Johnson argues, has just this orientation.[31] This emphasis on growth over democratization until recently has been tolerable to the extent that regimes actually delivered on promised growth, but the East Asian states face more complex and mobilized social forces today than they did a generation ago. As Jusuf Wanandi puts it: "The rising middle class is no longer content with physical and material progress alone and demands a higher quality of life, which among other things entails greater political rights, greater participation in deciding the future, and legal guarantees."[32] The challenge facing both authoritarian and reforming communist East Asian regimes is to give a political voice to the new classes and interest groups without disrupting either political stability or continued economic growth. The response to this challenge has ranged from varying degrees of accommodation in the Philippines, Taiwan, Singapore, and South Korea, to military repression in China, Myanmar, and Thailand.

Although careful accommodationist strategies are the most likely to deal successfully with these pressures for liberalization, the end result will not duplicate Western models of democracy and individual rights. Donald Emmerson has noted the domination of civil society by Southeast Asian states and their "bureaucratic-activist profile."[33] The reasons have to do with the timing and sequence of state formation in East Asia. For at least the past hundred years the transition from a traditional agrarian, village-based economy to an industrialized urban economy has been the goal of the modernizing national elites of East Asia. Unlike the Western democratic state, which developed with the rise of an anticlerical, antiauthoritarian middle class in Europe,[34] the sequence of state and societal formation in East Asia was reversed, resulting in a relatively autonomous developmental state. The Asian modernizing elites created new administrative structures not to preserve their respective traditional social structures, but to transcend them. This distinctive pattern of institutionalization has cast state-society relations in a different mold, and today, after the "autonomous," or "strong," or "tutelary" East Asian state has grown firm roots, simple replication of Western politics and political economy is ruled out, although one sees hope for widening participation.

———————————————————— *Japan's Leadership Prospects*

If the generalizations made about security, economic growth, and political development in the East Asian region are correct, then Japan may have better prospects for leadership than are commonly supposed. In the area of military security, Japan has serious barriers to expanding its role beyond its own local defense. Article 9 of the postwar constitution has been interpreted by the government to mean that Japan cannot participate in conventional security alliances or UN-sponsored collective security actions. Japan is not a permanent member of the UN Security Council, and so it lacks the diplomatic access to international security issues enjoyed by China, Russia, the United States, Britain, and France. Domestic opinion is against change in the constitution, and Japan's political leadership structure is ill suited to the management of international security crises, as evidenced by Japan's halting responses to the two latest Gulf crises.[35]

But the emphasis within the region is on resolving conflicts and broadening the concept of security to include political stability and economic security. Here Japan has developed a concept of "comprehensive security" that is relevant to the region's post–Cold War environment. We may expect Japan's economic power to influence regional stability by such means as the funding of peace settlements and the promotion of the shared regional interest in economic cooperation, with residual attention paid to increasing conventional military capabilities.

This broader approach is more relevant now that a Soviet or Chinese threat of attack or subversion is gone. The issue of maritime security is still important, but the firm commitment of the United States to the freedom of the seas—a commitment obviously in their own self-interest—resolves this issue. As the United States remains preoccupied with its military role, the region is freed to focus on developmental issues, which is precisely where Japan is building its leadership role. This U.S. commitment, rather than constraining Japan, may be just as significant as a liberating factor.

In the area of economic development, Japan aims to turn the region into an interdependent production zone. Japan has already incorporated Taiwan and Korea,[36] is finishing the job in the ASEAN countries, and is now turning to China and Indochina. In the process, Japan helps to meet the developing countries' need for capital, technology, and market access to Japan and the rest of the world. And as the United States moves in a more protectionist direction, even as a North American Free Trade Agreement and a stronger EC take shape, the importance of Japan to the region is leveraged upward (see Figures 5.2 and 5.3).

The related issue of Japan's dependence on energy sources and markets outside the region is a key constraint, and with roughly 70 percent dependence on Middle Eastern oil there is no prospect for autarkic policies. But the

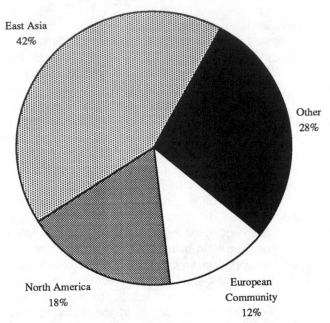

Figure 5.2   Origin of East Asian Imports, 1990 (percentage of total)
Source: Ippei Yamazawa, "Current Patterns of the Asia Pacific Trades," PECC Fifth
Trade Policy Forum, Kuala Lumpur, August 18–21, 1991.

Japanese have benefited from the fact that, by 1980, 80 percent of oil production had passed from multinational ownership into the hands of producer
governments, and using ODA and investment deals, by that year Japan secured 45 percent of its oil needs through direct deals with them.[37] With further
such efforts, oil stockpiling, and diversification of energy by sources and type
(as of 1987, 31 percent of Japan's generated electricity was nuclear fueled),
Japan has reduced its vulnerability to temporary oil supply interruptions.

In terms of trade orientation, Japan now depends less on the United
States for imports than on East Asia (23 percent versus 28 percent in 1989),
and in 1991 the Japan Foreign Trade Council estimated that Japan's exports
to the region exceeded those to the United States for the first time. Meanwhile, the United States has become more dependent on Japan for capital and
key technologies, as well as for the absorption of more U.S. exports. Nonetheless, Japan and the region as a whole still rely on access to the United
States and the European Community (see Figure 5.4.).

Japan is well suited to play the leadership role it desires in the region.
First, it can generate capital surpluses, which can then be channeled by the
Japanese government and corporations to meet regional needs such as infra-
structure, private investment, and technical assistance. Second, it can supply

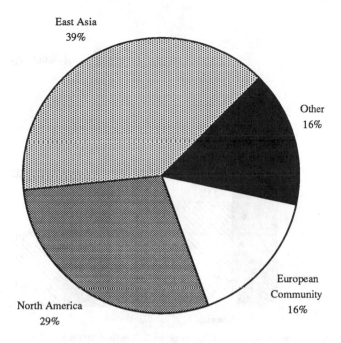

Figure 5.3 Destination of East Asian Exports, 1990 (percentage of total)
Source: Ippei Yamazawa, "Current Patterns of the Asia Pacific Trades," PECC Fifth
Trade Policy Forum, Kuala Lumpur, August 18–21, 1991.

key technologies needed by the region for industrial upgrading. Third, the
global reach of its corporate groupings means that affiliation with them gives
access to the global reach of their operations. Fourth, the liberalization of the
Japanese market and the growth of consumerism in Japan promise to absorb
more Asian exports.

As for Japan's political appeal, it has created a model of political
economy that may be more relevant to the region than Western models. In
their origins and logic, Japanese institutions bear structural similarities to
those of its East Asian neighbors, whereas their performance with respect to
growth and political stability is worthy of study and emulation. In a recent
speech inaugurating the new Centre for Japanese Studies in Kuala Lumpur,
Saburo Okita agreed with Chalmers Johnson's analysis of the East Asian
capitalist developmental state. Although Okita saw a need for Japan to reform
itself, he also stated that "the traditional methods have been effective and
should be preserved," whereas "for many other developing economies the
'catching up' strategy may still be relevant." Besides being a model, Okita
put Japan's contribution to Asia as follows: "I think that Japan's role in the
region is to contribute to their economic development by combining the three
elements of trade, investment, and ODA."[38]

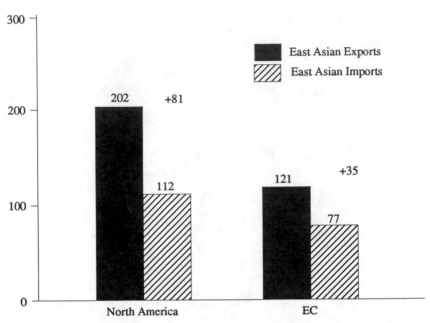

Figure 5.4   East Asian Trade Balance with North America and the EC, 1990.
Source: Ippei Yamazawa, "Current Patterns of the Asia Pacific Trades," PECC Fifth
Trade Policy Forum, Kuala Lumpur, August 18–21, 1991.

With regard to political assets, Japan's failing is that its political system
and political culture seem to produce relatively few charismatic individual
leaders. But Japan exhibits stability, unparalleled economic performance, and
continuity of purpose. As a political economy, Japan provides a model for the
region, and may have the combination of resources and the institutional capacity to plan and implement the construction of a regional division of labor.

The general political message that Japan is sending the region may be
more welcomed by its governments than that of, say, the United States, which
has stressed the liberal model of political economy, democracy, and human
rights. In contrast, the message given by Japan is that it would sympathize
with the political fragility of these regimes, and would continue to help them
plan their economic development so long as they had friendly, progrowth
relations with Japan. Thus, Japan promises resources to enhance the capacity
of Asian states, and will avoid adding to the legitimacy crises of regional
members by actively promoting democratization and human rights.

At the same time, the United States has been unable to address the
region's problems and aspirations, much less its own. One critique of U.S.
policy appearing in the *Bangkok Post* made the following assessment: "Does
this U.S. Administration have a strong policy direction in Asia? Or for that

matter, a real interest in the region at all? The answers it would seem are no, and maybe." Noting that the United States criticizes Japan for "checkbook diplomacy," it also points out that "Washington has come to depend on Japan fulfilling just this role, with the Gulf War and Cambodia being two prominent examples."[39] President Bush's last-minute cancellation of his long-awaited Asian trip in November 1991, followed by the ill-conceived 1992 presidential trade mission, cannot fail to have a disquieting effect in the region.

Thus, Japan has stepped into a de facto leadership role, and has the will and capacity to articulate a vision of the region's future that appeals to the member states. As memories of Japan's wartime behavior fade or become irrelevant to contemporary issues, Japan is well situated to become the region's acknowledged leader.

In this context the appeal by Prime Minister Mahatir of Malaysia for Japan to lead the so-called East Asian Economic Grouping is striking both because it marked a turnaround in Mahatir's attitude toward Japan (in 1981 he said he didn't want or need Japanese aid because it cost him money), and because it has earned an unexpected degree of support in the region. The impetus was the poor outlook for the Uruguay Round, the growing global scarcity of capital, and the formation of NAFTA. The core of this proposal is an inward-looking policy dialogue about coordinated industrial and trade development in the region. Dr. Noordin Sopiee, director of the Institute for Strategic and International Studies in Kuala Lumpur and a key foreign policy adviser to Prime Minister Mahatir, explained the character of the EAEG's policy coordination in part by referring to a Japanese policy study that proposed a scheme for coordinating East Asian economic development featuring a bureaucratic planning apparatus, called the "Asian Brain."[40]

The proposal sounds absurd except for the fact that important people in Japan and Malaysia take it seriously. The idea is to allocate roles in the regional division of labor according to each economy's emerging comparative advantage. The planning would be managed from Tokyo, which would use its trade, direct investment, and ODA in ways that would harmonize the region's industrial structure and eliminate wasteful overcompetition and trade frictions. This may seem preposterous to the U.S. public, who are predisposed to reject the values and methods of the developmental state, but to the East Asian states, which already recognize Japan's capabilities and accept without question the value of state-sponsored developmentalism, the attraction of joining what Saburo Okita has called a "flying geese" formation of East Asian economies led by Japan may be hard to resist, and certainly might be better discussed in a multilateral setting than in separate bilateral policy dialogues between Tokyo and each regional member.[41]

Protests from the United States blunted Mahatir's call, but, significantly, the United States has not entirely killed the idea. As of now the EAEG proposal has been transformed into an informal caucus within the APEC group, but the caucus may yet become more significant than APEC unless the

United States can find some way of making itself more relevant to the region.

An economic planning capacity is the basis for linking trade, investment, and ODA to strengthen the regional division of labor. A Japanese foreign ministry official discussing the Asian economies alluded to this capacity when he stated, "Laissez faire can't be recommended. . . . Careful utilization of market forces is always the ideal."[42]

Let me be clear that Japan's planning capacity is neither centrally directed nor comprehensively orchestrated by an individual mastermind or monolithic state. What I am suggesting is that key elements of Japan's bureaucracy, the ruling Liberal Democratic Party, and large private sector financial and industrial interests consult in the policymaking process to define a common agenda. This is in line with Peter Katzenstein's approach to identifying the roots of the foreign economic policies of the advanced industrial states. The focus is on the way societal interest groups form ruling coalitions with political structures (i.e., parties and bureaucrats). These coalitions are then able to define basic economic strategies and orientations, and they "find their institutional expression in distinct policy networks which link the public and the private sector in the implementation of foreign economic policy."[43]

The study of how the ruling coalition in Japan "finds its institutional expression" issue area–by–issue area has given rise to the literature on policy *zoku* in Japan.[44] Studied more from a macropolitical perspective, Ellis Krauss and Michio Muramatsu speak of "patterned pluralism."[45] Taking a more structural approach, T. J. Pempel explains that "a conservative network of technologically advanced industry, finance, and the state bureaucracy has been able to exploit the political exclusion of the left and organized labor to generate a foreign economic policy combining resistance to unwanted international stimuli and creative domestic resource extraction."[46]

Strategy or planning in this context does not refer to an individual mastermind or a secret conspiracy, but to an ongoing process of quiet consultation over basic policy between public and private actors, and in Japan this distinction often becomes blurred, although if I had to generalize I would say that on balance, policy initiative comes from the bureaucracy in line with Japan's statist traditions. Once consensus is reached, a rough division of labor can be constructed and implementation can start on a case-by-case basis with involvement by all major actors.

This does not mean that implementation is smooth, or that bureaucratic conflict does not occur, or that business and government see eye to eye. Study of these conflicts may be popular today, but they do not explain the basic structure of the policy process or the strategic direction of policy. A structural approach implies that what Haruhiro Fukui has called Japan's "conservative coalition"[47] determines the basic choice of Japanese strategy, and the coordination of consensus formation and implementation by the bureaucracy, messy as it usually is, is what passes for planning. The point, however, is that Japan is capable of a higher degree of public-private collaboration and purposeful resource mobilization than, say, the United States. This view is roughly consistent with the overriding features of Japanese policy-making found by Daniel Okimoto—that is, the importance of policy networks and the "practices of government-business consensus, government-led coordination, and selective intervention."[48]

———————————————————— *Conclusion*

Japan is taking up the challenge of leadership with quiet vigor and steady purpose. The East Asian governments are increasingly receptive to Japan's leadership, and there is no doubt that some positively welcome it. One significance of Japan's emerging leadership role in East Asia may be that the region is developing a very different kind of political economy premised not on free competition, but on official coordination of industrial policy and regional economic structure.

Another implication is that the new Japan-centered dynamic may find a firm institutionalized expression. The logic of an institutionalized East Asian grouping rests not just on economic interdependence, for the region as a whole is still economically dependent on access to other regions, but also on political factors and a perception that the United States is becoming irrelevant to regional aspirations.

A third point is that even though Japan may make only modest progress toward constitutional revision and military rearmament, it may nonetheless play a key role in regional security affairs. Its ability to deploy economic resources in ways that reshape the structure of interests in the region can affect prospects for peace and political stability.

Finally, the direction of Japanese initiative highlights the need for U.S. attention to Japan and East Asia. The United States will not effectively advance its global interest in economic and political liberalization in the region without Japan's support, and so efforts in this direction are needed. Furthermore, to the extent that Japan's new style of close economic coordination with others in the region is formalized, the United States may find itself disadvantaged in finding the new trade and investment opportunities needed to rectify a huge structural trade imbalance with the region.

———————————————————— *Notes*

1. Kenneth Waltz, *The Theory of International Politics*, Reading, Mass.: Addison-Wesley, 1979.

2. Stephen Krasner and Daniel Okimoto, "Japan's Evolving Trade Posture," in Akira Iriye and Warren I. Cohen, eds., *The United States and Japan in the Postwar World*, Lexington: University of Kentucky Press, 1989, pp. 117–143.

3. David Arase, "Pacific Economic Cooperation: Problems and Prospects," *The Pacific Review*, vol. 1, no. 2 (Summer 1988), pp. 128–144.

4. Mineo Nakajima, "Japanese Policies Toward the Soviet Union and China," in Gaston Sigur and Young C. Kim, eds., *Japanese and U.S. Policy in Asia*, New York: Praeger, 1982, pp. 81–96.

5. Richard Solomon and Masataka Kosaka, eds., *The Soviet Far East Military Buildup: Nuclear Dilemmas and Asian Security*, Dover, Mass.: Auburn House, 1986. See also Bruce Cumings, "The Conflict on the Korean Peninsula," in Yoshikazu Sakamoto, ed., *Asia, Militarization, and Regional Conflict*, Tokyo: United Nations University, 1988, pp. 103–121.

6. Mikhail Titarenko, "The Situation in the APR and Soviet–South Korean Relations," *Far Eastern Affairs*, no. 5 (1990), pp. 3–16.

7. Robert A. Scalapino, *Major Power Relations in Northeast Asia*, New York: Asia Society, 1987.

8. A 1985 RAND report estimated that by 1994 the North-South military balance would shift decisively in the South's favor, but this was before it was suspected that the North would have nuclear weapons by that time. *FBIS East Asia, Daily Report Supplement*, April 16, 1991.

9. *New York Times*, International Edition, February 16, 1990, p. A7.

10. *The Military Balance, 1990–1991*, London: International Institute for Strategic Studies, 1990.

11. "Soviet Military Planning to Cut Fleet by 20% to 25%," *Los Angeles Times*, July 26, 1991, p. A12.

12. Mikhail Kapitsa, "Yalta System and After: Stability and Change in Northeast Asia," *The Korean Journal of International Studies*, vol. 21, no. 4 (Winter 1990).

13. Shiro Saito, *Japan at the Summit: Japan's Role in the Western Alliance and Asian Pacific Cooperation*, London: Routledge, 1990.

14. *FBIS Daily Report, East Asia*, May 31, 1991, p. 3.

15. Takakazu Kuriyama, *New Directions for Japanese Foreign Policy in the Changing World of the 1990s*, Tokyo: Ministry of Foreign Affairs, May 1990.

16. The following are selected East Asian countries and the percentage of total bilateral official development assistance received from Japan in 1987–1988: Indonesia, 63 percent; Malaysia, 79 percent; Mongolia, 84 percent; Myanmar, 72 percent; Philippines, 54 percent; and Thailand, 69 percent. Ministry of Foreign Affairs, *Japan's ODA: 1989 Annual Report*, Tokyo: Association for Promotion of International Cooperation, 1990.

17. Ibid., p. 140.

18. David Arase, "Japanese Policy Toward the Two Koreas," in Robert H. Puckett, ed., *The U.S. and Northeast Asia*, New York: Nelson-Hall, 1992.

19. Shigemura Toshimitsu, "Nicchō-Chōso o Mimamoru Washinton no Embo" [Washington's long-range perspective of Japan-DPRK and Soviet-DPRK relations], *Chūō Kōron*, December 1990, p. 95.

20. *FBIS Daily Report, East Asia*, January 9, 1991, p. 19.

21. *Asahi Shimbun*, June 6, 1989, evening edition, cited in Motofumi Asai, "Japan's China Policy: A Pattern of Consistency," in George Hicks, ed., *The Broken Mirror: China After Tiananmen*, Chicago: St. James Press, 1990, p. 297.

22. David Arase, "Japanese Foreign Policy and Asian Democratization," in Edward Friedman, ed., *Democratization: Lessons from the East Asian Experience*, forthcoming.

23. Nakae Yosuke, "Nicchū 20-nen no Rikaido o Tou" [Questioning the level of understanding after 20 years of Sino-Japanese relations], *This Is Yomiuri*, July 1991.

24. China renounced its claim to war reparations from Japan in return for quick

normalization in 1972 and an informal Japanese pledge of positive economic cooperation.

25. "China's Plans To Expand Naval Fleet," *Washington Post*, February 19, 1989, p. A43.

26. *Far Eastern Economic Review*, July 11 1991, pp. 39–41.

27. *Los Angeles Times*, February 17, 1991, p. D 1.

28. *World Economic Survey, 1991*, New York: United Nations, 1991, p. 283.

29. *Los Angeles Times*, December 23, 1991, p. D3.

30. "The state is made up of, and limited to, those individuals who are endowed with society-wide decisionmaking powers." Eric A. Nordlinger, "Taking the State Seriously," in Samuel P. Huntington and Myron Weiner, eds., *Understanding Political Development*, Boston: Little, Brown, 1987, p. 362.

31. Chalmers Johnson, "Political Institutions and Economic Performance: The Government-Business Relationship in Japan, South Korea, and Taiwan," in Frederic C. Deyo, ed., *The Political Economy of the New Asian Industrialism*, Ithaca, N.Y.: Cornell University Press, 1987, pp. 136–164.

32. Jusuf Wanandi, "Sociopolitical Development and Institution Building in Indonesia," in Robert A. Scalapino et al., eds., *Asian Political Institutionalization*, Berkeley: Institute for East Asian Studies, University of California, 1986, p. 186.

33. Donald K. Emmerson, "Rediscovering the State: Political Institutionalization in Southeast Asia," in Scalapino, et al., *Asian Political Institutionalization*, pp. 138–156.

34. Maurice Duverger, *Modern Democracies: Economic Power Versus Political Power*, New York: Holt, Rinehart and Winston, 1974.

35. David Arase, "Japan in Post–Cold War Northeast Asia," paper presented at the workshop on Major Asian Powers and the Security of Southeast Asia: The Post–Cold War International Order, Kuching, Sarawak, September 4–8, 1991.

36. Bruce Cumings, "The Origins and Development of the Northeast Asian Political Economy: Industrial Sectors, Product Cycles, and Political Consequences," *International Organization*, vol. 38 (Winter 1984), pp. 1–40.

37. Fariborz Ghadar, "U.S.-Japanese Petroleum Investment Strategies: Cooperation or Conflict," in Charles K. Ebinger and Ronald A. Morse, eds., *U.S.-Japanese Energy Relations: Cooperation and Competition*, Boulder, Colo.: Westview, 1984.

38. Saburo Okita, "Japan's Strategies for and Future Commitment to the Changing World," *Japan Lecture Series*, Malaysia: Institute for Strageic and International Studies, 1991.

39. *FBIS Daily Report, East Asia*, November 19, 1991, p. 1.

40. "The Thrust for Greater Economic Ties," *The New Straits Times* (Kuala Lumpur), August 18, 1991.

41. Saburo Okita, "Pacific Development and Its Implications for the World Economy," in James W. Morely, ed., *The Pacific Basin: New Challenges for the United States*, New York: The Academy of Political Science, 1986, pp. 26–28.

42. *Wall Street Journal*, August 20, 1990, p. 1.

43. Peter J. Katzenstein, "Introduction: Domestic and International Forces and Strategies of Foreign Economic Policy," in Peter J. Katzenstein, ed., *Between Power and Plenty: Foreign Economic Policies of Advanced Industrial States*, Madison: University of Wisconsin, 1978, p. 19.

44. Takashi Inoguchi and Tomoaki Iwai, *'Zoku' Giin no Kenkyū* [Research into policy tribe Dietmen], Tokyo: Nihon Keizai Shimbunsha, 1987; Seizaburo Sato and Tetsuhisa Matsuzaki, *Jiminto Seikei* [The LDP in power], Tokyo: Chūō Kōronsha, 1986.

45. Michio Muramatsu and Ellis Krauss, "The Conservative Policy Line and the

Development of Patterned Pluralism," in Yasukichi Yasuba and Kozo Yamamura, eds., *The Political Economy of Japan, vol. 1: The Domestic Transformation*, Stanford, Calif.: Stanford University Press, 1987, pp. 518–526.

46. T. J. Pempel, "Japanese Foreign Economic Policy: The Domestic Bases for International Behavior," in Katzenstein, *Between Power and Plenty*, pp. 139–190.

47. Haruhiro Fukui, "Introduction," in T. J. Pempel, ed., *Policy and Politics in Japan*, Philadelphia: Temple University Press, 1982.

48. Daniel I. Okimoto, *Between MITI and the Market: Japanese Industrial Policy for High Technology*, Stanford, Calif.: Stanford University Press, 1989, p. 175.

Chapter 6

Soviet-Japanese Relations Under Perestroika: The Territorial Dispute and Its Impact
Alexei V. Zagorsky

Configuration of Soviet-Japanese Relations

Since the restoration of Soviet-Japanese diplomatic relations in 1956, there have been three major issues shaping their bilateral relations, with their respective importance changing from period to period. These issues are economic cooperation, security problems, and the territorial dispute over the southern Kuril Islands (or *Hoppō Ryōdo*—the "Northern Territories"—as the Japanese call them). This does not mean to imply that there were no other problems in Soviet-Japanese relations. It means that these were the major issues during the Cold War period and continue to affect the Soviet/Russian-Japanese relations during the perestroika period that began in 1985.

The economic dimension gained importance in the early 1960s, with the Japanese participation in Siberian development, and Japanese export of industrial machinery and capital and import of Soviet raw resources. The issue of economic cooperation is discussed by Akaha in Chapter 7. Suffice it to note here that the 1960s and the 1970s saw bilateral economic cooperation grow, largely as a result of Japanese participation in Siberian economic development, during the period of East-West détente. The most visible growth in trade came in 1960–1976, when the trade volume grew from $147 million to $3,419 million,[1] and again in 1978–1981, when the two-way trade grew from $3.9 billion to $5.3 billion.[2]

Security considerations have been of major importance since the early postwar period. U.S. and Japanese security concerns toward the Soviet Union have largely defined the essence and character of the U.S.-Japan security treaty and U.S. security strategy in Asia Pacific. The territorial dispute around the four islands of Iturup (Etorofu in Japanese), Kunashir (Kunashiri), Shikotan, and the Habomai group off the northeast coast of Hokkaido began with the Soviet occupation of the Kuril chain including these islands in the waning days of World War II and the San Francisco peace conference of 1951. The Japanese delegation to the peace conference insisted on excluding those four islands from the Kuril Islands chain to be abandoned by Japan as a condition of the peace settlement with the Allied powers. Japan has reserved its claims over the Soviet-occupied islands for the entire postwar period.

Although the Japanese territorial claims have existed during the entire postwar period and were raised to the highest level by Prime Minister Kakuei Tanaka during his visit to Moscow in 1973, the rigid Soviet position, discouraging any discussion of the problem and concentrating predominantly on economic matters, determined the shape of bilateral relations during the Cold War years. By the late 1970s, the situation had changed drastically due to structural changes in the Japanese economy following the oil shock of 1973–1974. Japan's growth had slowed and its resource import pressure relaxed. Consequently, the complementarity between the Soviet and Japanese economies had declined.

The transformation of Japan's security environment also altered the configuration of major issues in Soviet-Japanese relations in the 1970s and early 1980s. Several factors increased Japanese concerns over the "Soviet threat." First, beginning in the late 1960s the Soviet Union implemented the Gorshkov naval doctrine, aimed at achieving a Soviet-U.S. parity in the Pacific naval balance and encircling China. With major Soviet naval bases located in the Sea of Japan and the Soviet navy operating in major international sealanes in Southeast Asia, Japan's feeling of increased threat was certainly justified. Second, the Soviet ground force buildup in the Far East, which had begun after the Soviet-Chinese border clashes in 1969, intensified after the Sino-Japanese and U.S.-China rapprochement in the 1970s. Third, the Soviet Union's increased involvement in developing nations' affairs culminated in the Afghanistan invasion in 1979. Fourth, the Soviet Union deployed troops on the Iturup and Shikotan islands in retaliation against the Sino-Japanese Peace and Friendship Treaty of 1978. In addition, Japan's declaration as "a member of the Western camp," formulated in a period of deteriorating détente politics, also did much to accentuate Japan's critical view of the Soviet security policy. Thus, with the decreased importance of economic interests, security problems—formulated as the "Soviet threat"—became the top priority in Japan's policy toward the Soviet Union in the late 1970s and especially in the early 1980s.

The territorial dispute, although present throughout the postwar period, was not always on the top of the list of practical Japanese political aims vis-à-vis the Soviet Union. In fact, the issue became a focal point in Japanese policy only during the period of Soviet perestroika. The evasive Soviet promise to discuss "issues remaining unsettled since World War II" in the 1973 Tanaka-Brezhnev communiqué and the subsequent stubborn Soviet refusal to understand the Northern Territories issue as an outstanding problem between the two countries certainly had deprived Japan of any reasonable hope of progress on this issue. Although Japanese representatives stressed the significance of the territorial dispute at every meeting with the Soviets, the emphasis appeared to be largely symbolic. It was designed to preserve the unsettled status of the problem rather than to institute a practical attempt at substantive discussions.

The only exception to the Japanese approach of a rather symbolic nature was Tokyo's vehement reaction to the various moves on the part of Moscow in the second half of the 1970s to solidify the Soviet presence on the disputed islands. A political confrontation emerged in 1976–1977, when the Soviet Union and Japan established two-hundred-mile fishery zones including the waters off the disputed islands.[3] In the early 1980s the fishery issue around the area took on a disturbing meaning as some fishermen in Hokkaido began to support the abandonment of the Japanese territorial claims over the Northern Territories in favor of a special fishing regime in the area that would grant them special fishing rights.[4] Another sharp Japanese reaction was prompted by the Soviet deployment of troops on Kunashir and Shikotan in 1978 in retaliation against the Sino-Japanese Peace and Friendship Treaty, which was assessed in Moscow to be anti-Soviet due to its "antihegemony" clause.

From the late 1970s to the first half of the 1980s, however, the territorial issue generally looked like an additional irritating factor in Soviet-Japanese relations, rather than a focus of genuine and practical efforts at conflict resolution. The situation had radically changed with Mikhail Gorbachev's taking power in Moscow in 1985 and the proclamation of the principles of "new political thinking" in 1986.

_____ *Japanese View of the Gorbachev Administration*

Unlike Western Europe and the United States, Japan was never greatly impressed by the Gorbachev administration. The initial reaction was one of skepticism and caution. For example, according to the 1986 edition of *Asian Security*, edited by the influential Japanese Research Institute for Peace and Security, "An administration with a new image has emerged, but whether Gorbachev will try to make radical changes in the Soviet economic system or will merely attempt to make it more efficient remains to be seen."[5] The first notable public praise for the perestroika policy by a senior Japanese politician appeared only in April 1990, when Prime Minister Toshiki Kaifu, in an interview with the Soviet newspaper *Komsomolskaya Pravda*, said that he was "pinning great hopes on the policy of perestroika [which served] the cause of stability and peace on the planet."[6]

Japan experienced no "Gorbamania," as was witnessed in Europe and the United States, either in academic circles or in public opinion. Academic publications on the Soviet Union were consistent in their skeptical view of Soviet reforms.[7] Even liberal researchers tended to show a cautious view, stressing Gorbachev's origins in the pragmatic Kosygin faction of the Communist Party of the Soviet Union (CPSU).[8] Public opinion in Japan also continued to show its traditional coolness toward the Soviet Union. For the whole perestroika period, the index of friendly feelings toward the Soviet Union had a very slight increase, from 8.6 percent in June 1985 to 10.7 percent in October 1989. The proportion of those having unfriendly feelings remained at or more than 80 percent, 83.7 percent in 1985 and 81.1 percent in 1989. The Japanese attitude was to be explained by a combination of various factors. First, the Japanese Foreign Ministry officials, especially those charged with Soviet affairs, appeared to be some of the most hardline anticommunists in the Japanese government. Second, the Japanese animosity toward their northern neighbors was long-standing. Third, the anti-Soviet sentiment was a natural reaction to the Soviet declaration of war on Japan after the dropping of an atomic bomb on Hiroshima. The Soviet action was seen by the Japanese as a "stab in the back" when the Soviet-Japanese neutrality pact was still in force. Fourth, the Soviet Union was a communist country very different from Japan. Fifth, the Japanese resented the continuous and, in their eyes, illegal Soviet occupation of the northern islands and unwillingness to return them to Japan. Sixth, the Japanese perceived that the Soviet Union posed a military threat, and this view had been aggravated by the stationing of Soviet military garrisons on the disputed territories.[9] The list could be extended to include Japanese feelings about the fate of wartime prisoners detained in Siberia after Japan had surrendered, with tens of thousands dying there. Or we could add to the list the continuing fishing dispute in Soviet-Japanese relations and Soviet-imposed limits on Japanese catches in traditional fishery areas within the Soviet two-hundred-mile fishery zone (now exclusive economic zone) and even beyond it. But the most important issue was the unsettled territorial dispute. For more than forty years no Japanese nationals had lived on these islands, but the territories' value to Japan might be compared with that of Okinawa, which was returned to Japan from U.S. control in 1972. The area of the islands under Soviet-Japanese dispute is 4,909 square kilometers, more than twice the area of Okinawa and the Ogasawara islands combined (2,330.5 square kilometers).

The Northern Territories issue grew dramatically in importance with the introduction by Prime Minister Yasuhiro Nakasone in the early 1980s of the notion of "final settlement of postwar accounts" (*sengo sōkessan*). The territorial dispute with the Soviet Union was the last major problem of Japanese policy remaining unsettled since the end of the war, and it strongly affected the Japanese desire for a great power status. Despite the Japanese economic success, their expanding economic role in world affairs, and their increasingly active involvement in world politics, the defeat in World War II remained a psychological legacy to many Japanese. In this context, the "final settlement of postwar accounts" was a slogan designed to overcome the mistreatment of the vanquished. Thus, in the 1980s the problem of the Northern Territories was placed at the top of the list of foreign policy priorities for Tokyo.

For Soviet-Japanese relations in the period of the Gorbachev administration, the Soviet calls for improved bilateral relations and enunciation of "new political thinking" were to be assessed, first of all, on the basis of a new Soviet stand on the territorial dispute. The Japanese saw new possibilities for a favorable territorial solution both in Gorbachev's policy to expand Soviet relations with the West and in the increasing Soviet demand for Western economic assistance. The Japanese approach to the Soviet Union crystallized through the 1980s and was expressed thus:

> One of the goals of the Soviet Asian policy is normalizing relations with Japan, as Japan is the most appropriate nation to provide the Soviet Union with capital and technological know-how desperately needed to improve the economic situation in the Soviet Far Eastern and other provinces. Meanwhile, the Soviet Union should understand that there is a long-term problem in the way of normalization of relations with Japan; we need certain concessions on the problem of the Northern Territories. Until there is progress on the Northern Territories problem, the Soviet Union can not expect to normalize its relations with Japan.[10]

The possibility of paying greater attention to the territorial dispute emerged in the late 1980s against the backdrop of enhanced Japanese confidence in its national security. Although the level of Soviet military buildup and the modernization of Soviet armament in the Far East were persistent sources of concern to Japanese policymakers, the general view of the security situation had become more sanguine. First, thanks to the "balance of military power including nuclear mutual deterrence and to efforts to stabilize international relations in general," Japanese security analysts had seen a diminution of "the possibility of an overall military collision between East and West or large military conflict leading to such a collision." Second, although they did not rule out the possibility of a "limited military conflict," they expected "the balanced relations between the great powers and the existence of the Japanese-American security system will continue to play an important role in maintaining stability of international relations and in preventing a real aggression against our nation."[11] When Gorbachev's speeches at Vladivostok and Krasnoyarsk in 1986 and 1988, respectively, put a special stress on Soviet proposals for Asia Pacific arms control, the proposals were ignored by the United States and Japan. If Japan had emphasized security issues in its relations with the Soviet Union, it might have led to a genuine Japanese involvement in Soviet-initiated discussions in this area, although such a development would likely have complicated U.S.-Japan security relations. These developments, combined with the efforts to find an opening in the Northern Territories issue, resulted in the elimination of the notion of a "Soviet threat" from the 1990 and 1991 editions of Japan's *White Paper on Defense*.

Thus, if the 1960s and the first half of the 1970s could be assessed as a period of economic cooperation in Soviet-Japanese relations, the late 1970s to the first half of the 1980s saw a growing political alienation between the two nations against the backdrop of vanishing détente and growing concerns over security problems. And the years after 1985–1986 may be seen as a period dominated by the search for a solution to the territorial dispute.

The Northern Territories as a Legal Case

Japanese claims over the Northern Territories are based on the notion that the islands are an "integral part of Japanese territory." The Japanese argue that throughout the whole history of international relations in the Far East, the islands never formally belonged to any nation but Japan. They maintain that although Russia initially claimed the territories at the first Russian-Japanese talks on the delimitation of borders during the negotiations for a treaty of commerce in Nagasaki and Shimoda in 1854–1855, the trade treaty stipulated the northern border of Japanese territory as "the Iturup Island and the port of Aniwa at the southern end of the Sakhalin Island."[12]

In fact, however, the territorial dispute represents a highly complicated case with no clear-cut legal guidelines for an indisputable settlement. The situation prevailing before World War II certainly favors the Japanese view. Changes in the Russian-Japanese border in 1875 and 1905 never affected Japan's sovereign rights over the four islands. The Soviet government did not present any territorial claims to the Japanese government when the two sides established diplomatic relations in 1925. Moreover, the Soviet Union stated that it bore no political responsibility for the signing of the Portsmouth peace treaty that terminated the Russian-Japanese war of 1904–1905 and recognized all of the Kuril archipelago and Southern Sakhalin as Japanese territory.[13]

Origins of the Soviet claims to territories under Japanese rule can be traced only to the Yalta Conference among Stalin, Roosevelt, and Churchill in 1945. The final secret agreement among the Allied powers specified conditions under which the Soviet Union was to enter into the war against Japan. The terms included the return to the Soviet Union of the southern part of Sakhalin and all the islands adjacent to it, as well as the transfer of the Kuril Islands to the Soviet Union.[14] This secret agreement gave birth to the subsequent legal collision between Moscow and Tokyo. A previous international agreement describing guidelines for postwar settlement with Japan had provided that

> Japan shall be stripped of all islands in the Pacific which she has seized and occupied since the beginning of the First World War in 1914, and that all the territories Japan has stolen from the Chinese, such as Manchuria, Formosa, and the Pescadores, shall be restored to the Republic of China. Japan will also be expelled from all other territories which she has taken by violence and greed.[15]

Another relevant international document is the Atlantic Charter, signed in August 1941 by the United States and the United Kingdom and joined by the Soviet Union in September. The parties to the charter stated that they "seek no aggrandizement, territorial or other," and "desire to see no territorial changes that do not accord with freely expressed wishes of the people concerned." The same pledge was reproduced in the United Nations Declaration of January 1, 1942, and in the Cairo Declaration.

Taking these documents into account, it is clear that even at Yalta the three big powers regarded southern Sakhalin and the Kuril archipelago as two cases different in nature. The logic of the Cairo Declaration in promising restitution of the Chinese rights on Formosa (Taiwan) and the Pescadores, which had been acquired by Japan as a result of the Sino-Japanese War at the end of the nineteenth century, applies to the Soviet claims to southern Sakhalin. Russia lost these territories in the Russian-Japanese War of 1904–1905. Both cases are to be seen as those of "territories taken by violence." But the case of the Kuril Islands is fundamentally different. Japan acquired them peacefully, according to the 1875 treaty in which the Russian claims to southern Sakhalin were recognized by Japan in exchange for Japanese sovereignty over the Kuril Islands. Under no condition should this deal be considered an act of "violence and greed." The U.S. and British consent to the Soviet claims on the Kuril Islands at Yalta was a side payment for Soviet involvement in the war against Japan, differing little in nature from the earlier Soviet-German pact of 1938, which gave Nazi Germany a free hand in Poland in exchange for the Soviet occupation of the Baltic states, eastern Poland, and Bessarabia. The Kuril Islands provision in the Yalta agreement was a clear violation of the Atlantic Charter, the United Nations Declaration, and the Cairo Declaration, and was designed to legalize Stalin's policy of recovering former possessions of the Russian empire.

The circumstances of the Soviet Union entering the war and occupying the Kuril Islands also gave rise to the legal clash between the Soviet Union and Japan. The Yalta agreement, which provided that the Soviet Union would join the war against Japan within two or three months after Germany surrendered, ignored the fact that the Soviet-Japanese neutrality pact signed in April 1941 was valid until April 1946. The only right the Soviet Union had under these conditions was to declare unilaterally that it did not intend to resume the pact after its expiration in 1946, but the Soviet Union began operations against Japan on August 9, 1945, one day after declaring its intention to terminate the pact. Moreover, Soviet operations in the Kuril Islands continued even after Japan had surrendered. The four disputed islands were occupied on September 20; Japan had signed the act of capitulation on September 2.

Even from this brief analysis, it is obvious that the Yalta agreement from the beginning was a violation of international law accepted at that time and may be a very doubtful basis for today's discussion. If codification of the postwar settlement had stopped at this position, it could have been possible to argue that the Soviet Union had no legitimate claims to the four islands nor to the whole Kuril chain. But the situation evolved and the dispute became much more complicated with subsequent developments.

First, the Potsdam Declaration, accepted by Japan as the terms of capitulation, gave the Allied powers a full right to strip Japan of certain islands. The declaration stated: "The terms of the Cairo Declaration shall be carried out and Japanese sovereignty shall be limited to the islands of Honshu, Hokkaido, Kyushu, Shikoku, and such minor islands as we determine."[16] The Allied powers used this right at the San Francisco peace conference in 1951 and, according to chapter II, article 2, section (c) of the peace treaty, Japan renounced "all rights, title, and claim to the Kuril Islands, and to that portion of Sakhalin and the islands adjacent to it over which Japan acquired sovereignty as a consequence of the Treaty of Portsmouth of September 5, 1905."[17] Legal consequences of this formula were (1) that Japan accepted the loss of the Kuril Islands irrespective of its contradiction to the nonaggrandizement principle and the Cairo Declaration, and (2) that the Soviet Union did not acquire internationally recognized territorial rights, as this was not clearly indicated in the text of the San Francisco peace treaty, and moreover, the Soviet Union was not a party to the treaty (the Soviet delegation had walked out of the peace conference and refused to sign the treaty).

A strict legal logic would imply that only states-parties to the San Francisco peace treaty (except Japan) had a legitimate right to decide the future of southern Sakhalin and the Kuril Islands. This notwithstanding, two edicts by the Presidium of the Supreme Soviet of the Russian Soviet Federative Socialist Republic of 1946 and 1947 established South Sakhalin Province in these territories and later merged them into Sakhalin Province. These were fundamentally unilateral acts not valid from the viewpoint of international law. A proper legal approach by the Soviet Union would have been to enter into negotiation with states-parties to the San Francisco treaty on the future of southern Sakhalin and the Kuril Islands. This approach was strongly advocated by the U.S. Senate—the legislative body of the major architect of the San Francisco peace treaty.[18]

Another complicated aspect of the San Francisco treaty was that the text did not determine the limits of the Kuril Islands. This left Japan with a right to claim border delimitation between the Kuril Islands and Japanese territory. Japan saw the Northern Territories as an entity separate from the Kuril Islands, whereas the Soviet Union regarded them as a part of the whole Kuril chain. The issue itself poses several problems. There never was a uniform understanding of the geographical scope of the Kuril Islands among the Russians, the Japanese, and the Ainus.[19] The only formal definition of the Kuril archipelago in diplomatic history comes from the St. Petersburg Treaty of 1875 between Russia and Japan. The treaty is very explicit in excluding Iturup, Kunashir, Shikotan, and Habomai from a Kuril entity and in setting the boundary between Japan and the Kuril Islands as a boundary between Urup (Uruppu in Japanese) and Iturup.[20] Article II of the treaty states:

In exchange for the cession to Russia of the rights on the island of Sakhalin, stipulated in the first article, His Majesty the Emperor of all the Russians, for Himself and His descendants, cedes to His Majesty the Emperor of Japan the group of the Kuril islands which he possesses at present . . . so that henceforth the said group of Kuril islands shall belong to the Empire of Japan. This group comprises the following eighteen islands: (1) Shumushu . . . (18) Uruppu, so that the boundary between the Empires of Russia and Japan in these areas shall pass through the Strait between Cape Lopatka of the peninsula of Kamchatka and the island of Shumushu.[21]

The Soviet argument takes another direction. According to the Soviet position, the war of 1904–1905 unleashed by Japan abolished previous treaties and created a new situation after the signing of the Portsmouth treaty. But one may enter the objection that the Portsmouth treaty did not jeopardize Japanese rights over the Kuril Islands nor did it provide any new status for the archipelago. With the new realities after the San Francisco peace treaty, however, it is not possible to reinstall the provisions of the St. Petersburg treaty in their full meaning. It may be used only as a unique source of internationally accepted delimitation of the Kuril Islands.

The real problem is that the history of geographic determination did not stop with the provisions of the St. Petersburg treaty, as the scope of the entity under Japanese administration itself underwent several changes. The Japanese administrative structure in 1855–1875 did not treat the four disputed islands equally and uniformly. After 1875, the Kuril Islands were merely incorporated into Chishima *kuni* (Chishima Province) as three additional counties (*gun*) of Uruppu (composed of the Uruppu, Chirihoi, and Burotan islands), Shumushu (the Shumushu, Araido, Shirinki, and Paramushiru islands), and Shimushiri (the rest of the Kuril archipelago with Shimushiri Island as its center). In January 1885, Shikotan Island was separated from Hanasaki *gun* as a single county, Shikotan *gun*, and added to Chishima *kuni*. Since that period, the whole chain from Shumushu (Shumshu in Russian) to Kunashiri including Shikotan was treated in Japan as Chishima *rettō* (archipelago). For example, the 1934 edition of *Chishima Gaikyō* (the outline of Chishima) issued by the Hokkaido General Governorship (Hokkaido *chō*) defined the Southern Kurils as the three islands of Kunashiri, Etorofu, and Shikotan, the Middle Kurils as seventeen islands north from Uruppu, and the Northern Kurils as four islands up to Shumushu.[22]

Thus, the legal status of Chishima Province, or Chishima archipelago at the time of Japanese capitulation in 1945, included twenty-four islands from Shumushu in the north to Shikotan in the south. Moreover, the administrative division of Chishima *kuni* provides strong evidence that the Southern Kurils were treated as a major part of the whole entity (five counties out of eight in 1875–1885 and six out of nine later, or 62–67 percent of all administrative units in the entity) and included three of the currently disputed islands.[23] Even more impressive are the population figures of Chishima *kuni*. According to the 1934 edition of *Chishima Gaikyō*, the entire population of

Chishima Province in October 1933 was 14,524 persons, with 7,041 residents on Kunashiri, 5,842 on Etorofu, 953 on Shikotan, 19 on Uruppu, 31 on Shimushiri, and 638 on Shumushu.[24] This makes it clear that the population of the three southern islands accounted for 95 percent of the entire population of the province.

In the context of the San Francisco peace treaty, this situation poses a question: What are the "Kuril Islands" over which Japan waived all the rights? Are they an entity internationally recognized in 1875 or an entity within Japanese domestic administration as of 1945? There is support for the argument that Japan by its own will expanded the limits of the Kuril Islands to include the three southern islands.[25] So the only territory that doubtless is not a part of the Kuril Islands is Habomai, and this island should be regarded as a historically integral part of Hokkaido.

Another complicated legal issue within the context of the San Francisco peace treaty is the Japanese objection to what they claim was an unfair treatment of the Northern Territories. In fact, Japanese Plenipotentiary Representative Shigeru Yoshida at the San Francisco conference viewed the situation differently from how it is presented today. Yoshida stated:

> I can not accept the assertion by the Soviet representative that the Chishima Islands and Southern Karafuto [see note 26] were acquired by Japan as a result of aggression. At the time of the opening of Japan, Tzarist Russia had no objection to the fact that the two islands in the southern part of Chishima—Etorofu and Kunashiri—were a part of Japanese territory. At that time the Chishima Islands north to Uruppu and the southern part of Karafuto were under joint possession of Japan and Russia. On May 7, 1875, Japan and Russia agreed in peaceful diplomatic negotiations that the southern part of Karafuto would be a Russian territory, and as a compensation the Northern Chishima Islands became Japanese territory. The word compensation was used, but in fact, a compromise in negotiations had been achieved to cede the southern part of Karafuto. Later, on September 5, 1905, the southern part of Karafuto became a Japanese territory according to the Portsmouth Treaty signed under intermediary services of U.S. President Roosevelt. The Chishima Islands and the southern part of Karafuto were unilaterally acquired by the U.S.S.R. on September 20, 1945 immediately after Japan's capitulation. The islands of Shikotan and Habomai, which are a part of the main Japanese territory of the island of Hokkaido, were occupied by the Soviet Union at the end of the war while there were Japanese troops.[27]

There are several points to note in connection with Yoshida's objections. First, he indicated four areas under dispute: Southern Sakhalin, Northern Chishima, Southern Chishima, and Shikotan and Habomai treated as a part of Hokkaido. Taking into account the fact that Japan signed and ratified the San Francisco peace treaty with clear provisions for abandoning Southern Sakhalin and the Kuril Islands, it is hard to accept Yoshida's remark as a Japanese stipulation for the exclusion of the Southern Kurils from the provisions of the treaty. It looks more like a complaint against unjust treatment than a clear definition of the scope of the territories surrendered. Another point is that Yoshida used the expressions "Northern Chishima" and "Southern Chishima" but never mentioned Chishima as a single unit. This should be interpreted as indicating the Japanese view then current that the Kuril Islands were divided into two parts but that Japan abandoned both at the San Francisco conference. This interpretation is supported by later explanations to the Japanese Diet by the head of the Foreign Ministry Treaties Bureau, who stated that "the scope of the Chishima Islands under the treaty is supposed to include both Northern Chishima and Southern Chishima. At the same time, the historical fate of Northern and Southern Chishima differs, as it has been stated by Plenipotentiary Representative Yoshida at the San Francisco Conference."[28]

The next point has to do with a clear separation between Iturup and Kunashir as Southern Chishima, and Shikotan and Habomai as a part of Hokkaido and distinct from the Kuril Islands. Although the legal ground to separate Shikotan from the Kuril Islands does not seem very persuasive, the Yoshida remark may be interpreted to support the view that at the signing of the treaty Japan excluded Shikotan and the Habomai group from the notion of the Kuril Islands.

Legal consequences of the Potsdam Declaration and the San Francisco peace treaty in this sense are more in favor of including in the scope of the Kuril Islands at most three of the four islands under dispute, namely Iturup, Kunashir, and Shikotan, or at least two, Iturup and Kunashir. At the same time a controversial issue is whether the provisions of these documents may be seen as absolutely justified as they contradict the principle of nonaggrandizement stipulated in earlier valid international agreements. To my understanding, this dispute has no legal solution and should be dealt with on a purely political basis, taking into account both today's realities and the circumstances of the Soviet entry into the war against Japan.

Thus, legally, the problem of border delimitation between Japan and the Kuril Islands is an issue yet unresolved within the postwar settlement and a subject to be discussed by the two sides concerned. The legal paradox is that the parties politically concerned do not coincide with the parties entitled to make decisions on this issue. The political situation is clear. The dispute is between the Soviet Union, or Russia as successor to the former Soviet Union, and Japan. But the legal background is different. According to the provisions of the Cairo Declaration accepted by Japan, the Allied powers have the ultimate right to indicate which island territories belong to Japan and which do not. Japan has no say on the issue in these terms. But, generally, Japanese legal obligations from the postwar settlement are defined not by the Cairo Declaraton but by the San Francisco peace treaty. Japan may have a right to insist on clarification of the provisions that are not defined precisely, and as it is a party to the peace treaty, it may present its arguments. But legally this may be done only through negotiations between Japan and the other parties to the San Francisco peace treaty, which would exclude Russia. To become a part of these negotiations, Russia would have to sign an agreement with the parties to the peace treaty to take legal possession of Southern Sakhalin and the Kuril Islands, but even that agreement legally would not give the Russians exclusive rights to determine the scope of the Kuril Islands, including the disputed islands. So a strictly legal solution might be sought in two sets of negotiations, one between the parties to the San Francisco peace treaty and Japan and the other with Russia. But this would seem impractical, as the rights of Russia and Japan would be limited by the participation of the other parties, and any initiatives in this scheme would depend on those other parties. In this context the Japanese initiative to discuss the issue directly with the Soviet Union during the talks to restore bilateral diplomatic relations in 1955–1956 was politically reasonable, although lacking in strictly legal grounds.

However, the joint Soviet-Japanese declaration of 1956 further compounded the legal confusion. The final text of the joint declaration stated that the Soviet Union would transfer Shikotan and Habomai to Japan after a Soviet-Japanese peace treaty was signed. Exchanges of letters between then Soviet Deputy Foreign Minister Andrei Gromyko and head of the Japanese delegation Shunichi Matsumoto provided that the issue of Iturup and Kunashir was subject to further discussion. The declaration was ratified by both the USSR Supreme Soviet and the Japanese Diet and obtained the status of an international treaty. From a strictly legal viewpoint, the joint declaration of 1956 is the only international document creating specific Soviet obligations that cannot be denied unilaterally. So Russia, as successor to the Soviet Union, is still legally obliged to implement these provisions at the conclusion of a peace treaty. Nikita Khrushchev's 1960 statement that the Soviet Union would retract the Soviet pledge does not make any legal sense.

A further complication of the declaration is seen in Japan's position. A valid approach for Japan would be in terms of border delimitation, as was shown earlier. The text of the 1956 joint declaration does not even mention the words "border delimitation," and the separation of the two groups of Southern Kurils (Habomai-Shikotan and Kunashir-Iturup) is irreconcilable with the logic of the delimitation of the Kuril archipelago. A legal approach would be to separate Habomai as an indisputable Japanese territory and then to deal later with the remaining three islands.

These, then, were the complicating legal and political circumstances of the territorial dispute between the Soviet Union and Japan on the eve of perestroika.

Stagnant Bilateral Relations in the 1980s _____

Japan's assertion that the four Northern islands are an integral part of Japanese territory had been periodically reiterated by unanimous votes in the Japanese Diet in favor of a "simultaneous return of the four islands." The

Japanese position in the period of the Gorbachev administration was based on the assumption that the Soviet Union was weak and badly needed Japanese capital investment and economic assistance. The territorial dispute was supposed to be settled as a political, rather than a legal, problem, under Japanese economic pressure. This approach was expressed as a principle of "inseparability of economics from politics" (*seikei fukabun*); that is, there would be no significant Japanese economic assistance to the Soviet Union until the territorial dispute was settled, and the amount of assistance would depend on the extent of Soviet concessions on the territorial issue.

In the mid-1980s there was extensive discussion in Japan on whether the return of the disputed island territories was to be achieved by conditioning any improvement of bilateral relations on the solution of the territorial problem or if expanded bilateral ties would improve the chances of resolving the territorial dispute. Should the return of the four islands be a precondition for better Soviet-Japanese relations or should it be a result of improved relations? The first view, known as *iriguchi ron* (entrance approach), was advocated by the Foreign Ministry and left no room for independent Japanese initiatives in Soviet affairs, whereas the other approach, known as *deguchi ron* (exit approach), called for Japanese initiatives in areas outside the territorial dispute. In the Japanese debate of the 1980s, the entrance approach was dominant, and this made Japan dependent on Soviet initiatives. This explains the uncomfortable delay and passivity in Japanese policy toward the Soviet Union during the perestroika period, in comparison with the more timely response on the part of most other Western nations. In fact, by making the territorial dispute a top priority in Soviet-Japanese relations, the Japanese foreign policy bureaucracy excluded Japan from the mainstream of East-West relations in the latter half of the 1980s.

This does not mean, however, that there were no positive developments in Soviet-Japanese relations during this period. Japanese Prime Minister Yasuhiro Nakasone visited Moscow at Konstantin Chernenko's funeral and had a personal meeting with Gorbachev. In 1986, regular annual consultations between Soviet and Japanese foreign ministers were resumed after eight long years of no contact at that level, with Soviet Foreign Minister Eduard Shevardnadze paying a long-awaited visit to Tokyo. Starting in 1986, Moscow gradually liberalized Japanese visits to their relatives' graves in the Northern Territories without a Soviet visa, and the issue was fully solved during Gorbachev's visit to Japan in 1991.

However, the territorial problem showed no change until 1988. Following a meeting with Shevardnadze in Tokyo in 1986, Japanese Foreign Minister Shintaro Abe stated, "The two countries agreed on starting and continuing peace treaty negotiations which include the territorial problem," but the Soviet foreign minister said, "The issue of the Northern Territories was the one on which we did not reach any agreement. There are no changes in the Soviet stance on the issue on a historical and legal basis."[29] When Abe met with

Gorbachev in May 1986, Gorbachev reportedly rejected the Japanese foreign minister's insistence on discussing the territorial dispute. The Soviet leader said, "You've brought up an issue that you must not bring up. As a result of World War II, the present borders have already been given legitimacy."[30] In 1987, Soviet-Japanese relations deteriorated further in the wake of a series of incidents with national security implications. *Toshiba Kikai* broke the rules of the Coordination Committee for Multilateral Export Control (COCOM); intelligence information was leaked from a U.S. base in Yokota to the Soviet Union and China; Soviet spy activities at Japan Air Lines were disclosed; and the deputy head of the Soviet trade mission to Japan was expelled from Japan, and the Soviet Union retaliated by expelling Japanese Self-Defense Force officials at the Japanese embassy in Moscow along with several officers of Japanese trading companies. A meeting by Shevardnadze and his Japanese counterpart, Tadashi Kuranari, at the United Nations in New York produced a harsh Soviet reaction on the territorial debate, with Shevardnadze saying, "Japan has no ground to demand the return of the territories."[31]

Signs of possible improvement in Soviet-Japanese relations first became visible only in December 1988, when the eighth meeting of foreign ministers during Shevardnadze's second visit to Tokyo produced an agreement to establish three joint working groups, with one of them concentrating on the peace treaty. At the same time, prospects emerged for Gorbachev's visit to Tokyo in response to a 1986 invitation. The atmosphere improved for better relations as a result of growing Soviet flexibility and readiness to discuss the territorial dispute within the broader context of peace treaty negotiations. However, the successive sessions of the joint working group on the peace treaty in 1989–1991 proved to be rather ineffective and disappointing, with both sides rigidly repeating their established positions on the issue. In an apparent attempt to find an opening in bilateral relations, CPSU Central Committee secretary and Politburo member Alexander Yakovlev, heading a Soviet parliamentary delegation to Tokyo in October 1989, mentioned to LDP Secretary General Ichiro Ozawa what he called a "third option" in settling the territorial dispute. Yakovlev never clarified his "third option" proposal, but there appeared to be two implications. The option deviated from the official positions of both the Soviet Union and Japan, and it stressed the importance of broader Soviet-Japanese dialogue to overcome the difficult territorial dispute. In fact, the idea was close to the "exit approach," although it remained unclear how to deal with the dispute. However, subsequent discussions in the Soviet Union revealed that the Soviet leadership wanted to downplay the importance of the territorial issue and to leave the issue pending forever by silent agreement on both sides, and that they expected to be able to expand bilateral cooperation, especially in economic and security fields.

Changes in Japan's approach became visible only after the Soviet diplomatic offensive, but they proved to be rather substantial. In January 1989,

Shintaro Abe brought to Moscow an eight-point program for Japanese assistance to the Soviet Union, including economic, humanitarian, and technical assistance. Although his presentation linked prospects for enlarged bilateral cooperation to progress on the territorial issue, Abe's move was welcomed in the Soviet Union as a sign of change in the Japanese approach. Then, in May 1989, Abe's successor, Sosuke Uno, visited Moscow and announced Tokyo's new policy of "expanded equilibrium." The new Japanese foreign minister made it clear that although a peace treaty and the solution of the territorial dispute were Tokyo's major objectives, both nations should make progress on other issues.[32] This position was reiterated by Prime Minister Toshiki Kaifu in July 1990, when he told Japanese newspaper editors that Tokyo would press for a resolution of the territorial dispute while at the same time expanding cultural and personnel exchanges with the Soviet Union. He indicated that making the resolution of the territorial dispute a prerequisite for expanded ties would be "too tough" a stance.[33]

An important point to note about the new Japanese policy of expanded equilibrium was not so much the expansion of the list of issues addressed at the Soviet-Japanese consultations. The two sides had earlier discussed problems of mutual interest, including regional conflicts in Asia (e.g., Korea, Indochina, Afghanistan, and the Middle East). Even when bilateral consultations at the foreign ministers' level were suspended in 1976–1986 due to Andrei Gromyko's refusal to visit Tokyo, these issues still received attention in consultations between the two countries' deputy foreign ministers. The important point of expanded equilibrium was that Japan consented to discuss issues where Soviet interests were dominant. It should also be noted that on both political and diplomatic levels Japan was rather quick to respond to the Soviet initial push, especially after Yakovlev talked about a third option. In fact, since 1989, Japanese diplomatic activity seemed to move closer to the exit approach.[34] So, in fact, irrespective of the earlier Soviet initiatives, Japan proved to be the more flexible in meeting major Soviet requirements. By the time Gorbachev visited Tokyo in April 1991, Tokyo had come a long way from its initially rigid position.

An additional adjustment in the Japanese position was seen in spring 1990, when several prominent LDP leaders took a stance much more favorable to the Soviet Union. Abe reportedly said in April that he personally preferred to separate the fate of Shikotan and Habomai and that of Iturup and Kunashir, the latter to be settled later. This would be a return to the position Japan had taken in 1956. Abe even said that he would not mind Japan's buying the disputed islands, a view strongly rejected by the Japanese Foreign Ministry and the majority of public opinion.[35] Moreover, Ozawa, in his interview with the Soviet newspaper *Pravda*, indicated that he thought the Japanese official position was too rigid and that both sides should review their initial stands in order to reach a compromise.[36] In June, Shin Kanemaru, a former LDP secretary general and the leader of the LDP's largest faction, repeated Abe's idea.[37] Although these remarks were met by strong criticism from the Japanese Foreign Ministry and from Prime Minister Kaifu himself, they nevertheless indicated the emergence of a new vision among the Japanese political elite.

Alas, the apparent flexibility among Japanese politicians and certain changes in Tokyo's official approach to the Soviet Union were misunderstood in Moscow. Moscow emphasized the expansion of bilateral cooperation on the basis of expanded equilibrium, with a focus on economic and security issues. The Soviet Union also stressed the importance of a comprehensive system of bilateral confidence-building measures—mostly of a symbolic nature, such as notification on a large movement of troops, mutual visits of observers to defense exercises, and establishment of contacts between the two countries' military. The unusually warm Japanese reaction that followed, neither accepting the Soviet initiative nor flatly rejecting it, was perceived in Moscow as presenting a chance to dissolve the territorial dispute in the emerging broader framework of bilateral cooperation. Unfortunately, these perceptions reduced Moscow's incentive to search for a new formula for the resolution of the territorial dispute.

Gorbachev-Kaifu Summit, April 1991

Gorbachev's announcement in July 1990 that he would visit Japan early in 1991 stirred Japanese activities. The announcement was soon followed by a visit to Moscow by senior LDP politician Yoshio Sakurauchi, chairman of the Dietmen's League for Japanese-Soviet Friendship. However, Sakurauchi had nothing to add to the well-known Japanese territorial claims and was met very coolly by Gorbachev. According to the Japanese version of the meeting, Gorbachev even hinted he might cancel his scheduled visit to Tokyo if Japan was so insistent on placing the territorial issue at the top of the agenda for the summit.

The next Japanese attempt at a compromise was undertaken in October 1990 during a visit to Moscow by a senior LDP delegation to hold a "Japan week." The delegation was supposed to be led by former Foreign Minister Abe, but the architect of the new approach to Soviet-Japanese relations had fallen ill and could not join the delegation. Nonetheless, the meeting raised Japanese expectations when, according to Japanese media reports (in contrast to a conspicuous silence on the Soviet side), the Soviet side intimated readiness to resurrect the principles of the 1956 joint declaration. If implemented carefully, Abe's overture could have had far-reaching consequences, because the rejection of the joint declaration was one of the weakest legal points in the Soviet position. Unfortunately, however, Abe seemed so concerned about his own political life that, in an attempt to capitalize on a possible breakthrough, he publicized the expected compromise in an interview with the Japanese newspaper, *Yomiuri Shimbun*. As a result, the prospects for a compromise, still not adopted by official organs in Moscow or in Tokyo, were strongly denied by foreign offices in both nations.

Japan was so eager to break the territorial deadlock that even an obvious conservative shift in Soviet politics and Moscow's use of force in the Baltic states in January 1991 did not hinder Japanese preparations for Gorbachev's visit to Tokyo. In February 1991, Japan became the first and the only Western nation to send its foreign minister, Taro Nakayama, to Moscow. The last presummit Japanese attempt to find a solution came in late March 1991. LDP Secretary-General Ozawa brought to Moscow a plan for $26 billion in Japanese credits for the Soviet economy (larger than the total sum of the loans acquired by Gorbachev in Western Europe and Korea, but much less than the $250 billion rumored in Moscow in February 1991) in exchange for Soviet concessions on the territorial issue. The move did much to reinforce the impression in the Soviet Union that Japan was willing to settle a worrisome problem with money.

In analyzing the results of Gorbachev's visit to Tokyo in April 1991, it may be noted that Japanese efforts in 1990–1991 had the potential of producing real results, but Japan failed to convince the Soviet leader to make any dramatic decision. Gorbachev still was led by the erroneous notion that the abundant Soviet resources and markets were sufficient to make Japan forget the territorial dispute, and the extended meetings with Japanese politicians did not change his view.

At the Japanese Diet, the Soviet president admonished the Japanese formula of linking politics (i.e., the territorial dispute) to economics. He stated:

> I think that in case politics contributes to the development of economic relations, and economic relations establish a solid basis for political dialogue and stability in political relations, this formula is acceptable and we may welcome it. But in case only a part of the formula is taken, then it looks like a political dictate over economics or an economic dictate over politics. It often occurs that having some solid positions in the economy one or another side wants to use them as an instrument of political pressure. . . . But this is not acceptable from the point of view of normal cooperation to direct international relations in a new, healthy mode in the spirit of new thinking.

The Soviet president continued:

> I think that we have a tremendous potential for economic cooperation between our two nations. I don't know whether there is any other potential of that kind elsewhere. Because we are neighbors, everything is close. We can cooperate like within a family. But nevertheless our economic relations do not stand comparison with relations with other states. And that seems to be a consequence of undue political pressure upon economic relations.[38]

An important point of the summit was that several political issues outside the territorial dispute were settled. The most significant of these issues was the problem of Japanese war prisoners detained in the Soviet Union after August 1945. Gorbachev's stop at Khabarovsk to pay respects to Japanese victims of the Gulags before his arrival in Tokyo, as well as the completion of the list of Japanese war prisoners who died in Soviet camps and its delivery to Japanese authorities, did much to improve the psychological atmosphere surrounding Soviet-Japanese relations. The Soviets also granted to the Japanese the right to visit their ancestral sites in the Southern Kurils without applying for a Soviet visa. The move was reciprocated by Japan granting free entry to Hokkaido for Soviet permanent residents of the Southern Kurils.

Ironically, however, the improved psychological climate accentuated the territorial impasse. The issue was dealt with in three paragraphs of section 4 of the joint communiqué issued at the conclusion of the summit:

> Prime Minister of Japan, Toshiki Kaifu, and President of the U.S.S.R., M. S. Gorbachev, held detailed and extensive negotiations on the whole range of questions of preparation and conclusion of the peace treaty between Japan and the U.S.S.R., including the problem of territorial delimitation, taking into account positions of both sides on sovereignty over the Habomai Islands, Shikotan Island, Kunashir Island and Iturup Island.
>
> Joint work done earlier, and especially summit talks make it possible to state several conceptual positions: a peace treaty should become the document of the final postwar settlement, including the solution of the territorial problem, open long-term prospects for Japanese-Soviet relations on a friendly basis, and exclude damage to the other side's security.
>
> During the meeting the Prime Minister and the President stressed the ultimate importance of acceleration of the work to complete the preparation of the peace treaty and expressed their firm determination to act for this purpose in a constructive and dynamic way, using all the positive elements accumulated in bilateral negotiations in different years, starting from 1956 when Japan and the U.S.S.R. jointly declared the termination of war and reestablishment of diplomatic relations between them.[39]

Since 1960 the Soviet Union had been ready to discuss the peace treaty but evaded the expression "territorial problem" in any official documents. In a major shift in policy, the Soviet side officially recognized the existence of the territorial dispute and made a direct reference to the four islands in dispute.

Certain new trends could be seen in the Gorbachev-Kaifu communiqué. Both nations accepted the legal approach of territorial delimitation instead of the former Japanese demand for the "return of Japanese territories illegally occupied by the U.S.S.R.," or the Soviet-proposed formula of 1956, which talked about "a transfer of islands by the U.S.S.R." The first paragraph of the communiqué, quoted above, should be understood to mean that all four islands are to be the subject of talks on territorial delimitation. The second paragraph presented the situation as still unsettled from wartime, in contrast to the situation in Europe. The settlement would not be ruled by the principle of "irreversibility of the postwar results." At least theoretically, these positions implied that a final solution favorable to Japan was possible. The third paragraph referred to the "positive elements accumulated in bilateral negotiations since 1956" and was regarded by the Japanese side as an implicit recognition on the Soviet side of the provisions of the 1956 joint declaration.[40] This point reflected a major change in the Japanese position. Until the April summit, Japan had strongly denied any possibility of returning to the 1956 principles, and insisted instead on the discussion of all four islands as a single entity. At the summit talks, as was recognized by both Gorbachev and Kaifu, it was the Japanese prime minister who was doing his best to include a reference to the joint declaration in the summit statement.

From the joint communiqué one could deduce the following points:

1. The postwar accounts had not yet been settled in Soviet-Japanese relations, and today's status quo might not be regarded as a fully legitimate postwar reality.
2. A problem to be settled was the issue of territorial delimitation between Japan and the Kuril Islands, and this view did not infringe on the set of postwar arrangements between the Allied powers and Japan.
3. Territories under dispute, or territories with uncertain political status, encompassed the islands of Iturup, Kunashir, Shikotan, and the Habomais.
4. The issue was to be settled by successive Soviet-Japanese summits begun in 1991.
5. A two-stage approach, or separate consideration of the two groups of disputed islands (Shikotan and Habomais as one group, and Iturup and Kunashir as the other) might be acceptable.

A major problem with the official text of the summit statement was that all these points were not formulated clearly, and in certain aspects might be interpreted in different ways. Although the joint statement offered an alternative approach to start new negotiations on the territorial dispute, both nations continued, rightly or wrongly, to try to use economic incentives to modify the other side's position on the territories issue. The Japanese option was to offer substantial economic assistance in case of firm Soviet guarantees for a favorable territorial solution, accepting both the two-stage approach and prolonged negotiations. This approach seemed to be much more realistic and pragmatic than Gorbachev's option, which would give unconditional priority to doubtful economic cooperation, which might or might not lead to a reappraisal of the Soviet position on the territorial dispute.

In retrospect, the 1991 summit marked a distinct turning point in the bilateral relations. No doubt, the joint Tokyo statement was an important step forward, compared with the 1973 Tanaka-Brezhnev communiqué. But the progress was not big enough to reach even the stage of the 1956 joint declaration.

Conclusions _____

This review of Soviet-Japanese relations during the perestroika period of 1985–1991 indicates a Soviet failure to exploit the alleged Japanese interest in economic cooperation and the resurgence of the territorial dispute as a focal point in Japanese policy toward the Soviet Union. The Japanese approach to the Soviet Union during this period provides strong evidence that Japan still lacks the major attribute of a great world power, that is, a clear foreign policy oriented toward international responsibility. Japan is a great economic power but politically remains concerned mostly with its own parochial problems. As Chapter 7 by Akaha shows, the parochial approach continued even after the dissolution of the Soviet Union as a unified political entity in 1991.

Against the backdrop of the transition of world politics from East-West confrontation to "new political thinking" and the end of the Cold War, Japan proved itself to be politically unable to contribute to the solution of global issues. In the face of the dramatic turn in Soviet history, Mikhail Gorbachev's perestroika in 1985–1991, Japanese interests and efforts centered around the single issue of territorial dispute. Instead of developing a broader global vision regarding a possible new Russian role in the world, Japan was preoccupied with the territorial issue as the most important national concern vis-à-vis the Soviet Union.

It goes without saying that the dispute over the Northern Territories has long been a key determinant of the Japanese public's views of their neighbors to the north, and the issue cannot be ignored by any ambitious Japanese politician. No doubt, from the Japanese viewpoint, the territorial dispute is the core issue in any policy toward Russia, and any political initiative is judged from the point of view of whether it would contribute to a favorable territorial solution. In the wake of the Gorbachev-Kaifu summit, it appeared that Tokyo had become flexible enough to develop an alternative solution to the territorial problem that would be acceptable to the general public. At the same time, in contrast to the flexibility on the territorial issue, Tokyo continued to reject serious discussion of other problems on their own merit. Even Moscow's concern over a broader range of issues, primarily of an economic nature, was viewed by Tokyo in terms of how that concern could be exploited in Tokyo's attempt to obtain Moscow's concessions on the Southern Kurils.

Japan's apparent decision to give priority to national over global issues undermines Tokyo's professed desire to be recognized as a great world political power. In this context, one notes Japan's tendency to pursue a chosen policy line irrespective of important changes in the international political environment. This was indeed the case when, in the face of the rapid disintegration of the former Soviet Union and mounting Western concern over its global implications, Tokyo attempted to play the "Gorbachev card" in 1991.

To be fair, however, one needs also to recognize Soviet limitations and shortcomings. The two countries' failure to find solutions to the problems of mutual concern can be explained to an important degree by the lack of political will among the Soviet leaders and their misperceptions and misunderstandings about Japan and Soviet-Japanese relations. There is no doubt that Gorbachev's strategy was to outwit the Japanese by accelerating initiatives without seriously considering even minor concessions to Japan. This kind of strategy proved fruitless. It forced Japan to put all the eggs in Gorbachev's basket, overestimate his potential, and ignore opportunities offered by overtures from the growing democratic opposition in Russia. A balanced assessment of Soviet-Japanese relations during the perestroika period would thus see the largely unsuccessful bilateral diplomacy as a product of mutual failings.

What were the immediate consequences of the two countries' failures to accommodate each other? For the Gorbachev administration, the deadlock with the Japanese was but a local fiasco in its approach to only one, albeit important, nation. Although Boris Yeltsin of new democratic Russia inherited all bilateral problems from the Gorbachev era, the problems did not jeopardize either the general outline of the new Russian leader or his personal image in the West. Nor did Japan lose much in its policy toward the Soviet Union and Russia as it was able to keep its economic levers for a much longer period. Losing with Gorbachev, Japan may be able to afford to play the same game with Yeltsin or his future successor. If Japan had no desire to become a global political power, its tactics toward Moscow could be viewed as consistent and well calculated. The problem is that by defining the return of the Northern Territories as a national priority, Japan would continue to lag behind other major Western powers in dealing with the fast changes in the former Soviet Union and their impact on world politics. This fact gains greater importance as the Russian situation acquires greater salience in the world community. Japan's inability to offer internationally acceptable initiatives toward Russia adds to the rather long list of issues of international significance to which Japan has shown only delayed reaction. It also increases international doubts about the nation's qualifications as a world political power, despite its enormous economic might.

Notes

1. Munenori Akagi, *Nisso Kankei o Kangaeru: Gekidō no Taishō, Shōwa o Ikite* [Thoughts on Soviet-Japanese relations: My life in the turbulent eras of Taishō and Shōwa], Tokyo: Shinjidaisha, 1982, p. 307.

2. *Gaikoku Bōeki Gaikyō* [Outline of foreign trade], 1982, no. 12.

3. For more details on the dispute over fishery zones, see Tsuneo Akaha, *Japan in Global Ocean Politics*, Honolulu: University of Hawaii Press and Law of the Sea Institute, 1985, pp. 130–149.

4. Akagi, *Nisso Kankei*, pp. 211–212.

5. Research Institute for Peace and Security (RIPS), *Asian Security, 1986*, London: Brassey's Defence Publishers, 1986, p. 50.

6. *Komsomolskaya Pravda*, April 20, 1990.

7. For typical publications, see Shigeki Hakamada, *Shinso no Shakaishugi: Soren, Tōō, Chūgoku, Kokoro no Tampo* [Deep in socialism: The Soviet Union, Eastern Europe, China, search of the soul], Tokyo: Chikuma Shobo, 1987, pp. 221–227; Masamori Sase and Hiroshi Kimura, eds., *Gorubachofu Kakumei: Peresutoroika no Chōsen to Shōgai no Bunseki* [Gorbachev revolution: Analysis of the challenge and obstacles in perestroika], Tokyo: Saimaru Shuppankai, 1988.

8. For example, see Nobuo Shimotomai, *Gorubachofu no Jidai* [The era of Gorbachev], Tokyo: Iwanami Shoten, 1988; Kenji Iwata, *Soren no Naiseiryokugaku to Gaikō: Kosuigin, Burejinefu kara Gorubachofu e* [The dynamics of internal politics and foreign policy in the Soviet Union: From Kosygin and Brezhnev to Gorbachev], Tokyo: Tōshindo, 1989; Koji Sugimori, *Gorubachofu no Sekai Seisaku to Nisso Kankei* [Gorbachev's global policy and Japanese-Soviet relations], Tokyo: Tōkai Daigaku Shuppankai, 1989; Peter Berton, "The Impact of the 1989 Revolutions on Soviet-Japanese Relations," in Young C. Kim and Gaston J. Sigur, eds., *Asia and the Decline of Communism*, New Brunswick, N.J.: Transaction Publishers, 1991, p. 136.

9. Berton, "The Impact," p. 135.

10. Heiwa Anzen Hoshō Kenkyūjo, ed., *Ajia no Anzen Hoshō, 1989–1990* [Asian security, 1989–1990], Tokyo: Asagumo Shimbunsha, 1989, p. 107.

11. Bōeichō, ed., *Bōei Hakusho, Heisei Gannen* [White paper on defense, 1989], Tokyo: Okurashō Insatsukyoku, 1989, pp. 100–101.

12. *Dai Nippon Komonjo, Bakumatsu Gaikoku Kankei, Bunsho no Yon* [Public documents of great Japan. Documents on foreign relations in the Bakumatsu period, book 4], Tokyo: Tokyo Teikoku Daigaku, Bunka Daigaku, Shiryō Hensangakari, 1934, p. 22.

13. For more details on Soviet-Japanese relations in the 1920s, see George Alexander Lensen, *Japanese Recognition of the Soviet Union: Soviet-Japanese Relations, 1921–1930*, Tokyo: Sophia University, 1970.

14. The two conditions are contained in section 2 part (a) and section 3 of the agreement, respectively. U.S. Department of State, *Foreign Relations of the United States: The Conferences at Yalta and Malta, 1945*, Washington, D.C.: Government Printing Office, 1955, p. 984.

15. U.S. Department of State, *Foreign Relations of the United States: The Conferences at Cairo and Teheran, 1943*, Washington, D.C.: Government Printing Office, 1955, p. 869.

16. U.S. Department of State, *Foreign Relations of the United States: The Conference of Berlin, 1945*, vol. 1, Washington, D.C.: Government Printing Office, 1955, p. 892.

17. *Documents on American Foreign Relations*, New York: Harper, 1954, p. 471.

18. At the time of the treaty ratification, the U.S. Senate Committee on Foreign Relations adopted a special resolution stating:

> No provision of the treaty should infringe on rights and interests of Japan or allied powers as recognition according to the treaty indicated of any rights or claims by the U.S.S.R. on Southern Sakhalin and adjacent islands of Habomai and Shikotan, or on any other territory belonging to Japan as on December 7, 1941, as equally nothing in the treaty indicated or its ratification by the Senate presumes a recognition by the United States in favor of the Soviet Union of provisions concerning Japan in so-called Yalta agreement of 11 February 1945.

See *Documents on American Foreign Relations*, p. 459.

19. For the Ainu view, see Hokkaido Terebi Hoso, *Haikei, Gorubachofu-sama* [Dear Mr. Gorbachev], Sapporo: Nōmu, 1991, p. 106. For early Japanese views, see Haruki Wada, *Hoppō Ryōdo Mondai o Kangaeru* [Thoughts on the problem of the Northern Territories], Tokyo: Iwanami Shoten, 1990, pp. 58–59.

20. Wada, *Hoppō Ryōdo*, pp. 50–51. To my knowledge there is only one attempt, by Haruki Wada of Tokyo University, to provide a different interpretation of this clause. His interpretation would suggest the St. Petersburg treaty dealt only with those islands of the Kuril chain that were under Russian control, excluding any other Kuril islands that were outside Russian jurisdiction.

21. For an English translation of the text, see George Alexander Lensen, *The Russian Push Toward Japan: Russo-Japanese Relations, 1697–1875*, Princeton, N.J.: Princeton University Press, 1959, pp. 501–502.

22. Wada, *Hoppō Ryōdo*, p. 14.

23. Takeo Tanioka and Keiichiro Yamaguchi, *Konsaisu Chimei Jiten: Nippon Hen* [Concise geographical dictionary: Japan], Tokyo: Sanseidō, 1974, pp. 568, 756, and 964.

24. Hokkaidocho, *Chishima Gaishi* [Outline of Chishima], Tokyo: Kokusho Kankokai, 1977, p. 44. Reprint of *Chishima Gaikyō* of 1934.

25. In international practice there is an example of a Japanese-arranged transfer of a territory from one of its dependencies to another (Yanbian district transferred from Korea to Manchuria), which was recognized as valid at the postwar settlement.

26. Internationally, Karafuto is more commonly known by its Russian name, Sakhalin.

27. *Warera no Hoppō Ryōdo* [Our Northern Territories], Tokyo: Gaimusho, 1970, p. 43.

28. Cited in Hokkaido Terebi Hōsō, *Haikei, Gorubachofu-sama*, p. 88.

29. *Asian Security, 1986*, pp. 56–57.

30. Ibid., p. 57.

31. Heiwa Anzen Hoshō Kenkyūjo, ed., *Ajia no Anzen Hosho, 1989–1990*, p. 107.

32. The issues mentioned were Japanese visits to ancestral graves on the Soviet and Soviet-held territories in the Maritime Province, Sakhalin, and the Northern Territories; cooperation on fishery issues in the Japan Sea; and environmental protection. Peggy Falkenheim, "Moscow and Tokyo: Slow Thaw in Northeast Asia," *World Policy Journal*, Winter 1990–1991, p. 163.

33. *Mainichi Daily News*, July 28, 1990.

34. Falkenheim, "Moscow and Tokyo," pp. 164–165. Falkenheim noted that "although the Japanese Foreign Ministry still officially maintains a policy of not separating economics from politics, there has been some de facto change as well."

35. *Asahi Shimbun*, April 24, 1990.

36. *Pravda*, April 10, 1990.

37. *Yomiuri Shimbun*, September 3, 1990; Sophie Quinn-Judge and Charles Smith, "Island Fever," *Far Eastern Economic Review*, June 21, 1990, p. 23.

38. *Vstrecha Prezidenta SSSR s biznesmenami: Rech' M. S. Gorbacheva* [Meeting of the Soviet president with businessmen: Speech by M. S. Gorbachev], *Izvestiya*, April 18, 1991.

39. "Sovmestnoye sovetsko-yaponskoye zayavleniye" [Soviet-Japanese joint statement], *Izvestiya*, April 19, 1991.

40. *Asahi Shimbun*, April 24, 1991.

Chapter 7

The Politics of Japanese–Soviet/Russian Economic Relations

_____ *Tsuneo Akaha*

During the Cold War decades, Japan's economic policy toward the former Soviet Union was largely subordinated to its political-security alliance with the United States. Conversely, the Soviet Union hardly ever viewed Japan except from the vantage point of global strategic rivalry between the superpowers. Therefore, only during the periods of U.S.-Soviet détente did bilateral trade and other commercial ties receive serious policy considerations in Tokyo and Moscow on their own merit. Even during those periods, however, problems of a bilateral nature prevented Japan and the Soviet Union from fully realizing the potential benefits of economic cooperation. Politically, Tokyo and Moscow failed to find a mutually acceptable compromise on the Northern Territories dispute, and this clouded the atmosphere of bilateral relations and severely limited the scope of bilateral commercial transactions. Japan also viewed the growing Soviet military presence and political maneuvers in the Asia Pacific region as a threat to its national security. Economically, with the exception of the détente years of the late 1960s through the 1970s and the perestroika period since the mid-1980s, the centrally planned economy of the Soviet Union and the liberal capitalist economy of Japan presented formidable institutional and legal barriers to the development of commercial relations.

Now that the global Cold War is over, the Soviet Union has disappeared —first as a socialist hegemon and then as a unified political entity—and Russia has emerged as successor to the Soviet Union, will Japan and Russia be able to overcome problems of bilateral origins and expand their economic ties? This is the central question of the present chapter. To fully answer the question, I first analyze the impact of the Cold War on the Japanese-Soviet economic relations and separate it from the influence of other factors. Second, I examine Japan's response to the unfolding of perestroika and other related developments in the Soviet Union. Third, I assess the impact of the dissolution of the Soviet Union and the emergence of Russia on the Japanese-Soviet relations. And finally, I discuss the prospects of Japanese-Russian economic relations in the future and their implications for Japan's role in the posthegemonic world. More precisely, I will ask: Will Tokyo actively assist Russia in its economic reform by extending substantial official aid and private investments before the territorial issue is fully resolved, or will Japan continue to link the expansion of bilateral economic ties to the resolution of the territorial problem? Might there be a political compromise short of a complete resolution of the territorial dispute? Would such a compromise guarantee successful and substantial expansion of economic ties between the two countries? How important would improved economic relations be for Japan's role in the posthegemonic world?

Obstacles to Economic Ties in the Cold War Era ——————

The economic needs of Japan and the Soviet Union in the early postwar decades were largely complementary. A good part of Japan's fast-growing energy and other resource needs could potentially have been met by the enormous Siberian and Soviet Far Eastern resources, and the Soviet Union's chronic shortages of investment in its resource-rich regions could have been ameliorated by Japan's burgeoning financial and technological assets. However, as Zagorsky pointed out in Chapter 6, the historical enmity between the Japanese and the Russians, the ideological antagonism of the Cold War, and the Japanese-Soviet dispute over the Northern Territories prevented the two countries from developing potentially beneficial economic relations.

When diplomatic relations were established in 1956, Japan and the Soviet Union issued a joint declaration in which Moscow agreed to transfer Shikotan Island and the Habomai group to Japan after conclusion of a peace treaty and to further negotiate the status of the Kunashiri and Etorofu islands. The two sides failed to sign a peace treaty and the territorial dispute continued. Moreoever, when Tokyo concluded a revised security treaty with Washington in 1960, Moscow abandoned the "1956 formula" and declared there was no territorial dispute between the two countries. The Soviets officially maintained this position until Gorbachev's visit to Tokyo in April 1991.[1]

Despite the territorial stalemate, bilateral economic relations showed a steady growth after 1956. In 1957, a bilateral treaty of commerce was concluded and the five-year trade and payments agreement was subsequently renewed, which allowed the two sides to achieve modest gains in their commercial ties. Japanese exports to the Soviet Union expanded from a mere $760,000 in 1956 to more than $168 million in 1965, and Japanese imports from slightly less than $2.9 million to more than $240 million. The trade ties expanded further as Tokyo and Moscow concluded seven agreements between 1968 and 1975 on large-scale cooperative projects for resource development in Siberia and the Soviet Far East. The projects were the First Far East Forestry Resources Development Project (with a commitment of $163 million in government credits); the Wrangel Harbor Construction Project ($80 million); the Industrial Woodchip and Pulp Development Project ($45 million); the South Yakutia Coal Development Project ($450 million in initial contracts and $40 million in additional loans); the Second Far East Forestry Resources Development Project ($500 million); the Yakutia Natural Gas Exploration Project ($25 million); and the Sakhalin Continental Shelf Oil and Gas Exploration Project ($237.5 million). All these projects were to be conducted on a compensation basis, with Japanese low-interest credits enabling the Soviets to purchase Japanese industrial plants, machinery, and equipment.[2] Several commercial agreements were also concluded during this period, including contracts for Tyumen oilfield development, the Baikal-Amur (BAM) Railroad construction, and numerous construction projects for oil and natural gas pipelines, a gas liquefaction plant, timber-pulp mills, an iron-steel mill, fertilizer plants, petrochemical plants, a medical film manufacturing plant, a bulk oxygen plant, and an iron-ore pelleting plant.

Behind the resource development projects in Siberia and the Soviet Far East were Japan's economic and political interests. Tokyo's economic rationale was more pressing and realistic. The Japanese government, particularly the Ministry of International Trade and Industry, saw the potential of the vast untapped resources of Siberia and the Soviet Far East for meeting the nation's fast-expanding resource needs. MITI and the Ministry of Finance (MOF) decided to support the development projects with large credits and loans. The projects produced some visible results, and by 1979 the two-way trade had grown to $4,372 million from a mere $822 million in 1970. The Japanese-Soviet trade in dollar terms experienced growth every year during the 1970s except in the 1976–1977 period, when it experienced a small 1.9 percent decline. During the 1970s Soviet timber exports to Japan increased from $197.7 million to $732.1 million, coal from $43.7 million to $124.1 million, petroleum products from $23.9 million to $153.6 million, and nonferrous metals from $76.3 million to $323.4 million. Other Soviet exports to Japan that experienced growth during the 1970s were fisheries (increasing from $5.4 million to $42.4 million) and cotton (from $24.3 million to $151.8 million). Japan's effort to diversify its oil supplies in the wake of the 1973–1974 oil crisis also had a favorable impact on Japanese-Soviet trade, with Japanese crude imports from the Soviet Union jumping from a mere $7.7 million in 1972 to $30.6 million in 1973 and $20.9 million in 1974.[3] After Japan recovered from the oil shock, however, Japanese crude imports from the Soviet Union dropped to the pre-1973 levels ($5.1 million in 1975) and remained low through the remainder of the decade.

Politically, against the backdrop of the first U.S.-Soviet détente, Tokyo hoped that expanded bilateral economic ties might soften Moscow's tough stand on the territorial issue. Prime Minister Kakuei Tanaka visited Moscow in October 1973 and pressed Soviet leader Leonid Brezhnev on the territorial question. In the joint statement issued at the conclusion of their talks, the two leaders acknowledged that the resolution of issues remaining unsettled after World War II and the conclusion of a peace treaty would contribute to the establishment of good-neighborly and friendly relations between the two countries. They also agreed to resume negotiations for the conclusion of a peace treaty. Tanaka claimed the "unsettled issues" included the territorial dispute. However, the Soviet side never accepted this interpretation and continued to deny the existence of any bilateral territorial dispute. On the economic front, however, Tanaka and Brezhnev agreed the two countries should expand cooperation on the basis of reciprocity and equality in the areas of Siberian natural resource development, trade, transportation, agriculture, and fisheries.

No doubt, Tokyo's official support for the Siberian and Soviet Far Eastern development projects was crucial for the expansion of bilateral economic relations in the 1960s and 1970s. The Import-Export Bank of Japan extended loans enabling Japanese companies to participate in the large resource projects. In the latter half of the 1970s, the growing demand for natural gas pipelines and chemical plants in Siberia and the Soviet Far East was met by the extension of Import-Export Bank loans for Japanese exports of such plants and steel pipes.[4]

Notwithstanding these visible gains in bilateral trade relations, the political and military developments during the 1970s prevented the full realization of the potential of bilateral economic cooperation between Japan and the Soviet Union. The growing U.S.-Japan security cooperation, the steady arms buildup in Japan, and the Sino-American and Sino-Japanese rapprochement were all major concerns to the Soviet Union. The Soviet response of mixing political and economic overtures and relentless military buildup in Asia did not produce the desired effects. On the contrary, the Soviet policy toward Japan was a record of failure. Moscow failed to conclude a peace treaty with Tokyo and it failed to attract Japanese interest in its proposal for an Asian collective security system. It also failed to block the conclusion in 1978 of a Sino-Japanese Treaty of Peace and Friendship with the infamous antihegemony clause. Beijing insisted, for strategic reasons, that Japan not encourage the construction of a pipeline to carry oil from Siberia to the Pacific coast.[5] Most importantly, Moscow failed to drive a wedge between Tokyo and Washington by exploiting the growing Japan-U.S. trade friction.[6]

The 1980s saw Japanese-Soviet economic relations stagnate, with the two-way trade suffering year-to-year declines four times, and Japanese exports suffering year-to-year declines five times during the decade. The Soviet share of Japan's worldwide exports, which had reached 3.3 percent in 1976, dropped to 1.1 percent in 1989, a record low since the 1960s. Japanese imports from the Soviet Union also declined three years in a row between 1981 and 1984, and the Soviet share of Japan's total imports dropped from the 1970s' peak of 2.8 percent (in 1973) to 1.4 percent by the end of the 1980s.[7]

Behind this disappointing record were both political and economic developments. Politically, the Soviet invasion of Afghanistan in 1979 prompted Tokyo to join Western economic sanctions against Moscow in December 1979–April 1981. Tokyo suspended the extension of official credits to the Soviet Union. The West's economic sanctions against the Soviet Union in December 1981–November 1982 over the imposition of martial law in Poland also dampened Japanese business interest in the Soviet Union.[8] Results showed up in a 23.4 percent drop in Japanese exports to the Soviet Union and a 27.6 percent decline in Japanese imports in 1983. The "Toshiba incident" also disrupted bilateral trade. When Toshiba Machinery violated COCOM regulations in 1985 and became a target of U.S. sanctions in 1987, Tokyo tightened its control of exports to the Soviet Union.[9] Japanese exports to the Soviet Union dropped by 4 percent and imports plummeted by 18.6 percent in 1987.

China proved to be not only a political factor, as noted earlier, but also an economic factor affecting Japanese economic ties with the Soviets. Namely, Japan found China an easier economic partner than the Soviet Union. Following the restoration of diplomatic relations in 1972 and the conclusion of the Treaty of Peace and Friendship in 1978, relations between Japan and China improved quickly. Within ten yeas of the treaty, Sino-Japanese trade grew more than fourfold, far outpacing Japanese-Soviet trade.

The most important economic factor behind the rather stagnant commercial relations between Japan and the Soviet Union in the 1980s was the structural change of Japan's economy. By the late 1970s Japan had become a much more energy-efficient economy than at the time of the first oil crisis. Before the oil crisis, Japan's energy demand had continued to increase in direct proportion to the growth of its GNP, but after 1975 the nation's energy needs became smaller, despite the continuing GNP growth. Oil imports continued to decline, from 5,221 barrels a day in 1974 to 4,429 in 1988.[10] By the end of the 1980s, oil consumption per unit of real GNP was down more than 50 percent from 1973.[11] Japan's successful energy policy had dampened its earlier interest in the development of Siberian and Far Eastern resources, but Moscow failed to recognize this and continued eagerly (but unsuccessfully) to seek long-term bilateral economic agreements with Tokyo.[12]

There were other chronic problems on the Soviet side that limited Japanese-Soviet economic ties in the 1980s. They included harsh climate, the vast geographical distances required for transportation, and the rigidly centralized economic planning. Also problematic were the deteriorating hard currency earnings that could be allocated to development projects in Siberia and the Soviet Far East and the compensation agreements that locked Japanese project partners into unfavorable terms. Soviet officials' crude negotiating behavior did not help. Japanese investors also preferred business opportunities in the United States, Asian newly industrialized countries, China, and Western Europe.[13] Regional deficiencies in infrastructure and lack of experience in dealing with foreign businessmen posed additional problems. Moreover, the Soviets' growing deficit in trade with Japan weakened their ability to import from Japan during the early 1980s. By 1982 the Soviet trade deficit with Japan had reached $2,217 million—the largest trade deficit the Soviet Union had experienced with any capitalist country until that time.[14] The dominance in Japanese-Soviet trade of a small number of large Japanese general trading companies had yet another significant impact on the bilateral trade. *Sōgō shōsha*, as these firms are known in Japan, formed a part of the powerful business community in Japan, headed by Keidanren (the Federation of Economic Organizations), and generally cooperated with their government. Tokyo discouraged large business deals with the Soviets pending progress on the territorial issue.[15]

Perestroika and Rising Japanese Expectations

Gorbachev's rise to power in 1985 did not have an immediate impact on the bilateral economic relations. The new Soviet leader's glasnost and perestroika policies were initially met with considerable skepticism in Tokyo. Gradually, however, Gorbachev's "new thinking" diplomacy had a favorable impact on the atmosphere surrounding the bilateral economic relations.[16]

In his famed Vladivostok speech in 1986 and Krasnoyarsk speech in 1988, Gorbachev enunciated a new Asian policy based on new thinking. Now economics was to be "placed in command," security doctrine was to be based on the concept of "reasonable sufficiency," and "ideological considerations were to play no role in Soviet international relations."[17] However, it was China—not Japan—with whom Gorbachev wanted to achieve rapprochement first. Tokyo could not respond favorably to Gorbachev's call for the establishment of a comprehensive regional security framework and for arms control and confidence-building measures. To Japan (and to the United States) Gorbachev's proposals were extremely vague, clearly one-sided, and evidently suspect. Although the Sino-Soviet rapprochement quickly resulted in a substantial Soviet force reduction in Asia, Japanese defense planners were concerned about the qualitative improvements in the Soviet Far Eastern and Pacific forces that accompanied their quantitative reductions.[18] Moreover, the Soviets tended to undervalue the importance of economic power as a factor in international politics and thus underestimated Japan's importance in world affairs. By the time Gorbachev realized the potential value of Japanese economic power to his policy of perestroika, his domestic power base had eroded so much that he could not successfully extend the policy of new political thinking to the relations with Tokyo. As I will show in this chapter, this had an important bearing on the Northern Territories problem.

Following Soviet Foreign Minister Eduard Shevardnadze's visit to Tokyo in 1986 and the reciprocal visit by Japanese Foreign Minister Shintaro

Abe the same year, the tone of bilateral political talks improved gradually and steadily, and new signs of economic activity appeared. By the end of the 1980s, Japanese-Soviet trade had reached a historic high of $6,086 million. The rising value of the Japanese yen since the Plaza Accord of 1985 also helped the expansion of bilateral trade, with most growth coming in Japanese imports of fisheries, timber, coal, and nonferrous metals, and Soviet imports of chemicals and industrial and transport equipment. The increased Japanese purchases in turn improved the Soviets' ability to import from Japan. The two countries also set up joint ventures starting in 1987, with the number of business tie-ins increasing to 34 by September 1990,[19] and to 52 by the spring of 1992.

By 1990, the tone of overall Japanese-Soviet relations had improved considerably. In June, Prime Minister Kaifu optimistically declared, "Economic relations between Japan and the Soviet Union have the potential to develop to a level comparable to the existing economic relations between Japan and the United States."[20] Rising expectations led to a flurry of activities involving Japanese businesses and their Soviet counterparts in late 1990 and early 1991. In December 1990, for example, the general trading company Mitsubishi Corp. received a $308 million order for eighteen freighters from the privatized enterprise Sovkomflot. In the same month, another trading company, Mitsui & Co., and the U.S. engineering firm, MacDermott International Inc., agreed to conduct a feasibility study for a natural gas project off Sakhalin. Subsequently, in the spring of 1992, a consortium of these companies along with Marathon Oil won a bid to develop offshore Sakhalin natural gas. In January 1991, another giant trading firm, C. Itoh, concluded a barter-trade agreement with an oil-drilling concern in Sakhalin, marking the first time Moscow had agreed to allow an oil-drilling enterprise in the country to ship oil directly to a foreign agent. Achieving another first among Western companies was Daiwa Securities of Tokyo, which won a contract to advise the Soviet Union and Russian Republic governments on the establishment of a financial and market system.

However, the growing optimism among the Japanese commercial circles was severely threatened by the Soviet military crackdown in Lithuania and Latvia in January 1991. The Japanese government was afraid the military action in the Baltic states might boost the political influence of the Soviet military and the communists in Moscow, who by the way were opposed to any territorial concessions to Japan. Japanese Foreign Minister Taro Nakayama flew to Moscow and urged Gorbachev to solve the Baltic problem peacefully. Tokyo also warned it might halt the $100 million emergency assistance it had approved in December. The Japan-Soviet Joint Economic Committee meeting in Tokyo in early February produced no notable results except for an agreement to continue the planning of a Sakhalin oil and natural gas development project.

As disconcerting as the political developments in the disintegrating Soviet Union were and as potentially damaging as their impact on bilateral commercial ties were, the single most important issue in Tokyo's Soviet policy remained the territorial dispute over the Northern Territories. It is to this issue that I shall now turn.

The Irremovable Obstacle: The Northern Territories _____

The legal and historical background to the Northern Territories dispute is discussed extensively by Zagorsky in Chapter 6.[21] Therefore, I will discuss only the economic and political aspects of the problem here.

The value of the disputed islands—the Habomai group, Shikotan, Kunashiri, and Etorofu—had grown considerably since the Soviet establishment in 1977 of a two-hundred-mile fishery zone (now exclusive economic zone, or EEZ) encompassing rich fishing grounds around the island territories.[22] The total maritime area enclosed by the Soviet (now Russian) jurisdiction is about 57,000 nautical square miles. The total value of fishery resources in the area is difficult to estimate, but it is known that the spawning grounds for some commercially exploited species exist around all of the islands. The island chain proper has no petroleum potential, but potential is suspected in the South Okhotsk Basin underlying the Kuril Abyssal Plain and the continental shelf and continental slope offshore from southeast Sakhalin. No economically recoverable ores have been found on or around the Habomai group and Shikotan, but the area seaward of these islands is a likely locus of manganese nodules and crusts and barite nodules. Kunashiri and Etorofu are rich in minerals, including tin, zinc, lead, copper, nickel, sulfur, and metallic sulfides. Deposits of sulfur on the two islands are said potentially to produce enough sulfuric acid to satisfy the needs of the entire Soviet Union. Larger deposits of titanium and magnetite exist in the sandy shoals bordering Kunashiri and Etorofu; and nickel, copper, chromium, vanadium, and niobium also exist in the same shoals.[23]

For Russia, transfer of all four islands to Japan would mean losses of substantial titanium sand, sulfur, and metal sulfide deposits, along with productive fishing grounds. Joint sovereignty or UN administration of the four islands—propositions put forth by some in the former Soviet Union—would provide for a more or less equal division of resources between the two countries. Transfer of Shikotan and the Habomai group alone would still entail a major loss of fishing grounds because the Pacific EEZ of these islands is much larger and much richer. In contrast, no significant mineral deposits would be lost because Shikotan and the Habomai group contain only minor deposits of economic minerals. Transfer of Shikotan and the Habomai group and joint development of the other two islands would give Japan significant fishing grounds because the majority of fishery resources are located on the Pacific side of the islands. Japan would also obtain access to several economic mineral deposits, including the larger sulfur, sulfide, and titanium deposits.[24]

To most Japanese, however, the islands issue is of political and symbolic, rather than economic, importance.[25] After all, the Japanese economy has prospered without the islands. Therefore, the idea of joint development under Soviet jurisdiction (or joint jurisdiction) of some or all of the islands has little or no appeal in Japan. The vast majority of the Japanese, regardless of their ideological persuasion, support their government's claim that all the island territories belong to Japanese sovereignty. Disagreements among the Japanese relate primarily to the question of whether the territorial reversion should be simultaneous (all the islands at the same time) or sequential (e.g., the Habomai group and Shikotan first and then Kunashiri and Etorofu).

Starting in 1988, there were growing indications that Moscow was changing its attitude, if not its policy, toward the territorial issue, and this occasioned a policy shift in Tokyo in 1989. By late 1990, however, the Soviet Union had begun to show signs of political disintegration, and with them came confusing and often conflicting signals regarding Moscow's policy toward Tokyo.

In his Krasnoyarsk speech in September 1988, Gorbachev hinted at the possibility of limited Japanese access to the rich fishing grounds around the disputed islands and Japanese visits to the islands. He also encouraged Japan to expand its economic ties with the Soviet Union. In March 1989, Tokyo and Moscow began discussing the conclusion of a peace treaty. During Japanese Foreign Minister Sosuke Uno's visit to Moscow in April 1989, Shevardnadze reportedly raised the possibility of some kind of accommodation regarding the Habomai group and Shikotan.[26] In May, Tokyo responded to these signs of softening Soviet attitude by adopting a policy of "expanded equilibrium" (*kakudai kinko* in Japanese). According to the new policy, talks on the territorial issue and a peace treaty would proceed along with gradual expansion of economic and other ties.

By early 1991, however, the Soviet Union had begun to show serious signs of disintegration, with the Baltic states declaring independence and other Soviet republics demanding sovereignty amidst growing nationalism. With these signs came Soviet leaders' statements that indicated trouble for Soviet-Japanese territorial accommodation. For example, in January 1991, Gorbachev declared that the return of the Habomai group and Shikotan was once a possibility but the chance had been dashed.[27] The military leadership also expressed firm opposition to any territorial concessions to Japan.[28]

There were other quite confusing signs coming out of the Soviet Union. Boris Yeltsin, who had earlier supported the 1956 formula, retreated from that position after being elected to the presidency of the Russian Federation. On the eve of the Kaifu-Gorbachev summit in Tokyo in April 1991, Yeltsin warned Gorbachev against acquiescence and reiterated his own proposal for a five-step solution to the problem. According to his formula, Tokyo and Moscow would first acknowledge the existence of the territorial dispute. Subsequently, over a period of fifteen to twenty years, free economic zones would be established on the disputed islands, and Soviet troops and military equipment would be withdrawn from the area. At the same time, a peace treaty would be signed and Soviet civilian residents on the islands would be relocated. Valentin P. Fedorov, governor of Sakhalin,[29] proposed that Japan and the Soviet Union should establish and develop a free economic zone encompassing the Soviet-controlled islands and a part of Hokkaido—an idea totally unacceptable to Japan. A March 1991 nonbinding referendum in the disputed area indicated that more than 80 percent of the residents of Etorofu and more than 70 percent on the other three islands were opposed to the return of their islands to Japan.[30] Vladimir Zaitsev, deputy chairman of the Sakhalin Soviet of People's Deputies, told a visiting Japanese parliamentary delegation in March 1991 that he supported the return of the Habomai group and Shikotan. A similar view was expressed by Anatolii P. Aksenov, chairman of the Sakhalin Oblast Soviet of People's Deputies. Gorbachev's press spokesperson and aide to the Soviet president, Vitali Ignatenko, stated that the Soviet leader would come to Japan with a comprehensive package of proposals including one for the resolution of the territorial dispute.[31] The independent newspaper *Interfax* reported in March that the Soviet Foreign Ministry appeared to have decided to return the Habomai group and Shikotan to Japan if Japan would abandon its claims to the other two islands.[32] Finally, the chairman of the Democratic Party of Russia, Nikolai I. Travkin, said he would return the disputed islands to Japan not for money but for the sake of good relations with Japanese neighbors.[33]

As the April summit between Kaifu and Gorbachev approached, Tokyo floated a proposal to entice Moscow into a territorial concession. LDP Secretary General Ichiro Ozawa stated that the LDP favored the return of the Habomai group and Shikotan first and a phased turnover of Kunashiri and Etorofu in exchange for Soviet recognition of Japanese sovereignty over the entire Northern Territories. The LDP was also reportedly preparing an economic aid package amounting to three trillion yen (more than $20 billion), including $4 billion in emergency loans and another $9.3 billion in economic projects.

In early April, the Japanese government decided to abandon its longstanding demand for simultaneous return of all the disputed territories and decided to seek first the reversion of the Habomai group and Shikotan on the basis of the 1956 joint declaration on condition that the Soviet Union would recognize Japanese sovereignty over the other two islands as well.[34] This position was endorsed by the leading opposition party, the Social Democratic Party (SDP) (formerly the Japan Socialist Party), and the second largest opposition party, Komeito. A majority of the public also favored the phased return of the islands.

If anybody had expected Gorbachev to offer major concessions, however, such an expectation proved unfounded and quite unrealistic. In the face of rising nationalism in the Russian and other republics and the increasingly restless military and communists, Gorbachev would have risked his already weakening political power at home had he offered any important concessions to Japan in the spring of 1991. The joint communiqué issued at the conclusion of the talks in Tokyo acknowledged the existence of the dispute; it even named all the disputed territories. However, Gorbachev did not accept the 1956 joint declaration as a starting point for negotiations toward a peace treaty, nor did he recognize latent Japanese sovereignty over the disputed territories.

On the economic front, the summit produced similarly limited results. Although the two sides signed fifteen agreements pledging cooperation in wide-ranging areas, the level of cooperation envisaged was very modest. Areas of bilateral cooperation included political dialogue, Japanese technical assistance for Soviet economic reform, trade and payments, fisheries, civil aviation, environment, science and technology, cultural exchange, and the settlement of the issue of Japanese prisoners of war incarcerated in Siberia during World War II. The Soviet president also obtained Tokyo's pledge to support Soviet membership in the Pacific Economic Cooperation Council.[35]

Despite the lack of progress on the territorial issue and limited headway on economic cooperation, the Kaifu-Gorbachev summit clearly marked the beginning of a new era in Japanese-Soviet relations. Tokyo and Moscow finally found a common ground for conducting dialogue over political and security issues of mutual concern. On regional security issues, Kaifu welcomed the establishment of diplomatic relations between the Soviet Union and South Korea, and Gorbachev expressed appreciation of the start of talks between Japan and North Korea for the normalization of relations. Kaifu and Gorbachev also agreed that North Korea should promptly conclude a safeguards agreement with the International Atomic Energy Agency. Kaifu also spoke approvingly of Moscow's effort as a permanent member of the UN Security Council regarding the conflict in Cambodia, and Gorbachev favorably evaluated Tokyo's effort to bring about a comprehensive political settlement to the conflict.

The Economic Crisis and Dissolution of the Soviet Union

Throughout 1990 and 1991 there were signs of deepening economic crisis in the Soviet Union. Output of the Soviet economy had fallen 4 percent in 1990, the largest decline for any major nation in the postwar period; during the first quarter of 1991, Soviet national income dropped by 10 percent from a year earlier and GNP by 8 percent; public-sector productivity also declined by 9 percent and investment by 16 percent. The Soviet government's budget deficit amounted to 31.1 billion rubles and was fast growing. Hyperinflation was feared, with the prices of consumer goods rising by as much as 80 percent from a year before. Finally, the Soviet Union's foreign debt reached about $68–81 billion as of November 1991, and during the first quarter of 1991 foreign trade shrank by as much as 33.8 percent.[36] The production of oil, an important export item that accounted for 60 percent of foreign currency earnings in the first half of the 1980s, peaked at 12.5 million barrels per day in 1988 and had dropped to 10.4 million by early 1991.[37]

The economic woes in the Soviet Union also affected its economic relations with Japan. In 1990, Japan's exports to the Soviet Union plunged about 20 percent, to about $2.5 billion, resulting in the first Japanese trade deficit ($600 million) with the Soviet Union in sixteen years.[38] And the first half of 1991 saw Soviet exports to Japan drop another 20 percent.[39] Long delays in Soviet payments for Japanese exports impeded improvement of bilateral trade, the falling hard currency earnings by the Soviets were blamed for the delays, and growing Soviet arrears ($500 million as of June 1991) had reduced the Soviets' already precarious credibility as a trading partner. In May 1991, Japanese banks were forced to stop issuing loans to the Soviet Union because of the increased credit risk.

How did Japan respond to these developments? Tokyo initially refused to view Japanese-Soviet relations except from the narrow perspective of how the developments in the Soviet Union might affect the fate of the territorial dispute. Prime Minister Takeshita elevated the Northern Territories issue to the global level when he obtained the Western leaders' support for Japan's position on this issue at the G7 Summit in Houston in July 1990. Only after the United States, Germany, and the European Community approved emergency aid to the Soviet Union in January 1991 did Tokyo decide to extend humanitarian aid of food and medical supplies.[40] At the G7 Summit in London in July 1991, Prime Minister Kaifu joined U.S. President George Bush and British Prime Minister John Major in arguing against the Western economic aid that had been proposed by French President François Mitterand and German Chancellor Helmut Kohl. Major, as chairman of the G7 Summit, issued a statement in support of the full normalization of Japan-Soviet relations, including resolution of the Northern Territories issue. Following the summit, Kaifu met with Gorbachev and called for acceleration of talks on the conclusion of a peace treaty to solve the territorial dispute, and pledged Japanese technical assistance.[41] The "G7 plus 1" meeting between the summit leaders and Gorbachev in London produced an agreement in support of Soviet economic reform but stopped short of the financial assistance sought by Moscow.[42]

At the Bush-Gorbachev summit in Moscow in July 1991, the U.S. president stated twice that the Soviet-Japanese territorial dispute was one of the remaining obstacles to the full reconciliation between East and West and nudged the Soviet leader to concede on this issue. Bush realized that the transformation of the Soviet economy into a market economy was essential to its integration into the world economy and to the forging of a new world order. He apparently recognized that Western economic aid, particularly that of Japan, would be vital to the success of Soviet economic reforms, but that Japanese assistance was not forthcoming without progress on the Northern Territories issue.

Tokyo also argued that Western aid would be wasted in a Soviet Union that appeared either unwilling or unable to proceed with the development of a stable market economy. On the one hand, Japanese apprehensions seemed vindicated by the unsuccessful communist coup against Gorbachev on August 19–21, 1991, and by the dramatic political changes that ensued. On the other hand, the same developments increased international pressure for economic assistance to the Soviet Union and, following the dissolution of the Soviet Union, to Russia.

In the wake of the failed coup, Gorbachev resigned as general-secretary of the Communist Party of the Soviet Union and declared the dissolution of the party. In September, Gorbachev established a provisional governmental structure composed of a national council, an interrepublic economic committee, and a new Supreme Soviet. The Soviet Union recognized the independence of Latvia, Lithuania, and Estonia. In October, Russia and eleven other Soviet republics agreed to an economic union.[43] In early November the Russian Congress of People's Deputies gave Yeltsin sweeping powers to end government control of prices on nearly all goods, bring privatization of state enterprises, break up collective farms, and revamp the monetary system. Then came the final blow to Gorbachev. On December 8, Russia, Ukraine, and Byelorussia formed the Commonwealth of Independent States and declared the dissolution of Gorbachev's government.

The failed coup and the subsequent developments in the Soviet Union also convinced many in the West that economic aid would be crucial in saving the Soviet Union, and later Russia, from total collapse.[44] Although Tokyo wanted Moscow's concessions on the bilateral territorial dispute before it would extend economic assistance to the Soviet Union, it also wanted to avoid international isolation on the issue of Western aid.[45] Thus began Japan's formidable task of balancing its political interests vis-à-vis the former Soviet Union and Russia and its desire to be a leading member of the international community.

In October 1991 Tokyo joined the G7 agreement to help the Soviets devise a reform program. The Japanese government also announced an economic aid package valued at $2.5 billion, including $500 million in Export-Import Bank loans for food, medicine, and other humanitarian aid and tax breaks for private-level humanitarian aid. It also included measures to reduce the burden on Japanese companies trading with the Soviet Union, such as $1.8 billion in trade insurance to cover any Japanese commercial losses and $200 million in Export-Import Bank trade credit for Soviet exports to Japan.

Tokyo also announced a package of technical assistance programs in the fields of energy, conversion of military industries to civilian production, distribution, and nuclear energy.[46] Moreover, following the implementation of a sweeping economic reform in Russia in January 1992, and in the face of the deepening economic crisis in the CIS, Japan and forty-six other nations met in Washington, D.C., and agreed on five general action plans. The measures were designed to improve and expand the transfer of medicine, food, shelter, energy, and technical assistance to the commonwealth states. Japan also pledged an additional $50 million in humanitarian aid earmarked for the International Red Cross. At the same meeting, Japanese Foreign Minister Michio Watanabe revealed Tokyo's three-point policy. Tokyo conditioned substantial aid on (1) speedy economic reforms in the former Soviet republics, (2) acceleration of political reforms and a fundamental policy shift toward a nonmilitary big power, and (3) the application of diplomacy based on law and justice in Asia Pacific and early conclusion of a peace treaty between Japan and Russia.[47] To Japan, diplomacy based on "law and justice" meant, above all else, resolution of the territorial dispute to Japan's satisfaction.

Prospects for Japanese Economic Assistance to Russia

Of the factors that had influenced Japanese-Soviet economic relations in the Cold War decades, the relations of the United States with the former Soviet Union and with its successor today have a substantially diminished impact. The economic relations between Japan and Russia today are more heavily affected by the political and economic developments in Russia and by bilateral issues, the most important being the territorial dispute. Tokyo's most pressing economic policy question vis-à-vis Moscow is how much and what kind of economic assistance it should extend to Moscow in the absence of an acceptable settlement of the Northern Territories problem.

The domestic situation in Russia remains highly uncertain. On the one hand, there are some encouraging signs of democratization and liberalization. The ideological influence of the communists in the political process has largely disappeared, with communist members of the Russian Congress of People's Deputies constituting only a small minority.[48] In the wake of the failed coup in August 1991, the military has lost its unity and today is in no position to reverse the liberalization trends in the country, although the military-industrial complex can frustrate Yeltsin's efforts to convert the military industry to civilian production.[49] Most intellectuals, even those with only limited Western ties, are convinced that constitutional and legislative reforms are necessary to bring foreign capital-technological investments into Russia and to integrate the Russian economy into the international system.[50] The public is generally resigned to the need of further economic reforms, including privatization of property.[51]

On the other hand, political and economic problems continue to mount. The Russian parliament remains immobilized by the absence of a clear-cut balance of power among the diverse political orientations represented in the body. The jockeying for power between Yeltsin and the Russian parliament continues with no end in sight, and there is growing resentment among conservative and moderate members of the parliament over the Western countries' well-publicized support of Yeltsin and lack of contact with the parliament.[52] Russian intellectuals' support of Yeltsin has weakened substantially since his dramatic rise to power in the wake of the 1991 coup.[53] The Russian president's popularity among the general public is also bound to drop as the economy continues to slide.[54] Widespread social unrest cannot be ruled out.[55] Particularly problematic in this regard are the rigidities and inefficiencies of bureaucratic institutions that have continued in Russia long after the dissolution of the communist-controlled Soviet system.[56] The privatization of state assets continues with no effective parliamentary oversight.[57] Nationalism is on the rise and there is a growing sense of betrayal among the public, particularly among rural populations, that their leaders had reduced the great superpower Soviet Union to a weak Russia.[58] Moderate reformists find themselves handicapped against extremist elements who advocate national unity through either Bolshevik-style reforms or Russian nationalism as a solution to all problems, political or economic.[59] Finally, ethnic and nationalist tensions and conflicts sweeping across central Asia are likely to complicate Russian economic reforms and hamper any improvement in economic relations among CIS members.[60]

There is widespread belief among Russian intellectuals that Western assistance and investment are essential for successful economic reforms in the country. Many Russians, both in and out of the government, also believe that Russia's successful transformation from a centrally planned economy to a market-oriented economy is vital for the country's integration into the world economy as well as for its constructive participation in the development of a new world political order in the post–Cold War era. Many Russian intellectuals are hopeful that Western governments and business leaders share the same view.[61]

These hopes must be balanced by a sober analysis of obstacles to closer Russian economic ties with the West. The absence of a legal tradition in Russia is a major problem.[62] There is a dilemma in the fact that a stable domestic environment would be necessary to promote foreign investment but, conversely, investment by foreign businesses would be necessary to create a favorable domestic climate. It is also questionable whether the economic development models developed in the West can be effectively adopted in Russia's effort to move from a socialist to a capitalist economy.[63] Industrial monopolies continue in the wake of the gradual privatization of state industries, making it difficult for small and medium Russian enterprises to take full advantage of the growing entrepreneurial spirit in the country.[64]

Those in the Russian Foreign Ministry who are concerned with Japanese relations are generally agreed that the only significant obstacle to the conclusion of a peace treaty with Japan is the dispute over the southern Kuril Islands and that some Russian concessions are necessary.[65] There is no question that many Russian leaders would like to see a resolution of the territorial dispute with Japan and would be willing to offer concessions to achieve it. For example, Ruslan Khasbulatov, acting speaker of the Russian parliament, stated in September 1991 that the territorial dispute should be solved on the basis of the principles of law and justice. Yeltsin also appeared to want to speed up his five-step solution to the dispute.[66] Russian Foreign Minister Andrei Kozyrev hinted the territorial dispute might be solved either by submitting the case to the International Court of Justice or on the basis of the 1956 Japanese-Soviet joint declaration.[67]

However, the political situation in Russia severely limits the options available to the Russian leadership. Many Russian intellectuals are afraid that the Japanese side does not fully understand the domestic situation in Russia. They point out that the territorial dispute has become an object of power struggle in Russia, with anti-Yeltsin forces exploiting the issue to mobilize nationalist elements against any concessions to Japan.[68] Some in Moscow believe that the prospects for Russian concessions to Japan on the territorial issue today are worse than when Gorbachev visited Tokyo in April 1991.[69] Would Yeltsin offer a major concession to the Japanese if he was not confident that his political power was strong enough to withstand the domestic criticism that would follow any compromise on his part? Even if Yeltsin offered to return the Habomai group and Shikotan to Japan on the basis of the 1956 joint declaration, which he could argue was Soviet law that his government had inherited, would this be acceptable to Tokyo?[70] There would still be a big gap between this compromise and the Japanese position that Russia acknowledge Japanese sovereignty over all the disputed islands.[71]

It was against this uncertain background that Yeltsin announced on September 9, 1992, that he was postponing his visit to Tokyo. Although the possibility of postponement had been rumored earlier, it had been ruled out as both Tokyo and Moscow continued preparing for the scheduled visit. Therefore, the announcement, coming only four days before the scheduled visit, came as a diplomatic bewilderment and psychological disappointment in Japan. Some Japanese observers attributed Yeltsin's abrupt decision to Moscow's long-standing tendency to underestimate the importance of Japan[72] and a shift in the balance of power in Russia in favor of conservative, nationalist elements.[73] The cautious optimism that had characterized Japanese expectations prior to Yeltsin's startling announcement quickly gave way to widespread pessimism. Some analysts maintained Japan had no alternative but to wait indefinitely for a favorable turn of events in Russia,[74] whereas others called for a more flexible Japanese approach to bring about improvement of overall bilateral relations before a territorial solution could be found.[75] Nobuo Matsunaga, former Japanese ambassador to the United States and former vice foreign minister, acknowledged that Japan may have put too much public emphasis on the territorial dispute, to the detriment of Yeltsin's domestic position, and called on the two countries to move forward on both the territorial issue and economic cooperation.[76]

Developments since Yeltsin's postponement of his visit to Tokyo have been both discouraging and confusing to the Japanese. In September 1992, the Sakhalin government was reportedly seeking Moscow's legislative approval of its plan to develop a special economic zone in the southern Kuril Islands and invite foreign investment and other participation. As a part of this effort, the Sakhalin government announced in September its decision to lease 278 hectares of land in Shikotan to a Hong Kong–based company. The Sakhalin government was also reportedly seeking the cooperation of an Australian firm in developing golf courses on the island of Kunashiri.[77]

Whatever formula Tokyo and Moscow might ultimately adopt to resolve the territorial dispute, the timing of the settlement would be crucial. Against the rising tide of nationalism in Russia, any territorial concessions by Moscow would be intolerable to many Russians. In May 1992, Yeltsin had stated he would like to see a peace treaty concluded in 1993. It would seem that even if a peace treaty could be concluded, including the transfer of Kunashiri and Etorofu islands, the submission of the treaty to the Russian parliament and—as required by the Russian constitution—to national referendum might have to wait a few more years, until such time that Yeltsin's political position had substantially solidified and the domestic economic situation had considerably improved.[78] Any territorial agreement that might be reached without acceptance by a majority of the Russian people would be bound to generate lasting resentment among them, to the detriment of stable relations between the two countries in the long term.[79] Moreover, if Japan were viewed as taking advantage of the vulnerability of the Russian situation, it would be counterproductive.[80]

_____ *Conclusions*

It is clear that the economic reforms and stabilization of Russia, and Western economic involvement in the country, have political as well as economic significance. It is imperative that Western governments assist Russia. If Japan and Russia are to develop stable and lasting relations, Tokyo will have to take a more active part in this area. Needless to say, Tokyo must carefully balance its interests vis-à-vis the territorial dispute with Moscow and its larger international responsibilities. This is a formidable task indeed.

Tokyo will be well advised to actively pursue the policy of "expanded equilibrium," adroitly exploiting a partial divorce between political and economic issues. At a minimum, Japan will have to expand its package of technical assistance further. Japan is providing technical assistance in five areas: (1) dispatch of private-level missions in the field of military-to-civilian conversion; (2) dispatch of consultants and acceptance of trainees in the area of production and management modernization; (3) assistance in the modernization of a distribution system; (4) trade promotion through trade fairs; and (5) exchange of official personnel in industrial technology and fiscal and financial policies. However, the scope of the technical assistance is too limited; so is its potential impact.

So far, Japanese technical assistance has concentrated on Russia's Far Eastern region, an area of central interest to Japanese businesses. A number of developments in Siberia and the Russian Far East have attracted the attention of Japanese business circles. Vladivostok was open to foreign ships effective January 1, 1992. Efforts are under way to establish special economic zones in the Primorskii region. Japanese companies are considering cooperation with their Russian counterparts in developing communication infrastructure in the Far Eastern region. The Japan-USSR Trade Association is studying a plan to expand the capacity of the port of Vanino, located across the La Peruse Strait from Sakhalin. Japanese businesses believe that if and when the BAM Railroad expands its freight capacity and the railroad connecting Komsomolsk-na-Amure and Vanino is improved, the port in question may grow into a major point of exit for coal, petroleum products, and other bulk cargo. There is even a plan to construct a trade center in Vladivostok. The United Nations Development Program (UNDP) is actively promoting the development of a commercial and transportation center on the Tumen River, which borders northeast China, the Russian Far East, and North Korea. If these ideas and plans materialize, some Japanese firms are likely to come forth with investments in the region.[81] For now, however, they are awaiting their government's decision to step up cooperation in technical assistance with the United States and other governments.

Finally, even under the best of scenarios, economic relations between Japan and Russia are likely to be limited for some time, and this is largely due to the substantially wide gap in the level of private-sector development and attendant lack of economic complementarity between the two countries.[82] Japan's economic needs are dictated largely by its industry's capital- and technology-intensive character, whereas the Russian economy, despite the highly developed military sector, requires first and foremost the development of private markets and civilian industrial capacity to meet the consumer needs of the population. The development of market forces and expansion of civilian production in Russia will be a long-term process, perhaps requiring ten to fifteen years, and any immediate benefits to Japanese business concerns are likely to be limited.

As for the territorial dispute, the most promising solution seems to be a phased solution according to which a peace treaty will be concluded within a fairly short time (perhaps one to two years), committing Russia to the return of the Habomai group and Shikotan shortly thereafter. The treaty might either include a provision acknowledging Japanese sovereignty over the entire Northern Territories or be accompanied by a joint declaration of intent to work out the reversion of the remaining two islands and demilitarization of the entire Northern Territories within a reasonable time frame (five to ten years).

Should Tokyo rigidly stick to its position on the territorial issue, it would risk turning the rising Russian nationalism against Japan. Japanese-Russian animosities might well outlive the Cold War in Northeast Asia. It would also seriously hurt Japan's potential role in integrating Russia into the world. The worst scenario for Japan would be a continued Japanese-Russian territorial stalemate and substantially improved Russian relations with the other Western countries. Surely, this is a prospect that Japan cannot afford if it is to expand its political role in the posthegemonic world.

Notes

I wish to thank the Japan Foundation for granting me a professional fellowship in the summer of 1991, enabling me to conduct field research in Tokyo, Sapporo, and Niigata, Japan, in May-September. I am also grateful to the Center for Global Partnership of the Japan Foundation for awarding a research grant to the Center for East Asian Studies, Monterey Institute of International Studies, which allowed me to conduct a series of interviews in Moscow in May–June 1992. Thanks are also due to the many individuals in Japan and Russia who provided valuable time and information for my field research. Needless to say, I alone am responsible for the contents of this chapter.

1. Shigeo Natsui (consul, Consulate General of Japan, San Francisco), "Speech for Roundtable Discussions, Stanford University, May 15, 1991," mimeo.

2. For a summary of these projects, see Raymond S. Mathieson, *Japan's Role in Soviet Economic Growth: Transfer of Technology Since 1965*, New York: Praeger, 1979, pp. 12–13. A Japanese account can be found in Kazuo Ogawa and Takashi Murakami, *Mezameru Soren Kyokutō: Nihon no Hatasu Yakuwari* [The awakening Soviet Far East: The role Japan should play], Tokyo: Nihon Keizai Hyōronsha, 1991, pp. 204–224.

3. Crude oil exports to Japan during the 1970s were considerably less than during the preceding decade, with the Soviets showing more interest in exporting their oil to Europe. Soviet exports of crude even in the peak year of 1973 stood at a modest $30.6 million. These and the other trade statistics used in this chapter, unless otherwise noted, come from the Japan Association for Trade with the Soviet Union and Central–Eastern Europe (now Japan Association for Trade with Russia and Central–Eastern Europe), Tokyo.

4. Unlike most other Western aid to the Soviet Union, Japanese bank loans to the Soviet Union had ties in that they could be used only for Soviet purchase of Japanese products except when the Soviets desired products unavailable in Japan.

5. This point was brought to my attention by Alexei Zagorsky, the author of Chapter 6.

6. Herbert J. Ellison, *The Soviet Union and Northeast Asia*, Asian Agenda Report 13, Lanham, Maryland: University Press of America, for the Asia Society, 1989, p. 29.

7. Shinichiro Tabata, "The Japanese-Soviet Economic Future," *Acta Slavica Iaponica* (Sapporo), March 1991, table 1.

8. For a Japanese view on the economic sanctions, see Ogawa and Murakami, *Mezameru Soren Kyokuto*, pp. 199–203.

9. MITI directed Japanese companies trading with socialist countries to develop and strictly observe a compliance program. The Security Export Control Office in the Export Division of MITI's International Trade Administration Bureau closely monitored Japanese export activities.

10. Unyushō Unyuseisakukyoku Jōhōkanribu, ed., *Unyukankei Enerugi Yōran* [A summary of transport-related energy], Tokyo: Okurashō Insatsukyoku, 1991, pp. 44–45.

11. Masataka Sase, "Over a Barrel?" *Look Japan*, February 1991, p. 12.

12. Robert E. Rehbein, "The Japan-Soviet Far East Trade Relationship: A Case of the Cautious Buyer and the Overconfident Seller," *Journal of Northeast Asian Studies*, Summer 1989, p. 39.

13. Ibid., pp. 48–52.

14. The imbalance had all but disappeared by the end of the decade, and in 1990 the trade gap turned in the Soviets' favor by $788 million. Tabata, "The Japanese-Soviet Economic Future," p. 6. In 1991, the balance again turned in Japan's favor.

15. Susan L. Clark, "Japan's Role in Gorbachev's Agenda," *Pacific Review*, vol. 1, no. 3 (1988), pp. 281–282.

16. Hiroshi Kimura, "Gorbachev's Agenda for Asia," *Pacific Review*, vol. 1, no. 3 (1988), pp. 215–226.

17. Robert A. Scalapino, "The China Policy of the USSR and Asian Security in the 1990s," paper delivered at the conference on Superpower Détente and Localization of Conflict, Monterey Institute of International Studies, Monterey, California, March 12, 1991.

18. Bōeichō, *Bōei Hakusho* [Defense white paper], 1990, Tokyo: Okurashō Insatsukyoku, pp. 44–59.

19. *Keizai Sokuhō* [Instant economic report], Japan Association for Trade with the Soviet Union and Central–Eastern Europe, Tokyo, February 5, 1990. It should be noted, however, that virtually all ventures failed to turn in a profit. Among the problems were conflicting expectations between the Soviet and Japanese partners, unfounded speculations about business prospects, fraudulent business practices, hard currency shortfalls, lack of management experience and skills on the Soviet side, bureaucratic red tape, unclear Soviet legislation on foreign trade and joint ventures, and the uncertain political future of the Soviet Union.

20. Kaifu made the statement in his interview with *Literaturnaya Gazeta* on June 15, reprinted in "Japan-Soviet Relations: Current and Future Prospects. Excerpts from Interviews with Japanese Prime Ministers Published in the Soviet Press," Tokyo: Ministry of Foreign Affairs, March 1991, p. 6.

21. For other discussions of the territorial dispute, see Kenichi Ito, "Japan and the Soviet Union Entangled in the Deadlock of the Northern Territories," *The Washington Quarterly*, vol. 11, no. 1 (Winter 1988), pp. 35–44; Hiroshi Kimura, *Hoppō Ryōdo: Kiseki to Henkan eno Josō* [The Northern Territories: The locus and initial steps toward their return], Tokyo: Jijitsūshinsha, 1989; Toru Nakagawa, "Japan's Northern Territories in International Politics," *Japan Review of International Affairs*, vol. 2, no. 1 (Spring/Summer 1988), pp. 3–23; and Haruki Wada, *Hoppō Ryōdo Mondai o Kangaeru* [Thoughts on the problem of the Northern Territories], Tokyo: Iwanami Shoten, 1990.

22. Japan does not recognize the Soviet claims. For a detailed analysis of the Japanese response to the Soviet establishment of a two-hundred-mile EEZ, see Tsuneo Akaha, *Japan in Global Ocean Politics*, Honolulu: University of Hawaii Press and Law of the Sea Institute, 1985, pp. 110–149.

23. Mark J. Valencia and Noel Ludwig, "Minerals and Fishing at Stake in Northern Territories Talks," *Japan Times*, Weekly International Edition, February 25–March 3, 1991, p. 8.

24. Ibid.

25. On the political significance of the dispute to Japan, see Chapter 6 by Zagorsky.

26. "Further on Shevardnadze-Uno Meetings in Moscow: Hint at Partial Territory Settlement," *FBIS Daily Report/SOV*, March 22, 1989, pp. 17–18. There were a number of other signs of a softening Soviet stance on the territorial issue. In November 1989, Aleksander Yakovlev, a Politburo member and one of Gorbachev's principal foreign policy advisers, spoke in Tokyo of a "third way," implying the territorial problem could and should be resolved in concert with other issues on the Soviet-Japanese agenda. "Yakovlev Hints New Soviet Offer on Northern Islands Issue" and "Yakovlev: No Miracle Solution," *Daily Yomiuri*, November 14, 1989, p. 1, and November 16, 1989, p. 1, respectively. In mid-October 1990, Gennadii Yanaev, the Soviet Communist Party Central Committee member responsible for foreign relations, and Sergei Akhromeev, Soviet presidential adviser, supported a return to the 1956 joint declaration as a starting point in territorial negotiations. *Asahi Shimbun*, October 15, 1991, pp. 1 and 2; *Japan Times*, March 2, 1991, p. 1.

27. Gorbachev was reported to have made the statement during his meeting with Japanese Foreign Minister Taro Nakayama in Moscow in late January 1991. *Daily Yomiuri*, February 5, 1991, p. 1. Deputy Foreign Minister Igor A. Rogachev cautioned against growing optimism in Japan and stated that Gorbachev's visit to Japan alone would not resolve the territorial problem. *Tass*, January 22, 1991, reported in *FBIS Soviet Union*, January 24, 1991, p. 7.

28. Defense Minister Dmitrii Yazov warned that territorial concessions to Japan would compromise the security of the Soviet Union, and Commander of the Far East Military District General Viktor Novozhilov declared the Soviet Union could no longer be considered a great power if it gave up the disputed islands. *Japan Times*, April 13, 1991, p. 3; *FBIS Soviet Union*, April 17, 1991, p. 63.

29. Sakhalin has administrative jurisdiction over the Northern Territories.

30. Only 9.6 percent of the Etorofu residents and 21.9 percent of the Kunashiri, Habomai, and Shikotan islanders favored a return of the islands. *Japan Times*, March 19, 1991, p. 1, and March 20, 1991, p. 1.

31. *Yomiuri Shimbun*, February 7, 1991, pp. 1 and 2.

32. *Japan Times*, March 19, 1991, p. 1.

33. *Komsomolskaya Pravda*, March 19, 1991, p. 1; reported in *FBIS Soviet Union*, March 26, 1991, p. 4.

34. *Yomiuri Shimbun*, April 11, 1991, p. 1.

35. The Soviet Union was formally admitted into the organization in October 1991.

36. *Daily Yomiuri*, November 21, 1991; Tsuneaki Sato, "Soren Keizai ni Shohōsen wa Aruka" [Is there a prescription for Soviet economy?], *Sekai*, no. 555 (June 1991), pp. 64–66.

37. Thomas W. Lippman and Mark Potts, "From Oil Exporter to Giant Sponge," *Washington Post*, National Weekly Edition, February 11–17, 1991, p. 22; *Nihon Keizai Shimbun*, November 27, 1990, p. 5.

38. *Japan Times*, January 5, 1991, p. 7.

39. *Keizai Sokuhō*, no. 861 (August 15, 1991), p. 1.

40. Keisuke Okada, "LDP and Bureaucracy Battle over Economic Aid to Soviets," *Japan Times*, Weekly International Edition, December 10–16, 1990, pp. 1 and 8; "Japan Moves Toward Food Aid for Soviets," *Japan Times*, Weekly International Edition, December 24–30, 1990, pp. 1 and 5; "Tokyo to Lend Moscow $100 Million for Food," *New York Times*, December 19, 1990, p. A8; *Nihon Keizai Shimbun*, November 27, 1990, p. 2.

41. *Asahi Shimbun*, July 18, 1991, p. 1.

42. The agreement included the Soviet Union's "special association" with the IMF and the World Bank; cooperation with the Soviet Union by other international organizations, including the European Bank for Reconstruction and Development and the Organization for Economic Cooperation and Development; Western technical assistance in energy, transportation, and other fields; improved market access for Soviet goods and services; visits to Moscow by Prime Minister Major as G7 chairman in 1991–1992 and Western finance ministers.

43. The other republics joining the economic union were Byelorussia, Kazakhstan, Uzbekistan, Tadzhikistan, Turkmenia, Kirghizia, and Armenia. Ukraine joined the union a month later.

44. Some even believed that the West's failure to extend helping hands to the proreform forces in the Soviet Union was one of the background factors that prompted the coup attempt. *Asahi Shimbun*, evening edition, August 22, 1991, p. 2.

45. Hisao Kanamori, "Soren Keizai o Mite" [On observing the Soviet economy], *Keizai Sokuho*, no. 859 (July 25, 1991), p. 8; Kazuo Ogawa, "Gorubachofu Honichigo no Nisso Keizai Kankei" [Japan-Soviet economic relations after Gorbachev's visit to Japan], *Keizai Sokuho*, no. 859 (July 25, 1991), p. 12.

46. *Nihon Keizai Shimbun*, October 9, 1991, p. 6.

47. *Asahi Shimbun*, January 24, 1992, p. 1.

48. According to Sergei A. Michailov, a people's deputy and deputy chairman of the Russian Supreme Soviet's Committee for Foreign Affairs and International Economic Relations, only fifty of some one thousand deputies are communists. Author's interview with Michailov, Moscow, June 1, 1992.

49. Author's interview with Valery I. Gerasimov, a people's deputy and vice-chairman of the Russian Supreme Soviet's Committee on Health Protection, Social Security, and Physical Culture, Moscow, June 1, 1992.

50. This view was widely shared by the twenty-two individuals the author interviewed in Moscow in May and June 1992, including four Russian Foreign Ministry officials; five people's deputies in the Supreme Soviet of the Russian Federation; and thirteen researchers in the Diplomatic Academy of the Russian Foreign Ministry, Institute of the U.S.A. and Canada, Institute of World Economy and International Relations (IMEMO), Institute of Oriental Studies, Institute of Far Eastern Studies, Yavlinsky Institute, and Gorbachev Foundation.

51. This view was shared by those interviewed by the author in Moscow in May and June 1992.

52. Author's interviews with Sergei A. Michailov and Valery I. Gerasimov, Moscow, June 1, 1992.

53. Many of the individuals interviewed by the author said Yeltsin was a choice by default because a viable alternative to the Russian president to lead Russia during the transition period could not be found.

54. Yeltsin's price liberalization policy caused uncontrollable inflation, massive unemployment, and shortages of daily necessities in Russia generally and in the provinces particularly.

55. Author's interviews in Moscow, May and June 1992, with George E. Komarovskii, senior counselor, Russian Ministry of Foreign Affairs; Igor Tyshetsky, senior researcher, Diplomatic Academy of the Russian Ministry of Foreign Affairs,

and director-general, Russian-Japanese Medical Foundation; Alexei Bogaturov, senior researcher, Institute of the U.S.A. and Canada; and Mikhail Kozhokin, senior researcher, Yavlinsky Institute.

56. Problems of bureaucracies were pointed out by every one of the interviewees in Moscow in May and June 1992. The Russian government of 1992 had more ministries and state committees than the Soviet government during the Gorbachev years.

57. Author's interview with Sergei A. Michailov, Moscow, June 1, 1992.

58. Author's interview with Vassili I. Saplin, first deputy head, Asia-Pacific Department, Russian Ministry of Foreign Affairs, Moscow, May 25, 1992.

59. Author's interview with Valery I. Gerasimov, Moscow, June 1, 1992.

60. Author's interview with George E. Komarovskii, Moscow, May 25, 1992.

61. This observation is based on the author's interviews in Moscow in May and June 1992.

62. This was clearly recognized by many Russian intellectuals. Author's interviews with Yuri Baturin, adviser to Gorbachev, deputy director, Center for Political Studies, Gorbachev Foundation, Moscow, June 5, 1992; and Grigoryi S. Bondarev, a people's deputy and member of the Committee for Foreign Affairs and International Economic Relations, Supreme Soviet of the Russian Federation, Moscow, June 1, 1992.

63. Author's interview with George E. Komarovskii, May 25, 1992.

64. Author's interviews with Valery I. Gerasimov, Moscow, June 1, 1992; and George E. Komarovskii, Moscow, May 25, 1992.

65. Author's interviews with George E. Komarovskii, Vassili I. Saplin, and Andre M. Yefimov, chief of the Japanese Division, Russian Ministry of Foreign Affairs, Moscow, May 25, 1992.

66. *Asahi Shimbun,* September 10, 1991, p. 1. It was also reported that in his meeting with U.S. Secretary of State James Baker in Moscow in September 1991, Yeltsin indicated that he was prepared to expedite the resolution of the territorial dispute with Japan. *Asahi Shimbun,* September 12, 1991, p. 1.

67. *Asahi Shimbun,* September 21, 1991, p. 1.

68. Sakhalin Governor Federov is criticized by some, for example, as using his position against territorial concessions to promote his political status in his region. Author's interviews with Vassili I. Saplin and Andre M. Yefimov, Moscow, May 25, 1992.

69. Author's interview with Andre M. Yefimov, Moscow, May 25, 1992.

70. Russian Deputy Foreign Minister George Kunadze was quoted as indicating Russia's readiness to accept essentially the same compromise position in April 1992. *Asahi Shimbun,* May 2, 1992, p. 2.

71. On April 18, 1992, Japanese Foreign Minister Michio Watanabe stated that if Russia would recognize Japanese sovereignty over the entire Northern Territories, Tokyo would be prepared to recognize Russian administration of Kunashiri and Etorofu until the return of those islands. *Asahi Shimbun,* April 19, 1992, p. 1.

72. Fuji Kamiya, "'Taikokushugiteki Sondaisa' koso Mondai" ["Big-power arrogance" is the problem], *Asahi Shimbun,* September 18, 1992, p. 15.

73. Ibid.; Yutaka Akino, "Dai Roshia Shugi Shihai Shikanezu" [Dominance of great Russianism cannot be ruled out], *Asahi Shimbun,* September 15, 1992, p. 4.

74. Tadao Morimoto, "Tairo Gaiko Shizukani Matsu Igai Michi Nashi" [Diplomacy toward Russia offers no alternative but to wait quietly], *Asahi Shimbun,* September 15, 1992, p. 15.

75. Shigeki Hakamada, "Nichiro no Sōgo Shinrai Jōsei koso Hitsuyō" [Mutual confidence building between Japan and Russia is needed], *Asahi Shimbun,* September 17, 1992, p. 15; Takeshi Tomita, "Susumanu Nichiro Ryōkoku no Sōgo Rikai" [Ja-

pan-Russian mutual understanding showing little progress], *Asahi Shimbun*, September 16, 1992, p. 11.

76. Nobuo Matsunaga, "Dekirukagiri Tairo Shien o, Hōnichi o 'Ryōdo' Shuppatsuten ni" [As much aid to Russia as possible, let's make the visit to Japan the starting point of the "territories"], *Asahi Shimbun*, September 15, 1992, p. 4.

77. *Asahi Shimbun*, October 2, 1992, p. 5.

78. One Russian Foreign Ministry official told the author that if the parliament were to vote on any territorial concession to Japan in June 1992, only 20 percent of the people's deputies would support it. Author's interview with Vassili Istzatov, deputy director, Bureau of Congressional Issues, Russian Ministry of Foreign Affairs, Moscow, June 1, 1992.

79. Author's interview with George E. Komarovskii, Moscow, May 25, 1992.

80. Author's interview with Dmitry V. Petrov, chairman, Department of International Problems of the Far East, Institute of Far Eastern Studies, Moscow, May 27, 1992.

81. Author's interviews with representatives of small and large businesses in Niigata, Hokkaido, and Tokyo in the summer of 1991.

82. Dmitry V. Petrov suggested that Russian economic development was about fifteen years behind that of the Japanese and that Japanese technology was therefore inappropriate for Russian industrial infrastructure. Author's interview with Petrov, Moscow, May 27, 1992.

Chapter 8

Japan's Foreign Policy Choices for the Twenty-first Century: A Chinese Perspective

Zhou Jihua

Japan's Strategic Objectives

The national strategic objective of Japan after the Meiji Restoration was to catch up with and surpass the developed countries in Europe and the United States so as to secure for itself a seat amongst the world's big powers. To this end, Japan adopted a policy of militarism that guided the nation onto the road of strengthening the armed forces (leading to aggression) and making the country rich. This policy led Japan into ferocious contention with the Western imperialists for colonies in the Asia Pacific region, in a bid to build its own sphere of influence. This was also a road that pitted Japan against its Asian neighbors. In the end, Japan was completely defeated in World War II by the peoples of Asia and the world. After the war, Japan embarked on the reconstruction of the country from the war ruins. Japan still aimed at catching up with and surpassing the countries of Europe and the United States by adopting a policy of making the country rich through trade. Under the security umbrella of the United States and free from the disruptions of wars, Japan successfully realized its plan of doubling its national income and miraculously came abreast of the developed nations in Europe and the United States in the 1970s.

In the wake of the pronouncement of the Nixon doctrine in 1969, Japan experienced three shocks: Henry A. Kissinger's secret visit to China (1971), the U.S. dollar shock (1971), and the oil shock (1973). Japan felt a serious sense of crisis in the fields of security, diplomacy, finance, and energy. If the period of catching up with and surpassing Europe and the United States could be metaphorically described as "catching up with a patch of clouds on a mountain slope,"[1] then Japan at the time of the crises was lost in the clouds on a mountain slope. The question of "where Japan should go" was put squarely before Japan.

It was under the condition of the so-called Pax Americana that postwar Japan had smoothly carried out its strategy for economic development and

185

realized its objectives, which otherwise might have been reached by military means as once attempted before World War II. Now that the system of Pax Americana is being shaken, if not beginning to disintegrate, can Japan still manage to go along the road of development that it has followed for decades after the war? Or will Japan resort to a change of course and return to the prewar policy of making the country rich by strengthening its armed forces? The latter option has proved to be a dead end by numerous international events after the war. Only by striving to maintain a free and open international community free from the threat of war can Japan ensure its national survival, social stability, and economic prosperity. Japan has been determined to shake off its status as a junior partner unconditionally following U.S. leadership. It has tried to adapt to the situation, expand its international political role, and place itself on an equal footing with the other big powers of the world. This has been an inevitable strategic objective of the new Japan that had realized its goal of catching up with and surpassing Europe and the United States economically and technologically.

In the view of Japanese foreign policymakers, the ongoing changes in the international situation have been brought about against the background of the decreasing ability of the United States and the Soviet Union to maintain world order. As soon as the equilibrium built on the U.S.-Soviet confrontation breaks down, and in the absence of a new mechanism to maintain order, the destabilizing elements will be on the increase worldwide. The outbreak of the Gulf War was just a case in point. But then what should be the new mechanism for maintaining peace and by whom should it be established?

Japan's Vice Foreign Minister Takakazu Kuriyama elaborated on this when he proposed that as we move from the 1990s to the twenty-first century, and a new international order is being built, the biggest task facing the world is how to establish a structure of international coordination.[2] He holds that the trend of political democratization and economic liberalization is expanding worldwide and that the 1990s will be a decade of reforms on a global scale. The world has to tackle two major tasks: the construction of a global political order after the end of the Cold War and the establishment of an international trade system that can bear the pressures of both protectionism and nationalism. Kuriyama holds that the building of a new international order is basically the work of the big powers. The diplomatic mission of the medium and small countries is how best to fit themselves into the existing order so as to safeguard their own national security and economic interests. Postwar Japanese diplomacy has entailed making the best use of the international order that has been dominated by the United States and in which Japan has translated peace and prosperity into reality. This can be said to be the most successful model of diplomacy for the medium and small countries.

According to Kuriyama's account, of the $20 trillion GNP of the world in 1988, the United States and the European Community each took up $5 trillion and Japan made up for $3 trillion. Japan, as it has become a major member of the developed world, can no longer pursue a diplomacy of passively accepting an international order. Kuriyama maintains Japan has to switch from the diplomacy of the medium and small countries to big power diplomacy and ensure its own national security and prosperity by actively building an international order.

In Kuriyama's view, the common political values and economic principles of the United States, Europe, and Japan are the mainstay in the trend for democratization and liberalization in the world today because their total economic wealth makes up two-thirds of that of the entire world. The era in which the United States by itself sustained the world politically and economically is coming to an end, and a coordinated system among the United States, Europe, and Japan now holds the key to world peace and security. The responsibility of building a new international order for the 1990s must be jointly shared by the developed countries of Europe, the United States, and Japan. However, Japan knows that its own strength still is no match for that of the United States or Europe. Japan, in the number three position, has to cooperate with the other two and use its strength effectively in shouldering the responsibility for making international rules.

In January 1989, U.S. President George Bush and Japanese Prime Minister Noboru Takeshita decided jointly to transform their countries' relations into a "global partnership."[3] In March they also added Europe to this relationship, emphasizing that the United States, Europe, and Japan should engage in more frequent tripolar political consultations and coordination.[4] Kuriyama has put a footnote to this idea and unmistakably signaled that Japan has come to define its own international standing within this framework. In other words, the international order will be masterminded by the United States, Europe, and Japan under the tripolar system.

Whether the analysis and assessment of the international situation by the Japanese diplomat are correct may be subject to discussion, yet they at least reflect in one respect the decisionmaking tendencies of Japanese foreign policy authorities. As a matter of fact, no matter how the international pattern will unfold itself, the series of structural changes that are currently taking place in the political, economic, and military fields around the world have brought about serious challenges to all countries. Japan, the newly emergent economic superpower, is meeting the challenges of the era with a strategic posture of playing a more active global leadership role that corresponds with its economic status.[5]

Challenges Confronting Japan

The United States, Europe, and Japan possess two-thirds of the world's total economy, and their ability to influence the world economy and international affairs has increased in the current stage of world development where competition for comprehensive national strength is the predominant feature. During this period, however, political pluralism and military strength still command important international influence. Many medium and small countries, some of whom are big powers in terms of military might, are no longer in the weak and powerless position they once were in prewar time.

At present, the trend toward democratization in international relations is irresistible. Will the "rich nations club" of the United States, Europe, and Japan dominate the international order the way Japan thinks it might? Now that Japan has the ambition to be one of the poles of the world structure, it will unavoidably face some serious challenges. Kuriyama took note of this point. He stated that Japan's international position had been rapidly elevated in the latter half of the 1980s. What action Japan, which had become an economic giant in a twinkle of an eye, will take will have a profound impact not only on the world economy but also on international politics. But how will Japan use its colossal economic might? Many countries have realized that Japan has grown into a big power and today expect it to shoulder international responsibility commensurate with its economic status. At the same time they feel a sense of insecurity and apprehension lest the economic superpower shun its responsibility and seek to expand its power at the expense of other nations.[6] Kiichi Saeki, a noted Japanese scholar on international politics, has pointed out that both the United States and the former Soviet Union will do their utmost to regain their economic strength in the 1990s and that this will present two issues before Japan. On the one hand, Japan will have to do everything possible to prevent the disappearance of those conditions that have facilitated that nation's successful growth in the postwar period, namely the cooperation between Japan and the West and the Japan-U.S. alliance. On the other hand, Japan also will have to be prepared to pay the world some necessary remunerations for its success.

It is not difficult to see that Japan will face two kinds of pressures and challenges in securing its own place in the international system. Countries of the world will press Japan to commit itself more to international development and, at the same time, they will also be opposed to Japan's repeating its mistakes of national egoism and militarism. The two challenges reflect two aspects of current international developments. The first challenge stems from the reforms of the international economic order. At present, trends toward protectionism and economic integration are growing, which indicates a growing intensification of international economic competition. Because the upcoming competition will take place among the several economic blocs with the major developed nations as their centers, the intensity of the competition will be far greater than any in history. If, in the course of building a new international economic order in the early 1990s, the major countries and regions should fail to define a new set of rules for competition among themselves, an economic world war would be difficult to avoid. Japan, whose development depends on international trade, will have to strive in two aspects. First, it must coordinate its economic and trade policies with those of the other developed countries to prevent further intensification of international economic frictions. Second, it must continue to strengthen its own economic power and establish its own bloc so as to meet the challenges arising from the intensification of interbloc competition.

The other challenge facing the major powers of the world comes from the reform of the international political order. The ability of the United States and the former Soviet Union to maintain world order will continue to decrease, especially when the Warsaw Pact no longer presents a threat to the West and the united Germany grows rapidly in status. The developing trend of political pluralism in the world may be further enhanced and changes brought about in the strategic relations among the Western allies.

As far as Japan is concerned, both its diplomacy and its security are based on its alliance with the West, and it will have to do its utmost to maintain its relationship with its allies and iron out any major differences with them. On the other hand, Japan will strive to increase its independence in foreign and security policy pursuits so as to gradually reduce or eventually free itself from its dependence on the United States and seek more say in international affairs.

In summary, it can be said that Japan's central diplomatic task, in essence, is to seek to maintain its invincibility in the intensifying international economic competition and to enhance its ability to become a major political power more in line with its economic prowess.

Japan's Foreign Policy Tendency

Since the decline of the East-West conflict and the beginning of international efforts to build a new international order, Japan has gained more options for its foreign policy. In recent years, especially following the drastic changes in Eastern Europe, a heated debate has developed in Japan concerning its future foreign policy direction, with opinions varying widely from the dovish to the hawkish. Kuriyama's argument cited earlier can be seen as an expression of the basic viewpoints of the mainstream foreign policymakers in Tokyo.

The Japanese diplomat maintains that the kind of international order Japan seeks must be based on the fundamental values that the developed democratic countries commonly share and respect. Although Japan has become a big power, according to Kuriyama, it vows not to become a military power, and its international role will be limited only to the nonmilitary field. However, this does not mean that Japan does not share any responsibility for international security. It means that Japan will share the responsibility by nonmilitary means outside the domain of the Japan-U.S. security system.[7] In 1988, the Japanese government put forward its International Cooperation Initiative, which consists of three basic parts: promoting cooperation for peace, increasing international cultural exchanges, and expanding govern-mental development aid. This showed how Japan would play its role as a major keeper of the international order. After Prime Minister Kaifu's visits to Eastern and Western Europe in January 1990, Japan took an active role in support of the European Community's aid to the East European countries. That was an important part of Japan's effort to promote cooperation for peace.

In his policy speech before the Japanese Diet on March 2, 1990, Kaifu elaborated on Japan's foreign policy course. He stated that the new interna-tional order Japan seeks must take the following five points as its objectives: (1) to maintain peace and security; (2) to respect freedom and democracy; (3) to ensure world prosperity under the system of an open market economy; (4) to maintain a sound environment for human life; and (5) to build stable international relations on the basis of dialogue and coordination. Kuriyama emphasized that the prime minister's statement made it clear at home and abroad that, as a developed democracy, Japan is determined to participate actively in the building of a new international order. The statement also answered the question of where Japan would go after it became a big power.[8]

Kaifu's policy speech has indeed convinced many people of the irresist-ible desire of Japan to become a world power. But to judge what direction Japan will take in its foreign affairs one first has to further study the hidden connotation of the speech. Kuriyama elaborated on Kaifu's speech in a con-crete way when he wrote that each of the five points the prime minister raised has an important policy significance in its own right.[9] First, Japan will make an active contribution to the relaxation of tensions in the international arena and to the settlement of regional conflicts. Second, Japan will provide assis-tance to the democratic reforms spreading across the world. Third, Japan will contribute to the building of an open global economic system based on mar-ket principles. Fourth, Japan will tackle new problems facing the world, such as the issues of regional environment and drugs. Fifth, Japan will contribute to the establishment of the principle of international coordination to over-come narrow nationalism.

As a matter of fact, under the rubric of "making contributions to the world," Japan is now implementing the above-mentioned principles. For ex-ample, two-thirds of Japan's official development aid has been in areas of strategic interest to the United States,[10] and the emphasis on international coordination has been obtained at the annual summit meetings of the Group of Seven (G7). Japan also calls for a system of intensified policy coordination among Japan, the United States, and Europe. Tokyo has set democratic re-form as a target of the allies' sanctions against Beijing from 1989 to 1991. There also has been a tendency of Japan to apply this principle to other socialist countries and to Third World countries.

In summary, maintaining a peaceful international environment and a free and open international economic order will continue to be basic principles in

Japan's foreign policy. Japan will broaden its contacts with countries of the world to create a new international image, it will apply its economic-financial superiority in an effort to contribute to the world, and it will attempt to increase its independence and autonomy in foreign affairs and to bolster its ability to participate in the management of world affairs.

In formulating its foreign policy, Japan may lay its emphasis on the following four aspects:

1. Improve the Japan-U.S. alliance structure and, with this as the core, establish a world system with an international order dominated by the three Western partners—the United States, Japan, and Europe.
2. Influence the reform process in the socialist countries and integrate them into the capitalist market economy by way of granting economic assistance.
3. In the process of dealing with and easing contradictions between the developing South and the developed North, lay emphasis on the Asia Pacific region in an attempt to assume the leading role in the region, and in the meantime strive to build an economic community with Japan as its center to contend with other regional blocs.[11]
4. Continue to implement the comprehensive security policy it has adopted since the early 1980s while discreetly enhancing its independent defense capability, and increase its overall national strength.

The Desirable Direction for Japan's Foreign Policy

The economic rise and political enhancement of postwar Japan form a strong contrast with the relative decline of the United States and the disintegration of the Soviet Union. This fact has eloquently proved an ancient historical thesis: Peaceful development is the only correct road for all countries. The unrestricted development of armaments in peacetime will in the end undercut their fundamental national strength and, therefore, their own international position. No matter whether Japan has realized it, the pacifist practice by the Japanese people represents an enormous contribution to international politics. Its significance is a hundred times greater than that of the U.S.-Soviet INF Treaty.

However, there are some people in Japan who do not value or have forgotten this point and are actively arguing for arms buildup, and even some who are seeking to increase Japan's influence in international affairs through reliance on military means. The debate in the Diet on dispatching a UN peacekeeping cooperation corps during the Gulf War was a case in point. Kuriyama pointed out that the 5:5:3 ratio on the economic scale among the United States, Europe, and Japan today coincides with the 5:5:3 ratio of the number of principal ships the United States, Britain, and Japan were allowed to have under the Washington Naval Armaments Limitation Treaty of 1922. Prewar Japan's overconfidence in its military might led Japan to attempt to alter the international order by force, and consequently brought catastrophic results to the world.

Can Japan make full use of its new strength along the right course today? This is a good question to raise.[12] It must be noted that Japan now boasts of abundant economic and technological strength, but judging by its comprehensive national strength, its weaknesses are also quite apparent. It is known to all that Japan has a narrow strip of territory that lacks in natural resources and a limited population that is rapidly aging. These inherent weaknesses are difficult to overcome and will either undercut to a certain extent the leading edge Japan has gained or render it quite vulnerable. For example, because of these weaknesses, Japan relies heavily on international trade. Consequently, the development of its science and technology is mainly market-oriented, with emphasis on the goal of achieving instant results. Although Japan has made relatively great progress in applied and development research and has kept pace with the advanced levels of the world in many areas, it lags far behind the United States and Western Europe in the more risk-prone area of basic research. Furthermore, Japan's balance-of-payments surplus may be shrinking. As the number one creditor nation, Japan accumulated enormous amounts of capital in the 1980s on the basis of its yearly rising balance-of-payments surplus and its high savings ratio. From the mid-1980s to 1990, these two pillars have taken a downward trend. Its balance-of-payments surplus peaked at $94.1 billion in fiscal 1986 and dropped to $87 billion in 1987 and further to $79.6 billion in 1988. Its worldwide trade surplus peaked at $94.3 billion in 1987 and shrank to $79 billion in 1988. These downward trends have been pushed by the appreciation of the yen and the economic structural adjustment policy Tokyo has adopted to expand domestic consumption.[13]

As for the nontrade service income (including incomes from tourism, transportation, patent transfers and investment interests, among others), a downward trend appeared as early as 1986. This is due to the growing deficits on the balance sheets for tourism, transportation, and so on. Thanks to the appreciation of the yen in recent years, the number of Japanese making overseas trips has far exceeded foreigners visiting Japan. As for tourism, the deficit had increased from $5.6 billion in 1986 to $9.7 billion in 1987, and, according to a conservative estimate of the Japanese government, was expected to reach $13 billion by 1991. Because the Japanese shipping industry has lost some competitiveness on the international market, the deficit on the balance sheet for transportation increased from $2.5 billion in 1986 to $6.1 billion in 1987. Due to Japan's expanding overseas investments, the surplus from the interest balance sheet increased from $9.5 billion in 1986 to $16.6 billion in 1987. However, this could not offset the deficits on the balance sheets of tourism, transportation, and other items. The deficit in service trade grew from $4.9 billion in 1986 to $5.7 billion in 1987.[14]

There also has been a hidden crisis in Japan's domestic savings ratio. The downward trend, from 23 percent in 1975 to 16 percent in 1985, is likely to continue. This is because of three factors. First, pension saving as a big item has been greatly reduced since the social security system was reformed in the 1970s. Second, those who were born after World War II have now entered their mature consumption age and, unlike their elder generations who respect frugality and thrift, they are more inclined toward leisure and spending. Third, the aged population segments who spend more than they save are rapidly expanding. Taking the evolving trend of the age of the head of the household as the basis and the saving practices of all age groups at present as the index, it may be deduced that the savings ratio will fall from 16 percent to 13 percent during the years from 1995 to 2010. According to a U.S. investment bank estimate, social welfare expenditures in Japan will grow as the population ages. By 2010, the need for capital funds by the Japanese government, corporations, and individuals will exceed the amount of savings and the individual savings ratio in Japan will drop to the level of 3–5 percent, which is where the United States is today.[15]

Moreover, Japan has an international image problem. In a research report entitled "Japan's Comprehensive National Strength" published in 1987, the Japanese Economic Planning Agency held the view that Japan has two advantages, one of which is its friendly relations with other countries such as its allies. The assessment even gave Japan higher marks than the United Kingdom, France, and the United States in this regard.[16] However, this assessment may be suspect. It at least can be said that due to Japan's tarnished international image, this supposed advantage is more unreliable than the financial advantage the country currently enjoys.

Japan's negative international image is not only attributable to its prewar record of militarism and aggression but to its peculiar position in geopolitics. Japan is situated in Asia, but it maintains only loose relations with its Asian neighbors economically and politically. It has never been regarded as capable of representing Asia in international affairs. On the other hand, it styles itself as a loyal member of the Western alliance, but in the eyes of Europe and the United States, Japan represents both a rival and a threat from the Eastern Hemisphere. As an observer metaphorically put it, although Japan has a very influential economy internationally, it still remains a lonely island both culturally and politically.[17] Japan has neither a clear-cut identity with any region in the elections at international organizations nor a permanent electoral constituency. Japan even has a strong sense of isolation itself. An article in the *Tokyo Times* on September 6, 1987, had this to say:

> Recently, world public opinion strongly condemned Japan all of a sudden and with it, there even emerged a new acronym, "the ARCE Encirclement" (A for America, R for Russia, C for China, and E for Europe). The phenomenon of "Japan bashing" by these countries has become increasingly pronounced. Behind this phenomenon are apprehensions of and opposition to

Japan's growing power in the economic, high tech, and even political and military fields.[18]

Japan has come to see that it would be very difficult to turn its huge economic influence in the East Asian region into a strong political influence. No matter how moderate, an increase in Japan's political role will incur serious suspicion. Even the United States, which on many occasions has called on Japan to share the dual responsibilities for foreign economic assistance and defense, is reluctant also to share with Japan all of the benefits that will accompany those responsibilities.[19]

The Post–Cold War Asia and Japan _____

Two major events shook the world in 1991: the Gulf War and the dissolution of the Soviet Union. The events, particularly the dramatic disappearance of the Soviet Union, will have a wide-ranging, deep, and lasting impact on the transformation of the global framework and the development of international affairs.

The disappearance of one of the two superpowers spelled the unmistakable end of the old world order and the beginning of a truly new era in history. One of the key features of the new era is that competition of economic and national power replaces the conflict of military power and ideology as the central theme of international relations. Another characteristic of the new times is the growing trend of economic and political multidimensionalization of the world. The dissolution of the Soviet Union has resulted in a significant shift in the balance of power in favor of the West, but this has not necessarily meant a proportional increase in the real power of the West. On the contrary, the contradictions within the West that have been concealed under the East-West conflict will come to the surface one after another. In other words, the centripetal force of the West will grow weaker and centrifugal force will grow stronger as a result of the collapse of the East. The disappearance of the Soviet Union as the common adversary of the Western nations will naturally soften the foundation of the Western alliance that has been based on the military protection by the United States.

At the same time, the relative decline of the United States and the economic rise of the EC and Japan pose a strong challenge to U.S. leadership. Major contradictions in international relations are shifting to those among the advanced nations. The mounting competition for markets and advanced technology, the emergence of trade protectionism, and the growing trends toward regional economic blocs are all manifestations of these contradictions. President Bush in his 1991 National Security Strategy stated in no uncertain terms that the rise of Japan and Germany and their move toward economic and political leadership are the most important developments of the 1990s, with deep strategic significance. He also said that U.S. trade negotiations with these powers have a strategic significance similar to that of the U.S. arms control talks with the former Soviet Union.

During the Cold War era, Europe was the front line of East-West conflict and yet enjoyed relative stability whereas social turmoil and armed conflict continued unabated in the Third World. In the post–Cold War era, "hot points" in the Third World, which once invited superpower intervention, are cooling down, but the disappearing balance of power in Europe is turning that region into the most unstable area of the world.

As the Cold War ended, countries around the world began making adjustments in their domestic and foreign policies, with some countries embarking on major political reforms. Progress on domestic-foreign policy adjustments in many Asian countries has revealed both domestic contradictions and strong nationalist tendencies in their desire to protect national interests and sovereignty. At the same time, the countries of the region desire regional economic cooperation and are actively seeking improvement in regional international relations. In contrast to Europe, the Asian situation appears quite peaceful and calm.

A political solution to the Cambodian conflict has been found and the North-South Korean dialogue has shown some initial progress toward eventual reconciliation. China today enjoys the best relations with its immediate neighbors that it has experienced in more than a century, and its relations with other Asian countries are also improving. ASEAN countries are gradually reducing their economic dependence on the United States and strengthening their relations with Japan, although they desire a continued U.S. military presence in the region to counter Japan's inclination toward a big military-political power. ASEAN countries also want to strengthen their political and economic solidarity and, at the same time, bring the three Indochinese states and Myanmar into their fold, all in an attempt to play a larger role in the Asia Pacific region. India, in the wake of weakening ties to the former Soviet Union, is undertaking major domestic and foreign-policy adjustments and strengthening its relations with the United States, Europe, and Japan. Pakistan is losing some of its importance in the U.S. global strategy and is readjusting its relations with the United States.

Japan, with its fast-expanding economic power, today faces favorable opportunities it has never had before and is actively engaging itself in world affairs to attain the status of a big political power. It has indeed seen a moderate improvement in its international position. However, in the face of new contradictions of the emerging era, Tokyo is reviewing its relations and adjusting its foreign policy accordingly.

The Tokyo Declaration of January 1992 marked the beginning of a new era in Japanese-U.S. relations. The central feature of the new relationship is the maintenance of the bilateral alliance through coordination vis-à-vis escalating contradictions of the post–Cold War world. The dissolution of the

Soviet Union has lessened Japan's military reliance on the United States. Japan is also challenging U.S. leadership in the Asia Pacific region, shaking the foundation of the Japanese-U.S. alliance. However, the inescapable fact of economic interdependence with the United States and the fact that Japan cannot become a big political power without U.S. support cause Tokyo to continue to view its relationship with Washington as the cornerstone of its foreign policy. Washington, in turn, wishes to maintain and strengthen its ties with Tokyo because Europe, not Japan, is the most serious potential threat to U.S. leadership within the U.S.-European-Japanese tripolar framework that is now emerging.

The year 1992 marked the twentieth anniversary of the normalization of Japanese-Chinese relations and, with the exchange of visits between the two countries' top leaders, those relations would enter a new phase. Both sides emphasized the relationship of friendship and cooperation. Prime Minister Kiichi Miyazawa has referred to Japanese-U.S. and Japanese-Chinese relations as the two wheels of Japanese foreign policy. However, the two wheels are running on different tracks. Japanese-U.S. relations are running on a world order track but Japanese-Chinese relations are running on an Asian order track. For Japan to become a world political power, it must first become an Asian political power. To become an Asian political power, Japan must be so recognized by China. China, on the other hand, needs Japan's cooperation for its speedy economic development. Japan and China are at different levels of development and therefore their economic relationship is more accurately characterized as one of mutual complementarity than one of competition. Moreover, solid advancement of Japanese-Chinese relations will be beneficial not only to the two countries but to the peace and development of the whole Asia Pacific region.

And 1992 was also the first year of European integration and the first year of a new European century following the dissolution of the Soviet Union. Japan's ties with the EC are not as strong as its ties with the United States but, in preparation for EC integration, Japan has built an economic base in Europe. Japan's tasks in Europe for now are to build on that economic base, strengthen its political ties with Europe, play a role in the economic reconstruction of the former Eastern European nations and the former Soviet Union, and seek a voice in the forging of a new European order. If successful in these tasks, Japan will be able to become a coequal partner in the emerging tripolar world. One cannot expect any major advancement in Japanese relations with Russia until the latter stabilizes. Once the situation in Russia improves, however, Japan will lose no time in assisting in the economic-social reform of the Russian Federation, particularly in the economic development of the Far Eastern region.

In short, Japan's foreign policy in the new era will rid it of its passive character and transform it into one that contributes to the world. Japan's contributions to the world will not be limited to the economic field; they will be much more comprehensive, encompassing political, diplomatic, cultural, and military fields. Japan will direct its foreign policy course toward closer coordination with the United States, further improvement of relations with China, attainment of a permanent seat in the UN Security Council with due regard to the Group of Seven, strengthening of its Asia Pacific base, advancement into the Asian parts of the CIS, and forging of a new world order under U.S.-Japanese-European leadership.

_____ *Conclusions*

In the decades of the Cold War, regardless of the judgment other nations may reach about Japan's place in the world, Japan played a role it deemed appropriate for itself and, in my judgment, that role was as important as that played by any other nation. Japan also contributed to the ending of the Cold War. Its successful transformation from the prewar military aggressor to the postwar economic superpower, I suspect, influenced former Soviet President Mikhail Gorbachev in initiating his "new thinking diplomacy." Indeed, I would venture to say that Gorbachev had much to learn from Japan.

Whereas Japan successfully pursued its policy of economic expansion, the Soviet Union and the United States kept tasking themselves with heavy defense burdens and in the process brought about their own economic demise. In the mid-1980s, the United States became the world's largest debtor nation and Japan became the world's largest creditor nation. The economic fortunes of Japan and Germany came as something of a surprise to the Cold War superpowers. The spectacular economic performance of Japan and Germany was particularly shocking to the Soviet Union, which was faced with long-term economic stagnation. Soon after assuming power, Gorbachev warned his people that unless they reconstructed their economy, the nation would fall behind countries like Japan and become a third-class nation. The aim of Gorbachev's "new thinking" was to reduce his nation's military burden to a "reasonable and sufficient" level in order to strengthen its economy and retain its superpower status. The task required the signing of the INF Treaty with the United States and the termination of the financially bankrupt Cold War confrontation with the West.

If the Japanese learn from their peaceful experience of the postwar period, continue to follow the policy that has made it possible, and pursue it throughout the world, they will be making an important contribution to the world. That will also expand their political influence and prepare them for their rightful place in world politics. Should Japan be content with its current status as an economic big power, its international contribution will be limited and it will be criticized for selfishly pursuing its own peace and prosperity.

Japan's international standing today has been built on its economic strength. And in the future it will also mainly be relying on economic means to participate in international affairs and to play its role as a big political power. However, Japan can make real contributions to world stability and development by overcoming the negative tendencies in its foreign policy, by doing away with national egoism, by refraining from imposing its own values on others and from seeking to be a military power, and, finally, by treating its neighbors as equals in seeking common prosperity. Only in so doing can Japan's political status and its role be accepted by the Asian countries. This, therefore, is the direction that Japan's foreign policy strategy should follow.

Upon assuming premiership in 1991, Kiichi Miyazawa worked to expand his country's international role commensurate with its economic power and in response to the expectations of the international community.[20] As a concrete measure, he stepped up efforts to pass a peacekeeping bill to be able to play a bigger role in the Cambodian peace process under the United Nations. He also hopes to resolve the Northern Territories problem and sign a peace treaty with Russia, as the successor to the Soviet Union.[21] It remains to be seen whether Miyazawa and his successors will succeed in building a national consensus on the concrete policy measures to realize Tokyo's intention to expand its global role in the direction described in this chapter.

Notes

1. Yasuhiro Nakasone, *Atarashii Hoshu no Riron* [A new conservative thesis], Tokyo: Kodansha, 1987.
2. Takakazu Kuriyama, "Gekidō no Kyūjūnendai to Nihon Gaikō no Shintenkai" [The turbulent nineties and new directions of Japanese diplomacy], *Gaikō Forum*, May 1990, pp. 12–21. Kuriyama became Japanese ambassador to the United States in 1992.
3. *Asahi Shimbun*, February 3, 1989.
4. *Sankei Shimbun*, March 24, 1989.
5. Speech by Prime Minister Noboru Takeshita, delivered on June 22, 1988, in Chicago.
6. Kuriyama, "Gekidō no Kyūjūnendai."
7. Ibid.
8. Ibid.
9. Ibid.
10. *Gaikō Seisho* [Diplomatic bluebook], Tokyo: Foreign Press Center, 1988, pp. 411–419.
11. But, at the APEC meeting in Seoul in November 1991 the United States induced Japan to join in opposing just such a bloc, which Malaysia was sponsoring under the name of the East Asian Economic Caucus (EAEC). Japan and the United States also opposed it at the ASEAN postministerial meeting in Kuala Lumpur in July 1991.
12. Kuriyama, "Gekidō no Kyūjūnendai."
13. Trends are unclear, with external surpluses soaring again in 1991 and domestic demand sagging, particularly in the wake of the "bursting of the bubble" in Tokyo in 1991.
14. William Emmott, "Japan Pawā no Genkai: Shihon Taikoku Nihon no Jumyō

wa Mijikai" [Limits to Japan power: The life span of the capital power Japan is short], *Tōyō Keizai*, March 18, 1989, pp. 102–106.

15. Keizai Kikakuchō Sōgō Keikakukyoku, ed., *Nihon no Sogo Kokuryoku* [Japan's comprehensive national strength], Tokyo: Keizai Kikakuchō, June 1987.

16. Ibid.

17. Karen Elliott House, "The 90s and Beyond," *Wall Street Journal*, January 23, 1989.

18. *Tokyo Times*, September 6, 1987.

19. Stephen Wagsteel, "Japan's East Asian Moves Met with Suspicion," *Financial Times*, May 19, 1989.

20. Miyazawa's policy speech before the Diet, November 8, 1991.

21. *Daily Yomiuri*, November 9, 1991, pp. 1 and 2.

Chapter 9

Japan's Roles in the Posthegemonic World: Perspectives from Southeast Asia

Prasert Chittiwatanapong

At the start of the 1990s, it became clear that the Cold War era and the hegemonic world order were gone. Toward the end of 1991, the posthegemonic, or post–Cold War, international order was in the making, with elements of hope and concern, stability and disintegration, and constructive and destructive forces.[1] International relations scholars have agreed that at no time since the end of World War II has international change been as rapid and momentous as during the first years of the 1990s.[2] In this process of rapid change at the superpower level, countries in Asia have been forced to adjust their foreign policies in order to successfully ride over the streams of change.

Japan, a country that has long benefited very much from the relatively stable bipolar structure of international politics, has been affected by the global changes no less than any other country in East Asia. Of course, Japan views the new world order with less confidence and less optimism than before.

This chapter will answer two basic questions concerning Japan's role in the posthegemonic world from the perspective of Southeast Asia. Specifically, how has Japan responded to the new world order in the making? And how have the countries in Southeast Asia, particularly the ASEAN members, viewed Japan's political-security role, which has become increasingly more active? In this chapter, ASEAN is frequently used to represent Southeast Asia, although the three Indochinese states of Vietnam, Laos, and Cambodia, as well as Burma are unmistakably Southeast Asian nations. The discussion here touches mainly on the recent developments, covering the few years prior to the end of 1991. Finally, the perspectives from Southeast Asia here mean the perspectives from the governments rather than those of the opposing voices from among the region's articulate intellectual groups.

Japan's Responses to the
Posthegemonic World Order

Japan's foreign policymaking elite tend to view the posthegemonic world order in East Asia with feelings of uncertainty and concern. Unlike their European counterparts, Japanese leaders have not seen the Cold War coming to an end in the Korean peninsula, China, and Indochina and the threat from the communist Soviet Union disappearing. Japanese foreign policy experts have increasingly warned against Soviet military buildup and the continued potential Soviet threat. Seizaburo Sato, one of the more influential strategic thinkers, cited a finding that the Soviet Union had introduced the fourth generation of fighter planes since 1983, and that the number of new Soviet planes added per year spurted from about thirty for the first five years or so to more than a hundred in 1989, almost catching up with Japan's 120 F-15 fighters. He stated, "Even today we need to maintain our defenses against a Soviet attack, though the urgency of the situation has clearly lessened." He believed that Japan has a responsibility "to deter and resolve regional conflicts."[3] Japanese scholar-diplomat Hisahiko Okazaki argued in a similar vein that even though the Soviet Union lost the Cold War, and the United States, Europe, and Japan won, "they must remain on guard, keeping a close watch on events in the Soviet Union."[4] As a staunch realist and cautious strategist, Okazaki believed that defense spending should continue to increase despite the ending of the Cold War because Japan's new responsibility is enlarged. He insisted, "Henceforth Japan must maintain this capability to participate in the efforts to uphold international justice and protect the global community."[5]

The Gulf War stunned the Japanese and drastically changed their optimistic perception of the posthegemonic world order. That crisis came at a time when the Cold War was ending in Europe and tension in East Asia had been greatly reduced. If Saddam Hussein's dream were realized, the world's largest oil supplies would be controlled and the lifeline of the world's economy would be threatened. No doubt, Japanese industry would be seriously affected. Instead of discussing the necessity of participating in the U.S.-led forces to stop Saddam Hussein's occupation of Kuwait, the Japanese political leaders were somehow engaged in a debate over the constitutionality and legality of sending military personnel to the Gulf area. Certainly, such debate prevented a timely and needed contribution from being made.

The Gulf War, with its dreadful impacts on oil supply and environmental destruction, as well as the international pressures demanding Japan to contribute not only in cash but with armed personnel, had given many lessons to foreign policymakers in Tokyo. They reconfirmed their belief that the global security leadership of the United States was still essential and could not be substituted. They also concluded that Japan must from now on prepare to assume the responsibility of sharing costs in terms of armed personnel whenever there are international calls for greater burden-sharing, especially in and for the United Nations. Citing the constitutional constraint of article 9 is not convincing when international forces sacrifice their lives.[6]

The likely scenario that China, and perhaps India, may emerge as an active regional power in Southeast Asia is also a cause of concern for Japan.[7] As the Soviet Union began to withdraw its forces from Cam Ranh Bay and the future of the U.S. bases in the Philippines became increasingly uncertain, China remained the only military power capable of expanding its influence in Southeast Asia. The nations in Southeast Asia have reacted to the changing security climate in the region with continued high defense spending, especially for the purchase of modern weapons. Japan also has been concerned about the scenario of emerging territorial disputes and other regional conflicts among Asian nations, whose international behaviors were once controlled by the Cold War.[8] As China has various territorial disputes with countries in East Asia, the Chinese tendency to use arms in settling disputes is cause for concern. In the 1989 dispute with Vietnam over the right to the Spratly Islands, China used its more superior naval force to impose its terms on Vietnam. Currently, the Chinese navy is relatively weak due to the lack of a strong industrial base. With the return of Hong Kong in 1997, however, China will have the capability to move its navy southward.

No country in Southeast Asia will escape the sense of threat from a Chinese military buildup and naval power expansion program. For this reason the United States has been asked by Japan to maintain its military presence in the region. There is a possibility that in the future Vietnam may offer Cam Ranh Bay to the United States to counter Chinese threats. In that situation, Japan will probably move quickly to assist Vietnam's economic recovery and warn China against programs of arms export and production. Actually, in April 1991 Japan started giving an official warning to China when Prime Minister Kaifu announced that the level of military expenditure, arms export, and possession of destructive weapons of the aid-recipient country would be considered in Japan's aid decisions.[9]

Well before the end of the Cold War in Europe, Japan had expressed a desire to play a more active role in regional conflict resolution. Regardless of the source of the pressures, whether or not reluctantly, Japan had long been waiting for chances to play a more active role in the resolution of regional conflicts, especially in Southeast Asia. As the fighting in Cambodia began to subside and diplomatic efforts by ASEAN in the Jakarta informal meeting began to bear fruit, Japan moved quickly to play the role of a leading regional power.

The Vietnamese invasion of Cambodia in December 1978 changed Japan's policy from one of calling for ASEAN-Indochina peaceful coexistence to a new policy of putting pressures on Vietnam. Tokyo decided to throw its support behind ASEAN's position, namely, upholding the democratic Kampuchean government's right of representation in the United Nations, supporting ASEAN positions in the United Nations, cosponsoring

ASEAN resolutions, and lobbying for support for ASEAN. Japan also tried to bring this issue to international attention. At the expanded ASEAN foreign ministers' meeting in Bali in July 1979, Foreign Minister Sunao Sonoda proposed the holding of an international conference to restore peace in Cambodia. One source claimed that because of this proposal the UN-sponsored International Conference on Cambodia was convened in July 1981.[10]

The most decisive measure taken by Japan on Vietnam's invasion of Cambodia was the use of aid to pressure Vietnam to withdraw its troops. In April 1978 Japan promised economic assistance to Vietnam in the form of a 16 billion yen grant for four years, and a 20 billion yen loan for two years. Just before the Cambodian invasion in December, Foreign Minister Sonoda warned Vietnamese Foreign Minister Nguyen Duy Trinh in Tokyo that aid might not be given if Hanoi threatened the peace in Southeast Asia.[11] When Vietnamese forces invaded Cambodia late that month, Japan decided to freeze its promised aid package. With the exception of some humanitarian aid, Japan continued to withhold its aid to Vietnam until the peace settlement came at the Paris International Conference on Cambodia in late October 1991.

At the same time, the Japanese government decided to increase aid to Thailand, the frontline state bordering Cambodia, including aid for the refugees in Thailand. Between 1979 and the end of 1985, a total of $502 million was provided, making Japan the number one aid donor for Indochinese refugees.[12] Japanese aid also went to the construction of "new villages" along the Thai border near Cambodia. In April 1980, 57 billion yen was pledged to Thailand, an increase of 28 percent over the preceding fiscal year. In 1984, aid to Thailand went up to 82 billion yen. Also, Japan cooperated closely with the United States in this aid strategy. According to one well-informed source, the United States reportedly requested that Japan extend strategic assistance to about twenty countries.[13]

Japan's roles in the Cambodian peace settlement reflected its desire to play a more active political-security role in the region. In June 1990, Japan succeeded in getting understanding and support from ASEAN to hold a meeting on Cambodia by inviting the leaders of the four Khmer factions to Tokyo. The Ministry of Foreign Affairs of Japan worked successfully, with cooperation from Prime Minister Chatichai Choonhavan of Thailand, to convince Hun Sen and Prince Sihanouk to sign an agreement to establish a Supreme National Council and to start an immediate voluntary cease-fire. This agreement was actually the first after a series of many informal meetings in Jakarta. Key to the success of the Tokyo meeting was the support, cooperation, and technical advice from the Chatichai government, to which the Japanese ambassador to Thailand, Hisahiko Okazaki, was sincerely committed. Two Thai generals were sent by Prime Minister Chatichai to Tokyo to assist Japanese efforts so that a diplomatic success could be assured. These were the former army commander-in-chief and the then vice premier for security affairs, General Chavalit Yongchaiyudh, and then army chief-of-staff, General Suchinda Kraprayoon, who later succeeded the former as the army commander-in-chief.

As a major power in the region, Japan sought international prestige in hopefully contributing to the resolution of regional conflicts, not the least of which was the thirteen-year-long Cambodian conflict. By hosting the Tokyo meeting on Cambodia, Japan was proud to stand together with Indonesia and Thailand in organizing such meetings to convince the Cambodian factions to accept the UN peace plan. These meetings were held in Bangkok, Tokyo, and Jakarta, in February, June, and September 1990, respectively. A high-ranking Japanese Foreign Ministry official in Bangkok explained that to get a budget for the coming Indochina reconstruction work, Japan needed some publicity to show to the Japanese public so that the Ministry of Finance would allocate the needed budget.[14]

After the failure in passing the UN Peace Cooperation bill in late 1990, the Kaifu cabinet decided to submit a UN Peacekeeping Operations Cooperation bill to the Diet in October 1991 to enable the government to send the Self-Defense Forces overseas. The bill was expected to be passed and to become law after a new prime minister was chosen to replace Toshiki Kaifu, whose term as the president of the ruling Liberal Democratic Party expired in late October 1991. The second peacekeeping bill failed to pass soon after Miyazawa became prime minister in October 1991, but the third attempt in 1992 was successful and passed on June 15, 1992. The Japanese personnel from the Self-Defense Forces, as well as nonmilitary individuals, were dispatched to Cambodia in October 1992 to serve with UNTAC. The dispatch of personnel of the armed forces to perform various peacekeeping functions requested by the United Nations would greatly enhance Japan's international prestige and influence, as well as its acceptance by the West. Japanese diplomats refer to this dispatch of men in military uniform as *jinbutsu no men no kōken* (a contribution in the field of personnel). Soon after being elected as the new prime minister on November 5, 1991, Kiichi Miyazawa told the Japanese public, "We must recognize that our international role in the building of a global order for peace can only grow larger."[15] In his policy speech to the Diet, Miyazawa emphasized the importance of the United Nations as a framework for Japan's foreign policy: "Among the indispensable underpinnings of our U.N.-centered efforts for global order are close cooperation with the United States and friendly relations with other countries of Asia."[16]

At the Post-Ministerial Conference between ASEAN foreign ministers and the dialogue partners in Kuala Lumpur in July 1991, Japanese Foreign Minister Taro Nakayama surprised ASEAN foreign ministers with his proposal for using the PMC as a forum for discussion on security issues. Security had never been an issue included in the agenda of the PMC because ASEAN was established as an organization designed for regional economic cooperation, although security cooperation exists bilaterally among ASEAN members. Nakayama's proposal, if endorsed, would have provided Japan a forum for security policy initiatives, making known its concern and working more closely with ASEAN on regional security issues.

It could be interpreted that Nakayama's proposal aimed at moving toward closer security cooperation with ASEAN in terms of intelligence exchanges of military personnel, training, and education. Under the present constitutional constraints, it may be difficult for Japan to carry out these functions with ASEAN, but it was hoped that once the new UN Peacekeeping Operations Cooperation bill became law these functions might become possible if treated as part of a preparation for participation in UN-requested peacekeeping activities.

Apart from the above-mentioned views of the posthegemonic world and the active roles played in the past two years, Japan has also attempted to lay a foundation for its more active roles in the region. This is the attempt, in parallel with the expanded roles mentioned earlier, to heal the wounds in the minds of Asian peoples and the bitter memories of Japan's wartime aggression and atrocity. Prime Minister Kaifu was the first Japanese top political leader to express feelings of apology to Asian peoples in clear terms. He did so in May 1990 in his speech in Tokyo welcoming Korean President Roh Tae-woo. Emperor Akihito did the same at the imperial banquet on the same occasion. During his historic ASEAN visit in April and May 1991, while in Singapore, Kaifu expressed his deep sorrow to the victims of the Japanese Imperial Army's aggression in the following words:

> This year marks the 50th anniversary of the Pacific War. At this juncture, looking back upon the first half of this century, I express our sincere contrition of Japanese past actions which inflicted unbearable suffering and sorrow upon a great many people of the Asia-Pacific region. The Japanese people are firmly resolved never again to repeat those actions which had tragic consequences.[17]

Emperor Akihito's first visits to Asian countries, choosing Thailand, Malaysia, and Indonesia as the first destinations, are significant in various ways. The Japanese government's intention was to improve the image of the Japanese imperial institution in Asia and to start a new era of better relations between the emperor and the Asian peoples. This new diplomatic move produced very good results in the two countries with monarchies: Thailand and Malaysia. Although war compensation was demanded by a certain group, it produced an equally good result in Indonesia because the Japanese Imperial Army's invasion of that country helped the people of Indonesia gain national independence from the Dutch. Japanese-Indonesian ties, friendly and close since the wartime period, have been strengthened by the imperial visit. More than the previous visits of any prime minister of Japan, Emperor Akihito's visits captured the minds of the people of Southeast Asia. Japan won extraordinary admiration and praise. In Bangkok, the emperor was told the following:

> Nowadays, Japan is a prominent country which is strong and secure as well as successful and prosperous in all fields of endeavor. Japan today can indeed be said to be at least of equal power to any other nation of the world in the economic, social, political and technological areas, worthy to be placed in the front rank of nations in Asia and the world at large. [18]

In summary, Japan reacted to the changing international order with a decision to play more active roles in the security and stability of Southeast Asia. From the dominating position in the economies of the ASEAN countries, Japan has begun to extend its influence to the political-security field. Japanese leaders viewed the posthegemonic world order with uncertainty and concern. They remained cautious about the new world order, pointing to the continued Soviet potential threat, the Gulf War, and the likelihood of China playing more assertive security roles. Tokyo's desire to play a more active political-security role could be seen in the Cambodian initiative, the submission of the peacekeeping operations bill to the Diet, the proposal for a security discussion with ASEAN by Foreign Minister Taro Nakayama, and the efforts to clear the war responsibility issue. Japan did not hide its intentions. Prime Minister Kaifu made use of his historic visits to ASEAN during April 27–May 6, 1991, to announce Japan's determination to play more active roles in the field of security. Apart from reemphasizing Japan's basic policy of not becoming a military power, he made it clear to the ASEAN governments that Japan's roles would no longer be restricted to only financial contributions.

Quite surely, Japan has been undergoing a period of self-reflection about its international roles. The most popular theory has always been the danger of being isolated politically. And this has reappeared in security discussions in Tokyo time and again. One of the most well-informed Japanese politicians, Motoo Shiina, warned that two possibilities are awaiting Japan: participation or isolation. Recalling the dangerous historical experience in the early twentieth century, allowing Japan's alliance with Great Britian to lapse, he argued, "Japan is again treading the road to isolation." [19] He warned that Japan's insistence on being a "conscientious objector" will only serve to endanger Japan's survival. Parallel with the isolation theory was the emergence of a new trend of public opinion in Japan that the pacifist approach to the problems of global security was no longer convincing and that Japan must not think only of its own security but of regional and global security as well. That Japan must contribute in a more active manner toward a new world order was an emerging consensus in Japan. As the Social Democratic Party (formerly the Socialist Party) of Japan has changed its security policy to a more realist approach under the chairmanship of Makoto Tanabe, it is widely believed that the view of Japan as a conscientious objector will lose its influence among the Japanese public.

ASEAN's Views of Japan's Expanded Political-Security Role _____

The foregoing discussion suggests that Japan's political-security role in Southeast Asia has been expanded and will be increasingly active. One important question concerns how the ASEAN governments view and react to the process of Japan's expanded political-security roles. To address this question, one should first take a brief look at Southeast Asia's, or ASEAN's, importance to Japan.

The importance of Southeast Asia, particulary members of ASEAN, to Japan is obvious. For the steady growth of the Japanese economy, the supply of natural resources from Southeast Asia is crucial. Vital resources include rubber, tin, vegetable oil, nickel, wood, bauxite, copper, sugar, and crude oil. Oil exploration in the South China Sea and the Vietnamese shore will make this region more attractive, especially if another Gulf war breaks out. Southeast Asia is also an important market for Japanese exports. The population of ASEAN and Indochina is near 400 million, bigger than that of North America and the European Community. Partly due to yen appreciation, Japan-ASEAN trade has grown rapidly since 1985. Japan's exports to ASEAN in the years from 1986 to 1989 expanded annually at the rates of 7.69 percent, 28.47 percent, 50.12 percent, and 10 percent, respectively.[20] Although Japan's imports from ASEAN fluctuated, the growth rate rose from 18.54 percent in 1987 to 87.55 percent in 1988.[21] In the five years since the yen appreciation, Japanese exports to ASEAN and to the United States have grown by an annual average of 24.22 percent and 9.80 percent, respectively. On the basis of this growth rate, by the year 2000, ASEAN would become a bigger market than the United States for Japanese goods.[22]

The ASEAN countries are also important to Japan as a production base for Japanese investors. Due to the effect of yen appreciation, Japanese investment in the five ASEAN countries has increased rapidly. According to the Ministry of Finance of Japan, Japan's direct investment in Thailand jumped during the four-year period from 1986 to 1989 from 58 cases to 192, 302, and 403. In terms of value, it jumped from $124 million to $250 million, $859 million, and $1,276 million.[23] A similarly rapid rate of increase was seen in Japan's direct investment in Malaysia, although at a smaller value. In Singapore, Japanese direct investment did not increase in terms of the number of cases, but its value rapidly grew from $302 million to $491 million, $747 million, and $1,902 million during the same four-year period.[24] Indonesia did not attract much new direct investment from Japan during this period, but the cumulative base was so large that the country remained the largest recipient of Japanese direct investment, absorbing as much as 26 percent of Japan's total investment in Asia. Because Japan's direct investments during this period were mostly export oriented, its economy and that of the ASEAN countries became ever more intertwined, making the countries "mutual hostages" to each other.

Japan's official development assistance has contributed to the close economic ties between Japan and Southeast Asia and the improvement of Japan's image among Southeast Asian peoples. Traditionally, more than 60 percent of Japanese ODA has gone to Asia, with more than half of that to ASEAN. Indonesia long led the list of recipient countries before being overtaken by China in recent years. Thailand, the Philippines, and Malaysia have been, since the early 1960s, major aid-receiving countries. Before Japan decided to start offering massive aid to China in 1980, ASEAN's share of total Japanese aid was as high as 45 percent.

In the early 1980s Japan's aid became increasingly more security oriented, in close cooperation with the U.S. global strategy. In a U.S.-Japan joint statement in May 1981, both nations agreed to strengthen aid to strategic regions. Thailand, Pakistan, and Turkey were targeted as strategically important countries to receive aid from Japan.[25] In recent years, Japanese ODA was used to finance the construction of public utility facilities such as dams, electricity, water supplies, highways, expressways, telephone networks, railways, hospitals, human resource training centers, and various agriculture-related projects. At present, Japanese ODA amounts to about 0.33 percent of its GNP. Its impact will be much greater if this percentage is increased to 3 percent, as called for in the U.S. Senate resolution in 1987, or if $13 billion could be added to it, as made possible by its contribution to the Gulf War in 1991.

In terms of political-security considerations, Southeast Asia's importance to Japan is more obvious. Situated between the Indian Ocean and the Pacific Ocean, Southeast Asia is geostrategically important to Japan. Oil supply from the Middle East must depend on the sea-lines of communication that pass through Southeast Asian waters, especially the Strait of Malacca and the Lombok Strait. Roughly speaking, 60 percent of Japan's oil imports and 40 percent of Japan's foreign trade are transported through these two straits. Clearly, the free passage of Japanese ships through these sea-lanes is a condition to ensure Japan's economic vitality. But more importantly, Japan needs like-minded political friends outside the Anglo-Saxon world.[26] In Asia, ASEAN is the only dependable supporting base for Japan's expanding political-security roles, apart from its sharing basic values of market economy and anticommunism. Both Japan and ASEAN either are linked to or support the U.S. military presence in the region. To make this "constituency" a firm supporting base, the Japanese government and private sector have been making intense efforts to cultivate a new generation of ASEAN power elites who are more sympathetic to Japan and Japan's more active political-security role.[27]

Japan's active role in the political-security problems of the region date back to the 1960s. In June 1964, Japan organized a conference in Tokyo inviting leaders of Indonesia, Malaysia, and the Philippines to talk with each other to end the conflicts that had resulted from the creation of Malaysia. In 1970, when the Cambodia conflict broke out, Japan tried to work with Indonesia and Malaysia to stabilize the situation in Cambodia. Japan was much concerned about the future relationship between ASEAN and Indochina after the Vietnam War came to an end. Prime Minister Takeo Fukuda clearly spelled out Japan's Southeast Asian policy during his visit to the region in 1977—that Japan would seek to foster good relations with Indochina and looked forward to improved relations between ASEAN and Indochina. A Japanese security expert revealed that when officials of the Ministry of Foreign Affairs held a meeting in Hong Kong in March 1976 to discuss the situation in post–Vietnam War Southeast Asia, it was already agreed that Japan should contribute to peaceful coexistence between ASEAN and Indochina.[28] In this light, the much-heralded Fukuda Doctrine of August 1977 was not as historic as often interpreted. Psychologically, the friendly ties between Japan and ASEAN helped heal the wounds of Japanese aggression and atrocity, as the most bitter memories still existed in the minds of the Koreans and Chinese. An unfriendly ASEAN would be very costly to Japan's foreign policy initiatives. Japan's global roles need ASEAN support, especially in such regional economic cooperation organizations as the Pacific Economic Cooperation Council and the Asia Pacific Economic Cooperation forum. For any of Japan's international initiatives, ASEAN's understanding and support must be sought and the ASEAN countries must come first.

ASEAN's importance to Japan should not be exaggerated, however. Japan recognizes the importance of globalism as much as regionalism. Japan considers its relation with the United States the most important partnership in the world. The trilateral relations comprising the United States, Western Europe, and Japan are perhaps more important than Japan-ASEAN relations. It is not incorrect to conceive that ASEAN is considered important in the sense that it is a base for Japan to reach its global roles or its globalization strategy. As Japan's national identity is increasingly based on common and shared sentiments toward the future, ASEAN's importance to Japan cannot be overstated. The Japanese public's interest in ASEAN culture, society, and its peoples is still relatively low. According to a 1990 public opinion survey on Japan's foreign relations, 53.4 percent indicated that they have no feelings of affinity toward members of ASEAN, and only 35 percent indicated that they have such feelings.[29]

Recently the Japanese policymaking elites have increased their efforts to exchange views and seek international support for Japan's more active roles in regional conflicts. The efforts of the Ministry of Foreign Affairs of Japan and of certain groups of Japanese Dietmen have recently been noticeable. A research think-tank under close support from the Ministry of Foreign Affairs, and the Japan Forum on International Relations (JFIR) under the chairmanship of former Foreign Minister Saburo Okita, organized the First Japan-

ASEAN Roundtable, held in Tokyo on September 10–11, 1990. They co-sponsored two leading Southeast Asian think-tanks on security issues: the Centre for Strategic and International Studies (CSIS) in Indonesia, and the Institute of Strategic and International Studies (ISIS) in Malaysia. These two leading Southeast Asian think-tanks had prepared a draft policy statement to the roundtable, which was aimed at achieving "a complete partnership" between Japan and ASEAN. Among the nine policy proposals, several suggested that Japan, together with ASEAN, should play a more political role in international affairs. The first proposal stated, "Very obviously, both Japan and ASEAN should contribute to the process of global détente, using the diplomatic, political, economic, ideological, and other capabilities which they individually or jointly possess."[30] On the Gulf crisis, the draft policy statement proposed, "Both Japan and countries of ASEAN should consider initiatives aimed at restoring peace and stability in the Middle East, contributing according to our ability and comparative political advantage."[31] This statement suggested that Japan's participation in the UN peacekeeping activies is acceptable to ASEAN. The draft policy statement also mentioned that "country bashing" be jointly condemned.[32]

ASEAN's Welcoming of Japan's More Active Political-Security Role

ASEAN governments have rarely objected to Japan's moves to be a more active player in regional security problems. The Gulf War has convinced ASEAN leaders that Japan's security role can be an important contribution. No ASEAN government expressed views opposing the UN Peace Cooperation bill, which was shelved in late 1990, and the UN Peacekeeping Operations Cooperation bill, which met a similar fate in late 1991. With the end of the Cambodian problem and the beginning of Indochinese reconstruction, however, Japan's political influence is expected to increase.

The view that Japan needs to shoulder more responsibility in the posthegemonic world has been expressed by ASEAN, especially by the Thai leaders. Thailand's Foreign Minister Arsa Sarasin has argued that Japan's greater share of responsibility, matching its economic power, "is the burden that comes with being a big power."[33] In a speech on April 25, 1991, Foreign Minister Arsa Sarasin proposed, "Japan should become actively involved, diplomatically and politically, in the search for solutions to regional conflict and tension as Japan is currently doing in the case of Cambodia."[34] During a visit to Thailand as part of his ASEAN tour, Prime Minister Kaifu was reassured by Thai Prime Minister Ananda Panyarachun that Japan's increasingly active role in international politics, especially in the Cambodian problem, was welcomed by Thailand. In his speech at the dinner to welcome Mr. Kaifu in Bangkok, Ananda Panyarachun expressed his view that

in recent years, Thailand has been observing Japan's constructive role in the
international political arena, aimed at creating peace, stability, and happi-
ness for the peoples of this region. This was most evidently demonstrated by
her greater participation at the G-7 Summit in Houston as well as her efforts
to seek a solution to the Cambodian problem.[35]

"Pax Japonica" was not a very familiar term in Southeast Asia in the
1970s and early 1980s, but it could be expected to be mentioned more frequently in the post–Cold War era. For example, Amnuay Viravan, executive
president of the Bangkok Bank, has called for a stronger Japanese political
leadership commensurate with its economic power. In an article published in
1987, Viravan said, "Perhaps one can venture to say that 'Pax Japonica' has
dawned, and a staggering responsibility has now fallen on Japan with the
massive wealth it has accumulated."[36] Japan's international roles toward the
end of the twentieth century began to be characterized as "economic Pax
Japonica" and "economic Pax Nipponica" by two prominent strategic thinkers, Sukhumbhand Paribatra of Thailand and Noordin Sopiee of Malaysia.[37]
In his article, entitled "The Rise of Pax Nipponica: The Challenger to Japan,"
Noordin Sopiee predicted that an economic Pax Nipponica is coming but the
question is how to "ensure that we develop the mechanisms and processes for
enriching and managing the coming economic Pax Nipponica."[38]

Feeling disillusioned with the bipolar structure of world politics, which
caused millions of lives in the so-called proxy wars, ASEAN strategic thinkers look to Japan as a constructive new player in the multipolar international
politics. There are several expectations of Japan's roles in the minds of those
who talk about a Pax Nipponica, in both the economic and political senses.
First are Japan's efforts in solving regional conflicts by using its tremendous
clout as the world's largest aid-donor country to achieve positive changes by
making aid conditional. Second are Japan's attempts at making multilateral
organizations such as the United Nations more effective in solving regional
conflicts and preventing wars. Third is the applicability of Japan's peace
constitution, nonnuclear policy, and limited defense spending (as a percentage of GNP). Fourth is the possibility of turning Japan's economic power and
technological superiority into a means of peacemaking and conflict resolution. And last, but not least, is the expectation that Japan will be more active
in playing the diplomatic role of conflict mediator such as France did in the
Paris International Conference on Cambodia in late October and the United
States did in the Middle East peace talks in Madrid during late October and
early November 1991.

Japan's political-security role has been viewed by the ASEAN govern-
ments more as an international contribution than a military revival. After the
Gulf War, Japan's peace constitution has increasingly been viewed in South-
east Asia as an excuse rather than a guarantee. One prominent Thai editor in
Bangkok echoed this new thinking on Japan's international role and wrote,
"Tokyo should have acted more actively to send military personnel, armed or

not, to join the international force to demonstrate solidarity on all fronts—and not only in the traditional Japanese 'yen policy' with members of the world body."[39] The editor concluded, "Japan has no choice but to make the world realize, in a serious and consistent manner that she 'really cares' about the welfare of the global community and will play a role that can significantly contribute to lasting peace."[40]

As the role of the United Nations in maintaining international peace and security becomes accepted by both camps of ideology, Japan's security role will inevitably be expanded. More than the U.S.-Japan Treaty of Security and Cooperation, the UN framework has gained acceptance among the Japanese public. The Kaifu cabinet would not have decided to submit a bill to the Diet to allow sending Self-Defense Forces personnel to the Gulf had it not been for the request from the United Nations. In his policy speech to the Diet on October 12, 1990, in the wake of the Iraqi invasion and annexation of Kuwait in August, Prime Minister Kaifu proclaimed,

> It is crucial that Japan be able to cooperate effectively with such efforts both in personnel terms and in material terms. The issue is whether or not Japan will be able, rather than sitting idle just because there is no direct threat to Japanese territory, to respond as a key member of the international community in the post–Cold War international order to threats to international peace and justice.[41]

A leader of the Japanese business community observed that even though the United Nations had no substance in the real world of international politics, "Japan had been under the spell of the United Nations absolutism."[42]

Japan's political-security role, which centers around the United Nations, was recently symbolized by the election of Japan as a nonpermanent member in the Security Council. On October 16, 1991, the UN General Assembly voted by an overwhelming majority of 158 to grant Japan a two-year term of nonpermanent membership in the Security Council beginning in 1992. This is a seventh term for Japan, unmatched by other UN member nations apart from the permanent five. A year earlier, the post of the UN High Commissioner for Refugees was given to a Japanese professor of international relations, Sadako Ogata. In late October 1991, Professor Ogata of the International Christian University in Tokyo was dispatched to Burma by the United Nations to investigate the state of human rights after the announcement of the Nobel Peace Prize for Aung San Suu Kyi. These appointments suggest an increase in international confidence in Japan's political-security roles. In economic assistance for world development, Japan channeled a very high portion of its ODA, 32.1 percent, through multilateral organizations. The figures for the United States, Germany, France, and the United Kingdom were 16.8 percent, 18.8 percent, 10.8 percent, and 23.4 percent, respectively. The average for the Development Assistance Committee (DAC) of OECD was 22.5 percent.[43]

The ASEAN governments support Japan's more active security role under the UN framework for at least three reasons. First, the ASEAN governments believe that the UN role in maintaining international peace and security has so far not proved to be against the interest of the noncommunist world. Second, by supporting Japan's self-identification with the world body, ASEAN wanted to prevent Japan from pursuing an independent security policy, as happened in the 1930s and might happen again should the U.S.-Japan security arrangement break down. Third, it is thought that a more effective UN collective security role in regional conflicts and wars may be able to persuade Japan not to build up and modernize its armed forces with the high technology that Japan is now producing in the commercial field.

ASEAN's Cautious Attitude Toward Japan's Active Political-Security Role

The above discussion might have given the impression that ASEAN wholeheartedly supports Japan's more active political-security role. Compared to China and Korea, ASEAN is perhaps a more dependable support base for Japan's expanded international role, but we must be objective in our discussion about the ASEAN governments' and peoples' sensitivity to Japan's expanding international roles in the security field.

The unwillingness to admit the aggression and atrocities committed by the Japanese Imperial Army on the part of conservative politicians and authority in Japan have often irritated people in the ASEAN countries. Unlike the case in Germany, the present political leadership in Japan does not look at the prewar and wartime history as a mistake to be condemned, and it has not apologized to the Asian peoples. Remarks by certain conservative politicians in the ruling Liberal Democratic Party have often been protested and criticized in the press in many Asian countries. The Ministry of Education's control over school textbooks, particularly Japanese history textbooks, has often been viewed by ASEAN with suspicion, as trying to rewrite history and prohibiting historical facts to speak to the postwar generation. An ASEAN senior statesman has pointed out that the "welcoming of death as glorious for a Japanese soldier in war for his emperor" is a big problem, which makes the Japanese case different from other Western aggressors.[44]

No one in ASEAN has warned Japan of the mistake of avoiding war responsibility as clearly as Singapore's Senior Minister Lee Kuan Yew. He has often declared that Japan's neighbors "have unforgettable memories of Japan's militaristic culture which resulted in unnecessary cruelty and inhumanity."[45] As a sincere supporter of Japan's more active roles, he was deeply impressed by Prime Minister Kaifu's expression of "sincere contrition" for the "unbearable sufferings and sorrow" of many peoples in Asia caused by Japan. Lee Kuan Yew said, "This is a good beginning for a catharsis, a purification by purging her guilt, which will benefit both Japan and her former victims."[46] Lee Kuan Yew has often said that words alone are not enough. In a speech at the Asahi Shimbun Symposium in Tokyo on May 9, 1991, he repeated this stance and said that "young Japanese must be part of this catharsis through their teachers and textbooks. When this is done Japan will be able to play a fuller role for peace and stability in the world, especially in Southeast Asia."[47] Had an imperial apology been made during Emperor Akihito's visits to Thailand, Malaysia, and Indonesia in late September and early October 1991, it would have been a symbolic gesture on the part of the Japanese government to relieve Japan and her former victims from the burden of past history and suspicion about the future. Unfortunately, the conservative ruling Liberal Democratic Party did not take this first imperial trip as a chance to lift Japan from the terrible past memories.

A good example of ASEAN's cautious views on Japan playing a more active political-security role is ASEAN's cool attitude, noted earlier, to Japan's proposal for having a forum to discuss security issues. This move was not, as some ASEAN scholars have claimed, a sudden idea derived from a proposal put forward by ASEAN's Institutes of Strategic and International Studies at Jakarta.[48] It could be argued that this bold policy direction was decided by Japan's Ministry of Foreign Affairs as far back as early 1990. In an article by Vice-Minister Takakazu Kuriyama entitled "New Directions of Japanese Foreign Policy in the Changing World of the 1990s: Making Active Contribution to the Creation of a New International Order," it was made clear that one of the five pillars of international order that Japan was seeking was "active contribution to the mitigation of international tensions and to the settlement of regional conflicts."[49] Japanese officials at the Ministry of Foreign Affairs tended to credit ASEAN as the origin of the idea, but it would be naive to say that Japan had not long looked for an appropriate context in which to make this idea heard by its friends and allies.[50]

At the General Session of the ASEAN Post-Ministerial Conference (ASEAN-PMC) on July 22, 1991, in Kuala Lumpur, Malaysia, Foreign Minister Taro Nakayama delivered a thirteen-page statement explaining Japan's views and policy on various issues in the region. Toward the end of the speech, he made a bold proposal to the members of the ASEAN-PMC in the following words:

> I believe it would be meaningful and timely to use the ASEAN Post-Ministerial Conference as a process of political discussion designed to improve the sense of security among us. In order for these discussions to be effective, it might be advisable to organize a senior officials' meeting which could then report its deliberations to the ASEAN Post-Ministerial Conference for further discussion.[51]

According to the proposal, security issues would be discussed among ASEAN-PMC members, excluding the two important players in the region, namely China and the Soviet Union. Japan proposed a meeting at the expert level, which in effect meant the convening of another forum or mechanism in addition to the ASEAN-PMC. Foreign Minister Nakayama emphasized in particular that Japan and ASEAN should become more active together. In his statement at the 6+1 Meeting with ASEAN foreign ministers the following day, on July 23, he tried to convince ASEAN that "what is of utmost importance for safeguarding the peace in Asia is for Japan and ASEAN to be actively involved in the solution of the problems that afflict this region and speak out with louder voice for stability."[52]

Nakayama's proposal did not win support from ASEAN. Indonesian Foreign Minister Ali Alatas reportedly said that ASEAN did not want to have a new separate mechanism to deal only with security matters.[53] Support for the idea came from Australia, whose foreign and trade minister, Gareth Evans, said the Soviet Union's waning influence and the U.S. stand on its future presence in the region had created a need for some substantial dialogue.[54] ASEAN's cool response to the Nakayama proposal surprised Japan's Foreign Ministry officials and was thought to be a misunderstanding of Japan's true intention. The purpose of the ASEAN-PMC, according to the Joint Communiqué of the Twenty-fourth ASEAN Ministerial Meeting in Kuala Lumpur, is not for security discussion. To the contrary, the statement said, the future activities should focus on "human resources development, science and technology, trade, industry, investment, and environment." Other issues to be raised in the various consultative mechanisms that existed within the framework included market access, trade disputes, and the promotion of joint ventures.[55]

Foreign Minister Nakayama perhaps did not expect that Indonesia would not be responsive to his call. As a strictly nonaligned country and playing a leading diplomatic role in the Cambodian peace settlement, the Indonesian government deemed it unnecessary to discuss security in view of the disappearance of the military threat coming from China and Vietnam. General Sudomo, the coordinating minister for politics and security, made a remark in October 1991 that "Indonesia has stopped thinking about the danger from the North and put aside any idea of setting up a military or security pact among ASEAN."[56] Mochtar Kusuma-Atmadja, former minister of foreign affairs of Indonesia, explained that Indonesia's tradition of nonalignment has its origin in the late-1940s' history of fighting against both contending power blocs. In his view, "The low level, non-institutionalized form of military co-operation at present between Indonesia, Singapore, and Malaysia is all that Indonesia . . . can afford."[57] Japan perhaps expected that support would come from Thailand, which was true but with certain reservations.

The Thai government has a tradition of supporting Japan's active political-security role in Southeast Asia. In the reconstruction of Indochina, Thailand will find itself working more closely with Japan, similar to the peace settlement of Cambodia during the Chatichai administration. It is a prevailing view in Bangkok that Thailand will benefit both politically and economically by supporting Japan's more active roles. The dilemma is China, a country with which Thailand has become half-allied since the Vietnamese invasion of Cambodia. For Thai policymakers, a forum discussing security problems in Southeast Asia without China's participation is unrealistic, given China's tremendous influence in the settlement of the Cambodian problem and its influence over Vietman after Sino-Vietnamese normalization following Du Muoi's Beijing visit in early November 1991.[58]

The Japanese foreign minister's proposal failed to get ASEAN support for another reason: such a fixed forum, excluding China and the former Soviet Union, would induce suspicion from those powers at a time when regional tension had been greatly reduced. Both China and the Soviet Union sent their representatives to the ASEAN Post-Ministerial Conference for the first time as guests and did the same in the 1992 meeting in Manila.[59] Although Australia and Canada have supported Nakayama's proposal, ASEAN would not like to see the PMC forum become a place where tension could be heightened due to differences between the regular dialogue partners and the invited guests. ASEAN would also find it difficult to allow Japan to use the forum to reassure ASEAN of its intention not to become a military power while continuing to expand its military capabilities and preparing itself for a more assertive security role as the United States reduces its economic and security presence in the region.[60]

ASEAN does not view the emerging new world order in Asia as a cause for alarm the way Japan tends to. The policymaking elites in Japan have repeatedly voiced the issue of the potential Soviet threat. North Korea's nuclear capability and the tension in the Korean peninsula preoccupy the minds of Japanese foreign policymakers. On the contrary, ASEAN is more optimistic about changes in the former Soviet Union. Once the support from China and the former Soviet Union is drastically diminished, ASEAN does not see North Korea as a source of trouble in Asia. Only a few, if any, ASEAN leaders will view the former Soviet Union and North Korea as posing any threat. Actually, soon after the outbreak of the Gulf War, Thailand quickly moved to establish diplomatic relations with North Korea. As the prime ministers of North and South Korea met in October 1991, the fourth of such meetings, and as the two Koreas became members of the United Nations in 1991, ASEAN does not feel concerned about the Korean peninsula as a source of instability disrupting international order in East Asia.

The ASEAN governments have tended to take the view that Japan's expanded political-security role need not entail the expansion of defense spending and military buildup. Miyazawa and his successors will have to take into account the new environment of détente, defense-spending cuts, and rapprochement among capitalist and socialist countries. Still, Japan's cut in defense spending will be smaller in proportion to that in the other major powers because the Japanese economy can easily afford the planned defense buildup program. A prediction made in 1989 said that Japan would become a military power by the year 2020, and that by 1990 Japan's military spending would be more than 60 percent as large as the combined military spending of the three European powers: the United Kingdom, West Germany, and France.[61] The ASEAN governments preferred the enlargement of Japan's comprehensive security program, which included efforts for self-help, efforts to render the whole international system conducive to Japan's security, and intermediate-level efforts to build a favorable security environment in the region.[62] ASEAN leaders also opted for having Japan's security roles limited under the framework of the United Nations. The Gulf War has influenced the public in the ASEAN countries to accept the shift from the concept of comprehensive security to the concept of active contribution in terms of armed personnel under the UN framework.

The Preference of U.S. Military Presence _____

Japan's cautious views about the posthegemonic world and her desire to play a more active political-security role are closely related to the issue of U.S. military presence in East Asia. More than before, Japan wants the U.S. military commitment to continue. The call for Japan's independent security policy has declined. Replacing that view is the emergence of a broad-based consensus of tying the Japanese security policy even more closely to the United States. To the Japanese ruling elite, it is in the European front that U.S. military presence might be withdrawn or substantially reduced, not in East Asia.

Both Japan and the ASEAN members favor continued U.S. military presence in the region even though the Cold War has waned and tensions among major powers have been eased. Both Japan and the ASEAN members believe that sources of regional tension still exist. Thai government leaders favor continued U.S. military presence in the region even though in 1975 the Thai government requested the United States to withdraw its military bases from Thailand. Prasong Soonsiri, the former Secretary-General of the National Security Council, for example, argued, "There are also other unresolved problems among Southeast Asian states. Dangerous potential conflicts may arise in the South China Sea due to territorial claims, especially when involving extra-regional powers."[63] He concluded that

> too rapid a change in the existing security agreements could upset the regional balance of power and lead to escalation in regional conflict. Under the present circumstances, the U.S. military presence still remain[s] vital to maintain the equilibrium and the balance of power in the region. The eventual U.S. troop withdrawal should be a step-by-step process.[64]

This view is widely shared among strategic thinkers in Japan, in whose views China and other communist states of East Asia are much less affected by the impact of perestroika reforms in the former Soviet Union and Eastern Europe.[65]

There are many reasons that the ASEAN governments support the continuation of the U.S. military presence in the region, including smooth U.S.-Japan security cooperation. The withdrawal or substantial reduction of the U.S. military presence will open the way to rivalry between Asian powers—namely, China, Japan, and India—to expand their political-military influences in Southeast Asia. Specifically, regarding Japan, ASEAN wants Japan's expansion of security roles to be put under the framework of the U.S.-Japan security treaty. Moreover, ASEAN fears that the strain in U.S.-Japan economic relations could easily worsen should there be any conflict in their security relations. The most likely consequence would be more pressures on exports from ASEAN countries in which Japan has invested heavily. The so-called U.S. unilateral approach and the principle of reciprocity will certainly threaten ASEAN's export-led industrialization. Experience shows that whenever U.S. criticism of Japan's trade policy and practice brings tension, the ASEAN countries have been targeted by U.S. trade representatives. Japanese leaders seem to understand this very well and are well aware that once the time comes, Japan would be asked by ASEAN to open more of its domestic markets. Any worsening of U.S.-Japan security cooperation not only would affect overall U.S.-Japan relations, but also would seriously affect ASEAN security and economic interests. The present economic situation, in the view of the United States, is already at the brink of a trade war: Japan provides the capital and technology ASEAN needs whereas the United States absorbs the bulk of ASEAN's exports.[66]

ASEAN also plays the opposite role, supporting the United States in pressuring Japan to open its domestic market. The Structural Impediments Initiative (SII) talks have greatly benefited the ASEAN countries; they have enjoyed both more open Japanese markets and an improved U.S. economy. With the opening of Japan's rice market, expected to be around 5 percent of the total Japanese rice consumption, Thailand may benefit as much as, if not more than, the U.S. rice exporters. The cost of production is much lower in Thailand. The problem is, however, that the price of U.S. rice exported to Japan will be relatively low because of heavy federal subsidies, an issue on which the ASEAN governments hope Tokyo will take a tough stand in negotiating with Washington.

Among the many functions performed by the U.S. military presence in East Asia is that of providing a buffer between Japan and its neighbors, including Southeast Asia. It is no exaggeration to say that were it not for the U.S.-Japan alliance, Japan's bilateral relationships with Korea, China, and ASEAN might have experienced more regional tensions and instability. By having the United States present economically, culturally, and politically in the region, ASEAN can better balance the Japanese presence and the coming of Japan's active political-security roles. Jusuf Wanandi, one of the most prominent strategic thinkers in ASEAN, correctly put it when he stated, "For ASEAN, the U.S.-Japan alliance is the most important guarantee that Japan will not go it alone in defense."[67] Japan seems to feel insecure when its presence in the region becomes too dominating and conspicuous. Anti-Japanese movements happened several times in Thailand and in Indonesia during the 1970s and early 1980s.[68] The Japanese government's reluctance to support the concept of East Asia Economic Grouping proposed by Malaysian Prime Minister Mahathir, which excludes the United States as a member, shows clearly Japan's fear of becoming too dominant a member in such a regional grouping. Japanese foreign policymakers have always been cautious and have warned that Japan should avoid conspicuous political initiatives for the reason that anti-Japanese sentiments could be easily whipped up under certain conditions.

Without the U.S.-Japan security arrangement, the ASEAN countries would find Japan's role in regional conflicts more a source of instability than a contribution to the region's peace and stability.[69] ASEAN would be alarmed to see Japan, without the U.S. security umbrella, expanding its military forces or allying itself with another power, probably China. One U.S. scholar on Southeast Asian security issues observed rightly: "An important connection between Japanese and ASEAN security lies in the fact that both rely on a strong regional American security presence. Leadership in Japan and ASEAN want that presence to continue."[70] For this reason U.S. bases in the Philippines have performed several political and military functions not only for the Philippines but for the entire Asia Pacific region. It is not an exaggeration to say that the nearly successful military coup in the Philippines in 1989 was narrowly defeated when U.S. military aircraft began flying over Manila and threatened the rebellion with higher destructive forces from the air.

The contributions of the U.S. military bases in the Philippines to the entire Asia Pacific region have been widely recognized by ASEAN and Japan. They provided a security umbrella to this region and facilitated dynamic economic growth. They supported, from the security viewpoint, various regional economic cooperation organizations, such as PECC and APEC. In the analysis of a Singaporean scholar, the U.S. military bases in the Philippines have contributed to the region by (1) forming an integral part of a deterrent system; (2) supporting the U.S. capabilities throughout the Pacific, the Indian Ocean, and the Gulf; (3) protecting strategic air- and sea-lanes; (4) providing a visible manifestation of U.S. power in an area of growing interest to the Soviet Union; (5) representing a part of the worldwide defense system; (6) demonstrating U.S. commitments to the security of the Philippines and the region; and (7) functioning as a counterbalance to the growing naval power of the Soviet Union, India, and China.[71] Singapore's leader, Lee Kuan Yew, has always preferred the continued U.S. military presence to Japan's regional security role. He has often been quoted as saying that supporting Japanese armed peacekeeping would be like giving liqueur chocolates to an alcoholic, and that whatever the Japanese do, they go to the limit.[72]

Fortunately or unfortunately, the trend of declining U.S. security commitments to Southeast Asia is obvious. U.S. economic aid to the Philippines, Thailand, and other strategically important countries has been steadily reduced. U.S. assistance to Thailand in recent years is on average only 4–5 percent of the total bilateral aid Thailand has received, whereas Japan's aid has accounted for about 65 percent. The proposed U.S. military and economic aid to the Philippines for fiscal year 1988 was $260 million compared with $406 million in 1986.[73] Economic assistance to Israel and Egypt, by contrast, amounted to 49 percent of the total U.S. aid budget of $6.1 billion.[74] Japanese aid officials have discovered an unbelievable statistic regarding Japan's largest aid-recipient country, Indonesia, and the largest U.S. aid recipient, Israel. In per capita terms, Indonesia receives fifty times less from the United States. Not only in Thailand and Indonesia but in other Southeast Asian countries, U.S. aid has been constantly declining, demonstrating less and less U.S. economic and security presence in the region. By the end of 1991, it became conclusive that the U.S. forces in the Philippines would have to be withdrawn by the end of 1992 with[75] no extension of the bases treaty. Economic issues would now become the main focus. In the Multilateral Assistance Initiatives (MAI), Japan's share is not small: a total of $3.5 billion would be offered to the Philippines for a period of five years; the U.S. contribution would be $160 million per year, but Japan's contribution of $100 million per year would not be small.[76]

To deter the threat from the Soviet Union (and now Russia) and to alleviate Asia's fear of Japan's military buildup, the Japanese government has decided to share more of the cost of the presence of U.S. forces in Japan in order to convince Washington to continue its military presence in Japan. According to an explanation from a high-ranking official of the Ministry of Foreign Affairs, Japan now pays $3.7 billion, or about 40 percent of the cost, for the U.S. military presence in Japan. It has been decided that by 1995, Japan will pay up to $4.4 billion at the exchange rate of 1991, or about 50 percent of the cost (about 73 percent of nonsalary cost).[77] It is ironic that Japan pays so much just not to become a military power. Put in another way, in order not to cause any fears among its Asian neighbors, Japan pays more and more every year.[78]

_____ *Future Prospects and Conclusion*

It is likely that toward the end of the twentieth century Japan's international roles will not be restricted to the economic, cultural, and diplomatic areas, but also will include an active political-security role. In Southeast Asia in particular, Japan will assume more roles and responsibilities. True, there are several enduring domestic constraints that are constitutional, political, and psychological, but once the Cold War framework is gone it will be easier to convince the Japanese public of the necessity to play a stabilizing role in the region. This is not burden-sharing with the United States in the old concept of Cold War, but burden-sharing with the United States and surrounding Asian neighbors in the new concept of post–Cold War joint responsibility. Already in action is Japan's attempt to persuade Indochina and ASEAN to live in peaceful coexistence. At the ASEAN seminar on "ASEAN and the World Economy" in Bali, Indonesia, in March 1991, an influential Japanese politician urged ASEAN to renew and expand trade and economic ties with Vietnam. According to Michio Watanabe, Vietnam should not be viewed as a potential threat to ASEAN.[79]

With the rebirth of Cambodia as a member of the international community and the improvement of Vietnam's relations with its ASEAN neighbors, Japan will increasingly play an active political-security role in the post–Cold War era. In Prime Minister Kaifu's words during his tour of ASEAN in May 1991, "We need to go beyond the economic realm and work in political, social, and foreign realms, as well as to become a major force for stability." Japanese leaders hope that through a more active role in the political-security realm, Japan will no longer be criticized as "a nation with the primary aim of maximizing profits while accepting little of the responsibility."[80]

The failure to respond effectively to the sudden crisis in the Gulf has pressed the Japanese political elite to try to make a major shift in Japan's foreign policy. Before the Iraqi invasion and annexation of Kuwait in August 1990, no student of Japanese foreign policy believed that it would be possible for Japan to send its Self-Defense Forces to a foreign area of conflicts and disputes. No experts on Japanese domestic politics thought it would be possible for the Japan Socialist Party (now the Social Democratic Party) to change its foreign policy stance to accept the dispatch of armed personnel overseas, albeit with strict limitations. None saw any likelihood of the above twin changes during the same period of time. But all experts were correct in pointing out that if such changes were to come one day, the source of such changes would be an external rather than an internal factor. Finally, Foreign Minister Nakayama's proposal would have been viewed as totally unlikely in the 1970s and 1980s. Who would have pictured a Japanese foreign minister proposing a security discussion with ASEAN with a U.S. secretary of state sitting there listening?

The Southeast Asian region is one of the main beneficiaries of the ending of the Cold War and the disappearance of the hegemonic world. The Cambodian problem had finally been settled at the Paris International Conference on Cambodia in October 1991. Unfortunately, the intrasigence of the Khmer Rouge faction in 1992, delaying its disarmament under the supervision of the United Nations Transitional Authority in Cambodia, threatened to disrupt the implementation of the Paris accords. The faction also attacked a village in central Cambodia twice in April and May. As most of the villagers were Vietnamese, the intention was to frighten them into leaving Cambodia. Vietnam has moved quickly to improve its relations with ASEAN. Prime Minister Vo Van Kiet of Vietnam visited Indonesia, Thailand, and Singapore during October 24–November 1, 1991, the first such visit in thirteen years. The joint communiqué signed in Bangkok on October 30 declared that Vietnam and Thailand would refrain from actions affecting the security interests of the other countries in the region. Prime Minister Anand Panyarachun of Thailand said after the signing of the joint communiqué at the end of Vo Van Kiet's visit to Thailand: "The atmosphere of the region has changed. It is the beginning of a new era not only for Thailand and Vietnam but also for a region that will include Laos and Cambodia. It will be a new era of cooperation, peace, and understanding."[81] Both Vietman and ASEAN now share the view that the countries in the region are presented with an unprecedented opportunity brought about by the end of the Cold War and the decline of the hegemonic world order. Surely, the adherence of all countries in the region to the 1976 Treaty of Amity and Cooperation in Southeast Asia would be the framework of peaceful coexistence and constructive cooperation in Southeast Asia. Vietnam expressed its intent to comply with the treaty, which called for mutual respect for independence, sovereignty, equality, and territorial integrity, and renounced the threat or use of force to settle differences or disputes. At the Manila ASEAN foreign ministers' meeting on July 21–22, 1992, the foreign ministers of Vietnam and Laos handed over their instruments of accession to the Treaty of Amity and Cooperation in Southeast Asia. They have not yet been accepted as members of ASEAN—this may take several years. On the other hand, the improvement of relations between Vietnam and China is moving equally quickly. Vietnam's Communist Party Secretary General Dr. Muoi headed a delegation of government and party officials, including Premier Vo Van Kiet and Foreign Minister Nguyen Manh Can, and visited China on November 5, 1991, to seal the full normalization of relations. Indeed, the end of the Cold War in Southeast Asia is coming in the very near future. The tragedy of one and a half million Vietnamese boat people and the one million victims of the Khmer Rouge's genocide will become a story of the past as peace finally comes to the entire region and economic reconstruction in Indochina becomes the agenda of the day. This hopeful image was marred in 1992 by China, which occupied another one of the Spratlys claimed by Vietnam and gave a contract to a U.S. oil company to start prospecting in a sea area belonging to Vietnam. In addition, a new law in China in February 1992 included the Spratlys as well as the Senkaku Islands belonging to Japan as Chinese territories.

ASEAN, of course, does not want to see Vietnam isolated any more. At the Twenty-fourth ASEAN Ministerial Meeting in Kuala Lumpur on July 19–20, 1991, a joint communiqué was announced. It stated, "The non-ASEAN South East Asian nations could find it possible to participate in the activities of the region." Prime Minister Anand Panyarachun of Thailand on various occasions expressed his hope that this ultimate goal should be achieved. He told Prime Minister Goh Chok Tong of Singapore at a dinner in Bangkok in honor of the latter, "Thus, as we look ahead to the post-Cambodia period, the challenge that we face is to work towards a regional order that embraces all nations of Southeast Asia in peace, progress, and prosperity as envisioned by the founders of ASEAN."[82]

Japan will definitely play a leading role in the economic field in the post–Cold War era. The end of the war of ideology has at last produced its impact: the Cambodian peace settlement. On October 23, 1991, representatives of nineteen nations signed their names to the Cambodian peace agreement at the Paris International Conference on Cambodia. Undoubtedly, Japan's economic influence and, of course, its political influence, too, was so dominating that no country could challenge it. The United States was still preoccupied with the issues of human rights in Cambodia and Vietnam, and the so-called prisoners of war (POWs) and those missing-in-action (MIAs) in Vietnam. The U.S. trade embargo on Vietnam is still imposed. On the contrary, Japan will play a leading role in the Indochina reconstruction through its aid programs and its joint ventures based on the countries surrounding Indochina, especially Thailand.

Another direction or area of Japan's more active political-security role will be the so-called United Nations diplomacy.[83] Japan will start to look for a permanent seat on the Security Council. Japan is now the number two financial contributor to the United Nations, in 1990 paying $90 million toward the UN budget, second only to the United States. The Japanese government has agreed to raise its share of the burden in 1992 from 11.38 percent to 12.45 percent of the total costs.[84] Japanese holding prominent positions in UN organizations include Professor Sadako Ogata, the UN High Commissioner for Refugees; Hiraki Nakajima, head of the World Health Organization; and Yasushi Akashi, Deputy UN Secretary General for Disarmament Affairs. But with its higher contribution to UN costs, it is likely that Japan will be allowed to control more prominent positions and to send more personnel to staff UN organizations.[85] Japan's more active political-security role within the framework of the United Nations will have the support of the ASEAN governments. ASEAN has also supported Japan's status as a member of the Security Council and Japan's sending of its armed forces personnel to UN peacekeeping activities. Under the leadership of Prime Minister Kiichi Miyazawa, Japan may be more assertive in its UN diplomacy,[86] including the successful push for a resolution to require arms traders to register their sales at the United Nations. Miyazawa will perhaps try to put an end to the image of Japan as an economic giant but a political dwarf.[87]

Recently, Japan-ASEAN relations have been characterized by such words as mature partnership, in contrast to the images of exploitation, dependency, and economic animal of the 1970s and early 1980s. A likely scenario would be the United States playing an opposition role in championing the value of human rights and democracy and watching with trepidation the Japan-ASEAN partnership working more closely together in the economic reconstruction of Indochina and in the region's security.

The posthegemonic world order during the past few years has revealed several positive changes: reduction of tension between old enemies, warming of relations between antagonistic neighbors, arms reduction between the two superpowers, exchange of visits between leaders of different ideologies, and other optimistic changes including peace in Cambodia. The end of the Cold War and the demise of the hegemonic world order have at the same time accentuated the magnitude of various problems that had been contained or managed by the old world order: ethnic unrest, territorial disputes, disintegration of old empires, massive migration, and other forms of instability and sources of insecurity. The new world order is, of course, difficult for Japan to manage. Indeed, it is difficult for any nation to manage.

In such a fluid, dynamic, and uncertain process of dramatic changes, Japan has both reiterated the necessity of the continuation of Pax Americana and prepared to assume a more active political-security role. The potential Russian threat, the disparity between the Russian and Japanese defense capabilities, and the unpredictable nature of changes in the former Soviet Union have been cited time and again as causes for concern by foreign policymakers and the ruling elite in Tokyo. Japan's concern about the uncertainty of the new world order was accentuated by the unexpected Gulf crisis. Japan has also been concerned about the prospect of China, and perhaps India, playing an active political-security role in the region as the U.S. military presence in East Asia has gradually been reduced and its forces in the Philippines are being withdrawn.

The Japanese government has not hidden its intention to have a say in the settlement of regional conflicts in Southeast Asia. The desire for a more active political-security role was shown in Tokyo's Cambodian initiative, the submission of the UN Peacekeeping Operations Cooperation bill, and Foreign Minister Nakayama's proposal. Japan also attempted to clear the bitter memory of its postcolonial policy and its aggression and occupation of its neighbors. In its preparation to assume a more active political-security role, Japan wants the U.S. military presence in East Asia to continue, fearing Japan's conspicuous presence in the region as destabilizing.

From the perspectives of Southeast Asia, Japan's more active role in the region is generally welcomed. Japan-ASEAN relations have become much closer than ever after the yen appreciation in 1985, so that "mature partnership" has recently been characteristic of their ties. Southeast Asia is important for Japan in the economic, political, and security senses. Their ties have been strengthened through the U.S. military presence and their economic relations with the United States. ASEAN, however, has been cautious of Japan playing a role that might be viewed as dominating, leading, or insensitive to their feelings. That is why Foreign Minister Nakayama's proposal was received coolly at the ASEAN-PMC despite the fact that foreign policy experts in ASEAN have long suggested that it is most appropriate to use that forum to discuss political-security issues. The January 1992 Summit of ASEAN did decide to use the annual meeting of foreign ministers as a security consultative organ and the dispute over the South China Sea islands was the chief topic at the Manila meeting in July, thus justifying Nakayama's proposal. At any rate, the ASEAN governments still feel more secure with the U.S. military presence than with its disappearance or drastic reduction in a short time frame.

In the final analysis, in the 1990s we are going to witness Japan becoming a more important player in the problems of security and regional conflicts in Southeast Asia. This is inevitable. The only question is how. From our discussion, we can conclude that Southeast Asia will support the expansion of such roles within three frameworks: the U.S.-Japan security arrangement, the United Nations, and the ASEAN-PMC. And this is also Tokyo's strategy. It would be too dangerous for Japan to pursue an active political-security role without such restraining frameworks. The governments and peoples of Southeast Asia will never allow Japan an unrestrained role in the region. Fifty years later, the Greater East Asia Coprosperity war is still vivid in our memories.

Notes

1. See Kuniko Inoguchi, "Ten Characteristics of the Post–Cold-War World," *Economic Eye*, Tokyo: Keizai Koho Center, vol. 12, no. 2 (Summer 1991), pp. 24–26. In this chapter, the terms "posthegemonic" and "post–Cold War" are used interchangeably, although their meanings differ greatly.

2. See Chin Kin Wah, "Changing Global Trends and Their Effects on the Asia Pacific," *Contemporary Southeast Asia*, vol. 13, no. 1 (June 1991), pp. 12–13.

3. Hisahiko Okazaki and Seizaburo Sato, "Redefining the Role of Japanese Military Power," *Japan Echo*, vol. 18, no. 1 (Spring 1991), p. 21.

4. Ibid., p. 25.

5. Ibid.

6. See the criticism about Japan's limited contribution in Kenichi Ito, "Force Versus Sanctions in the Middle East," *Japan Echo*, vol. 18, no. 1 (Spring 1991), pp. 26–31; and Kenichi Ito, "Japan's Limited Contributions to a Legitimate War," *Economic Eye*, Tokyo: Keizai Kōhō Center, vol. 12, no. 2 (Summer 1991), pp. 5–8. A reinterpretation of article 9 of the constitution has recently become a trend in Japan. It is interesting to note a younger generation scholar's remark:

> True, our Constitution bans us from the direct use of force to settle international disputes, but there is nothing in the Constitution that bars us from participating in internationally sanctioned military action. Such participation actually advances the cause of the "international peace based on justice and order" that Japan, in the war-renouncing Article 9 of the Constitution, claims to support.

Shinichi Kitaoka, "What Nonmilitary Assistance Can and Cannot Accomplish," *Economic Eye*, Tokyo: Keizai Kōhō Center, Summer 1991, p. 19.

7. Robert S. Ross, "China's Strategic View of Southeast Asia: A Region in

Transition," *Contemporary Southeast Asia*, vol. 12, no. 2 (September 1990), pp. 101–119; Lee Lai To, "Domestic Changes in China Since the 4 June Incident and Their Implications for Southeast Asia," *Contemporary Southeast Asia*, vol. 13, no. 1 (June 1991), pp. 17–43; Pervaiz Iqbal Cheema, "Indian Naval Build up and Southeast Asian Security: A Pakistani View," *Contemporary Southeast Asia*, vol. 13, no. 1 (June 1991), pp. 86–102.

8. See Chang Pao-Min, "A New Scramble for the South China Sea Islands," *Contemporary Southeast Asia*, vol. 12, no. 1 (June 1990), pp. 20–39.

9. In his speech delivered in Beijing on August 11, 1991, Prime Minister Kaifu told the Chinese government that "upholding the fundamental human rights of its people is a path that will in the end strengthen the nation's ties with the rest of the world." "Japan-China Relations in a New World, Address by Prime Minister Toshiki Kaifu," press release, August 11, 1991, Bangkok, p. 18.

10. Shigekatsu Kondo, "Political and Security Cooperation between ASEAN and Japan," in Francis Fung Wai Lai and Charles E. Morrison, eds., *Political and Security Cooperation: A New Dimension in ASEAN-Japan Relations?* The JCIE Papers, Tokyo: Japan Center for International Exchange, p. 13.

11. Ibid., p. 14.

12. Ibid.

13. Ibid.

14. Author's interview with Tadashi Ikeda, minister of the Japanese embassy in Thailand, at his office, Bangkok, October 8, 1991.

15. *Bangkok Post*, Bangkok, October 30, 1991, p. 4.

16. Ibid.

17. "Policy Speech by Prime Minister Toshiki Kaifu, Japan and ASEAN: Seeking a Mature Partnership for the New Age," Singapore, May 3, 1991.

18. "His Majesty's Address of Welcome on the Occasion of the State Banquet Given in Honour of Their Majesties the Emperor and Empress of Japan," Chakri Throne Hall, September 26, 1991, mimeograph, p. 1.

19. Motoo Shiina, "Japan's Choice in the Gulf: Participation or Isolation," *Japan Echo*, vol. 18, no. 1 (June 1991), p. 19.

20. Noordin Sopiee, "The Rise of Pax Nipponica: The Challenger to Japan," *Japan and the World in the Post Cold War Era*, Tokyo: Foreign Press Center of Japan, The Japan Times, 1990, p. 80.

21. Ibid.

22. Ibid.

23. *Tai Okoku Gaikyō* [General outline of Thailand], Bangkok: JETRO Bangkok Center and Japan Chamber of Commerce and Industry, 1991, p. 23.

24. Ibid.

25. Kondo, "Political and Security Cooperation," p. 15.

26. Masashi Nishihara, "Japan's Security Interests in Southeast Asia," paper presented at the International Conference on ASEAN and the Asia-Pacific Region: Prospects for Security Cooperation in the 1990's, organized by the Department of Foreign Affairs of the Philippines and the Ministry of Foreign Affairs of Thailand, at Hotel Intercontinental Manila, Manila, June 5–7, 1991, p. 2.

27. Anny Wong, "Japan's National Security and Cultivation of ASEAN Elites," *Contemporary Southeast Asia*, vol. 12, no. 4 (March 1991), pp. 306–330.

28. Kondo, "Political and Security Cooperation," p. 12.

29. "1990 Public Opinion Survey on Japan's Foreign Relations, January 1991 (Summary), by Prime Minister's Office," Tokyo: Foreign Press Center, January 1991, p. 9.

30. "The Draft Policy Statement of the First Japan-ASEAN Roundtable," in *Nihon to ASEAN: Kanzenna Pātonāshippu Kakuritsu Mezashite* [Japan and ASEAN: Aiming

at the establishment of a complete partnership], Proceedings of the conference organized by the Japan Forum on International Relations, Tokyo, September 10–11, 1990, p. 2.

31. Ibid., p. 3.

32. Ibid.

33. *Thailand Foreign Affairs Newsletter*, Bangkok, May 1991, p. 11.

34. Ibid.

35. Ibid., p. 5.

36. Amnuay Viravan, "Pax Japonica: Japan's Growing Global and Regional Responsibilities," *Speaking of Japan*, November 1987, p. 7.

37. Sopiee, "The Rise of Pax Nipponica," p. 79.

38. Ibid., p. 84.

39. Suthichai Yoon, "Japan That Can Say We Care," *Japan and the World in the Post Cold War Era*, Tokyo: Foreign Press Center of Japan, The Japan Times, 1990, p. 111.

40. Ibid., p. 110.

41. *Policy Speech by Toshiki Kaifu, Prime Minister, to the 119th Session of the National Diet* (October 12, 1990), Policy Speech Series 35, Tokyo: Ministry of Foreign Affairs, pp. 7–8.

42. Gaishi Hiraiwa (chairman, Keidanren), "In This Uncertain World Japan Must Carve Out Its Own Future," *Keidanren Review*, no. 130 (August 1991), p. 3.

43. Gerald L. Curtis, "America's Evolving Relationship with Japan and Its Implications for ASEAN," paper presented at the Fifth U.S.-ASEAN Conference, Singapore, June 11–16, 1989, p. 27. This conference was organized by the Institute of East Asian Studies, University of California, Berkeley, and the Singapore Institute of International Affairs.

44. Michael Richardson, "But Many in the Region Are Uneasy, Lee Says," *International Herald Tribune*, May 4–5, 1991, p. 1.

45. "Speech by Mr. Lee Kuan Yew, Senior Minister of Singapore, at the Asahi Shimbun Symposium in Tokyo, May 9, 1991," Singapore Government press release, no. 8 (May 1991), p. 6.

46. Ibid.

47. Ibid., p. 7.

48. See "A Time for Initiative, Proposals for the Consideration of the Fourth ASEAN Summit, ASEAN Institutes of Strategic and International Studies." The initiative proposed to "urge Japan to consult ASEAN regularly and systematically, thus avoiding misunderstanding and paving the way for mutually beneficial cooperation" (p. 21).

49. Takakazu Kuriyama, "New Directions of Japanese Foreign Policy in the Changing World of the 1990s: Making Active Contribution to the Creation of a New International Order," mimeograph distributed by the Japanese embassy in Bangkok. Also published in Japanese in *Gaiko Forum*, May 1990, pp. 12–21.

50. For example, Yukio Sato, director general of the Bureau of Information, Analysis, Research and Planning, Japanese Foreign Ministry, explained that the idea was picked up from an ASEAN-ISIS proposal but Japan added a new dimension to it. According to Sato, Japan's main purpose is to use this forum to reassure that Japan will not become a military power and to allay any suspicions or doubts. The author's interview with Yukio Sato at the Grand Hyatt Erawan Hotel, Bangkok, November 6, 1991. See also Yukio Sato, "Asian-Pacific Process for Stability and Security," paper presented at two seminars: ASEAN and the Asia-Pacific Region: Prospects for Security Cooperation in the 1990's, Manila, June 5–7, 1991, sponsored by the Department of Foreign Affairs, the Philippines; and the Fifth Asia-Pacific Roundtable, Kuala Lumpur, June 10–14, 1991, organized by the Institute of Strategic and International Studies, Malaysia.

51. "Statement by His Excellency Dr. Taro Nakayama, Minister for Foreign Affairs of Japan, to the General Session of the ASEAN Post-Ministerial Conference," Kuala Lumpur, July 22, 1991, mimeograph, p. 12.

52. "Statement by Minister of Foreign Affairs Taro Nakayama at the 6 + 1 Meeting with ASEAN Foreign Ministers," Kuala Lumpur, July 23, 1991, mimeograph, p. 2.

53. "ASEAN at Odds over Security Plan, *Nation*, July 24, 1991, p. 8.

54. Ibid.

55. *Thailand Foreign Affairs Newsletter*, August 1991, p. 10.

56. "Indonesia Says No to Military Pacts," *Bangkok Post*, October 12, 1991, p. 4.

57. Mochtar Kusuma-Atmadja, "Some Thoughts on ASEAN Security Cooperation: An Indonesian Perspective," *Contemporary Southeast Asia*, vol. 12, no. 3 (December 1990), pp. 162, 164. Kusuma-Atmadja personally suggested in August 1989 that "ASEAN should at least start thinking about an organized forum of security cooperation to be realized (perhaps) in the next five to ten years."

58. It was widely believed by ASEAN experts on security problems that China will become more assertive in the post–Cold War era, especially in contiguous areas such as the South China Sea. But China's security policy will continue to be low cost and low risk. See, for example, the Chairmen's Report of the 1990 ASEAN-ISIS Meeting, held in Bangkok, May 10–13, 1990, in *A Time for Initiative: Proposals for the Consideration of the Fourth ASEAN Summit*, ASEAN Institutes of Strategic and International Studies, a document for the 1991 Meeting in Jakarta, p. 14.

59. From the perspectives of China and the Soviet Union, a more desirable "forum" might be one to which all major players in the region's international politics should be invited to exchange viewpoints on security issues. China is, of course, an important player and geographically closer to Southeast Asia than Japan. ASEAN should listen to all the viewpoints and compare them. The above view came from the author's interviews with a division director in the Department of Political Affairs, Ministry of Foreign Affairs of Thailand, and V. P. Fedotov, ambassador for special assignments, USSR Ministry of Foreign Affairs, at Grand Hyatt Erawan Hotel, Bangkok, November 6, 1991.

60. For example, ASEAN leaders will find the ASEAN-PMC a forum that increases, rather than decreases, tension in the region if Japan, with U.S. support, announces that it is now considering the possibility of exerting "a stabilizing influence" in Asia Pacific, or the U.S.-Japan alliance serving as "an anchor for the Asia Pacific region." See such ideas in Masashi Nishihara, "New Roles for the Japan-U.S. Security Treaty," *Japan Review of International Affairs*, Spring/Summer 1991, p. 40.

61. U.S. Information Service, wireless text, May 16, 1989, quoted in Kavi Chongkittavorn, "Japan and Southeast Asia: Searching for Acceptable Roles," paper presented at the Fifth U.S.-ASEAN Conference, Singapore, June 11–16, 1989, p. 20. This conference was organized by the Singapore Institute of International Affairs.

62. See more discussion on comprehensive security in Tsuneo Akaha, "Japan's Comprehensive Security Policy: A New East Asian Environment," *Asian Survey*, April 1991, p. 324–340; Muthiah Alagappa, "Comprehensive Security: Interpretations in ASEAN Countries," in Robert A. Scalapino, Seizaburo Sato, Jusuf Wanandi, and Sung-joo Han, eds., *Asian Security Issues: Regional and Global*, Research Papers and Policy Studies, no. 26, Berkeley: Institute of East Asian Studies, University of California, 1988, pp. 50–78.

63. Prasong Soonsiri, "Prospects for Defense and Security Cooperation in ASEAN," paper presented at the International Conference on ASEAN and the Asia-Pacific Region: Prospects for Security Cooperation in the 1990's, Manila, June 5–7, 1991, p. 6. The conference was organized by the Department of Foreign Affairs of the Philippines and the Ministry of Foreign Affairs of Thailand.

64. Ibid., p. 7.

65. See, for example, *Final Report*, Tokyo: Politics and International Relations Research Group, Committee for Asia-Pacific Economic Research, Foundation for Advanced Information and Research, May 1991, pp. 18–19.

66. Curtis, "America's Evolving Relationship," p. 38.

67. See Jusuf Wanandi, *ASEAN and Security Cooperation in Southeast Asia*, IIGP Special Report, Tokyo: International Institute for Global Peace, March 1991, p. 10.

68. See more details about anti-Japanese movements in Thailand in Prasert Chittiwatanapong, "The History of Anti-Japanese Movements in Thailand," *Proceedings of the Joint Symposium on Thai-Japanese Relations: Development and Future Prospect*, January 15–16, 1987, pp. 35–45. This symposium was organized by the Core University Committee of Thammasat University and Center for Southeast Asia Studies, Kyoto University.

See also an interesting interpretation of anti-Japanese movements by Japan's ambassador to Thailand, Hisahiko Okazaki, who suggested that anti-Japanese sentiments are more myth than reality. According to Okazaki, they were part of a fashionable anti-Western movement, which included anti-U.S. protests at the time, rather than a manifestation of pure animosity toward the Japanese. See his views in Cimi Suchontan, "Shifts in Asia Cloud Investment Plan," *Bangkok Post*, September 30, 1991, p. 5.

69. One careful writer on international politics in Southeast Asia assessed, "While some ASEAN governments may not wish to be too open in expressing their interest in a continuing American presence in the region, none has really indicated a wish to see a withdrawal of that presence," Chin Kin Wah, "Changing Global Trends," p. 13.

70. Charles E. Morrison, "ASEAN-Japan Political and Security Relations: An Overview," in FungWai Lai and Morrison, *Political and Security Cooperation*, p. 6.

71. S. Bilveer, "The United States Without Clark Air Base: Its Meaning and Implications," *Asian Defense Journal*, September 1991, p. 24.

72. Michael Richardson, "But Many in the Region Are Uneasy, Lee Says," *International Herald Tribune*, May 4–5, 1991, p. 1.

73. Kusuma Snitwongse, "Meeting the Challenges of Changing Southeast Asia," in Scalapino et al., *Asian Security Issues*, p. 336.

74. Ibid.

75. The author's interview with Alan T. Ortiz, assistant secretary, National Security Council, Office of the President, the Philippines, at Grand Hyatt Erawan Hotel, Bangkok, November 4, 1991.

76. Ibid.

77. The author's interview with Yukio Sato, director general, Bureau of Information, Analysis, Research and Planning, Ministry of Foreign Affairs of Japan, at the Grand Hyatt Erawan Hotel, Bangkok, November 6, 1991.

78. Ibid.

79. *Thailand Foreign Affairs Newsletter*, February–April 1991, p. 19.

80. Editorial, *Bangkok Post*, October 30, 1991, p. 4.

81. "Anand to Make Reciprocal Trip to Vietnam," *Nation*, Bangkok, October 31, 1991, p. 1.

82. *Thailand Foreign Affairs Newsletter*, July 1991, p. 4.

83. Eugene Moosa, "Japan May Take on Wider Role," *Bangkok Post*, November 7, 1991, p. 4.

84. There are only ninety-one Japanese among the UN staff, much less than the allotment of two hundred to which Japan is entitled. Yasushi Akashi, who is Japanese and a Deputy Secretary-General of the United Nations, was appointed as head of UNTAC, which is implementing the Paris accords in Cambodia with a large number of military personnel, including members of the Japanese Self-Defense Forces. Ibid.

85. In the words of the new Prime Minister Kiichi Miyazawa, "Among the indis-

pensable underpinnings of our U.N.-centered efforts for global order are close cooperation with the United States and friendly relations with other countries of Asia." From his policy speech delivered to the Diet, *Bangkok Post*, Bangkok, November 9, 1991, p. 6.

86. Soon after being elected on November 5, 1991, the new prime minister warned the Japanese public, "We must recognize that our international role in the building of a global order for peace can only grow larger." *Bangkok Post*, Bangkok, November 9, 1991, p. 6.

87. Actually, Japan's desire to play a more active political-security role was recently seen in Japan's expression of its interest in joining the Middle East peace talks following the U.S.-arranged conference in Madrid, Spain. *Bangkok Post*, Bangkok, November 11, 1991, p. 6.

Chapter 10

New Dimensions of Japanese Foreign Policy: A Latin American View of Japanese Presence

Charlotte Elton

As Latin America emerges from the lost decade of the 1980s, it does so with a keener appreciation of changing economic and political realities. There is greater uncertainty in the world, with the formation of regional trading blocs; the reemergence of the projection of U.S. power in the Gulf War; and the precipitate decline in the military, ideological, and economic power of the former Soviet Union.

Within the newly emerging framework there is increasing awareness of the role that Japan plays internationally and particularly of the contributions it could make to a new international economic order and to Latin America's economic development. There are very high hopes for advances through trade with Japan, loans, investment, aid, and technology transfer beyond the present levels.

In this chapter, I examine some dimensions of relations between Latin America and Japan in the political and economic spheres. Emphasis will be placed on distinguishing between direct relations and those that should be analyzed within the broader context of either Latin America's relations with the United States, or U.S.-Japan relations. Latin America's interaction with Japan throws light on the central theme of this collection of studies concerning the nature of Japan's leadership role in the new world order.

Japan's Political Relations with Latin America

Latin American countries traditionally have concentrated on the United States and Europe in their political and economic relations. In fact, Latin America has been more closely associated with one single major power, particularly in the twentieth century, than any other developing region. The dominance of the United States, followed by Western Europe, will probably continue, although there is great interest in the rise of Asia Pacific countries as strong growth areas, and much prominence given to Japan's influence in the world.

233

The expectations of Japan in Latin America are largely in the economic rather than the political field. However, as a positive aspect in the political arena, Japan approaches Latin America with a clean slate.[1] There is no background of invasions, colonialism, interventions, and war damage, such as continues to be a source of constant friction, deep suspicion, and opposing views in Japan's relations with many Asian countries.[2] This relatively uncomplicated relationship is the basis for Japanese bureaucrats' contentions that one reason for giving aid to Latin America is to obtain favorable votes for Japan's positions at the United Nations.

This unidimensional relationship may seem somewhat surprising, given the large number of descendants of Japanese immigrants in Latin America today—well over one million, particularly in Brazil. In addition, there are estimated to be more than 70,000 Japanese descendants in Peru, 30,000 in Argentina, and maybe 10,000 each in Mexico and in Bolivia. Although there have been instances of economic relations between Japanese investors and local Japanese immigrant communities in Latin America, there had been no high-profile political implications to this migration until the election of Alberto Fujimori to the presidency of Peru in 1990.

However, the very success of Fujimori's electoral bid realized the worst fears of Japanese bureaucrats. It showed up their inability to respond meaningfully to such a potentially important development in Japan–Latin America relations and could be interpreted as leading to an anti-Japanese backlash. Although Japanese Foreign Minister Taro Nakayama told the Peruvian president during a visit to Tokyo in April 1991 that Peru was a "top priority country" for aid in Latin America, in fact aid from Japan has not been on a scale sufficient to dent Peru's problems;[3] and in July 1991 three Japanese consultants working in Peru were assassinated, leading to the decision to withdraw all field personnel from the country. Isolated attacks on local Japanese-Peruvian descendants followed the assassinations.

Although the Japanese immigrant communities themselves were first encouraged by Fujimori's success, they are experiencing a reverse migration process of *dekasegi*, or moving to find work. This exodus back to Japan is decimating local cultural organizations, including schools in Latin America for Japanese descendants. The combination of the economic crisis in Latin America and the labor shortage in Japan has made it possible for descendants of Japanese emigrants to work for relatively high wages doing unskilled jobs in Japan for a few years. In general, although relatively well educated, the Latin Japanese do the "dangerous, dirty, and low-paid" jobs that the native Japanese do not want.

Latin America has had almost no experience of Japan taking a political initiative in the region, so any discussion surrounding a potential political role for Japan is necessarily extremely speculative. In fact, at most there are only a few instances in which Japan has taken a position slightly different from the United States in the region. Examples are the Argentina–United

Kingdom war over the Malvinas Islands, the continuation of sugar imports from Cuba even after the United States implemented an embargo on trade with Cuba, and the recognition of Manuel Solis Palma effectively as president of Panama after his predecessor was ousted by General Manuel Noriega in February 1988. This came after the Federal Republic of Germany announced its recognition of the new Panamanian president, and after completion of a particularly tough set of negotiations between Japan and the United States concerning beef and orange imports. The implication in this last case is that, to avoid aggravating difficult negotiations with the United States, the Japanese government put off taking a political decision in Latin America that was in its own interests.[4]

Economic Relations: The United States, Europe, Japan, and Latin America

Trade

To exemplify the relative importance of the United States, Europe, Japan, and the rest of Asia for Latin America, analysis of trade flows between the regions for 1981 and 1987, as illustrated in Figure 10.1, is most revealing of the intensity of the relationships.[5] Latin American trade with Japan was of less importance than its trade with either the United States or Europe, and was not increasing.

In 1981, Latin America's trade with the United States was estimated at nearly $80 billion, compared with $50 billion with Western Europe and $14.8 billion with Japan. Intraregional Latin American trade was valued at $23.1 billion. Other trans-Pacific trade flows with Latin America were valued at a total of $5.8 billion in that year.

Looking at the 1987 figures, one can see clearly the dramatic "lost decade" of Latin American development, after the debt crisis of the 1980s. Most of the countries' economies suffered from the deterioration of commodity prices, lack of foreign exchange to import, and slow—if not negative—growth.[6] Intraregional trade almost halved to $12.1 billion; the value of trade with the United States, Western Europe, and Japan diminished slightly in each case, but maintained proportions similar to those of 1981. Despite the deterioration, Japan was still the second largest trading partner for Mexico, Colombia, Peru, and Brazil in 1989.

Meanwhile, other trade flows across the Pacific increased enormously in value. For example, U.S.-Japan trade rose from $60.7 billion to $113 billion; East and Southeast Asian trade with the United States rose from $40 to $71 billion; and East and Southeast Asian trade with Japan rose from $52 to $66 billion.

This comparison tells a story of the importance of the United States and

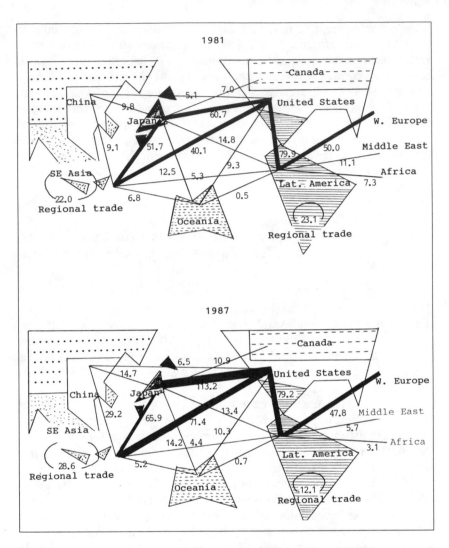

Figure 10.1 International Trade in the Pacific Basin, 1981 and 1987 (exports and imports in US$ billions, FOB)
Source: International Monetary Fund, *Direction of Trade Statistics Yearbook*, 1988, in K. Horizaka, "La Nueva Situación Económica Japonesa y América Latina y el Caribe," *Integracion Latinoamericana, INTAL*, no. 153 (January–February 1990), pp. 40–41.

Europe in Latin American trade, relative to Japan. There was also a generalized reduction in the economic interaction of Latin America with the rest of the world, including Africa and the Middle East, during the 1980s. Exports from Latin America had been 5.8 percent of world exports in 1982; by 1988 they dropped to 3.9 percent. Simultaneously, there was a great boom in world trade and much talk about "globalization," and the new "global" economy. It was only at the end of the decade that the main Latin American countries began their painful reinsertion into the global economy.

One reason for the reduction in Latin American trade with Japan during the 1980s was the suspension of, or restrictions on, trade insurance after the outbreak of the debt crisis in the 1980s.[7] By the mid-1980s, Japan's Ministry of International Trade and Industry had either suspended trade insurance or restricted its availability for more than fifty indebted countries. Japan's exports of plants and equipment to the Third World in general contracted between 1981 and 1984 from $13.7 billion to $4.8 billion. Japan, along with Europe and the United States, continued to restrict trade insurance even after new debt repayment schedules were agreed upon for some countries.[8] By 1989, MITI was adopting a case-by-case approach to providing insurance for trade with debtor countries, charging extra premiums for the high-risk countries. Obviously, this has had an inhibiting effect on recuperation of Japanese exports to Latin America.

During the 1980s, as pressure built from the United States for Japan to reduce its trade surplus, Latin America was included in Japan's recycling plan, as proposed at the Ottawa summit in 1987, to help reduce this pressure. The idea was to provide funds for Latin American countries that would finance the purchase of U.S. goods so as to reduce the U.S. trade deficit. Such a reduction would help improve U.S.-Japan relations.

_____ *Investment*

It is more difficult to compare direct investment trends by the United States, Europe, and Japan in Latin America because of noncomparability problems in the data. In particular, the host country data are often different from those reported by the investing country. Another difficulty arises with respect to direct foreign investment in services, such as financial tax havens, which are common to both the United States and Japan in their investments in Latin America.

Panama traditionally has been the main country identified as host to this kind of investment, but since 1986, with deregulation of the Japanese banking system, Japan has increasingly been using the Cayman Islands, Bermuda, the Antilles, and the Bahamas. It is notable that Japan's foreign direct investment (FDI) in Latin America during the 1980s was concentrated in those countries, rather than the traditional ones for its productive investment, such as Brazil, Mexico, Peru, Chile, and Argentina (see Table 10.1). There has been very little Japanese productive investment in Latin America in the last decade.

Table 10.1 **Japan's Foreign Direct Investment in Latin America, FY 1984–1990 (in US$ millions)**

Country	FY 1984	FY 1985	FY 1986	FY 1987	FY 1988	FY 1989	FY 1990	Total 3/31/91
Panama	1,671	1,533	2,401	2,305	1,712	2,044	1,342	16,244
Brazil	318	314	270	229	510	349	615	6,560
Caymans	1	132	930	1,197	2,609	1,658	588	7,332
Bahamas	97	298	792	734	737	620	121	3,459
Mexico	56	101	226	28	87	36	168	1,874
Bermuda	29	148	16	36	337	228	380	1,578
Netherlands Antilles	66	62	66	199	172	38	9	795
Peru	6	10	—	1	—	—	—	696
Latin America total[a]	2,290	2,616	4,737	4,816	6,428	4,973	3,223	38,538

Source: Japanese Ministry of Finance
Note: a. Including Caribbean and other regional territories.

Data available from the investor countries indicate that the United States is still by far the largest investor in Latin America in general, followed by Europe and then Japan.[9] According to the U.S. Department of Commerce Survey of Current Business, the cumulative U.S. investment in Latin America in 1987 was $42.3 billion. Of this, $11.5 billion was in Mexico, followed by $8.3 billion in Brazil. Comparable figures for Japanese investments are a total of $31.2 billion, with the largest amount of productive investment in Brazil ($5.6 billion) and Mexico ($1.67 billion). Excluding the tax-haven type of investment from both the U.S. and Japanese figures, total investments in Latin America turn out to be in the order of $25 billion for the United States compared with only $10 billion for Japan.

It is estimated that the European Community investment in Latin America is about $32 billion, although individual EC countries have less investment than does Japan. In Brazil, for example, West Germany has about a $5.4 billion investment, comparable with Japan's, but in Mexico, Japan's total share in foreign direct investment is about 5.5 percent, lower than the share of the United Kingdom (7.3 percent) or West Germany (6.6 percent).

A look at the types of Japanese investment in Latin America and the reasons for such investment since World War II is revealing and helpful to project what may be in store in the 1990s. A breakdown by one analyst shows that during the 1950s and 1960s the motivation was largely to secure a market within the host country, exemplified by the Usiminas steel plant and the Ishibras shipyards in Brazil, or the textile plants in the Central American common market, or the Nissan plant in Mexico. This was a time when income levels in Latin America were higher than in Japan's Asian neighbors and the prospects for further market growth seemed good.[10] Due to distances involved and to the higher wages in Latin America, the motivation could not be the search for cheap wage labor, as was the case for Japanese investment in Asia.

During the 1970s, the main motivation was to secure natural resources, either raw or semiprocessed for direct use by Japan or to increase the world supply. Either form of investment would help maintain availability and lower prices. Japan had many joint ventures in Brazil during this time, particularly with the Companhia Vale do Rio Doce (CVRD), such as NIBRASCO (iron ore pellets), CENIBRA (pulp), ALBRAS (aluminum), and Carajas (iron ore). Other large resource investments included zinc, lead, and copper smelting in Peru; aluminum in Venezuela; and coffee and soybeans in the Cerrado in Brazil.

In more recent years, Japanese productive investment in the region has dropped drastically. The main motivation behind any such investment was to secure an export production base for entry into the U.S. market. The typical case is that of investment in the maquiladora industry along the Mexican border with the United States. There is obviously some overlap in time, and in kinds of investment, but this breakdown is supported by analysis of trends in Japan's industrial adjustment in preparing for regionally integrated production strategies.[11]

_____ *Loans*

Japanese financial institutions have been relatively active in Latin America compared with those of Europe and the United States, considering the smaller size of the trade relationships. Particularly noticeable is the fact that the debt exposure of Japanese banks since 1982 has increased considerably in dollar values, whereas that of U.S. banks has diminished. Tables 10.2, 10.3, and 10.4 illustrate the loan exposure of Japanese, U.S., West German, and British banks to the debtor countries of Latin America between 1982 and 1990.[12]

U.S. bank loans to Latin America decreased from $82.9 billion in 1982 to $74.7 billion in 1987, whereas Japan's private bank loans to the region increased from $18.2 billion in 1982 to $40.8 billion in 1987. The United Kingdom had a total $40 billion exposure to Latin American debt in 1987, and West Germany had $18 billion.[13] Both of these countries increased their exposure in the 1980s, compared with the U.S. banks, as can be seen in Table 10.3.

Part of the increase in the exposure of Japanese banks is due to the more than $4 billion increase to Panama (not to the government, but to Japanese businesses registered in that country); it is also partly the result of yen appreciation with respect to the dollar and partly due to the addition of unpaid interest to the capital amount. The Japanese banks did not take part in any debt reduction schemes, nor initially in debt-equity swaps. They tended to follow the guidance of the IMF and the World Bank, and followed as a group any rescheduling schemes.

It was not until 1989 that the Ministry of Finance allowed an increase in reserves against bad debts, but as soon as they did Japanese banks began an exit strategy regarding Latin debt. As a result, in September 1990 Japanese

Table 10.2 Private Mid- and Long-term Outstanding Loans of Japan to Foreign Countries, 1982, 1986, and 1987 [in US$ millions (percent of total)]

Country	September 1982		September 1986		September 1987	
Latin America	18,216	(37.9)	36,419	(23.9)	40,778	(19.8)
Brazil	5,397	(11.2)	8,930	(5.8)	9,132	(4.4)
Mexico	5,904	(12.3)	10,768	(7.1)	11,058	(5.4)
Argentina	1,968	(4.1)	5,043	(3.3)	4,982	(2.4)
Venezuela	1,753	(3.6)	2,334	(1.5)	3,791	(1.8)
Panama	954	(2.0)	4,270	(2.8)	5,246	(2.5)
Chile	692	(1.4)	1,547	(1.0)	1,570	(0.8)
Other developing countries	7,696	(16.0)	29,902	(19.5)	36,056	(17.5)
Other countries	22,151	(46.1)	86,360	(56.6)	128,996	(62.7)
Total	48,063		152,681		205,830	

Source: Country Risk Report, Tokyo: Nihon Keizai Shimbun, 1988.

Table 10.3 Mid- and Long-term Loan Exposure to Selected Latin American Countries of U.S., West German, and British Banks [in US$ millions (percent of total)]

Creditor Country	Brazil		Mexico		Argentina		Venezuela	
United States								
1984	26,315	(6.6)	34,885	(8.7)	11,050	(2.8)	11,017	(2.8)
1986	25,716	(5.8)	30,698	(6.9)	12,091	(2.7)	11,108	(2.5)
1987	25,288	(5.5)	29,526	(6.4)	11,987	(2.6)	10,998	(2.4)
United Kingdom								
1984	9,344	(6.0)	8,746	(5.6)	3,394	(2.2)	2,771	(1.8)
1986	9,515	(4.9)	8,674	(4.5)	4,110	(2.1)	2,642	(1.4)
1987	9,673	(4.5)	8,773	(4.1)	4,206	(2.0)	2,625	(1.2)
West Germany								
1984	1,976	(2.6)	536	(0.7)	641	(0.8)	501	(0.6)
1986	3,925	(2.2)	1,001	(0.5)	1,663	(0.9)	722	(0.4)
1987	4,792	(2.0)	1,193	(0.5)	2,220	(0.9)	842	(0.4)

Source: Country Risk Report, Tokyo: Nihon Keizai Shimbun, 1988.

Table 10.4 Latin American Medium and Long-term Debt Outstanding to Japanese Banks, 1982–1990

Calendar Year[a]	Latin America (US$ billions)	Total (US$ billions)	Latin American Share (percentage)
1982	21.3	67.1	31.7
1983	23.9	77.5	30.8
1984	28.6	94.4	30.3
1985	30.1	107.9	27.9
1986	36.8	152.2	24.2
1987	40.9	213.5	19.2
1988	45.5	282.5	16.1
1989	44.7	336.9	13.3
1990	31.2	360.5	8.7

Sources: Japanese Ministry of Finance; Barbara Stallings and Kotaro Horizaka, "Japanese Relations with Latin America: New Patterns in the 1990s," in Abraham Lowenthal and Gregory Tevertan, eds., *Latin America and the United States in the New World*, forthcoming 1992.
Notes: Figures include yen-based lending, which is converted into dollars at the end-of-year exchange rate.
a. As of December 31 of each year.

banks held a total of $34 billion in developing country debt, down from $45 billion the previous year, according to unpublished Japanese government estimates.[14] This exit strategy is clearly illustrated in Table 10.4.

The Brady plan for Latin American debt took on many elements of the Miyazawa plan previously proposed by then Japanese minister of finance and later prime minister, Kiichi Miyazawa. In its implementation, in Mexico, for example, the Japanese banks generally took a risk- and exposure-reducing option, by taking the discount option rather than providing new money. They later followed the example of U.S. and European banks by reducing their holdings through secondary market sales. One financial analyst commented in early 1991: "Gone for good? With new money out of the question and the banks bent on exit strategies, the question is whether Japanese banks have any residual interest in Latin America. The best response is a big 'maybe'."[15]

From the point of view of official debts, as Japanese ministers of finance have repeatedly pointed out, there could be either debt forgiveness or new loans, but not both. Japanese initiatives may have contributed to some containment of the debt crisis in terms of taking measures to protect the stability of the international banking system, but little contribution toward solving the growth crisis of Latin American countries. The region made net transfers to the developed world from 1982 to 1990 to the tune of $16 billion to $32 billion a year, as can be seen in Table 10.5.

Currently there is some recycling of funds from Japan to countries that have signed agreements with the World Bank and the IMF, such as Mexico,

Table 10.5   Net Inflow of Capital and Transfer of Resources for Latin America, 1975–1991 (in US$ billions)

Year	Net Inflow of Capital	Net Payments of Profit and Interest	Transfer of Resources
1975	14.3	5.6	8.7
1976	17.9	6.8	11.1
1977	17.2	8.2	9.0
1978	26.2	10.2	16.0
1979	29.1	13.7	15.4
1980	32.0	18.9	13.1
1981	39.8	18.5	11.3
1982	20.1	38.8	−18.7
1983	2.9	34.5	−31.6
1984	10.4	37.3	−26.9
1985	3.0	35.3	−32.3
1986	9.9	32.6	−22.7
1987	15.4	31.4	−16.0
1988	5.5	34.3	−28.8
1989	9.6	37.9	−28.3
1990	18.4	34.4	−16.0
1991[a]	36.0	29.3	6.7

Source: Gert Rosenthal, *Balance Preliminar de la Economía de America Latina y el Caribe, 1991*, Chile: CEPAL, 1991.
Note: a. Preliminary figures

Costa Rica, and Venezuela. The Export-Import Bank of Japan is the vehicle for this recycling, with structural adjustment programs supervised by the international financial institutions as the guarantee. Bank officials express preference for natural resource export projects in which the foreign exchanges earned from the sales are automatically used to pay the loan.

Aid

Japan's aid program managers officially adopted a 7-1-1-1 formula for dividing aid between Asia, Latin America, the Middle East, and Africa in 1980, although Latin America's share has been below 8 percent most of this decade. With large quantitative increases, however, Japan is an important source of technical cooperation for many countries in the region.

The aid program is another field in which Japan often reacts to U.S. pressure for collaboration, as, for example, in extending loans to Jamaica in 1980 after the electoral defeat of the incumbent socialist prime minister, Michael Manley, and to Honduras as support for that country during the war in Nicaragua during the 1980s.[16] Honduras has the most Peace Corps volunteers of any country in the world; it also hosts the largest number of Japanese volunteers in the Americas, after Paraguay.

More recent examples are U.S. requests for aid to Panama after the invasion, Nicaragua after the Sandinista defeat, and El Salvador after the end of the civil war. There is a questioning among members of Japan's bureaucracy who are familiar with the region as to the wisdom of acceding to such requests, insofar as it could lead to Japan being tarred with the same brush as U.S. aid sometimes is. But the desire to smooth the U.S.-Japan relationship overrides these doubts.

Japan has shown its willingness to contribute to Latin American development by participation in some multilateral efforts, as through its support for the Inter-American Development Bank. Japan agreed in May 1991, for example, to participate in a new Multilateral Investment Fund proposed by President Bush as part of the Enterprise for the Americas Initiative, with contributions of $100 million for five years. Although there was some muttering as to why Japan should contribute the same amount as the United States, that was the amount finally committed, whereas the European Community was less forthcoming in its commitment to the new fund.[17] In the 1990 State Department initiative for Central America, the Partnership for Development and Democracy (PDD), again Japan showed greater willingness to cooperate with the United States than did the European representatives.[18]

Japan's aid program usually attempts to incorporate private sector interests, too. For example, Japan approved loans to Mexico in 1990 to help reduce air contamination in the capital; the money will be used partly to purchase fuel additives from Japanese manufacturers. Prior to the debt crisis, there were joint government–private sector projects in natural resource development, in which the Japan International Cooperation Agency (JICA) would help pave the way for official and private sector financing. The Greater Carajas development program in the Amazon is one such example.[19]

This panorama of the relative economic importance of the relationships between Latin America and the main regions of the industrialized world helps to set the background for expectations and views regarding the relative power positions of those regions. At the very least, there are indications of ambiguity in the Japanese private sector's attitude toward Latin America, and strong indications that many official actions in the region are the result of frictions and pressures within the U.S.-Japan relationship.

One preliminary conclusion of the situation in which Latin America found itself at the beginning of the 1990s regarding the so-called globalization of the economy and international system, is that "from the Japanese perspective, the region suffers from three key problems: marginality, credibility, and viability."[20]

Relations in the Pacific Basin

The large Pacific Rim countries of Latin America are showing increasing interest in strengthening their links across the Pacific Basin, with Australia and New Zealand as well as with China, Taiwan, and Japan. The reality of the intensity of economic links is still very small for Latin America compared with those between other areas across the Pacific. However, Chile, for example, in 1991 exported 10 percent of its total exports to Japan, and another 4 percent to China. In that year, Chile's trade with Japan exceeded its trade with the United States for the first time. New Zealand is also investing in Chile's natural resources, particularly in fruit production and in the forestry sector, as is Japan.

Mexico, too, has been making great efforts to reach across the Pacific as a way to diversify its economic and political relationships. However, with the approval of the North American Free Trade Agreement with the United States and Canada similar to the U.S.-Canada free trade agreement, it is not yet clear what effect such a pact will have on Mexico's relations with Asian countries. The East Asian states other than Japan fear it will decrease their crucial exports to the United States.

In Japan there are mixed views with regard to this agreement. There is concern that it represents the establishment of a trade bloc from which Japan will be excluded. Similarly, the Bush Enterprise for the Americas is interpreted by some Japanese analysts as a modern version of the Monroe Doctrine. It reconfirms the view very commonly heard in Japan that Latin America is the backyard of the United States, and this view gives more power to those who see Asia as Japan's area of influence.

There is some Latin American participation in the general meetings of the Pacific Economic Cooperation Council. Peru, Chile, and Mexico are members of the group first established in 1980, and Chilean and Peruvian businessmen are also active in the Pacific Basin Economic Council (PBEC), an industrialists' consultative group first organized in 1968.[21] In 1988 the first joint Inter-American Development Bank (IADB) and Asian Development Bank (ADB) conference was held to discuss comparative development experiences, and the Institute of Developing Economies (IDE) in Japan held a similar symposium in 1989.[22]

Both China and Taiwan have been taking a more active economic and political role in Latin America in recent years, although possibly as much for their own political reasons as for economic ones. For example, Taiwan is extremely active in Central America, where it enjoys diplomatic recognition by Guatemala, El Salvador, Honduras, Costa Rica, Nicaragua, and Panama. In South America only Paraguay recognizes Taiwan.

Nicaragua under the Sandinistas recognized China in 1984, but President Chamorro changed back to recognition of Taiwan soon after her election, to receive more economic aid as well as for ideological reasons. After relations between Panama and the United States began to deteriorate in mid-1987, Taiwan became actively involved in support of the Noriega government, as it sensed the possibility of a change in diplomatic recognition. The support extended to the dispatch of a new ambassador to Panama, the former defense minister and strategic adviser to the president of Taiwan; $60 million to the government at the end of 1987; supplies for the Panama Defense Forces when U.S. supplies were cut; and plans for the construction of an export processing zone. Despite these efforts, at the time of the Tiananmen Square crackdown in June 1989, the Panamanian government expressed its solidarity with the government of China, and in November that year discussions were under way to establish diplomatic relations. The invasion of Panama by the United States in December 1989 saved the Taiwanese as one of its side effects.

The interest of Taiwan goes well beyond economic assistance and investment. There are strong links with the military throughout Central America in supplies and training, particularly at the School of Political Warfare in Taiwan.

An example of China's involvement with the region is the establishment of close links with the Chilean government after General Pinochet overthrew President Salvador Allende in 1973. The reason for this was China's desire to avoid encirclement by the Soviet Union; Pinochet's strong anti-Soviet position led to the rapprochement between China and Chile.[23]

In general, Latins feel that linking with China, Taiwan, and Japan offers an alternative to the traditional linking with the United States, and hence a diversification of dependence. Japan's role with regard to Latin America is perceived as exclusively economic, "resulting in a very smooth relationship." Regarding the pressures on Japan to take on a more political role and to increase its defense spending, one analyst of Pacific Basin integration has noted, "this evolution is of course being observed from the distance in Latin America, where no opinion has been officially expressed. However, it would not be unwarranted to assume that Latin America much prefers the kind of economic relationship existing at present." The same analyst has stated that Latins show some preference for doing business with Japanese transnational companies, as they are free from government political interference such as often affects their North American or European counterparts.[24]

Although Brazil is not a Pacific Rim country, it does enjoy a special relationship with Japan, not least because of the estimated one million descendants of Japanese immigrants living there. Due to Brazil's vast natural resources and tendency toward a development state role for the government, a kind of "strategic alliance" developed over nearly thirty years between Japanese investors, trading companies, and banks with the Companhia Vale do Rio Doce, one of the most important state-run companies.[25]

However, the "special relationship" also suffered as a result of the debt crisis and concern in Japan's business and financial circles about economic mismanagement. Lack of political sophistication in Japan regarding Brazil was also shown in the proposal made public in 1989 to cancel Brazil's foreign debt in exchange for rights to gold in the Amazon. The proposal was purportedly made by members of a Mitsubishi subsidiary in Japan.

_____ Latin Americans' Views of Japan's Future Role

Latin Americans continue to have a very positive view of Japan's economic power and also favorable expectations regarding the potential for Latin America's own development, despite the relative slowdown in interaction in the past decade. During the late 1980s there was a "Japan fad" in Mexico, for example, to the extent that "decision-makers suggested and public opinion believed that large amounts of Japanese investment would come, and that a strategy of reducing Mexico's dependence on the United States was being successfully implemented."[26] There was the belief that "Japan would establish an independent political presence in Latin America, and thus alleviate pressure and domination by the United States."[27] The surprise election of Fujimori over the favorite candidate, Mario Vargas Llosa, in Peru was attributed to a belief that Japan's "Midas touch" could provide a quick solution to the country's economic problems.

The president of the Association of Latin American Industrialists, Pedro Kohn, stated:

> Latin America will not be able to move forward without Japan's help. We admire that country because of its philosophy of life, great industriousness, tenacity, concerted action between government and the people to achieve national objectives, its leadership in the world and its rapid growth. We are pleased to emphasize that Japan is that economic power that is providing the

greatest help towards the development of the countries of the Third World.[28]

A survey regarding the image of Japan was carried out in 1990 in eight Latin American cities in seven countries. Those questioned included businessmen, politicians, journalists, and university students as representatives of future elites.[29] The results show that 46 percent of the respondents consider that the growth of Japan's economic power will be favorable for Latin America (see Table 10.6). On the other hand, only 21 percent consider that the growth of Japan's political power in the future will be favorable for Latin America. Nearly one-third consider that it will be neither favorable nor unfavorable, and another 29 percent have no opinion at all. That result is indicative of the low level, among educated Latin Americans, of careful consideration or knowledge concerning Japan's potential political role.

On the other hand, the response to a question about Japan's future role in the international community showed very high expectations. In answer to the questions, "Will there be any country that can take the place of the United States in the twenty-first century? If any, which country will it be?" the countries listed most in the responses were Japan, the European Community, and the Soviet Union, in that order. "Only 11.2% of respondents answered that there would be no country which could take the place of the United States. This general view applied to non-students as well, indicating their expectations of the multipolarization of foreign relations which currently center on the United States."[30]

These results are an indication of the sources of information about international affairs, which generally arrive in Latin America from the United States, in which analysts in the late 1980s tended to adopt the view "the Cold War is over, and Japan has won," and also of the particular time when the survey was carried out—in 1989, before the U.S. military might was displayed in the Middle East.

The other side of the coin, namely Japanese impressions regarding Latin America, shows less interest or expectations. In a Japanese public opinion survey on diplomacy carried out by the Prime Minister's Office, only 25.4 percent of the respondents expressed an affinity for Latin America, compared with 76.4 percent for the United States, 51.6 percent for China, and 29.7 percent for Southeast Asia (see Table 10.7).[31]

Even more revealing, when asked about the need for increased diplomatic effort on the part of Japan to ensure Japan's peace and security, only 1.9 percent urged more diplomatic effort toward Latin America, even lower than regarding Africa, which was 3.6 percent (see Table 10.8). It is painfully obvious that for the Japanese public, Latin America is very much *taigan no kaji*, "the fire on the other shore." In general, Japan considers Latin America to be within the U.S. sphere of influence, and both bureaucrats and businessmen weigh any action in the region with one eye on Washington.

Table 10.6 Latin Americans' Views on the Growth of Japan's Power (percentages)

	Economic Power	Political Power
Favorable for Latin America	46.1	20.9
Unfavorable for Latin America	11.8	18.8
Neither	26.8	31.4
Don't know	15.3	28.8

Source: Kotaro Horizaka, "Japan's Image in Latin America and Future of Japanese–Latin American Relations," paper presented at the University of California–San Diego, February 1991.

Table 10.7 Feelings of Affinity Within Japan for Various Countries, October 1989 (percentages)

	Percentage Expressing Affinity
United States	76.4
China	51.6
South Korea	40.7
Southeast Asia	29.7
Latin America	25.4
Poland	20.7
Soviet Union	13.2

Source: Prime Minister's Office, *Public Opinion Survey on Diplomacy*, Tokyo: Foreign Press Center, April–May 1990, pp. 9–11.

Table 10.8 Japanese Support for Increased Diplomatic Effort Toward Various Countries, January 1989 (percentages)

	Percentage Urging More Effort
United States	73.3
China	63.7
Soviet Union	38.4
Canada	5.3
Africa	3.6
Latin America	1.9

Source: Prime Minister's Office, *Public Opinion Survey on Japan's Peace and Security*, Tokyo: Foreign Press Center, August–September 1989, p. 7.

Latin Americans view Japan as a different kind of world power than the United States or Europe. The sources of that power are considered to be in the financial, technological, organizational, and economic fields. Although there has been discussion of Japan increasing its political clout through greater use of international organizations, Latin Americans have not seen policy changes as a result of Japan's increasing contributions to the World Bank, the IMF, or the IADB, which are the key international institutions in the region.

Many Japanese economists in banks, and indeed in the Foreign Ministry, view with some circumspection the structural adjustment policies promoted by those international institutions. They are more inclined to favor policies that would promote integration of the internal markets, with less regressive income distribution, and have little quarrel with a greater role for the state and a managed economy. However, these views are privately expressed and have not made their way into the policymaking circles of the international financial institutions.

There is a desire among Latin Americans to seek alternatives to the reemergence of U.S. domination in the region. It is seen as positive that Japan cannot use "hard power," as Joseph Nye has called it, but has great potential to develop its "soft power" to promote greater economic integration, true globalization, and a more harmonious economic division in the world.[32] They see an important role for Japan as the first non–Western Hemisphere country to gain industrial and economic world power status.[33] There is hope that Japan, which is currently debating its political future, as a country that seeks nonmilitary ways of solving conflicts and that has developed and applied advanced technology so successfully, could play a role as a bridge between North and South, helping to close the increasing gap and to promote a truly new international economic order.

Notes

1. The other side of the coin, however, is that when economic interest flags, there are few other dimensions along which to keep up the interest between the regions.

2. When Japan and North Korea began talks in February 1991 to establish some kind of ties, the question of reparations for damage done during colonial exploitation from 1910 to 1945 was one of the main items on the agenda.

3. Japan turned down Fujimori's request for financial support in July 1990, pending successful negotiations with the international financial institutions and the meeting of those commitments. Japan became a member of the support group to assist in Peru's reinsertion into the international financial community, once it was formed. To help fight the cholera epidemic, Japan's prime minister promised Fujimori $266,700 in medical aid, during the latter's visit to Japan for the Inter-American Development Bank meeting in Nagoya, April 1991. "Japan Pledges Additional Assistance for Latin America," *JEI Report*, no. 15B (April 19, 1991), p. 8.

4. Examples are cited in Hiroshi Matsushita, "La Política Japonesa Hacia América Latina en la Postguerra, Discrepancias y Colaboración con los Estados Unidos," paper presented at the Seminar on Japan's Relations with Latin America: Implications for the United States, held at the Center for the Americas, University of California, San Diego, April 1990. In Kotaro Horizaka, Barbara Stallings, and Gabriel Székely, eds., *Raten Amerika tono Kyōzon; Atarashii Kokusai Kankyō no Naka de* [Japanese involvement with Latin America in the new international environment], Tokyo: Dobunkan, 1991.

5. See Kotaro Horizaka, "La Nueva Situación Económica Japonesa y América Latina y el Caribe," in *Integración Latinoamericana*, no. 153 (January–February 1990), pp. 35–54.

6. Growth rates per capita are particularly alarming for the 1980s. According to the Economic Commission for Latin America and the Caribbean (ECLAC, *Balance Preliminar de la Economía Latinoamericana–1988*, Santiago, Chile, 1989) they showed plus figures from 1981 to 1988 only in Brazil and Chile, each by 1–2 percent, and high negative growth rates occurred in Argentina, Venezuela, Peru, and Mexico.

7. "Japan's Trade Insurance Program: Responding to the Third World Debt Crisis," *JEI Report*, no. 14A (April 12, 1991), p. 7.

8. Ibid.

9. Akio Hosono, *Latin America and the Industrialized Countries (Japan, USA, and Europe) in Changing International Relations*, unofficial translation, Tokyo: The Institute of Overseas Investment, Export-Import Bank of Japan, May 1990, p. 11 (original in Japanese).

10. See Kotaro Horizaka, "Japan's Economic Relations with Latin America: Frameworks in the Past, Present, and Future," paper presented to the Seminar on Japan's Relations with Latin America: Implications for the United States, held at the Center for the Americas, University of California, San Diego, April 1990. In Horizaka, Stallings, and Szekely, *Raten Amerika tono Kyozon* (in Japanese).

11. Toru Nakakita and Shujiro Urata, eds. "Industrial Adjustment in Japan and Its Impact on Developing Countries," paper prepared for the Symposium on Industrial Adjustment in the Developed Economies and Its Implications for the Developing Economies, Institute of Developing Economies, Tokyo, February 1–2, 1991. In *Japan's Natural Resource Strategies and Their Environmental Impact in Latin America*, VRF Series, no. 195, Tokyo: Institute of Developing Economies, 1992, I analyze trends over time in Japan's interest in natural resource extraction from Latin America.

12. See discussion in Hosono, *Latin America and the Industrialized Countries*, pp. 12–13; also see Neantro Saavedra-Rivano, *Recent History and Future Prospects of Economic Relations Between Japan and Latin America*, VRF Series, no. 162, Tokyo: Institute of Developing Economies, 1989, pp. 17–20; and Kotaro Horizaka, "Japanese Banks and the Latin American Debt Problems," *Revista de Economía Política*, vol. 10, no. 3 (July–September 1990), pp. 95–113.

13. Hosono, *Latin America and the Industrialized Countries*, p. 13; data are from "Information on Country Risk," *Nihon Koshasai Kenkyujoho*, August 15, 1988.

14. Steven Murphy, in "The Purge Is On," *Latin Finance*, no. 25 (March 1991), pp. 69–74.

15. Ibid., p. 70.

16. Edward Farmer, "Latin America in Japan's Foreign Aid Programme," *The Pacific Review*, vol. 3, no. 4 (1990), pp. 325–334.

17. "Some Observers Speculate That Tokyo Agreed to Contribute the Full Amount to Help Smooth Tensions with Washington," *JEI Report*, no. 21B (June 7, 1991). By June 1992, the U.S. Congress had approved less than one-quarter of the amount President Bush requested.

18. The PDD was constituted at a meeting in Belem, Costa Rica, in April 1991. It is unclear how it will operate.

19. Dave Treece, *Bound in Misery and Iron: The Impact of the Grande Carajas Programme on the Indians of Brazil*, London: Survival International, 1987, documents the involvement of JICA in formulating plans for the Carajas region of the Amazon. Japanese private and public funds were invested in the iron ore development and other natural resource–based projects in the area. See also the report by Friends of the Earth, Japan, "Destruction of Rainforest in the Brazilian Amazon and the Role of Japan," briefing paper for the International People's Forum on Japan and the Global Environment, Tokyo, September 8–10, 1989.

20. Carlos Juan Moneta, *Japón y América Latina en los Años Noventa* [Japan and Latin America in the 90s], Argentina: Planeta, 1991, p. 128.

21. See Francisco Orrego Vicuña, "Pacific Cooperation: The View from Latin America," *The Pacific Review*, vol. 2, no. 1 (1989), pp. 57–67.

22. The IDE papers and proceedings were published in Takao Fukuchi and Mitsuhiro Kagami, eds., *Perspectives on the Pacific Basin Economy: A Comparison of Asia and Latin America*, Tokyo: Asian Club Foundation and Institute of Developing Economies, 1990.

23. Orrego Vicuña, "Pacific Cooperation," p. 62.

24. Ibid., pp. 62–63.

25. See remarks by the executive vice-president of CVRD, in Inter-American Development Bank and the Export-Import Bank of Japan, *Second Latin America–Japan Business Cooperation Symposium*, Tokyo, September 28–October 2, 1982, pp. 133–134. Leon Hollerman quotes from many interviews with Japanese businessmen in Brazil that give insight on the Japan-Brazil relationship in Leon Hollerman, *Japan's Economic Strategy in Brazil*, Lexington, Mass.: Lexington Books, 1988.

26. Wilson Peres, quoted in Peter H. Smith, *Japan, Latin America and the New International Order*, VRF Series, no. 179, Tokyo: Institute of Developing Economies, December 1990, p. 24.

27. Ibid., p. 24.

28. Quoted by Peter Smith, ibid., from *Hemisfile*, March 1990, p. 12.

29. The survey was financed by the Toyota Foundation and organized in Japan by a team of academics from three universities, headed by the Iberoamerican Institute at the University of Sophia. The results are to be published in Hajime Mizuno and Kotaro Horizaka, "La imagen de los latinoamericanos sobre el Japón y los japoneses," *Latin American Monograph Series*, no. 5-2, Iberoamerican Institute, University of Sophia, forthcoming. I have used results presented in a preliminary paper, Kotaro Horizaka, "Japan's Image in Latin America and Future of Japanese–Latin American Relations," paper given at the University of California, San Diego, February 1991.

30. Horizaka, ibid., p. 9.

31. Prime Minister's Office, *Public Opinion Survey on Japan's Peace and Security*, Tokyo: Foreign Press Center, August–September 1989.

32. For "hard power" and "soft power," see Joseph Nye, Jr., *Bound to Lead: The Changing Nature of American Power*, New York: Basic Books, 1991.

33. One example of this thinking is Xabier Gorostiaga, "Central America: Between Disaster and Hope," paper presented at the First International Japan–Central America Seminar, Tokyo, September 1990.

Chapter 11

Japan as Number Two: New Thoughts on the Hegemonic Theory of World Governance

Koji Taira

Historically, the question of how the world should be governed in the absence of a world government has been answered by the rise of a hegemonic power from anarchic competition for global leadership among major nation-states. But if a hegemonic power rises, it also falls when its ability to lead is spent. Thus the rise and fall of a hegemonic power define a cycle, and there have been a few such hegemonic cycles in history since the beginning of the nation-state era around 1500 A.D.: the world has been led, in chronological order, by the United Provinces, the United Kingdom, and the United States.[1] For some years, U.S. hegemony has been thought to be in decline, giving rise to a variety of speculations about the successor hegemon to the United States.

The decline of the United States is often linked to the rise of Japan. As a consequence, Japan's hegemonic qualifications are being carefully examined by many analysts.[2] Usually Japan passes the economic test but evokes doubts on other aspects of leadership. Especially, Japanese hegemony suffers from a lack of legitimacy; it is simply unacceptable to many states. Taking note of this state of world public opinion, Japan has settled down to a modest view of its role in the world, second fiddle to the United States.

This chapter is a commentary on the nature and implications of the Japanese strategy for a number two role in cooperation with the United States. By humbling itself as a number two, Japan can avoid nationalistic objections of other states to Japan's role in world affairs. A number two position is not necessarily damaging to Japan's pride because its history and culture attach appropriate honor and power to such a position. From the U.S. point of view, sharing the burden of leadership with Japan is also an optimal solution, given the economic difficulties of the United States. The military prowess of the United States against the backdrop of looming economic weaknesses smacks of an "imperial overstretch," arguably the last symptom of a declining hegemon before its fall.[3] A wise use of Japan's economic resources overcomes these weaknesses of the United States.

Economic Qualifications of Japan as a Hegemon

A few basic economic indicators quite clearly imply Japan's great-power status. First, Japan's GNP per capita is now higher than that of the United States and keeps increasing steadily. This comparison is based on a straight-forward conversion of Japan's GNP into U.S. dollars by the foreign exchange rate. This is an acceptable method of national power comparison, although different methods, such as purchasing power parity, are needed to compare standards of living. Japanese critics of the notion of Japanese hegemony tend to emphasize that Japan's standard of living is lower than that of the United States by purchasing power parity. Japanese hegemony is premature in their eyes. Second, Japan recently was the world's largest net creditor country (in 1985–1989, although overtaken by Germany in 1990), whereas the United States since 1985 has consistently been the world's largest net debtor. In 1989 and in 1991, Japan was the world's largest donor of official develop-ment assistance to less developed countries, a position briefly reclaimed by the United States in 1990. Third, Japan has a large well-educated, well-disciplined population. Although the population size of Japan is the world's sixth and half as large as that of the United States, the UN human resource quality index places Japan at the top and the United States at eighteenth.[4] Thus, in terms of quality-weighted human resources, the numerical superior-ity of the United States over Japan must be severely discounted as an element of national power.

Japan's hegemonic economic power, if not already obvious, will convince the worst doubters in a couple of decades, given Japan's superior propensity to save and its technological innovativeness. Japan's annual savings are more than enough to keep its rate of economic growth higher than that of the United States. The balance of savings not used for domestic investment in Japan flows out to the rest of the world as foreign invest-ment. The United States, with its chronic shortage of savings relative to its investment requirements, is a major beneficiary of Japanese savings exports.

From the interactions of Japan's macroeconomics with that of the rest of the world, an astounding scenario arises. Dietrich has graphically described this scenario.[5] To summarize his predictions: around 2015 Pax Nipponica has arrived; Japan enjoys uncontested dominance in every leading-edge industry; Japan's per capita GNP is four times that of the United States; Japan controls the world economy; Japan's Asian neighbors are the second-tier nations in the global economic pyramid with Japan at the apex; the United States and Europe belong to the third tier; the third-tier nations are consuming nations and provide a huge, stable, and profitable market for the ever-increasing flow of Japanese and East Asian high-tech products.

Fortunately, the benefits to the U.S. economy are also considerable under Pax Nipponica. Says Dietrich:

> Our economy is no longer mismanaged because the Japanese are managing it for us. The Japanese now own over 40 percent of American manufacturing assets [and] . . . fifteen percent of American bank assets. Through a combination of strategically placed manufacturing investments and overwhelming financial leverage, Japan is able to move the U.S. economy in concert with Japan's strategic economic world vision.[6]

There is little backlash from the United States against Pax Nipponica because politicians, academics, and journalists are richly subsidized by Japan. Japan has also silenced the complaint of a free ride on defense because a modest percentage of Japan's enormous GNP generates an astonishing level of defense budget.

To those who might consider this scenario preposterous, Dietrich retorts by saying that what had happened to U.S. steel, automobiles, and electronics by 1980 surely would have seemed preposterous if anyone had suggested it in 1955. If the United States wants to avoid the predicament of a fallen giant, according to Dietrich, it needs a comprehensive industrial policy, a strong central state, and a top professional bureaucracy; that is, "There is one way, and only one way, out of our current predicament: fundamental institutional change."[7]

The end product of the world's economic evolution during the next quarter century as depicted above certainly sounds alarming. What is fortunate about it, however, is that the process of reaching that stage is market guided and as subtle as the process that has made some of the Japanese industries world class in the last twenty-five years. Adjustments to the market forces are incremental and piecemeal. Even though the results of the adjustments over time may amount to a revolution, it only surprises the people after the fact, not during the process in which events are unfolding toward consummation. From this point of view, Pax Nipponica may become a fait accompli before anyone notices it. The Japanese themselves would be astonished to see their country at the top of the global economic pyramid. From the standpoint of their chosen number two strategy, clear evidence of their being number one would be as destabilizing to them as the end of U.S. hegemony would be to the United States.

The market-guided evolution of the world order as a process of restructuring international relations passes the democratic test for the reallocation of political power and leadership. But the United States appears to be determined to retain world leadership regardless of economic conditions. Apparently, which country one favors as a world hegemon is much like electing a candidate to a high office in one's own country. The United States has been the world hegemon for half a century. The political instinct of its citizens compels them to prefer continued U.S. hegemony over that of a newcomer. This instinct sometimes drives many U.S. opinionmakers into negative campaigns against Japan. Their message is that Japanese leadership is unacceptable. Their rhetorics are those of quadrennial presidential elections. Naturally negative campaigns ("Japan bashing") abound.

A Sampling of Negative Campaigns ————————————

Inconsistencies among the negative campaign themes against Japan as well as faulty understandings of history on the part of the Japan critics paradoxically indicate that there is no reliable reason for rejecting the hypothesis that Japan, given the opportunity to lead, may have more legitimacy on its side than commonly alleged. Some critics of Japan really are not thinking, but only reacting emotionally on the basis of whatever hidden private feelings compel them to do so. A couple of examples would make the point clear.

According to R. Taggart Murphy, what is allegedly wrong with Japan's financial power is as follows:

> Japan lacks the *ideology* and *political commitment* necessary to fulfill the
> obligations that go with financial power. To turn sheer financial strength
> into leadership, a country must be able to think in global terms, to view
> itself as a world central banker, to sacrifice certain short-term gains to
> maintain stable financial and trading systems. Japan does not have this
> world view. [Emphasis added.][8]

Britain and the United States were the world's financial leaders (the United States still is, although with decreasing strength). On the ideology and political commitment by which they justified their leadership, Murphy observes:

> The political elites in Great Britain and the United States were possessed of
> a sense of mission. The British elite in the last century fervently believed in
> their divinely appointed task of spreading Christian civilization and Anglo-
> Saxon concepts of the rule of law to the farthest corners of the globe. The
> U.S. "Atlanticist" elite of the immediate postwar world felt it their mission
> to prevent the Western democracies from making economic mistakes like
> the Hawley-Smoot Tariff Act or geopolitical mistakes like Munich.[9]

Such an unqualified praise of the British and U.S. "missions," as if these were the very embodiments of unquestionable ideals of mankind, can hardly be considered an objective understanding of history. If these are examples of the "ideology and political commitment" that should go with financial power, any country can generate it out of their sheer national pride or prejudice. If Japan, to qualify as a hegemon, should emulate the British and U.S. examples, Japanese leadership would only perpetuate historical tragedies of traditional hegemonies. Humanity has the right to expect something much better from the future world order than endless replications of old hegemonic mistakes. Japan's financial power was acquired quietly under the guidance of the market forces together with Japan's apparent lack of geopolitical ambition. If this is "power without purpose," it is far more humane than the arrogant British claim to the Christianization of the world or the overreactions of the United States to its own Hawley-Smoot fiasco, which destroyed the then international economic order.

For another example, one might consider the unusual emotionalism displayed in a lecture by a well-known economist before an academic audience. Dornbusch describes a likely course of events following "Japan's success and increasing visibility" in this manner:

> It is no secret that there is worldwide resentment against Japan. Among the reasons is the perception of a very closed Japanese society, apparent lack of a genuine and sincere interest in the progress of the world economy, and the sheer envy of Japan's success. . . . Japan is an outsider in the western world, and just as it cannot make up its mind to play the game full out, the major industrialized countries and their electorate cannot get accustomed to treating Japan as other than a very distant, rich, and awkward relative who shows up at a family gathering mostly unwelcome and uninvited. . . . There is resentment, and there is insecurity and fear in America that we are no longer number one.[10]

These negative reactions to Japan's economic power are clearly based on a lack of understanding of the characteristics of the Japanese economy and society. Even the economists, to whom rationality is ostensibly a supreme value, have not yet outgrown the irrationality of flagwaving nationalism born of the nation-state rivalries of the last five hundred years.

_____ *The Japanese Ideology and Commitment*

Japan has the ideology and political commitment by which it can relate to the rest of the world. Unfortunately, these are not fully articulated and expounded, giving rise to misgivings on the part of foreign Japan-watchers that Japan has neither of them. With the help of Asian and Japanese studies, however, one can infer them from observed characteristics of Japanese life.

Japan's success in economic development and modernization is often attributed to Confucianism, and its widely recognized moral foundations in Japanese life.[11] One prominent aspect of the Japanese ideology must then be a Confucian imperative, which is, to paraphrase, "Put your own house in order." In a Confucian society, leadership is conferred on the individual who has put his own house in order and complied with other requisite virtues. Leadership should not be aggressively sought after or acquired by stratagems. This Confucian dimension of the Japanese ideology, then, appears to fit well with how the Japanese have achieved economic self-reliance at home and how Japan apparently forswears pretension to power or leadership despite its extensive economic linkages with the rest of the world. A Confucian leader waits quietly to be put in the leadership position by a general consensus.

A large portion of the world, however, is not Confucian in the logic or process of leader selection. Power politics and nationalist rivalries dominate international relations even when nations' interests would be better served by the market forces. An overt un-Confucian ambition for leadership is recognized as normal. Thus, there is a lack of fit betweeen the Japanese ideology and rules of world politics. Fortunately, East and Southeast Asia share varying forms of Confucianism with Japan. Here prewar Japan sinned against its own ethics by overzealous imitation of Western imperialism. Chastened postwar Japan has returned to the ethical fold of Asia.

The Logic of Number Two

In view of Japan's Confucian modesty, which makes Japan's low profile a virtue, and the widespread misgivings that the rest of the world harbors about the legitimacy of Japanese hegemony, an optimum solution would be for Japan to use its economic capability for the good of the world and to submit to U.S. political leadership, which the world apparently accepts as legitimate. It would also be cost-effective for Japan to keep the Pax Americana alive as a world order and to help the United States through economic and technological cooperation. In other words, Japan should "contribute to" world peace and prosperity, but should not attempt to "lead" the world by its own vision and designs. This implies Japan as a number two. In Japan, the choice of a number two role in this manner is widely accepted.[12]

The acquisition of legitimacy takes time because it depends upon the gradual transformation of others' perceptions of the would-be hegemon. Before Japanese hegemony becomes legitimate, world public opinion has to change. During this waiting time, Japan as an apprentice hegemon can improve its knowledge of and involvement in international government. Much has already been learned about the ways of managing the global economy from the well-structured hegemony of the United States.[13] The global market forces are watched and assisted by international organizations (GATT, IMF, World Bank, OECD, UN, etc.). In designing, organizing, and maintaining these institutions, U.S. leadership has been indispensable. Because of its transparency and objectivity, U.S. hegemony has given rise to theories that can be learned and applied by hegemonic candidates.

Today these international organizations collectively constitute a rudimentary form of international government. The hegemon that takes over after the United States is spared the pains of having to start from scratch. An important part of hegemony today is a leading role in international government through the existing international organizations. A new hegemon can rise through the ranks in the established international order, rather than through "succession war" as in the past.

In terms of economic contributions to the maintenance of the existing international organizations, Japan can clearly afford an extensive involvement in them. But the actual role Japan plays is considerably below the potential. Part of the reason for this discrepancy is historical; that is, the "grandfathers" who won the last war are still in control. If voting power in international organizations were aligned to various countries' economic weights in the world and their ability and willingness to contribute, it would be strange that Britain, China, and Russia (as successor to the former Soviet Union) are still among the permanent members of the UN Security Council (arguably the most prestigious political organ of the world), whereas Germany, Italy, and Japan are not. Indeed, reform of the Security Council membership has been a sporadic topic of discussion among scholars. Recently, Adekunle Ajala of Nigeria argued in favor of adding Germany and Japan as permanent members.[14] Japan is now serving as a non-permanent member of the Security Council.

Generally, as world public opinion goes at present, Japan's money is welcome but its voice is not. Often international organizations forgo benefits from Japan's larger contributions because money translates into voice through rules that tie voting power to the quota of capital subscription. Japan's money was for a long time not welcomed by the incumbents, whose voting power was to decrease in the shuffle. Only as recently as in 1990, Japan was "promoted" to the long-overdue second rank in voting power in the IMF, equal to West Germany and next to the number one United States. The political economy of hegemonic transition understandably involves both political and economic considerations, even in well-established economic organizations. The participation of Japanese nationals in the bureaucracies of world organizations is also extremely low, further disadvantaging Japan through office politics.

There is one international economic organization in which Japan is clearly the leader—the Asian Development Bank. Whether Japan's position makes any difference may be answered by a comparative analysis of the performances of the ADB and other similar institutions. Unfortunately, such comparative studies are not available. In Asia, Japan's leadership is generally acknowledged. This encourages Japan to be cautious about its leading role in Asia, although it is still reticent about leadership on a global scale. In the global arena, the United States still is the hegemon. Its political leadership and military power are unmatched. Its domestic economy, however, is debt laden and falling behind Japan in growth rates. The world is caught in a peculiar chemistry of Japan's economic power and the political and military power of the United States.

_____ ***Japan's Political Commitment: Peace***

Owing to the unchallengeable military superiority of the United States, the need for other powers to have military power has been considerably reduced.

The Gulf War demonstrated how effective the United States was as a military "Leviathan." Just as the Hobbesian Leviathan has pushed brutish, quarrelsome individuals into a consensus on the desirability of a peaceful civil society, the U.S. Leviathan has successfully proved the futility of warlike nation-states' obsession with military power as an indispensable means of national security. Once nations are cured of this obsession, enormous amounts of economic resources are released from military expenditures and become payable as "peace dividends." This simple truth of how beneficial peace is and how easy it is to generate and maintain peace has long eluded mankind. Now it is given the first effective global recognition as a moral, as well as utilitarian, principle that should guide resource allocation in every nation.

A further benefit of global arms reductions, hopefully leading to a total global disarmament, is that the United States itself can now cease to be a military Leviathan. The United States now can afford a substantial reduction in its military expenditures and its military power. This leads to a substantial revision of the theory of hegemony as an international government.

An important role of hegemony is the production of international public goods, of which peace is paramount.[15] Peace as an international public good has been costly hitherto, and the hegemon's qualifications included sufficient economic resources by which to maintain military expenditure and military power. With a universal peace by consensus among nation-states, however, peace becomes an international public good without costing economic resources. The hegemon's role must then change from ensuring peace by military threats to a moral leadership to ensure peace without arms. Would the United States be able to remain a hegemon capable of maintaining world peace and to eliminate, in stages, its military power at the same time?

Global peace results from rejections of arms by individual states. If states really want a lasting peace, a conceivable political action would be a constitutional ban on war as a sovereign act of a state, which would be a quantum jump in the transformation of the conventional, archaic principles of state sovereignty. In this respect, Japan is one of the most advanced countries. Article 9 of the Japanese constitution states: "Aspiring sincerely to an international peace based on justice and order, the Japanese people forever renounce war as a sovereign right of the nation and the threat or use of force as means of settling international disputes."

During the Gulf War (August 1990 to March 1991), this peace article of the Japanese constitution effectively prevented Japan from "using force" in conjunction with the UN military action to remove Iraqi troops from Kuwait. By orchestrating the UN action, the United States demonstrated the rights and obligations of a hegemon to ensure peace in the Gulf region. The main point of the UN-U.S. achievements is the security of Kuwait's territorial integrity, which derives from a larger principle that every member-state of the United

Nations is protected by world collective security against invasions by other states. Japan is also a beneficiary of the collective security system and in exchange should contribute to the maintenance and strengthening of this system. In the case of the Gulf War, under its own constitutional ban on military contribution Japan made a generous financial contribution.

Japan's role in the Gulf War has been subject to intense controversy inside and outside Japan. Many unkind views of Japan's rejection of military participation, despite its financial generosity, have been heard in the West. Ostensibly, the type of Japanese contribution most desired by the West was the sending of Japanese troops to the Gulf. Failing in that contribution, whatever Japan did for peace in the Gulf seemed to have no value in the Western view. Japan was made a laughingstock of the world for its inability and ineptitude to seize upon a great political opportunity to demonstrate its world-leadership capability. More than two years after August 2, 1990, however, those Western views sound more like irresponsible harassments of Japan than objective assessments of Japan's role or capability in international relations.

Japan's choice of peaceful contributions in the case of the Gulf War was a result of intense political debate in Japan. It was a victory of Japan's democratic politics in conformity with the peace constitution. Furthermore, it was also the choice that Japan's Asian neighbors then favored. Large-scale troop movements over Asian waters on the way to and from the Gulf would have threatened Asian peace. In this case, the outcome of Japan's domestic politics was compatible with Asia's wishes and contributed to the reduction of the lingering Asian suspicion of Japan's geopolitical intentions. By not participating in the Gulf War with troops, Japan improved its credibility in the eyes of Asians with respect to the common cause of peace.

Since the end of the Gulf War, the Japanese have been intensifying the study and debate of Japan's contribution to world peace not only by writing checks but also by sending participating personnel to the UN peacekeeping operations (PKO). In May 1991, the Japanese parliament sent a multiparty mission to Europe and the United States to study how other countries were participating in UN PKO. Alternative plans were then widely debated concerning the reconciliation of human participation in UN PKO and the constitutional ban on "the threat or use of force" for international conflict resolution. In October 1991, the warring factions of Cambodia signed an agreement on comprehensive political settlement, and the new Phnom Penh regime subsequently asked for Japan's participation in UN PKO in Cambodia. Because the UN PKO came to a region of vital interest to Japan, it was pressed to make up its mind as quickly as possible. In June 1992, the Japanese parliament passed a PKO cooperation bill approving the sending of SDF personnel, although virtually unarmed, for peaceful assistance in PKO. The law also stipulates numerous safeguards to ensure that under no circumstances would Japanese personnel be drawn into military action.

The End of History

The Japanese commitment to peace is also broadly in accord with the long-run historical forces, which, however enigmatic, have brought history itself to an end. Although the philosophical concept of an "end of history"[16] is an update of Hegel with no particular regard to Japan, it has a special significance for the evaluation of Japan's hegemonic qualifications at the present juncture of history.

According to Fukuyama, all the requisite ideas that would put an end to history were produced during the Age of Enlightenment. These were the concepts of freedom, equality, and democracy supported by free enterprise and the market. When democratic polity and market economy pervade the world, history comes to an end in the sense that all thoughts and experiments in search of a better world are exhausted and that historymaking clashes of ideals and ideologies, often accompanied by armed struggles, can no longer be justified. In the last two hundred years, a variety of ideologies promising a better world appeared and disappeared. None of them could arrest the relentless growth of democracy and markets over wider and wider areas of the world.

Fukuyama has described the state of the world after the end of history as follows:

> The struggle for recognition, the willingness to risk one's life for a purely abstract goal, the worldwide ideological struggle that called forth daring, courage, imagination, and idealism, will be replaced by *economic calculation, the endless solving of technical problems, environmental concerns, and the satisfaction of sophisticated consumer demands*. [Emphasis added.][17]

Military heroism dies with the end of history and much less glamorous economics becomes the centerpiece of posthistory life. Japan appears to be well suited for a leading role in this state of affairs.

There is one more disruptive legacy of the nation-state era with which the world has to cope: nationalism. Although market forces and technological progress essentially know no geographical boundaries, nation-states are territorially defined. At times, "local" sentiments restrain "global" economic forces, as may be seen in clashes between nationalism and multinational enterprise. After all other ideologies and movements are safely defeated, nationalism may still remain as a source of inspiration for the protection of territorially confined national interest.

However, as Fukuyama says, "the vast majority of the world's nationalist movements do not have a political program beyond the negative desire of independence from some other group or people, and do not offer anything like a comprehensive agenda for socioeconomic organization."[18] So long as democracy allows free expressions of aspirations and interests of different groups, nationalism is unlikely to stand in the way of global economic forces.

It may even thrive as an aspect of cultural diversity that adds color and entertainment to life after the end of history.

To paraphrase Fukuyama further, as all regions and countries are peacefully integrated by global market forces, the nation-states with their conventional "sovereign" rights will become obsolete as basic units of world organization. When the concept of sovereignty becomes more hollow, states will increasingly take on the character of administrative units subordinate to a unified world and submit to the rules and procedures of negotiation for the adjustment of differing interests or conflicting rights.

_____ *An Interim Role for Japan*

Japan has become a hegemonic candidate when a major hegemonic function, "production" of peace, is no longer needed because the end of history has made peace a sort of "free good" rather than a costly public good that has to be produced and maintained by the hegemon. Other important hegemonic functions are largely economic. They have to do with the creation and maintenance of international institutions embodying principles, norms, rules, and procedures consistent with the market forces. The cost of global leadership consists in taking up a major share in the financing of these institutions. The hegemon must also efficiently respond to emergencies arising from imbalances in the balance of payments, shortages of development capital, misalignments of exchange rates, conflicting economic policies of various countries, and so on.

With the end of history and the likelihood of peace as a global free good, a crucial factor in world governance over the medium term is the quality of U.S.-Japanese cooperation. For a while, there may continue to be intermittent outbreaks of local skirmishes initiated by errant leaders of minor nation-states that are lagging behind the march of history. Today the United States alone has and is willing to use international policy power to put down and prevent these international incidents from disrupting global peace. Eventually, democracy and markets will invalidate armed conflicts between nations, giving rise to the primacy of peaceful negotiations for adjustments of national interests.

In the meantime, the United States as number one may continue to enjoy maximum freedom in the pursuit of its strategy based on its global vision, which is well known and even credited for bringing history to an end. But Japan's economic power is a critical factor that may make or break the success of the U.S. world strategy. Thus, for its own good, the United States cannot ignore Japan. Neither the United States nor Japan can afford the luxury of a nationalist notion of sovereignty. When production depends on interdependence and teamwork, the parties involved must subordinate themselves to superordinate goals.

Japan and the United States have complementary strengths and weaknesses. They need each other in close cooperation for the stability of the world order. U.S. opinion leaders, appreciating Japan's economic strengths, suggest that a closer economic integration of the two countries (a *Nichibei* economy) would generate a more effective hegemony.[19] Instead of lamenting the further fall of the U.S. share in world GNP, which was widespread in the 1970s, U.S. policymakers now link the strategy of the United States to the sum of Japanese and U.S. economies. It is no longer a matter of either U.S. or Japanese hegemony; it is cohegemony (bigemony) or, a little more generally, a "Pax consortis."[20]

Conclusion

Although the weight of the Japanese economy is on a hegemonic scale, this does not make Japan a full-fledged hegemon. The world is still full of armed nation-states, and some of them may stumble into war in the name of national honor. The world apparently still needs a hegemon with superior military power to restrain other states' ambitions. Fortunately, the world's need for a hegemonic state to ensure the peace and stability of the world order is one of the history-bound concepts and is sure to disappear with the end of history. When all political units, including the nation-states, are thoroughly democratized and disarmed, all political power devolves to the individual. Then all the individuals of the world might wish to reorganize a superordinate world community by a new global social contract. The world community may still be divided into geographical units of administration ("former" states), but political competition among these units for hegemony will be checked by internal forces of democracy and the global interdependence of markets. The dialectic of contradictions will finally come to rest under permanent peace and lose its historymaking power.

Notes

1. A. Immanuel Wallerstein, *The Politics of the World-Economy*, New York: Cambridge University Press, 1984.

2. A. Ezra Vogel, *Japan as Number One*, Cambridge, Mass.: Harvard University Press, 1979; C.P. Kindleberger, "International Public Goods Without International Government," *American Economic Review*, vol. 76, no. 1 (March 1986), pp. 1–13; Robert Gilpin, *The Political Economy of International Relations*, Princeton, N.J.: Princeton University Press, 1987; Paul Kennedy, *The Rise and Fall of the Great Powers*, Lexington, Mass.: Lexington Books, 1987; John H. Makin and Donald C. Hellmann, eds., *Sharing World Leadership?* Washington, D.C.: American Enterprise Institute, 1989; William S. Dietrich, *In the Shadow of the Rising Sun*, University Park, Penn.: Pennsylvania State University Press, 1991; Koji Taira, "Japan, an Imminent Hegemon?" *The Annals of the American Academy of Political and Social Science*, vol.

513 (January 1991), pp. 151–163; Koji Taira, "Disadvantages of Success: Pains of Behavior Adjustment to Role Changes," *Proceedings of the Symposium on Japanese and Third-World Development*, Cambridge, Mass.: Reischauer Institute of Japanese Studies, 1988, pp. 22–39.

3. Kennedy, *Rise and Fall of Great Powers*.

4. United Nations Development Program, *Human Development Report 1990*, New York: Oxford University Press, 1990.

5. Dietrich, *In the Shadow*, pp. 263–266.

6. Ibid., p. 265.

7. Ibid., p. iv.

8. R. Taggart Murphy, "Power Without Purpose: The Crisis of Japan's Global Financial Dominance," *Harvard Business Review*, vol. 67, no. 2 (March–April 1989), p. 74.

9. Ibid.

10. Rudiger Dornbusch, "The United States in the World Economy," *Quarterly Review of Economics and Business*, vol. 31, no. 2 (Summer 1991), p. 21.

11. Michio Morishima, *Why Has Japan "Succeeded"?* London: Cambridge University Press, 1982.

12. Minoru Morita, *Keizai Taikoku no Kessei* [A great economic power without policy], Tokyo: Nihon Hyōronsha, 1989; Atsushi Kuse, *Super–No. 2: Nippon*, Tokyo: Shōdensha, 1990 (in Japanese).

13. Gilpin, *The Political Economy*.

14. Adekunle Ajala, "Aratana Jōnin Rijikoku no Keisei o" [Proposed: A new organization of the Security Council], *Gaikō Forum*, no. 40 (January 1992), pp. 32–33.

15. Kindleberger, "International Public Goods."

16. Francis Fukuyama, "The End of History?" *National Interest*, no. 16 (Summer 1989), pp. 2–18.

17. Ibid., p. 18.

18. Ibid., pp. 14–15.

19. Gilpin, *The Political Economy*, pp. 336–339.

20. Steve Chan, *East Asian Dynamics*, Boulder, Colo.: Westview Press, 1990, pp. 102–107.

Conclusion

The Posthegemonic World and Japan

Frank Langdon
Tsuneo Akaha

Perhaps the most crucial question raised about the posthegemonic world is whether it has moved into a period when economic power is more important than political-military power.[1] In the early 1990s the answer was yes, at least among the major powers. The world clearly moved into a period of relatively cordial relations among the United States, Russia, Germany, France, Britain, Japan, and China. Compared to any time during the Cold War, they were less divided by strong ideological differences and were all more absorbed in economic problems than military ones vis-à-vis one another. China and the successor states of the Soviet Union became willing to accept more Western-type economic or political institutions, and the Western major powers became more willing to assist them. The Western major powers collectively tried to provide the benefits the U.S. hegemon was once able to supply by itself to enhance international military and economic security. These changes raised hopes of a more peaceful global environment devoted to economic reform and development.

Those events reduced the threat of major wars, but also reduced the incentive of fear of attack to stimulate the strong military and economic cooperation that had inspired the major powers during the Cold War. In the 1990s, less widely disruptive regional, ethnic, and religious conflict took the place of the Cold War, even in Europe. Particularly dangerous was the proliferation of nuclear weapons and weapons of mass destruction to smaller powers from the major powers unable or unwilling to check it.

The dominance of economic affairs was aided by continued disarmament moves. Arms control and disarmament were accelerated by the unilateral steps of both military superpowers, Russia and the United States, to reduce or destroy nuclear and conventional weapons as well as to take steps to adhere to various disarmament agreements such as the Strategic Arms Reduction Treaty (START). The states that fell heir to some of the Soviet strategic nuclear weapons—Ukraine, Belarus, and Khazakhstan—adhered to the START treaty and, further, agreed to become nonnuclear weapons states.

Those steps all reduced the lingering threat to the West from the former Soviet Union's weapons and forces. Acceptance of the less threatening Soviet "defense sufficiency" military doctrine seemed likely to continue after the Gorbachev era, further reducing the importance of military affairs among the major powers due to the decline of a Russian threat. However, Russia succeeded to the Soviet seat on the UN Security Council and retained a substantial portion of the nuclear and conventional military capability of the former Soviet Union. If cordiality and cooperation continue to characterize Russian-U.S. relations, rivalry and enmity may become a thing of the past, as happened between Britain and the United States. Russia is one of the only two major powers with which the United States has never fought a war. If Russia manages to weather the transition to prosperity and liberalism without a war with Ukraine and without separation of its regions, it will probably become a full superpower of the future.

Despite the relatively favorable international conditions at present, it is probably too soon to conclude that the world is due for a lengthy period of peace among the major powers. Hopes of utilizing the cooperation of the major powers with each other to convert the United Nations into an effective peacekeeping institution, as envisaged in drafting the UN Charter, is unrealistic. The multilateral action against Iraq in 1991 led by the United States did resemble something like the old U.S. hegemonic role, which neither the Soviet Union nor China tried to oppose. But the United Nations was not in command and no moves are even contemplated to utilize the provisions in the charter for a UN military staff or forces. The continuing danger of regional wars is illustrated by Iraq's use of a one-million-man army in the Middle East to commit aggression against its neighbors, to say nothing about the ethnic fighting in the former Yugoslavia or Azerbaijan. Although East Asia was comparatively quiet at the beginning of the 1990s with peace breaking out in Cambodia and Korea, tensions remain over disputed territories and contested regimes. The intractable Northern Territories problem between Japan and Russia can be solved only by long-term economic cooperation, which Tokyo is loath to accept. The comparative unimportance of the territories in which no Japanese has lived for nearly fifty years only emphasizes how seriously a symbolic issue of national pride can still poison relations among the major powers themselves.

Nevertheless, in the early 1990s, except for the ethnic clashes in Europe and the usual local wars in Africa, the world was unusually peaceful and it looked in the medium term like the major powers would not be engaged in much military competition with each other and would be absorbed in their economic problems for a long time. Economic disputes were intense among the Western powers, especially the United States, Japan, and those in the European Community, but did not prevent considerable economic cooperation and continuation of their close interdependence. The world really looked like it might be ready to grapple with its looming development and environmental problems, and finally had a breathing space in which to begin to transfer some of the assets wasted on military preparations to global social welfare. The only ingredient lacking was political leadership. It seemed unlikely that one could look to the United States as the previous hegemon, or to another hegemon such as Japan to take its place. What was needed was collective leadership, a theme taken up by U.S. Secretary of State Baker at the Seoul meeting of the Asian Pacific Economic Cooperation in 1991, or even the Pentagon in a policy document in May 1992, and exemplified to some extent in the Gulf War coalition against Saddam Hussein in 1991.[2]

Hegemony, which has been the major theme of this book, has been treated by different authors in slightly different ways, indicating some disagreement about what it involves. But there is almost no disagreement that the United States was a hegemon after World War II and in the first half of the Cold War. Then, international conditions were quite different from the 1990s in the unique economic and military superiority of the United States and in the economic and military threats to its much weaker major power allies.

Questions are often asked about whether the United States can regain the hegemony it once enjoyed and whether Japan can become a hegemon, perhaps a new kind that can lead by its economic power without an enormous military capability. In this decade the answer to both questions appears to be "no." The former weakened major powers no longer need the protection, either military or economic, for which they once depended upon the United States. The United States has let its economic capabilities be seriously drained by its prodigal behavior in the 1980s when it bought so much on credit and consumed it as though there was no tomorrow. It can no longer easily provide direct benefits to other countries or such generous free public goods, although it still provides a huge affluent market to major powers and developing countries alike, despite its increasing protectionism. It is limited in the use of military threats or force except against aggressive terrorist states.

In the 1990s, Japan is much more independent and confident in using its economic power and influence both regionally and globally, but the pacifist inclination of its population and its major political institutions make it impossible to arm on a large-scale basis, and difficult to use its military power outside its own borders. The continuation of the Japanese pacifist inclination was strongly demonstrated in the tortuous attempt to allow Japanese military forces to participate in international peacekeeping under the United Nations in the early 1990s.

It is also very unlikely that Japan can convert its economic influence into the sort of international hegemonic leadership shown by the United States in creating international public goods, such as the formation of global institutions like the Bretton Woods financial system, the International Monetary Fund, the Organization for Economic Cooperation and Development, and a host of other regimes and institutions. Nor has Japan exerted much significant positive leadership in international organizations outside of its own region. In something as basic to a hegemon as making its market truly open and welcoming to its trading and investment partners, only a few of Japan's leaders have begun to realize the necessity of that course to reduce the friction and criticism directed at it by the rest of the world, let alone induce the world to cooperate more.

In Chapter 11, Koji Taira paints an appealing utopian picture of Japan as an unarmed economic hegemon, relying on the military power of the United States to gradually make large-scale armament unnecessary, and converting the world to concentration on peaceful development and prosperity for all nations. For want of anything better, collective leadership of the major powers is necessary to take advantage of the probable temporary retreat of the dominance of military means to assert a kind of collective leadership that relies more on economic means to solve the world's most pressing problems.

The seven Western summit powers—the United States, Japan, Britain, France, Germany, Italy, and Canada—have attempted global collective macroeconomic cooperation by exhorting one another, but it is usually ineffective. The Trilateral Commission has tried to move the major powers in the same direction by a network of their elites, but the U.S. government has been especially obdurate in ignoring the commission's advice. A realistic perspective is apt to dominate in Washington whereby officials are only too ready to resort to threats and sanctions in economic affairs rather than to rely on conciliation and compromise with its partners. Neither the United States nor Japan is a benevolent hegemon that induces other states to cooperate by giving large rewards to meet their most pressing needs.

To clearly respond to the question of whether the United States is a declining hegemon or whether it can regain its hegemony, it is necessary to say that the United States is the strongest of the major powers. It is not declining in the classic sense that it will become like Britain, Spain, or the Netherlands, which were once unrivaled great powers. They followed an almost inevitable historical process of creating a strong technically superior economy that was able to support a superior military power for a time, but in that process the growth of their political and military responsibilities became more expensive than they could continue to support and the "imperial overstretch" fatally weakened the economy—the scenario derived by historian Paul Kennedy.[3]

The United States still has a strong economy and the largest output of goods and services of any country. It also has the most extensive military power, with bases and forces all over the world—more than Britain in the nineteenth century but something akin to ancient Rome with respect to the classical world. Its economy has been clearly weakened by letting the infrastructure run down, neglecting education and training of the labor force, and making insufficient investment in its leading industries. Probably the most serious of these self-inflicted injuries is a bad fiscal policy. Since the Johnson administration the federal government has not paid for its wars with taxes but resorted to increasing government borrowing. It should be remembered that after World War II and after the Korean War the federal government actually had a balanced budget. And it should be balanced again after the Cold War. But the Reagan administration greatly increased military expenditures and actually reduced taxes, with the resulting colossal budget deficit. The defense budget to enable the United States to get ahead of the Soviet Union at the height of the Cold War in the mid-1980s has scarcely come down.

The United States differs from the declining great powers described by Kennedy. It still has the world's most innovative and productive economy, even if its renewal and upkeep is being neglected. It also has the lowest tax rate of any developed country in the OECD. It only requires political will or some stimulus such as a military threat to raise taxes to the needed level. The economy can easily bear the high military burden by simply raising taxes to reduce the government's unnecessary borrowing, and the government can encourage private industry to invest more in upkeep and renewal without any fatal weakening of the country's economic base. Therefore, if the United States is declining, it is a long-term trend that can be reversed. Its basic economic strength is still there.

But the nondecline does not mean the United States can continue as a hegemon, at least not in the 1990s. The hegemonic conditions of the early Cold War period are gone. The other major powers are strong and not threatened militarily or economically, except for Russia and China, which may soon become strong as well. The best way to induce the major powers to cooperate in global management is by persuasion, conciliation, and compromise. Their comparative military or economic weaknesses may soon be remedied, so threats and force have very limited utility against them. The idea of leading by example and persuasion, which may be part of the scenario as envisaged by Koji Taira's pacifist economics and giant Japan as hegemon, is not altogether a fantasy. The resort to persuasion and conciliation to induce states to cooperate has long been an idealist view based on the cooperative aspects of human behavior, which exist as well as the combative aspects. Japanese society and its economic success are strongly based on just that collective and cooperative aspect of its people.

The United States is in a better position to continue to lead as a kind of benevolent persuasive first-among-equals on the basis of its past hegemonic record as well as its present economic and cultural potential. The other rich major powers have not provided as many public goods or exercised such a strong cultural influence internationally. By mobilizing its talent, the United States could provide considerable moral leadership and give real substance to the good intentions expressed at the summit meetings. The Tokyo Declaration of Miyazawa and Bush in January 1992 contains partnership ideas and ideals, but they need to be backed by concrete actions not only to enable the two biggest economic powers to cooperate internationally, but also to inspire the kind of collective leadership needed to be shown by the other major powers. If the Western major powers put adequate support behind cooperation with Russia and China, those countries, too, will fall in line for the time being because their needs, like those of most of the Western powers in the 1940s and 1950s, are now so great.

To bring together the analyses in this volume, we need to look at some of the key elements of the posthegemonic world order: (1) the primacy of economic development and security over military confrontation and rivalry, (2) the emergence of Japan as a new breed of world power, (3) the changing role of the U.S.-Japanese alliance in regional stability, (4) Japan's important role as a link between the global economy and the Asia Pacific economy, and (5) the uncertain Japanese-Russian relations.

The Primacy of Economic Development over Military Rivalry

When the United States was an unchallengeable military and economic superpower, it tended to concentrate on military and political affairs, the so-called "high politics." The Europeans and Japanese reversed those priorities to strengthen their economies first and put their slower and more limited defense efforts second. They still rely on the United States for a major share of their military security. In the meantime, the U.S. economy was weakened, whereas its allies experienced growing economic strength. In the 1991 collective security coalition against Iraq, the United States for the first time obtained large money contributions to cover its war costs from its rich allies, Japan and Germany, who were unable to contribute their own armed forces. Japan, whose armed forces are the most restricted in their theater of deployment, gives the greatest priority to economic growth. For Japan, clearly, the high politics of security is a poor second to the economy.

With the fading of the Soviet threat, the United States itself is reversing its long-standing security priority to favor its economy, but it is too tempted to indulge in protectionist retaliation against its trading partners, rather than economic reform and cooperation with them. In the Uruguay Round of trade reform under the GATT, Washington has championed the struggle to reduce agricultural subsidies and restrictions against the protectionism of the European Community, especially France and Germany, as well as against the agricultural protectionism of Japan and Canada. In addition to its effort in the reform of the global trading regime, the United States has mounted a regional drive to create a liberal trade bloc in the Americas, starting with the Canada-U.S. Free Trade Agreement. Australia and Malaysia have even proposed a regional Western Pacific–East Asian trade bloc without the membership of the United States and Canada from the Eastern Pacific. Although the regional economic cooperative movements of the Asia Pacific region and of North America have been devoted to open regimes that welcome global trade in principle, intraregional preferences exist against those outside the region. In addition, the sharp trade friction of the early 1990s could lead to even more protectionist regional blocs, which would further reduce global trade and disrupt the globalization of industrial production.

With the decline in the salience of military force, the economic dynamism of the Asia Pacific region takes on added importance and attractiveness to those outside of it. Japan's role as a model and source of investment, aid, and as a potential market only adds to its influence. The United States, despite its own capital needs, remains a major market and investment source for Asian states, which still depend on its market for their export-led economic development. Japan's imports from ASEAN (the Philippines, Indonesia, Malaysia, Thailand, Singapore, and Brunei), not counting Singapore, actually declined from 1980 to 1989, but its imports from the Newly Industrializing States of South Korea, Taiwan, and Hong Kong rose slightly in that same period.[4] Only 5 percent of Japanese manufacturing took place outside of Japan, compared to 21 percent for the United States and 17 percent for West Germany. In the Philippines, Taiwan, and Singapore, the United States remains the largest investor. In China, Japan has invested only $2.2 billion, 1.1 percent of its worldwide total. The United States is still more important than Japan as a market and often as the source of capital. Japan only hurts itself by refusing to buy more East Asian products. Even Japan's new factories in East Asia ship more to third countries such as the United States and Europe than to Japan.

In circumstances where U.S. military protection has less significance due to perceptions of lower military threats in the Asia Pacific region, the Pentagon probably does not need to retain military forces based in East Asia to keep U.S. political influence there. Its trade, investment, and technology are still eagerly sought by regional states and even by the communist countries, just as in the case of Japan. Yet, the Japanese government is eager to retain the U.S. forces in Japan and is even willing to increase its share of the local U.S. basing costs. The Pentagon is equally eager to stay. Japan has a solid defense guarantee from the world's strongest military power as long as U.S. military personnel are present in Japan. It also alleviates Asian fear of Japan's rearmament. It provides the Pentagon with a rationale for holding on to overseas bases and a large defense budget. But it is also Murphy's Law that officials anywhere are apt to oppose any changes that jeopardize their budgets. There are almost always potential military threats that can be adduced to justify a large military establishment. The U.S. role as a policeman within the region may be preferable only to that of other regional major or minor powers.

The U.S. leaders should ask themselves if it is in the best interest of the United States to keep playing such a far-flung military-political role on the world stage. Why not concentrate on the prestige of solving the world's economic problems that cry out for attention when its military protection and influence are less needed? Its wealthy allies are even more capable of mounting large-scale defense efforts, and the United States has an urgent need to spend far more to strengthen its own economy and society. Depending on loans from other countries such as Japan should be a temporary expedient. Continued massive borrowing and consumption may soon put the United States in the position of the Latin American states, which are apt to be insolvent and mired in social breakdown and unrest. The riots in Los Angeles are an ominous portent of the future. It is significant that Japan attained its own successful development almost entirely with its own internal savings and capital accumulation.

A New Breed of World Power

Yoichi Funabashi wrote, "Japan's unorthodox power portfolio ('economic giant and military dwarf') should not be viewed as an unstable and transitional phenomenon; its deep-rooted pacifism should not be treated as mere escapism, . . . on the contrary this very portfolio presents Japan with the opportunity to define its own power and role in the radically changing world ahead."[5] Insofar as Japan represents a new breed of world power, it could be a useful model for other countries, which might want to follow its example in emphasizing economic development without putting such great effort into acquiring arms and using them against its neighbors.[6] In East Asia, other countries, such as Korea, Taiwan, and Thailand, have consciously imitated Japan in their economic development. Although they too benefit from the U.S. military presence, they are under greater threat from stronger neighbors against whom they have made a bigger defense effort than Japan. But those military costs have not prevented impressive economic development.

Regarding defense, Japan represents an extreme example of a lightly armed major world power. By relying on the U.S. military support it spends only 1 percent of its GNP on defense.[7] But at the same time the post–World War II Japanese antimilitarism continues to be stronger than elsewhere. In countries such as the United States or France antimilitarism can be said to scarcely exist. In Japan's case, it continues to be strongly championed and maintained by the opposition political parties and leading news media, supported in turn by popular pacifist leanings. The agonizing attempts of the opposition Social Democratic Party of Japan to adopt a more realistic (less pacifistic) defense policy, while clinging to its basic belief that the Japanese defense forces are unconstitutional, are probably unique in the world.[8]

Such pacifistic attitudes and institutional barriers prevent the defense forces from exercising much domestic political influence or receiving priority in government budgetmaking, a crucial test of influence. Few of Japan's talented individuals and economic efforts are devoted to military purposes, in contrast to the situation in the United States. Because Japan's chief defense industries are also much more involved in production of nonmilitary products, there is only a moderate-sized military industrial complex, which is not dependent on a huge military budget as is the case in Washington. South Korea, like the United States, is at the opposite extreme from Japan, spending about 6 percent of its GNP on defense. North Korea spends an even higher proportion of its GNP on defense. South Korea makes for an interesting comparison because it has followed the Japanese example in much of its economic development. Its record suggests that if Japan had agreed to a much larger military budget, Japan, too, might have managed to achieve the same impressive economic growth, contrary to the common generalization that large military expenditures are likely to have an adverse impact on the economy.

An old but neglected message is sent to other countries by Japan's example. Reliance on economic rather than military capabilities can foster a high standard of living and still permit an influential and constructive foreign policy. It also spares people the pain of war casualties and impoverishment due to the pursuit of ambitious military aims. Indeed, the economic emphasis of Japan is the model Zhou hopes Japan will continue to present to the rest of the world. The United States has not been such a good model because it has been neglecting its domestic economy and social needs while participating in an ever more expensive high-technology arms buildup, which has only moderately slowed since the end of the Cold War. But the United States is in the enviable position whereby only a moderate tax increase and lowering of defense costs will still permit both a strong defense and a strengthened economy.

The Japanese still tend to regard their strong trade and financial impact abroad as a challenge, not as an economic attack on the United States or Europe. Some of the present fear of Japan's economic impact is quite excessive, and such a strong contrast to the admiration for Japan expressed in the 1960s and 1970s. The unjustified extreme is represented by the statement of Joseph Alioto, a lawyer and former mayor of San Francisco. He represented a U.S. video company that is a competitor of Matsushita Company, and accused Matsushita of monopoly in the purchase of MCA for $6.13 billion. He said the MCA purchase "was another example of Japanese industrialists embarked on a deadly, dangerous, ten-year program to unlawfully control and dominate the economy of the United States by the end of the century."[9] By contrast, the larger ownership of U.S. assets by Britain has not aroused such paranoia at all, nor do the large holdings of France, Canada, or the Netherlands.

Japan offers a good model for emulation, but it suffers from a legacy of militarism and colonialism, on the one hand, and from a mercantilist reputation, on the other, both of which foreigners never let it forget. Japan thus has a difficult time getting other countries to take its world vision seriously.[10] According to Chittiwatanapong, Japan is on its way to overcoming the first of these handicaps in Southeast Asia. To counter the residual fears of Japanese militarism, however, Japan should declare unequivocally, even in the face of international criticism such as it faced in the Gulf crisis, that it will not alter its strategy of acting as a global civilian power. It should seize every opportunity to proclaim it will not resort to military means to exert its political power.[11]

In order to overcome the second impairment, Japan must pursue its own market-opening measures more vigorously and render its internal economic processes more transparent. Reliance on external pressure to force its hand is damaging to its desired role as a liberalizing force in the international economic system. It also gives undue influence to the right-wing elements in Japan, which are only too eager to exploit the public's growing irritation over the government's acquiescence in what they consider misguided foreign political pressure from the United States. *Kenbei*, or dislike of the United States, is growing, particularly among the more articulate younger generation of adults who have no memory of World War II or of the U.S. role in the postwar demilitarization, democratization, and international rehabilitation of Japan.

Japan's third shortcoming, the inability to articulate universalizable norms, values, and principles, has been partially overcome by Japan's "soft power," the demonstration effect of Japan's postwar performance on its Asian neighbors' search for a model. In the Cold War decades, Japan was in no position to project its political views onto its neighbors. However, by example, Japan demonstrated that economic development can lead to political stability and to international political influence. That message has been heeded by other Asian countries. It is also remarkable that the economic growth of East and Southeast Asia occurred, unlike in Europe, "without the benefit of a comprehensive regional political framework designed by the region's major economic and political powers."[12]

In addition, in the posthegemonic world, Japan's difficulty in articulating a universalizable philosophy can be partially overcome by its active and constructive participation in a collective leadership system in which Japan, the United States, and Europe can complement each other.[13] It is to this issue that we shall now turn.

Japan as Number Two

Contrary to the almost hysterical sensationalism of some of the media in warning of the coming disastrous Japanese attempt at global dominance, the analyses in this volume amply demonstrate that Japan is neither capable nor desirous of a hegemonic role in the post–Cold War world.[14] Meeks' analysis of various indicators of economic power shows some of the areas in which the United States still leads the rest of the world, including global exports and imports. As Taira observes, Japan is content and comfortable with being in a number two position, exercising "supportive leadership" rather than seeking a regional, much less global, hegemonic role. It will be optimal for Japan and the rest of the world if it uses its economic power to provide benefits to the world and cooperates with the U.S. political leadership, which the world apparently accepts as more legitimate.

In the summit between Prime Minister Miyazawa and President Bush in Tokyo in January 1992, the two leaders confirmed Japan's supportive role for U.S. leadership. Following that summit, Miyazawa told the Japanese parliament, "In the talks with the United States, we agreed that it is imperative that the United States continue to play a leadership role in the building of the international order and that Japan has a shared responsibility to cooperate fully with this effort."[15]

As Langdon maintains, the European Community (led by Germany), Japan, and the United States, all as equals, could provide the leadership the world desperately needs. This was effectively demonstrated after the stock market collapse in October 1987 when they all closely coordinated their economic policies to almost instantaneously resolve the world financial crisis. It contrasts dramatically with the beggar-thy-neighbor policies that brought depression and war after the 1929 stock market crash, when it was every man for himself, not cooperation or harmonization of policies by the economic major powers. The action of the Nixon administration in launching economic attacks on its closest allies in 1971 was the beginning of the abdication by Washington of its role of the good hegemon, perhaps realizing that its economic capacity to absorb its allies' exports as the market of last resort or of acting as a macroeconomic locomotive for the world had already eroded away. In fairness, it must be said that the responsibility for the collapse of the Bretton Woods financial system at that time was equally that of the U.S. allies, who refused to revalue their currencies to reflect the changed world economic conditions as the system demanded.

According to Zhou, even from the perspective of China, which is the regional power that could potentially challenge Japan's regional political-security role, Japan, the United States, and Europe together hold the key to world peace and security and have the responsibility to build a new international order for the 1990s and beyond.

However, as Akaha shows in his analysis of the impact of the second Gulf crisis on the Japan-U.S. relations, it has been a formidable task to construct a genuine coequal relationship between the United States and Japan, to say nothing of all three power centers, including Europe, acting together. Japan is most unlike the other two in its comparatively minor military power and greater cultural distinctiveness. As economist Lester Thurow has pointed out, all the costs of the Gulf War could easily have been paid by the United States with a $6 trillion output of goods and services per year. The financial aid requested from Japan and Germany was to convince the people of the United States and other countries that the war was an allied effort, not just a U.S. effort. For U.S. troops to have been killed defending the oil supplies of Germany and Japan without any contribution on their part would have been politically disastrous.[16]

When the United States, as the largest economy, is unable to harmonize its economic policies with either of its two "global partners," Japan and the European Community, no world cooperation is likely to be achieved. Nor can the kind of cooperation that resulted in the multilateral international force against Iraq in the Gulf War be repeated in the economic sphere, as the deplorable disunity over the GATT world trade reforms shows. The formation of the tighter European union in 1993 will further weaken the global most-favored-nation principles of the GATT trading system and make Europe the largest and wealthiest power center in the world. Europe thus will be able to set the world's trade and financial rules in the future. Both the United States and Japan will have to adapt to those rules if any significant global economic cooperation or harmonization is to succeed. They will have to conform to Western European patterns if they are to continue to trade with those nations. The result will make it easier for both of them to get along together. The European pattern of political management of the economy is closer to that of Japan, and the European culture has a common origin and similar development to that of the United States. The idea of a Japanese hegemony is pure fantasy.

Nevertheless, the emergence of Japan as a new breed of world power is very important. As Zhou points out, the example of Japan's peaceful economic development into a major power without reliance on military power is a hundred times more significant than, for example, the Soviet-U.S. Intermediate Nuclear Forces Treaty, which inaugurated the disarmament moves that brought about the end of the Cold War. That is especially so when Japan tried to compete head-to-head militarily with the Western imperial powers, then to drive them out of East Asia, and to take their place. The emergence of Japan as a new kind of world power, when the United States has declined relatively and the Soviet threat has vanished dramatically, changes the political function of the Japan-U.S. security alliance. Strained economic relations will have an adverse effect on regional security if they spill over into the political-military relationship. Japanese Foreign Minister Michio Watanabe acknowledged as much when he stated before parliament in January 1992:

> Close cooperation with the United States is the foundation of Japan's foreign policy. The firm and extensive cooperation between our nations, as underpinned by the Japan-U.S. security arrangements, ensures peace and stability in the Asia-Pacific region and is effective in *enhancing international credibility of Japan's position of not becoming a major military power capable of threatening other nations*. Despite reports of various points of friction and confrontation between Japan and the United States, we must therefore strive to strengthen our cooperative relations centred on the Japan-U.S. security arrangements. [Emphasis added.][17]

It is true, as Arase, Zhou, and Chittiwatanapong observe in their respective chapters, that Japan's growing political-security role in Asia Pacific is increasingly appreciated.[18] However, it is equally true that Japan's regional neighbors, including South Korea, China, and Southeast Asia, usually favor a continued U.S. military presence in Japan to discourage any unnecessary defense buildup on the part of the Japanese.[19] A potential problem is that the U.S. taxpayers' support of the U.S. military presence in the region may weaken in the future as they become more focused on domestic economic problems. They would also question the wisdom of their government's security commitments in the Asia Pacific region if they came to believe that the commitments only enhanced Japan's economic power and that the United States was losing the competition in the region's markets.

To prevent such an eventuality, Japan will have to assist the United States in reducing its burden of regional security. It can do so both by delivering on its pledge to increase the host-nation support and by contributing to the region's stability through further economic development. As Akaha and Chittiwatanapong note, it is indeed ironic that Japan will be paying up to 50 percent of the cost of maintaining U.S. troops in the country in order, in effect, to prevent itself from becoming a major military power. Akaha points out the potentially destabilizing effect of continued U.S. military presence in the context of diminished foreign threats to Japanese national security. It will also be imperative for Japan to ensure that the Asia Pacific region will provide open markets for U.S. and other extra-regional exports and investments. This brings us to the issue of Japan's regional economic role in the posthegemonic era.

Japan as a Link Between the Pacific and World Economy

Economic dynamism in the Pacific region, particularly in Asia Pacific, and Japan's leading role in it are well documented.[20] Between 1980 and 1989, Japan's exports to other Pacific Rim nations excluding Latin America grew from 49.2 percent to 60.3 percent of its worldwide exports. The region's share of Chinese exports jumped from 60.5 percent to 75 percent. South Korea's exports in the Pacific region accounted for 56.5 percent of its global exports in 1980 and 69.4 percent in 1989. Hong Kong's regional exports grew from 53.7 percent to 69.4 percent of its worldwide exports, and the region's share of Australia's and New Zealand's exports increased from 56 percent to 61.5 percent and from 39.9 percent to 44.2 percent, respectively. Only the ASEAN countries' exports to the other Pacific Rim countries dropped, but only slightly, from 75 percent to 74 percent.

Japan's role as a market for Asia Pacific exports has grown significantly as a result of the appreciation of the Japanese yen since 1985 and Tokyo's domestic demand expansion policy, as well as by the expanding intrafirm trade between Japanese subsidiaries in the region and their parent companies in Japan. Japan's imports from East Asian–Western Pacific countries excluding China, Australia, and New Zealand accounted for 20 percent of its total imports in 1986, but this figure jumped to 29 percent in 1990. In contrast, U.S. exports to Japan as a share of Japanese imports declined from 38.5 percent to 31.5 percent during the same period, whereas West European exports' share grew from 17.9 percent to 22 percent.

During the same period, Japan's global economic presence has also grown and the nation has become an important link between the Pacific Rim economy and the global economy through its trade and investment activities. Between 1985 and 1989, Japan's share of capital supply in the international financial-capital markets jumped from 8.0 percent to 24.7 percent. In contrast, the U.S. share plummeted from 23.9 percent to 11.9 percent. Japan's foreign direct investment has also grown both in value (from $22 billion in 1986 to $57 billion in 1990) and in geographical distribution. In 1986, Japan invested $10 billion in the United States, $3.5 billion in Europe, and $2.3 billion in Asia. By 1990 these figures had jumped to $26 billion, $14.3 billion, and $7.1 billion, respectively. The only region receiving less investment in 1990 than in 1986 was Latin America (from $4.7 billion to $3.6 billion). As Elton documents, the focus of Japan's trade, investment, loans, and aid, especially in Brazil, was to gain access to essential raw materials, but it shrank drastically after the insolvency crisis of the 1980s. High hopes of Japan's developmental assistance still linger despite the demonstrated shallowness of Japan's economic commitment and political understanding of the region that comprises the southeast part of the Pacific Rim.

The chief threats in a post–Cold War world seem to be the global threat of a breakdown of international economic cooperation under the GATT among the United States, Japan, and the European Community. It is compounded by the likelihood of antagonistic and protectionist action under the regional economic blocs dominated by each of the three. It is crucial, therefore, that the Asia Pacific markets remain open and Japan continues to play a leading role as promoter of "open regionalism" there.[21]

The chief threat to the Asia Pacific region is a breakdown of economic cooperation between Japan and the United States. It would probably also make the military cooperation between them untenable. As Langdon points out, such a double blow would probably revive major power military rivalry in the Pacific. Zhou has also observed that China wants Japan to continue to play a leading role in maintaining a peaceful international environment and a free and open global economic order.

_____ _____ *Uncertain Japan-Russian Relations*

The inability of Japan and Russia to find a mutually acceptable compromise on the territorial issue severely hampers the two countries' contribution to the forging of a posthegemonic regional order in the Pacific. The complexity of any legal solution to the problem of the Northern Territories is overwhelming and a military solution is wholly out of the question. Therefore, Tokyo and Moscow will have to find a political solution to break the territorial deadlock.

Unfortunately, however, as Zagorsky documents, Japan has been unwilling to take independent initiatives in response to the fast-changing developments in the Commonwealth of Independent States and Russia. Tokyo's rigid position on the territorial issue excluded Japan from the mainstream of international political developments in the field of East-West relations during the perestroika period of the latter half of the 1980s. Akaha concludes that Tokyo must apply the policy of expanded equilibrium more aggressively and more flexibly. Most urgently, Tokyo must extend larger humanitarian aid in concert with the United States and Europe to avert the devastating consequences of a total collapse of the CIS economies. Japan must then extend major technical and economic aid to assist in its neighbors' difficult economic reforms. The comparatively intrinsic unimportance of the disputed islands underlines their symbolic significance. Unlike other nearby islands, the four disputed island territories were never occupied by Russia or the Soviet Union until August 1945. The few Japanese inhabitants were repatriated to Japan and the islands now contain several thousand Russian citizens who are determined to stay. The determined opposition to concessions by conservative and military elements in Russia stays the hand of the Russian government anxious to resolve the territorial issue with Japan.

Zagorsky and Akaha agree that the bilateral relations have importance not only for the two countries involved but also for the whole region, and perhaps for global peace and security as well. Tokyo must resist the temptation to take a parochial, bilateral view of the situation but instead must see Japan-Russia relations within the broader regional and global context. Regional and global problems such as nuclear and missile proliferation, global warming, ethnic unrest, and political tensions arising out of economic disparities within and among nations demand multilateral cooperation, including that between Japan and Russia. Reduction of regional tension is essential if Japan is to be responsible for its own territorial defense in ways that will neither impose costly defense on the Japanese nor destabilize its relations with the region's powers.[22] However, until Tokyo and Moscow can find a mutually acceptable political compromise on the territorial issue, their contribution to the reduction of tension in Northeast Asia will be severely limited. Moreover, should the Russians come to view the Japanese as opportunists bent on extracting Russian concessions in times of crisis, the two countries' longer-term relationship will suffer. Obviously, Tokyo must avoid this.

Conclusion

In conclusion, the posthegemonic era presents Japan with greater opportunities than at any point in the entire Cold War period to play a leading political role in the world, particularly in the Asia Pacific region. Its political influence will depend on soft power based on successful demonstration of national growth through economic strength. Unlike in Eastern Europe and Central Asia, the end of the Cold War is not likely to generate uncontrollable ethnic and national conflict in the Pacific region, although the possibility cannot be totally ruled out. This is largely due to the dynamic growth the region's economies have experienced over the last two decades. Japan has contributed to this process both directly—through trade, investment, and economic assistance—and indirectly, by demonstrating an economic model for achieving greatness. As long as Japan continues this successful performance, its political and even security roles in the region are likely to grow. However, as long as there remain possibilities of international conflict and pre–Cold War legacies of Japanese colonialism and militarism, Japan's soft power must be accompanied by U.S. military presence in the region. The most formidable task, then, is how to stabilize the Japanese-U.S. relations characterized by discrepant power capabilities. If Japan can successfully share its growing economic surplus with the United States and the other regional powers, difficulties can be minimized if not totally eliminated. Similarly, the development of a regional or subregional framework to complement the existing bilateral security arrangements in the region and to address Japan's and other regional powers' security concerns would contribute much toward the containment of a potentially very destabilizing arms race or races between Japan and its East Asian neighbors.

In essence, a pacifist yet active international role in collective regional and global leadership will be Japan's best answer to the challenges of the posthegemonic world.[23]

Notes

1. This question was answered in the affirmative in Richard Rosecrance, *The Rise of the Trading State: Commerce and Conquest in the Modern World*, New York: Basic Books, 1986.

2. Shinzo Yoshida, "Jūnan na Takokukan Kyōgi o, Shin Ajia Anpo Bei-Kokumu Chōkan ga Taian, Chōsen Mondai Kyōgi Nanboku to Beisonicchū de" [Toward flexible multilateral discussions, new Asian security proposals of the American secretary of state, the Korean problem should be discussed among North and South Korea,

America, the Soviet Union, Japan, and China], *Yomiuri Shimbun*, November 10, 1991, p. 5. Susumu Awanohara, "The Lone Ranger, Pentagon's Blueprint for the New World Order," *Far Eastern Economic Review*, vol. 155, no. 12 (March 26, 1992), p. 11. New York Times Service, "New Pentagon Strategy Promotes Cooperation," *Globe and Mail*, May 25, 1992, p. A8.

3. Paul Kennedy, *The Rise and Fall of the Great Powers: Economic Change and Military Conflict from 1500 to 2000*, New York: Random House, 1987.

4. Nigel Holloway, ed., *Japan in Asia*, Hong Kong: Far Eastern Economic Review, 1991, pp. 10–14.

5. Yoichi Funabashi, "Japan and the New World Order," *Foreign Affairs*, vol. 70, no. 5 (Winter 1991/92), p. 65.

6. For an insightful discussion of the theoretical and policy implications of Japan's successful economic development model, see Henrik Schmiegelow and Michele Schmiegelow, "How Japan Affects the International System," *International Organization*, vol. 44, no. 4 (Autumn 1990), pp. 553–588.

7. Although 1 percent of Japan's gross national product (GNP) of goods and services is very large, the amount spent on defense by Japan is still quite small when compared to that of the United States, which is about ten times greater. Also, the valuation of the yen upward in 1985 and 1986 virtually doubled the value of the Japanese military budget in dollars, but the yen, in which most of the money was spent, had not changed at all. Because Japan makes most of its own weapons in small runs that are very expensive and the living costs of its volunteer force are very high, defense expenditures do not go as far as similar ones elsewhere.

8. "Shakaitō Taikai, Tō Kaikaku Girigiri no Kōbō, Yōkyū Zokushutsu de Shusei, Anpo Jieitai Minaoshi, Tanabe-shi, Kurushii Tachiba ni" [Social Democratic Party congress, excruciating conflict over party reform, amendments under numerous demands, on reconsidering security and the Self-Defense Forces, Mr. Tanabe (the new chairman) is in a painful position], *Yomiuri Shimbun*, July 31, 1991, p. 2.

9. Edith Terry, "The Samurai Take Hollywood," *Globe and Mail*, December 12, 1990, p. A21. Michael Creighton utilizes the same theme of an insidious Japanese attempt to take over the United States in his mystery novel, *Rising Sun*, New York: Alfred A. Knopf, 1992. A more sober and constructive approach to the rivalry is presented by the academic economist, Lester Thurow, in his *Head to Head: The Coming Economic Battle Among Japan, Europe, and America*, New York: William Morrow and Company, Inc., 1991. Robert B. Reich has located thirty-five recent books aimed at identifying Japan as a threat to the U.S. way of life and freedom, just as Nazi Germany and the Soviet Union once were. Robert B. Reich, "Is Japan Really Out to Get Us?" *The New York Times Book Review*, February 9, 1992, section 7, pp. 1, 24, and 25.

10. David P. Rapkin, "Japan and World Leadership," in David P. Rapkin, ed., *World Leadership and Hegemony*, International Political Economy Yearbook, vol. 5, Boulder, Colo.: Lynne Rienner, 1990, pp. 196–199. For a Japanese analyst's response to this critique, see Hideo Sato, "Japan's Role in the Post–Cold War World," *Current History*, vol. 90, no. 555 (April 1991), pp. 145–148 and 179.

11. See Funabashi, "Japan and the New World Order."

12. Masaru Tamamoto, "Japan's Uncertain Role," *World Policy Journal*, vol. 8, no. 4 (Fall 1991), p. 593.

13. Sato, "Japan's Role," p. 146.

14. It should also be added that the authors in this volume are not in the pay of any Japanese organizations or dependent upon them for favors.

15. Foreign Press Center, Tokyo, "Policy Speech by Prime Minister Kiichi Miyazawa to the 123rd Session of the National Diet (January 24, 1992)," mimeographed, pp. 5–6.

16. Lester Thurow, *Head to Head*, p. 20.

17. Foreign Press Center, Tokyo, "Foreign Policy Speech by Foreign Minister Michio Watanabe to the 123rd Session of the National Diet (January 24, 1992)," mimeographed, pp. 5–6.

18. Tamamoto, "Japan's Uncertain Role," pp. 575–597.

19. See for example Sato, "Japan's Role."

20. A few examples of the growing discussion of Asia Pacific economic dynamism and Japan's role include Keizai Kikakuchō Sōgō Keikakukyoku, *Taiheiyō Jidai no Tenbō: 2000-nen ni Itaru Taiheiyō Chiiki no Keizai Hatten to Kadai* [Prospects of the Pacific age: Economic development and agenda in the Pacific region toward the year 2000], Tokyo: Okurashō Insatsukyoku (Finance Ministry Printing Bureau), 1985; S. B. Linder, *The Pacific Century: Economic and Political Consequences of Asia-Pacific Dynamism*, Stanford, Calif.: Stanford University Press, 1986; James W. Morley, ed., *The Pacific Basin: New Challenges for the United States*, New York: The Academy of Political Science, 1986; Arfin Bey, *Ajia Taiheiyō no Jidai* [The age of Asia-Pacific], Tokyo: Chūō Kōronsha, 1987; Kan Taiheiyō Kyoryoku Nihon Iinkai, *21-seiki no Taiheiyō Kyōryoku: Genjō to Kadai*, [Pacific cooperation in the twenty-first century: The present situation and agenda], Tokyo: Jiji Tsushinsha, 1987); and Steve Chan, *East Asian Dynamism: Growth, Order, and Security in the Pacific Region*, Boulder, Colo.: Westview Press, 1990.

21. For recent discussions of Asia Pacific regionalism, see Stuart Harris, "Varieties of Pacific Economic Cooperation," and Andrew Elek, "The Challenge of Asia Pacific Economic Cooperation," *The Pacific Review*, vol. 4, no. 4 (1991), pp. 301–311 and 322–332, respectively.

22. Takashi Inoguchi, "Change and Response in Japan's International Politics and Strategy," in Stuart Harris and James Cotton, eds., *The End of the Cold War in Northeast Asia*, Boulder, Colo.: Lynne Rienner, 1991, p. 232.

23. The fiscal year 1992 budget, approved by the cabinet on December 28, 1991, earmarked $33.7 billion (at ¥ 135 = $1.00) for defense. This represents a mere 3.8 percent increase, the smallest rise in defense spending in thirty-two years. In contrast, Tokyo plans to boost its foreign aid budget by 7.8 percent over the previous year.

About the Authors

Tsuneo Akaha

An associate professor of international policy studies and director of the Center for East Asian Studies at the Monterey Institute of International Studies, California, Akaha received his Ph.D. in international relations from the University of Southern California. He has been a visiting research fellow at Seikei University in Tokyo and at Hokkaido University's Slavic Research Center in Sapporo, Japan. He is the author of *Japan in Global Ocean Politics* and coeditor of *International Political Economy: A Reader*. His areas of research include Japanese foreign and security policy, political economy of Asia Pacific, international and comparative ocean policy studies, and international political economy. Akaha is currently directing a research project on U.S.-Japanese cooperation in the development of Siberia and the Russian Far East.

Frank C. Langdon

Langdon received his Ph.D. from the University of California, Berkeley. He is a professor emeritus of political science and research associate at the Institute of International Relations, University of British Columbia, Vancouver, Canada. Among his numerous publications on Japanese politics and foreign policy is *Sengo Nihon no Gaikō*. His current research interests relate to Japanese foreign policy and the impact of global and regional developments on Japan's foreign relations in political, economic, and security areas.

David Arase

Arase received an MA in international relations from the School of Advanced International Studies, Johns Hopkins University, and a Ph.D. in political science from the University of California, Berkeley. He is currently an assistant professor in the Department of Politics of Pomona College. His published works have examined Japanese foreign and security policies and Asian political economy.

Prasert Chittiwatanapong

A recipient of an MA degree in Japanese history from Waseda University (Tokyo), Prasert Chittiwatanapong is an associate professor of political science at Thammasat University in Bangkok, where he teaches Japanese politics and foreign policy. His current areas of research are Japanese aid policy and Japan's political-security role in Southeast Asia. His publications include *Japanese ODA to Thailand and Thai Management of Japanese ODA* and *Japanese Official Development Assistance to Thailand: A Study on Construction Industry Aspect.*

Charlotte Elton

An Oxford University graduate in philosophy, politics, and economics, with a masters' degree in development economics from Sussex University, Elton has been a research associate of the Harvard University Program on U.S.-Japan Relations and a visiting research fellow of the Institute of Developing Economies, Tokyo. Currently a research coordinator at the Panamanian Center for Research and Social Action (CEASPA), Elton has written extensively on Japanese interests in the Panama Canal and in Central and South America. Her recent publications include *Rivales o Aliados? Japón y Estados Unidos en Panamá* and *Japan's Natural Resource Strategies in Latin America and Their Environmental Impact* (in Spanish).

Philip Meeks

Associate dean of arts and sciences and professor of political science at Creighton University, Omaha, Nebraska, Meeks received his Ph.D. in political science from the University of Texas, Austin. His publications include *Space and Society: Challenges and Choices* (coeditor and contributor). His current areas of research include international political economy, international security, and comparative public policy in advanced industrial states.

Koji Taira

Koji Taira, Ph.D., is a professor of economics and industrial relations at the University of Illinois at Urbana-Champaign. Previously he has taught at the University of Washington, Stanford University, Keio University, and Hokkaido University. Recently he coedited a special issue of *The Annals* of the American Academy of Political and Social Science on Japan's external economic relations.

Alexei Zagorsky

Zagorsky got a Ph.D. in history from the Moscow Institute of International Relations in 1985. In 1987 he joined the Center for Japanese and Pacific Studies of the Institute of World Economy and International Relations (IMEMO) in Moscow, where he now heads the section for Japanese political studies. He is the author of about 60 publications in Russian, English, Japanese, and Korean, including *Japan and China: Patterns of Societal Development as Seen by Japanese Historians* (in Russian) and *Soren wa Nihon o Dō Miteiruka* (co-author, in Japanese).

Zhou Jihua

Zhou is a senior fellow and director of the Department for Japanese Politics, Institute of Japanese Studies, Chinese Academy of Social Sciences, Beijing. He is also director of the Beijing Center for East Asian Studies, Society for Comparative International Studies, and a professor at the China World Watch Institute. He is author of *Reisengo no Nihon Gaikō Seisaku no Chosei* (in Japanese). His current research areas are Japanese foreign and security policy and East Asian security.

Index

About the Book

The emerging "posthegemonic world," characterized by the diffusion of political power and the growing importance of economic relative to military strength, requires a collective global leadership the likes of which the world has never seen. This book examines the requirements of posthegemonic leadership and considers Japan's ability—as well as its own expectations regarding its ability—to meet the challenge in the political, security, and economic spheres.

A particularly appealing feature of the book is its reflection of the perspectives of a range of Pacific Rim countries, including those in Northeast Asia, Southeast Asia, and the Americas.